ANCIENT TOWN RECORDS
Volume IV

NEW HAVEN TOWN RECORDS
1769 - 1819

ANCIENT TOWN RECORDS

Volume IV

NEW HAVEN TOWN RECORDS

1769 - 1819

Compiled and Edited by

PETER J. MALIA

The Connecticut Press
Cheshire, CT

2020

© 2020 Peter J. Malia

Inquiries should be addressed to:
The Connecticut Press
36 Wildlife Court
Cheshire, CT 06410
www.connecticutpress.com

First Edition

Cataloguing-in-Publication Data
Malia, Peter J., 1951 - Editor
Ancient Town Records, Volume IV: Town Records of
New Haven, 1769 - 1819, 470 pp.
Includes annotations and index
ISBN 978-0-9977907-5-7 (soft-cover edition)
Library of Congress Control Number: 201991097

1. History |United States| Connecticut | New Haven | Colonial
| American Revolution | Early National
2. Genealogy | Connecticut | New Haven

Dedicated to

Celeste H. Malia

wife, best friend, life counsel

CONTENTS

NEW HAVEN TOWN RECORDS

ACKNOWLEDGMENTS

The first initiative to publish the manuscript records of the Colony of New Haven began in 1857. In that year, Connecticut State Librarian Charles J. Hoadley edited and supervised the publication of the *Records Of The Colony And Plantation Of New Haven: From 1638 To 1649*. In 1858, the *Records of the Colony Or Jurisdiction of New Haven, from May, 1653 To The Union*, appeared under Hoadley's editorship. These two volumes completed the State of Connecticut's publication of extant records of the New Haven Colony from its founding until its union with the Connecticut in 1665.

More than a half century later, the consummate Franklin B. Dexter, Yale University's Assistant Librarian and University historian, edited two new volumes of the Records of New Haven for the years 1649 - 1684. The New Haven Colony Historical Society published these volumes in 1917 and 1919, respectively, as Volumes I and II of the Ancient Town Records series with the expressed hope that additional records might "soon find a place in this printed series."

Some 42 years passed before Zara Jones Powers, Yale University's Manuscripts Librarian, edited the *New Haven Town Records, 1684 - 1769*. Once again, the New Haven Colony Historical Society rose to the occasion and published Powers's seminal work as Volume III of the Ancient Town Records series. Powers's last entry concluded with the New Haven Town Meeting of April 10, 1769.

This latest volume of *New Haven Town Records, 1769 - 1819* appears as Volume IV in the Ancient Town Records series. It commences with the New Haven Town Meeting of September 19, 1769 and concludes with the meeting of December 27, 1819. As did its predecessors, the volume includes the New Haven Freemen's Meetings from 1769 - 1826. The terminal date of 1819 for the records themselves was chosen for two reasons. First, it provides a full half-century of New Haven Town Meetings that span from colonial New Haven through the passage of the historic Connecticut Constitution of 1818. Ratification of that document ended Connecticut's official ties to the Congregational Church, reorganized its government into three separate but equal branches, and offered suffrage to all free white males age 21 and over.

The original manuscripts that comprise this latest volume of New Haven's Town Records are drawn from two successive journals housed at the Whitney Library at the New Haven Museum. To protect their fragile pages, the original leather-bound journals were dis-bound and their pages encapsulated between sheets of inert polyester plastic. To preserve a sense of the original pagination of the journals, however, this edition provides original page numbers using italicized brackets, such as *[p. 1]*.

While excerpts and passages from these Town Records have occasionally appeared in print through the years, this edition is the first complete transcription of the New Haven Town Records for the years 1769 – 1819. I stress the word *Town* for a reason. As of January 8, 1784, the Connecticut General Assembly enacted legislation allowing a portion of the more expansive Town of New Haven, which then included East Haven, West Haven, North Haven, Hamden, Bethany, Branford, and part of Amity (now Woodbridge) to incorporate as a city. The newly created City of New Haven comprised an area that roughly equates to its modern-day counterpart. Once incorporated, the City of New Haven also appointed its own municipal officials, who in many instances held office in the more expansive town government. Consequently, manuscript records of the City of New Haven's Alder Meetings also reside at The New Haven Museum and will hopefully join the published Ancient Records series in the future.

In compiling this volume, I am indebted to a long list of institutions and individuals who have provided assistance and support of this project through its many years in the making. Primary among them are the past and present staffs of New Haven Museum; Yale University's Sterling Library and Beinecke Rare Book and Manuscript Library; the New York Public Library; the Young Men's Institute of New Haven; the New York Public Library; the Library of Congress; The Connecticut Historical Society, and the Office of Town/City Clerk of New Haven.

Special recognition is extended to the late Professor Rollin G. Osterweis of Yale University and Floyd Shumway, late Director of the The New Haven Museum. Both individuals were avid supporters of this project when I first started it as a graduate student in Early American History in the late 1970's. Due to a lack of funding, the manuscripts resided on a shelf until 2017, when I ended my career as a corporate writer to resume my passion for history. In doing so, James Campbell, former Librarian and Curator of Manuscripts at the Whitney Library at the New Haven Museum, has also been a longtime supporter of the Town Records project. Under his guidance and that of his wife, Bonnie Campbell, Reference Librarian at The New Haven Museum, this project benefitted from, among other things, their expert supervision and guidance of two gifted graduate students, Barbara Ghildardi and Matthew

Green, who each spent many hours copying, proofreading, and compiling information for this publication.

Special thanks also go to Frances Skelton, Reference Librarian at the New Haven Museum, for providing me with access to her personal research on New Haven men serving in the American Revolution. Aside from the historical significance of these town records, Frances shares my appreciation of the genealogical treasure trove these documents present historians and researchers interested in learning what public offices New Haveners held during these critical formative years of the city and the nation.

Most important of all, however, is the appreciation I have for my late father, Donald J. Malia, Sr. In an era predating personal computers and word processors, he spent many hours typing and retyping handwritten transcriptions and notes into a presentable format.

Celeste H. Malia, my wife, has also provided invaluable help in preparing this publication over the past 40 years. She labored alongside me in the New Haven City Clerk's office hand copying these records for the better part of six months in 1978. More than four decades later, she continues to support my efforts to see what we both long ago simply started calling "the records" into print. On behalf of everyone involved in this project, I hope *The Records of New Haven, 1769 - 1819* will help future generations understand that true history is best told by those who lived it. As Samuel Bishop wrote at the end of the Revolution, New Haveners hoped "that future generations not being influenced by our passion ...[but] from their ideas of our character [...] which a faithful historian shall have recorded, and not from our passions of which they can have no history."

Finally, as editor of *The Records of New Haven, 1769 - 1819*, I take full responsibility for the accuracy of this transcription and any shortcomings or errors it may reveal.

Peter J. Malia CSG #19794
Cheshire, CT, 2020

INTRODUCTION

This volume of New Haven Town Records, 1769 - 1819 spans what is arguably the greatest epoch in New Haven's storied history. Over the course of a single lifetime, New Haven grew from a small colonial seacoast town on the edge of the British Empire into a vibrant American city and leader of its Industrial Revolution. Throughout this half century of revolutionary change, New Haven's time-honored town meeting remained the cornerstone of self-government.

In many respects, New Haven's first "revolution" began in the decade before the actual War of Independence. From 1756 - 1774, the greater New Haven area grew from 5,085 to 8,295 residents—a 65 percent increase, making it one of the largest towns in colonial America.[1] With names like Sherman, Arnold, Hillhouse, Darling, Austin, Lyman, Wooster, among many others, these "new men" in town, as historian Rollin Osterweis called them,[2] were drawn to New Haven to seek their fortunes in a bustling seaport that seemed destined to become an economic powerhouse for southwestern Connecticut.[3] Merchants, seamen, tradesmen, lawyers, doctors, scholars, and professionals of every stripe poured into the co-capitol of Connecticut and changed everything. Young, talented, and ambitious, they soon rose to positions of prominence to exercise an outsized influence over New Haven's social, religious, political, and economic future.

As this volume opens with the Town Meeting of December 11, 1769, New Haven's future appeared unduly bright. Despite a colonial boycott of British goods that took effect nearly two years earlier in response to the British Parliament's bungled efforts to tax the colonies, many Connecticut seacoast towns continued to operate as they pleased under the illusion that they were already semi-independent. In New Haven, that meant the newcomers continued to push for a series of internal improvements at town meetings, from new roads and bridges, to an even longer Long Wharf, all in an effort to make New Haven—and themselves—more competitive. Some of the more brazen merchants, including New Haven's Benedict Arnold and several others, went a step further and growing

---

1. Albert E. Van Dusen, *Connecticut* (New York, 4th printing, 1988), p. 105. See also, https://www.quora.com/What-were-the-largest-cities-in-the-13-colonies. New Haven at the time included Branford, North Branford, Hamden, West Haven, East Haven, Woodbridge, and Amity.
2. Rollin Osterweis, *Three Centuries of New Haven* (New Haven, 4th printing, 1975), p. 102.
3. Ibid, 104.

NEW HAVEN TOWN RECORDS

rich smuggling prohibited goods into the colonies from Europe and the West Indies in the years just before the Revolution. Smuggling, in fact, became so commonplace that many New Haveners turned a blind eye to the practice. Others in town were so upset by what was happening that they circulated a petition against "the growing immoralities ... especially in the rising generation."

Their pleas were wasted as New Haven's sense of self-aggrandizement was on full display at the December 9, 1771 town meeting. Having just completed a massive redevelopment of their waterfront, merchants and professionals wanted to showcase the town. They selected Roger Sherman to head a committee of prominent citizens charged with drafting a proposal calling for New Haven to become Connecticut's first chartered city. Even Sherman's magic failed him. The proposal never materialized as New Haven's overblown bowstrings quickly faded before the realities of a deepening colonial crisis.

The opening phase of that crisis involved Connecticut's westward expansion into the Wyoming Valley of Pennsylvania. The creation of the Susquehanna Company attracted both land speculators and investors as a solution to the growing problem of too many poor farm families and too little available land in Connecticut. To reduce the colony's financial burden of supporting these families, and possibly realizing a handsome profit in the process, a group of New Haven merchants and professionals (including a vocal Roger Sherman) supported the idea of resettling these poor families to the Wyoming Valley area. New Haven's conservative landed gentry worried such a bold move to expand Connecticut into a contested territory courted disaster and the possiblwe loss of its Royal Charter. Radicals in New Haven led by Sherman accused the conservatives of being greedy landowners who wanted to deny average citizens the right to own their own property. Spirited debates in the local press led to a show down at the April 11, 1774 New Haven town meeting. After more heated exchanges, a vote was taken. Conservatives won the day in an extremely close contest, 102 to 99. Aside from casting a light on just how divided New Haven had become, the results did not matter. New Light radicals throughout eastern Connecticut voted overwhelmingly in favor of Governor Jonathan Trumbull's administration and the Susquehanna settlement in what was a preview of Loyalist versus Patriot.

The divide only grew wider six weeks later. In the hurried handwriting of

---

4. Thomas M. Truxes, "Connecticut in the Golden Age of Smuggling," Connecticut Explored (Spring, 2010); also https://www.ctexplored.org/connecticut-in-the-golden-age-of-smuggling/
5. Benjamin Trumbull Papers, Box 22, Yale University Manuscript Collection.
6. Van Dusen, p. 130.

Samuel Bishop, himself a radical patriot and New Haven's town clerk for a remarkable 56 years, his recording of the May 23, 1774 town meeting was both matter-of-fact and revolutionary in its content. New Haven's "radicals" had gained control of the town meeting and named 18 of their colleagues to a Committee of Correspondence. The Committee's responsibilities were two-fold: coordinate a relief effort in response to a direct plea from the citizens of Boston, who were suffering after the British Navy closed their port as punishment for staging the infamous Boston Tea Party. More significantly, New Haven's Committee of Correspondence also reached out to neighboring towns and adjacent colonies calling for "a general union." At the very next town meeting on June 23, 1774, Bishop recorded that New Haveners voted in favor of a Continental Congress "to promote the wellfare and Happiness of all the american Colonies."

New Haven townsmen would not officially meet again until October 18, 1774. While there was no mention of the what transpired at First Continental Congress, Bishop's entry still spoke volumes. In his neat, forceful script, he recorded that town authorized a subscription be taken in support of Boston's suffering inhabitants. He then added ominously that the selectmen also ordered that a powder house be built and a stock of gunpowder be secured for New Haven's use.

In a last-ditched effort to forestall the drift towards war, New Haven conservatives turned out in force at the November 14, 1774 town meeting. As recounted in Bishop's minutes, the conservatives succeeded in requiring that the majority of the newly formed Committee of Association be members of the conservative First Society. The push back was immediate, with three town meetings held over course of the next 10 days. On December 20, 1774, New Haveners agreed to choose one selectman from each of the three Congregational societies in town to ensure equal representation. Then at the December 26, 1774 town meeting, Bishop noted that several additional citizens were added to New Haven's Committee of Inspection "so that there be peace and unanimity in this town." Only four days later, the townsmen met again, this time, Bishop recorded, to raise taxes to pay the £100 owed for gunpowder. On April 21, 1775 a post rider named Israel Bisssel galloped into New Haven with news of the Battles of Lexington and Concord. Stunned New Haveners

---

7. New Haven Town Meeting, June 23, 1774, see p. 36.
8. New Haven Town Meeting, November 14, 1774, see p. 37.
9. New Haven Town Meeting, December 20, 1774, see p. 39.
10. New Haven Town Meeting, December 30, 1774, see p. 43.

called an impromptu town meeting at Center Church. Unfortunately, Samuel Bishop was in Hartford at the time as New Haven's representative to the General Assembly. Amid the collective angst of nervous townsmen, no one thought to act as town clerk this fateful meeting. Anecdotally, however, New Haven's established conservatives turned out in force to vote against sending military aid to Boston.[11]

That all changed the following morning. On April 22, 1775, Captain Benedict Arnold and 50 local members of the newly formed Second Company of Governor's Foot Guard mustered on the New Haven Green. Learning that the town selectmen were meeting at Beers's Tavern, Arnold and his troops marched to the inn and demanded the keys to the town's powder house. The selectmen hesitated. Arnold gave them five minutes to change their minds or threatened to have his men break down the supply house door and help themselves. The keys were surrendered. After taking what supplies they needed, Arnold and his men marched off to war.[12]

Over the next seven months of 1775, and again from September to December, 1779; May through November, 1780; and mid-January until December 9, 1782, Samuel Bishop was absent as town clerk. In all but the last instance, he was serving in the Connecticut General Assembly with no acting substitute as New Haven town clerk. Large gaps and entire pages in the Town Records were subsequently left blank. Bishop likely intended to fill in the missing information, but never did. Readers need to consult other sources for accounts of what transpired in New Haven during those critical periods when Bishop's quill fell silent.

The New Haven Town Records that do exist during the Revolution offer invaluable insights into the life of a town on the front lines of a long and brutal war. In many of New Haven's town meetings from 1775 - 1783, the impact of that war and the extreme stress it placed on civilians ran undercurrent much of the public policies and actions that were adopted. For example, entries recorded during this period revealed New Haven's increasing anxiety over its precarious location within easy striking distance by British and Loyalist troops. Pleas to improve New Haven defenses, such as those documented in the Town Records of November 6, 1775 led to the construction of Black Rock Fort. Throughout the course of the war, the records also reported on a

11. Edward E. Atwater, *The History of the City of New Haven*. New York, 1887, p. 42.
12. Ibid., pp 42 - 43.

series of ongoing defensive measures, from arms purchases, and new powder mills built to tax increases to pay enlistment bonuses for new recruits.

Under the guise of patriotism, blood feuds also occasionally fueled New Haven's efforts to root out the disaffected. Samuel Bishop, for instance, mentioned in his summary of the November 6, 1775 town meeting that the townsmen voted that anyone "bound by conscience or choice to give intelligence to our enemies... or otherwise take an active part against us... be desired peacefully to depart from the town." As the war wore on, any semblance of politely asking suspected Loyalists to leave town gave way to outright interrogations, forced exiles, and the eventual confiscation of their personal property.

In the weeks following the British invasion of New Haven in 1779, enraged and traumatized citizens demanded an accounting from those who either remained in town or failed to show up in its defense. Bishop carefully recorded the names of every inhabitant interviewed. According to his entries, most of those who were questioned were excused, although he noted that the committee conducting those interviews believed a number of residents were not telling the truth. Reasons provided by still more of the suspected townspeople were judged "intirely insufficient." Sixteen New Haveners left town with the British, while eight others simply ignored calls to appear before the committee at all. No mention was ever made in the Town Records as to what further actions, if any, were ever taken against these inhabitants. Perhaps the committee felt that Bishop's immortalizing their names for history to judge was punishment enough.[13] More likely, they were just too emotionally drained by so many years of violence and death to seek any further retribution on their own neighbors.

Indeed, throughout the Revolution, the New Haven Town Records provided contemporary evidence that literally thousands of ordinary citizens went about their everyday business serving their town as surveyors, grand jurors, clerks, citizen soldiers, constables, pound keepers, tax collectors, selectmen, and in many other roles. Patriots and Loyalists alike did so based on their implicit social contract as citizens of New Haven who also, willingly or not, abided by the principles of Connecticut's established church, which defined being good as doing good. Gradually, almost imperceptibly, that sense of social contract provided New Haven's underrepresented inhabitants with the opportu-

---

13. New Haven Town Records, August 16, 1779, pp. 81 - 83 of this volume.

nity to gain real-life experiences, build self-confidence and community standing, and instill within themselves a realization that they, too, deserved to share in the political, civil, and religious rights they had just fought and sacrificed so much for through the Revolution. Even before the official end of the war, this growing sense of self-determination led a number of local parishes around Greater New Haven to seek out their independence. In the Town Records of February 12, 1781, for example, the citizen farmers of Amity, Bethany, North Haven, and Mt. Carmel all applied for separate town status. They would soon be followed by East Haven, Branford, and Woodbridge. All of their petitions were initially rejected, but the seed was sown. Life, liberty, and the pursuit of happiness as described in the Declaration of Independence were no longer just words on paper that applied only to a handful of privileged townsmen. Increasingly, they would inspire another revolution fueled by the prescient dream of ordinary citizens peacefully demanding that they finally be heard.

Meanwhile, the Town Records bore witness to another more immediate dream about to come true for New Haven. On October 20, 1783 over 200 of New Haven's leading citizens signed a petition asking the Connecticut General Assembly for a city charter. Then in a bold move forward, Town Clerk Samuel Bishop recorded yet another historic first for New Haven on March 3, 1784: the creation of a blue-ribbon committee inviting former New York Loyalist merchants to resettle in New Haven. Some actually came. Anxious to push forward with their plans , the New Haven Town Meeting voted on January 5, 1784 to again reach out to the General Assembly for its decision to become a city. Three days later, the request was granted. What roughly comprised the original nine squares of the town center was now officially recognized as the City of New Haven, complete with its own city government, board of alders, common council, and first mayor in the person of Roger Sherman. The new city was ultimately answerable to the larger Town Meeting of New Haven in a peculiar arrangement that lasted until 1855, when the town meeting form of local government finally entered into the history books.

In one of its first orders of business on October 5, 1784, the City of New Haven authorized that a new wharf be built that would eventually extend out even further into the channel. Nearly 150 years after their Puritan ancestors first set foot on the shores of Quinnipiack, the City of New Haven was about to enter its golden age as an international seaport.

It would not last very long. One by one the surrounding villages gained their independence, reducing New Haven's core population by nearly half to slightly more than 4,000 souls by 1788. Most of those remaining were in some way involved in the new city's burgeoning trade with the Caribbean, other American ports, parts of Europe, and even Asia. While the Town Records documented the phenomenal growth of the port from 1785 - 1808–thanks in no small part due to strong Federalist support for the economy, tariffs, and the assumption of state and local debts–they also painted a darker picture in the background. Accompanying the growing trade, increasing wealth, and the literally hundreds of vessels with thousands of sailors passing through New Haven each year, instances of disease, crime, and poverty were soon recorded. Yellow fever, Small pox, and Typhoid epidemics swept through New Haven in the 1780's and 1790's, and again in 1814, claiming hundreds of lives, including Mayor Roger Sherman in 1793. Ever the jack-of-all-trades, Town Clerk Samuel Bishop succeeded Sherman as mayor and simultaneously held the offices of town clerk (until 1801), judge of county probate, and was appointed by President Jefferson as Collector for the Port of New Haven serving from 1801 until his death in 1803.

Following Bishop's retirement as town clerk in 1801, 40-year-old Elisha Munson assumed the post of Town Clerk until his retirement in 1832. Munson remained as New Haven City Clerk until his death at the age of 81. While Munson's flourishing penmanship embellished the physical appearance of the New Haven Town Records, his reporting was a simple and sometimes gripping recital of New Haveners emotional pathos over a series of pivotal events that forever altered the future of New Haven.

Primary among these issues was the ill-conceived Embargo Act of 1809. Instead of punishing England and France as intended, the Embargo slowly choked the life out of New Haven's once thriving maritime economy. On January 10, 1809, Elisha Munson noted the passion and despair of the city's merchants who petitioned Congress to repeal the law. Again on May 4, 1811, Munson documented the meeting's heated opposition to America's non-importation laws, which by this point, had turned New Haven's one-time dream into a nightmare. A deep recession idled hundreds of New Haveners and the Long Wharf, noted Rollin Osterweis, "took on a ghostlike appearance."[1] When war was finally declared against England in 1812, the Town Records made no mention of it then... or ever. Neither was there any official discussion recorded in the Town Records of New Haven's support of the infamous Hartford Convention that nearly led to New England's succession from the

---

1. Osterweis, 201

United States decades before the South actually did so.

Following the end of the War of 1812, the New Haven Town Records consciously avoided any official entries of its wartime activities. Other sources, however, painted an unsavory picture of a that increasingly turned to smuggling to survive. Even after the debacle of the Hartford Convention and the national disdain it brought upon Connecticut Federalists, the City of New Haven would stubbornly retain its Federalist mayor until 1822. Old dreams, it appears, die hard. And new dreams are eventually fulfilled. On October 15, 1818, New Haveners voted 430 to 218 in favor of a new state constitution. In addition to extending the vote to all free men 21 years of age, the Congregational Church was disestablished and religious freedom beame the law of the land.

Through these remarkable 50 years, the New Haven Town Records revealed something more telling about New Haveners beyond what either Samuel Bishop or Elisha Munson consciously recorded. Meeting after meeting, year after year, from one generation to the next, the New Haven Town Records showed a people engaged in an ongoing, historic struggle of competing visions of the future. Old versus new. Commercial or agrarian. Pious or sectarian. Federalist or Republican, Connecticut First or America First. In its telling, the story of New Haven never lacked a sense of drama, a shortage of compelling personalities both good and bad, or a determined purpose to not only survive but to thrive.

As this primary resource stands as witness, the New Haven Town Records represent history in the making and provide a rare contemporary look into the countless lives of the famous, infamous, and forgotten who all lived, sacrificed, suffered, celebrated, and shared in the common experience of being New Haveners. It is history in its rawest form—as it happened. These records have important stories to tell and lessons to teach—if only we are all wise enough to read, to listen, and to learn from them.

EDITORIAL METHODOLOGY

This edition of *The New Haven Town Records, 1769 - 1819* adopts what Julian P. Boyd, the esteemed editor of *The Papers of Thomas Jefferson*, once called the middle course of historical editing. It is neither a total facsimile nor a complete moderation of this largely eighteenth-century manuscript. The transcription is as close as is reasonably possible to the original document. Its orthography, grammar, and capitalization have been preserved in order to convey the common phonemic, speech, and orthographic mannerisms of eighteenth-century New Haven. Consequently, raised letters and abbreviations have been retained, including the ampersand *(&)*, etcetera *(&c)*, and *yᵉ* and *yᵗ*, which are archaic forms of the *and* that, respectively.

Readers will also notice variations in spelling, capitalization, and the use of abbreviations, sometimes even in the same sentence. As with all handwritten historical documents, these particular points can be highly stylized and sometimes ambiguous. In those instances where the editor found it impossible to decipher the author's intent, modern rules were applied.

It also soon becomes apparent to readers of these records that New Haven's two successive town clerks during the half-century covered by this volume, Samuel Bishop, Jr. (1723 - 1803) and Elisha Munson (1760 - 1841) relied heavily on phonetics in spelling proper names. It is also clear that both men occasionally failed to record every entry in their proper sequence or sometimes not at all. Bishop, in particular, served as town clerk for a 53 years. During that time, he compiled a remarkable record as a public servant, including serving several terms in the Connecticut General Assembly, a probate judge, as New Haven's second mayor (1793 - 1803), and appointed by President Thomas Jefferson as Collector of the Port of New Haven from 1801 until his death in 1803. It should come as no surprise to learn that Bishop and later Munson also occasionally relied on meeting notes likely taken by someone else. In combination with their busy public schedules and advancing age, their penmanship and record keeping skills also gradually suffered through the years.

Rather than arbitrarily apply modern usage throughout these records, every effort has been made to preserve the orthography and stylization of the original manuscripts' authors in order to provide readers with the most accurate transcription possible. In those rare instances where spelling may be impossible to decipher absolutely, the use of *[?]* is employed, while *[...]* is employed to designate an omitted word and/or missing entries. All editorial insertions and corrections are designated by italics and enclosed by italicized brackets.

Despite every effort to provide a facsimile reproduction of the town records, doing so without exception would make for some difficult reading. The town clerks who were responsible for these records frequently made irregular and crowded entries — often well after the fact — and added subject notes in the margins to facilitate faster reference points. These were, after all, considered the official, historical records of New Haven. In other instances, the clerks made errors in dating the minutes of some meetings.

To enhance the overall readability of this volume, each town meeting in this volume is introduced in italics within italicized brackets, which was adopted by Zara Powers in Volume III of these records. The initial introduction of each town meeting is also capitalized, which does not conform with the original document until after 1801, when a new town clerk actually adopted the practice. In addition, all subject notes entered into the margins by the clerks have now been incorporated into the text and appear in italics to designate them as such. Additional notes not original to the manuscript appear in italics within brackets.

For the sake of clarity, punctuation — such as commas between proper names, periods at the end of sentences, and paragraph breaks — have been added silently. Superfluous dashes at the end of sentences in the original document have also been eliminated. In all other instances, added punctuation appears within italicized brackets.

Since the original town records were unbound and encapsulated in mylar as separate pages for their preservation, this edition provides the journals' original pagination scheme, which appears in italics within brackets throughout the text, such as *[p. 1]*. Also noted in italics within brackets are extended blank entries and blank pages that appear in the original documents. As noted previously, the town clerks occasionally left spaces to backfill with entries that were either recorded elsewhere or not recorded at all.

As for annotations, they are numerous, are meant to provide essential information and context, and are hopefully not overly distracting. Being both a genealogist and historian, the editor is aware that these records will hopefully prove to be of value in both disciplines. Consequently, every effort has been made to provide vital statistics for everyone mentioned in this volume. Short biographies are provided for many of those named in the records. Veterans are identified with an asterisk after their names in the index, while known graduates of Yale are also noted.

Inevitably, a number of individuals cited in the records could not be positively identified, due to either a duplication of names, lack of details, or editorial oversight. I offer my apologies here for any shortcomings my research may reveal. With the rise in reliable genealogical information and other resources that are now widely available on line, historians, genealogists, students, and casual readers can consult a vast array of primary and secondary resources that will hopefully augment, update, and correct the research that appears here. When deemed appropriate, sources and hypertext links from the internet as of this edition's publication are provided for further reference. I can only hope that such electronic references escape the fate of traditional library card catalogs and that future researchers will build on this humble effort to pre-serve a primary source of New Haven and American history.

ABBREVIATIONS OF MAJOR SOURCES

Ancestry.com   https://www.ancestry.com/search/

Atwater   Atwater, Edward E., *The History of the City of New Haven* (New York, 1887).

Dexter   Dexter, Franklin B., *Biographical Sketches of the Graduates of Yale College* (6 vols. (New York and New Haven 1896 - 1912).

Jacobus   Jacobus, Donald L., *Families of Ancient New Haven* (Vols. 1-5, Rome NY, 1922 - 1929; vols. 6 - 8, New Haven, 1930 - 1832).

LDS Online   https://www.familysearch.org
Family Seach

Malia   Malia, Peter J., *Visible Saints: The Colonial History of West Haven, Connecticut, 1648 - 1798* (Monroe, 2009).

NHCHS *Papers*   New Haven Cololy Historical Society, Papers (New Haven, 1865 -   )

NHCR   *Records of the Colony ... of New Haven, 1638 - 1649*, Charles Hoadley, ed., 2 vols. (New Haven, 1857).

NHTR   *New Haven Town Records, 1649 - 1769*, F. B. Dexter and Zara Powers, eds., 3 vols. (New Haven, 1917, 1919, 1962).

Osterweis   Osterweis, Rollin G., *Three Centuries of New Haven*, (New Haven, Fourth Printing, 1975).

PRCC   *Public Records of the Colony of Connecticut*, 15 vols. (Hartford, 1850 - 1890).

PRSC   *Public Records of the State of Connecticut*, 15 vols. Hartford, 1894 -1991).

New Haven Town Records
1769 - 1819

[DECEMBER 11 , 1769]

AT A TOWN MEETING HELD IN NEW HAVEN DECEMBER 11TH ANNO DOM 1769.

Clerk. Voted that Samuel Bishop J[r] be Town Clerk.[1]

Moderator. Voted that Col: John Hubbard be moderator.

Selectmen. Voted that Mess[rs] Stephen Ball, Nathan Whiting Esq[r] Phins. Bradly, Jeremiah Atwater, John Woodward, Joshua Chandler Esq[r 2] and Andrew Bradly be Selectmen the year Ensuing.

Overseers of the poor. Voted that the above Selectmen together with M[r] Jonathan Smith, Cap[t] Joel Hotchkiss and Simon Bristoll Esq[r] be overseers of the poor the year Ensuing.

Constables. Voted that Stephen Peck, Jonathan Mix, Joseph Holt, Silas Kimberly, Richard Brocket, Amos Thomas, Phin[s] Castle and Timothy Ball be Constables the year Ensuing.

Collector. Voted that Stephen Peck be Collector of the Country Rate the Ensuing year.

Grandjurymen. Voted that James Basset, Benjamin Douglass, David Beecher, Jabez Colt, Jacob Barney, Aaron Page, Jacob Bradly, Elip[t] Beecher, John Horton J[r], Gideon Todd Ju[r], Lawrence Clinton, Abram Carrinton, Thomas Pardee and Lamberton Painter[3] be grandjurymen the Year Ensuing.

1.Samuel Bishop, Jr. (1723 - 1803) served as town clerk from 1747 - 1801. A veteran of the French and Indian War, Bishop held several additional public positions, including serving as New Haven's second mayor and as Collector of the Port of New Haven in 1803.

2. Joshua Chandler (1728 - 1787) was a one-time member of the town's committee of correspondence. Originally from Woodstock, CT, his loyalties to the Crown led him to flee with the British during the July 5 - 6, 1779 invasion of New Haven. Chandler reportedly drowned off the coast of Nova Scotia in 1787. Dexter, II: 108 - 109.

3. Lamberton Painter (1740 - 1795) of West Haven was an ardent patriot and Revolutionary War veteran. See, https://www.findagrave.com/memorial/66645678/lamberton-painter.

Listers. Voted that Stephen Jacobs, Thomas Cooper J^r, Amos Sperry, Abram Chidsey, Jeremiah Ives, Erastus Bradly, Henry Toles J^r, Joseph Dorman, Jesse Leavinworth, Levi Clinton, Philip Dagget and Reuben Sperry be Listers ye year Ensuing.

List. Voted that the making up of the Grand List shall be paid out of the Town Treasury.

[p. 2] Surveyers of Highways. Voted that Isaac Beers,[1] James Rice, Isaac Atwater, John Beecher, Hezekiah Sabin, Asa Todd, Elisha Booth, John Potter, Moses Strong, Daniel Alling, Henry F. Huse, Stephen Smith, Joseph Russel, Jared Robinson, Saml Clark Jr., John Prindle, James Heaton J^r, Joel Basset, Isaac Brocket Ju^r, Elihu Rogers, Oliver Blackslee, Samuel Osborn, Charles Bradly, David Perkins, Reuben Beecher, Enos Hitchcock, Joseph Murwain, Joel Bradly, William Basset, Ezra Sperry, Aaron Smith, Epheram Turner and Jesse Beecher be Surveyers of highways the year Ensuing.

[Districts] Voted that the Selectmen give the Surveyers of highways their Districts.

Highway. Voted that ye Selectmen Lay out and purchase a highway from the Neck lane so Called into the New Township or Oystershell field so Called in Such place as will best accomodate the Publick and be least Detrimental to Private Property and that if they Cannot find waste Land, or needless highways to Dispose of for the purchase of the Same whatever Sum Shall be found wanting they are ordered to draw out of the Town Treasury.[2]

Highway. Voted that the Selectmen view the place where Capt Joel Hotchkiss proposed to have a highway purchased to go to Bethany meeting house and make Report of their opinion thereon unto the Town at their next meeting.

Committee. Voted that Col: whiting,[3] Saml Bishop J^r, Mr Hillhouse and Phin^s Bradly be a Committee to transact the affair of Mr Sabin on flowing the highway by reason of his Damm at Todds mill, and Settle ye Same in a Just & Equitable manner.[4]

---

1. Isaac Beers (1742 - 1813) inherited Beer's Tavern, a combination inn and bookstore, opened by his father in 1751. Beers eventually served as president of the New Haven Bank from 1798 - 1812.
2. This highway ran from what is presently upper State Street (Neck Lane) to a point southeast of the New Haven harbor (New Township).
3. Col. Nathan Whiting (1724 - 1771) graduated from Yale in 1743, served with distinction in the 2nd Connecticut Militia Regiment during the French and Indian War and served in the Connecticut Assembly until his death in 1771. See, Dexter,I: 750.
4. This highway is now Whitney Avenue, as Todd's Mill was located near Lake Whitney.

This meeting adj^d to the Last monday of Instant Decr at 1 of ye Clock in the afternoon.

[December 25, 1769]

[p. 3] AT A TOWN MEETING HOLDEN IN NEW HAVEN BY AD-JOURNMENT UPON THE 25TH DAY OF DECEMBER 1769.[1]

Moderator. Thomas Darling Esqr Chosen moderator.[2]

Key Keepers. Voted that Joseph Munson, Noah Potter, James Thompson, Joseph Gilbert, Aaron Gilbert, John Thompson, E.H. *[East Haven]*, Joel Tuttle, Sam^{ll} Candee J^r, James Bishop, Enos Granis, William Adams, Elisha Bradly, Joseph Beecher J^r, Ben^j Pardee, Mt. C. *[Mt. Carmel]*, Joseph Turner and Noah Ives be key keepers the year Ensuing.

Branders. Voted that Theophilus Munson, Elisha Booth, Simeon Bradly, Roger Alling, Thomas Mansfield, Joseph Peck, Jonathan Ives and Roger Peck be branders of horses the year Ensuing.

Culers of Lumber. Voted that John Miles, Newman Trowbridge, Robt Brown and John Beecher of W. H. *[West Haven]*, be Surveyors and Culers of Lumber the year Ensuing.[3]

Sealer [of weights & measures]. Voted that Theophilus Munson be Sealer of weights and measures the year ensuing.

Sealer [of dry measures]. Voted that John Miles be Sealer of Dry measures the year Ensuing.

Committee of Incroachments. Voted that John Potter, Caleb Hotchkiss Ju^r, Benjamin Wooding, Jonathan Alling J^r and Jared Robinson be a Committee to Remove Incroachments of from the Highway the year Ensuing.

---

1. Christmas in 18th century Connecticut was deemed a day of "pagan revelry" and "papist idolatry" and was not celebrated by the Congregational Church. Christmas was not made a federal holiday until 1870.
2. Thomas Darling (1720 - 1789), originally from Newport, Rhode Island, remained in New Haven as a tutor following his graduation in 1740. A successful entrepreneur, he ran a number of businesses, from a rope walk manufacturer to a printing business — the first in New Haven, See, Dexter, I: 643.
3. Laws enacted to protect over cutting of wood in New Haven date back to 1652. See *NHTR I; passim.*

Town Treasurer. Voted that Samuel Bishop J[r] be Town Treasurer the year Ensuing.

Leather Sealer. Voted that Stephen Bradly be Leather Sealer the year Ensuing.

[p. 4] Tythingmen. Voted Stephen Alling J[r], Caleb Gilbert, John Heminway, Ezra Ives, Benj. Brocket, Sam[l] Smith, Joseph Hotchkiss, Titus Smith, George Smith and Gamaliel Benham be Tythingmen the year Ensuing.

Coll[r]. Voted that Col: Wooster[1] be Collector of the Duty of five per C[t] on goods the year ensuing.

Bridge. Voted that the Selectmen Lay out forty Shillings on y[e] bridge over the mill river East from Bazel Munsons if they just best and needful.[2]

Swine. Voted that Swine be allowed to go upon the highways & Commons within this Town the Ensuing year and Shall not be Imported from thence Provided they are ringed all the year and Sufficiently yoaked from the 10th of march to the 10th of Nov[r] next.

Highway. *Voted that Joshua Chandler Esq[r], Col: Nathan Whiting, M[r] And[r] Bradly, Dan[l] Lyman Esq[r],[3] and Samuel Bishop J[r] be a Committee to Lay out and Purchase a highway where it is necessary from Cheshire Road to Bethany meeting *[house]* in Such place as will accommodate the Publick and Such Particular persons as Shall have Occasion to use the Same, three of them to be Sufficent to act in Laying out and Purchasing y[e] Same.

Voted that this meeting be adjourned to the first monday of January Next at one of y[e] Clock in the afternoon.

[JANUARY 1, 1770]

AT A TOWN MEETING HOLDEN IN NEW HAVEN BY ADJOURN-
MENT UPON THE FIRST DAY OF JANUARY 1770.

1.David Wooster (1710/11 - 1777) a 1738 Yale graduate, pursued a military career and served as a brigadier general in the Continental Army during the Revolution. He died of his wounds sustained at the Battle of Ridgefield in 1777. See, Dexter, I: 616 - 620.

2. This bridge was first erected by Ithamer Todd (1712 - 1785) in 1762.

3. Daniel Lyman (1718 - 1788), a native of Northampton, Massachusetts, remained in New Haven following his graduation from Yale in 1745. A prosperous merchant and political force in the Connecticut Assembly, he was also a leading New Light advocate. See, Dexter, II: 48 - 49.

Highway. *The Last vote passed about the highway from Cheshire road to Bethany meeting house was passed in this meeting.

[p. 5] Rate. Voted that there be a Rate of two pence on the pound paid by this Town upon the present List to Defray the Necessary *[costs]* arising within the Same the year Ensuing.

Coll^r. Voted that Thomas Punderson be Collector of said Rate.

Voted that s^d Punderson Shall have fifteen pounds for Collecting said Rate.

Rate to be paid. Voted that s^d rate be paid on the first Day of march next.

Surveyer. Voted that Jared Bradly be ~~Collector~~ Surveyer of highways.

Grandjuryrman. Voted that Peter Johnson be Grandjuryman in the Room of Mr Douglass who refused to Serve.

This meeting adjourned without *[day]*.

[APRIL 9, 1770]

AT A TOWN MEETING HELD IN NEW HAVEN UPON THE 9TH DAY OF APRIL 1770.

[Moderator.] Voted that Col: Nathan Whiting be moderator of this meeting.

Surveyer. Voted that Hezekiah Basset be Surveyer of highways in Room of William Basset.

Surveyer. Voted that Stephen Sanford J^r be Surveyer of highways in the Room of Aaron Smith.

Oyster act. Whereas the Catching of oysters in the Harbour of this Town In the Summer months and with Drags any Time in the year is found to be very Prejudicial to the growth and increase of that very usefull article of Subsistance. Thereupon voted and ordered that no person whatsoever do Catch any oysters in s^d Harbour or Cove of this Town in ye months of May, June, July, and August nor with Drags at any Time in the year and y^t ye waste shells taken with the oysters Shall be Severed from ~~them on pain of forfeiting ye Sum of Twenty Shil-~~

~~lings Lawfull money for every offence,~~ the oysters at the Place where taken in the Harbour or Cove and not Carried and Cleaned on the Shore or Land, on pain of forfieting *[p. 6]* Sum of Twenty Shillings Lawful money for every offence above mentioned Except that of Catching with a Drag and for that offence the Sum of forty Shillings, one half to him or them who shall sue for and Recover the Same and the other half to the use of the Town Treasury.[1]...Provided nevertheless that the Selectmen or any two of them may give leave and Licence to Catch oysters within the s^d four months in Case of Sickness only the Same being Certified under their hands and not to Exceed one bushel at any one time.

Further voted that Jacob Pardee Josiah Bradly, John Hemiway, Amos Morris, Jererniah Osborn, Benj Pardee, Abram Tuttle, Dan^ll Tallmadge, E1ip^r Stevens, Phileman Potter, Daniel Thonas, Jehiel Forbs, Thomas Davis & Benj Brocket be and they are hereby Specially Desired to take Care to prosecute all and ~~Every~~ any breachs of this order, this Special request not to hinder any other of the inhabitants from prosecuting as they may have opportunity.

This meeting adjourned without Day.

[SEPTEMBER 10, 1770]

AT A TOWN MEETING HOLDEN IN NEW HAVEN UPON THE 10TH DAY OF SEPTEMBER 1770.

[Moderator.] Col: John Hubbard Chosen moderator.

Committee. Voted that Col: Nathan Whiting, Mr Adam Babcock, Joshua Chandler Esqr, Danl Lyman Esqr, Mr Jesse Leavenworth, Mr Ralph Isaacs, Cap^r Joel Hotchkiss and Deacon David Austin be a Committee to meet the Gentlemen who may be appointed in the other Towns in this Colony to meet on the 13th Day of Instant Sepr to Consider what may be done towards promoting the Commercial Interest of ye Colony.[2]

---

1. On orders from the Connecticut Legislature, New Haven first regulated the taking of oysters in the off-season in 1762 and annually renewed those regulations. New Haven eventually banned the use of drag nets altogether. See, https://connecticuthistory.org/oystering-in-connecticut-from-colonial-times-to-today.
2. This committee was named to meet with representatives from other Connecticut towns to reaffirm their support of a 1767 non-importation agreement in protest of the Townshend Acts, including the tax on tea.

This meeting adjourned to the 3ᵈ Tuesday of Sepʳ Instant at three of the Clock in the afternoon.

[SEPTEMBER 18, 1770]

AT A TOWN MEETING HELD IN NEW HAVEN BY ADJOURNMENT UPON Yᴱ 18ᵀᴴ DAY OF SEPTEMBER ANNO DOMNI 1770.

[p. 7] Committee. Voted that Messʳˢ Thomas Darling, Adam Babcock, David Wooster, Joshua Chandler, Daniel Lyman, Roger Sherman,[1] John Hubbard, Simeon Bristoll, Samuel Heminway, Benj Smith, Andrew Bradly, Thos. Howel, Joseph Munson, William Granough, Nathan Whiting, Joel Hotchkiss, David Austin, Samuel Bishop Jʳ, Ralph Isaacs, Phenias Bradly, John Whiting, Stephen Ball, Jeremiah Atwater, John Woodward, James Thompson, Jesse Leavenworth, Enos Alling, Willᵐ Grigory, Jacob Pinto, Hezʳ Sabin, Samuel Sacket, Caleb Beecher, Willᵐ Douglass, Jared Ingersoll,[2] James A. Hillhouse,[3] Isaac Beers, Tim° Jones Jʳ and Amos Botchford — be a Committee to take into Consideration the present State of the commercial Interest of this place, and Report their opinion What they Judge is best and needfull to be done Relative thereto.[4]

This meeting adjourned unto the 3ᵈ thursday of octʳ next at two of the Clock in the afternoon at the brick meeting House.

There was not any meeting at the Time to which it was adjourned.

[DECEMBER 10, 1770]

[p. 8] AT A TOWN MEETING HELD IN NEW HAVEN UPON THE 10ᵀᴴ DAY OF DECEMBER 1770.

Clerk. Voted that Samuel Bishop Jʳ be Town Clerk.

---

2. Roger Sherman (1721 - 1793), originally of Newton, MA, needs little introduction beyond the fact that he was among the nation's most prominent Founding Fathers.

2. Jared Ingersoll (1722 - 1781) is best remembered as Connecticut's ill-fated stamp collector, who was forced to resign his office at the hands of a threatening mob in 1765.

3. James A. Hillhouse (1730 - 1775), of Montville, CT, graduated from Yale College in 1749, opened a law practice, and was the first Hillhouse in New Haven. He was the uncle of the U.S. Congressman and Senator James A. Hillhouse (1754 - 1832) of New Haven. See Dexter, II: 208 - 210.

4. According to Edward Atwater, this committee never filed a report. Soon after Parliament repealed most of the taxes in Townshend Acts except for a three pence per pound tax on tea.

Mod'. Voted that Col: John Hubbard be moderator.

Selectmen. Voted that Mr Stephen Ball, Nathan Whiting Esqr, Mr Phenias Bradly, Mr. Jeremiah Atwater, Mr John Woodward,[1] Joshua Chandler Esqr and Mr. Andrew Bradly be Selectmen the year ensuing.

Constables. Voted that Joel Gilbert, Stephen Peck, Jonathan Mix, John Denison, George Smith, John Gilbert,[2] N. H. *[North Haven]* Amos Thomas, Lemuel Bradly and Aaron Smith be Constables the year Ensuing.

[Constable.] Voted that George Smith be released from being Constable and Lamberton Painter Chosen in his Stead.

Grandjurymen. Voted that Abel Burret, Jonathan Osborn, Nath^ll Spencer, Rutherford Trowbridge, Jeremiah Parmale, Stephen Bradly E.H. *[East Haven]*, Saml Davenport, Jesse Stevens, Benjamin Pierpont, Ithamer Tuttle, Elip^t Beecher, Samuel Alling, Nathan Alling J^r and Peter Perkins be Grandjurymen the year Ensuing.

Listers. Voted that Isaac Bishop, Isaac Beers, Amos Balisford, Sam^ll Horton, Benj. Woodin, Seth Blackslee, Jesse Ford, Asa Goodyear, Nat^ll Beech, Samuel Thompson J^r, Andrew Smith Ju^r and Isaac Sperry be Listers ye year Ensuing.

[p. 9] Surveyers. Voted that James Rice, Ralph Isaacs, John Beecher, Nathan Mansfield, Lemuel Umberfield, Saml Horton, Hez^r Sabin, Mathew Gilbert Ju^r, Jabez Munson, Stephen Morris, Israel Potter, Joshua Austin, Timothy Thompson, Edward Russel, Samuel Tuttle, Saml Clark J^r, John Prindle, Samuel Candee J^r, Joshua Chandler Esqr, Jesse Todd, Saml Hitchock W. H. *[West Haven]*, Joel Blackslee, Elias Beech, Joseph Humaston Ju^r, John Johnson of Amity, David Ford, Charles Bradly, Amos Perkins, Reuben Beecher, Noadiah Carrinton, Alvan Bradly, David Sperry Mt. C. *[Mount Carmel]*, Amos Hitchcock, Thomas Johnson, Edward Perkins, Thomas Beecher J^r and David Clark be Surveyers of highways the year Ensuing.

Districts. Voted that the Selectmen Give the Surveyers their Districts.

Rate books. Voted that the Rate books for Collecting ye Country rate be made up by the Town Clerk at the Towns Cost.

---

1. John Woodward (1742 - 1810).
2. Capt. John Gilbert (1731 - 1779) was killed during the British invasion of New Haven on July 5, 1779, along with his brother, Michael Gilbert.

This meeting adjourned to the Last monday of Instant December at 10 of the Clock in the forenoon.

[DECEMBER 31, 1770]

AT A TOWN MEETING HELD IN NEW HAVEN BY ADJOURNMENT UPON THE 31 DAY OF DECEMBER 1770.

Key keepers. Voted that John Thompson E. H. *[East Haven]*, Joseph Munson, Noah Potter, James Thompson, Joseph Gilbert, Aaron Gilbert, Joel Tuttle, Sam^ll, Candee J^r, James Bishop, Enos Granis, Will Adams, Elisha Bradly, Joseph Beecher J^r, Ben^j Pardee,[1] Jos^ph Turner and Noah Ives be key keepers the year Ensuing.

[Cullers of Lumber.] Voted that John Miles, Newman Trowbridge, Robt Browne and John Beecher of W. H. *[West Haven]*, be Cullers of Lumber the year Ensuing.

[p. 10] Branders. Voted that Theop^s Munson, Elisha Booth, Simeon Bristol, Thomas Mansfield, Joseph Peck, Jonathan Ives, Roger Peck and George Smith be branders of branders of horses the year Ensuing.

Sealer. Voted that Theop^s Munson be Sealer of w^ts & measures.

Sealer. Voted that John Miles be Sealer of Dry measures.

Committee of Incroachm^ts. Voted that Caleb Hotchkiss J^r, Jonathan Alling J^r, Jared Robinson, Joseph Dorman and Stephen Ford be a Committee to remove incroachments of from the highways the Ensuing year.

Sealer. Voted that Stephen Bradly be Sealer of leather.

Treasurer. Voted that Samuel Bishop J^r be Town Treasurer the year Ensuing.

Tythingmen. Voted that Danl Tuttle, Jonathan Bradly, Joseph Thompson, Eben^r Townsend J^r, John Heminway, Willliam Granis, Isaac Beecher J^r, John Catlin, Epheram Humaston, Samuel Smith, Ambros Peck, John Ives, Stephen Lounsbury, Newman Trowbridge, John Gilbert Jr., Eben^r Barns, Tim° Bradly N.H.

---

1. Benjamin Pardee (1716 - 1776) and his wife, Hannah (1727 - 1767), among the first residents of Centerville, Hamden. His tombstone carries a curiously tragic epitaph: "He was crushed to death in an instant." Rachel M. Hartley, *The History of Hamden, 1786 - 1959* (Hamden, 1959), p. 220.

[North Haven], be Tythingmen the year Ensuing.

Fence viewers. Voted that John Mix, Nathan Mansfield, Obediah Hotchkiss, Ep-heram Humaston, Thomas Mansfield, Josiah Bradly and Sam[l] Thompson be fence viewers the year Ensuing.

Surveyers. Voted that Thomas Cooper J[r], and Job Blackslee be Surveyers of high-ways the year Ensuing.

[p. 11] Swine. Voted that Swine be allowed to go upon the Commons and high-ways within this Town y[e] Ensuing year and Shall not be Impounded Form thence Provided they are ringed all the year and Sufficiently yoaked from the 10th of March to y[e] 10 Day of Nov[r] next.

[Smallpox] Ben[j] Dorchester. Voted that y[e] Selectmen Provide Suitable house to Re-move Benj Dorchester unto, he being, he being *[sic.]* so broken out with the Small pox which is to be at s[d] Dorchester Cost.[1]

Rate. Voted that there be a rate or Tax Collected of the Inhabitants of the Town upon the present list of two pence half penny on the pound, to Defray the nec-essary charges arising in this Town the Ensuing year.

Voted that the s[d] rate be paid on the first Day of march next.[2]

Coll[r]. Voted that Thomas Punderson be Collector of the abovesaid Rate, and that he Shall have fifteen pounds for Collecting the Same.

Constable Voted that John Miles be Constable y[e] Ensuing year.

Geese. Voted y[t] if geese be found *[and]* Damages pasent, *[they will]* be Inpounded, and Impounded the owner thereof Shall pay four pence p[r] head.

Listers. Voted that there Shall be paid unto the Listers y[e] Sum of Three pounds out of the Town Treasury for making up the Grand List.

---

1. New Haven officials worried that inoculation might further spread the disease. It was not until 1792 that Dr. Levi Ives won town approval to erect an inoculation hospital in the city.
2. As there were roughly 240 pence to a pound in the late 18th century, this tax equated to roughly 1 1/4 percent.

Committee. Voted that Capt Abiather Camp[1] and James Rice be a Committee to remove the Incumbrances and Nusences in the highways and Streets in the Town.

Saml Horton. Voted that ye Selectmen Lease to Mr Samuel Horton part of the highway Near his house For Some of his Land for use of a highway During the Pleasure of ye Town.

[p. 12] Oysters. Whereas the catching of oysters in ye Harbour of this Town in the Summer months and with draggs at any Time in ye year is found to be very prejudical to ye growth and increase of that usefull article of Subsistance.

Therefore voted and ordered that no person whatsoever do Catch any oysters in the Harbour or Cove of this Town in the months of May, June, July, and August annually Nor with a Dragg at any Time in the year and that the waste Shells taken with oysters Shall be Severed from the oysters at the place where taken in the harbour or Cove and not Carried and Cleaned on the Shore or Land, on pain of forfieting the Sum of Twenty Shillings Lawfull money for every offence above mentioned Except that of Catching with a Dragg and for that offence the Sum of forty Shillings one half to him or her who Shall Sue for and Recover the Same and the other half to the use of ye Town treasury; Provided nevertheless y^t ye Selectmen or any two of them may Give Leave and Licence to Catch oysters within s^d four months in Cases of Sickness only the Same being Certified under their hands and not to Exceed one bushel at anyone Time — Further voted that Jacob Pardee, Josiah Bradly, John Heminway, Amos Morris, Jermiah Osborn, Benj Pardee, Abr^m Tuttle, Danl Tallmadge, Elip^t Stevens, Phileman Potter, Danl Thomas, Jehiel Forbs, Thomas Davis & Ben^j Brocket be and they are hereby Specially Desired to take Care to prosecute all and any breaches of this order this Special Request not to hinder any other of the Inhabitants from prosecuting as they may have the opportunity.

Voted that the Same Regulation under the Same Penalty Shall Extend to Stoney River.

[p. 13] Also voted y^t Jacob Bradly and James Thompson of East Haven be added to the forgoing persons and y^t ye whole of them be Desired to prosecute in s^d Stoney River in the Same manner as they were Desired to prosecute in the Harbour and Cove.

---

1. Abiathar Camp, Sr. (1732- 1787) was a prosperous New Haven merchant and Loyalist who left New Haven with the British during the invasion of New Haven in 1779. He died in St. John's, Canada in 1787.

Committee. Voted that Benj: Woodin and Elisha Booth be a Committee to view the Shot way So Called near the west Rock and Clay pits,[1] and Report whether it is needfull *[if]* there Should be a bridge built over the brook at that Place.

D[eacon Jonathan?] Mansfield.[2] Voted that any two of yᵉ Selectmen be desired to view yᵉ Land Deacon Mansfield hath thrown out for a highway on the west side of his Land North of his Son Nathan Mansfields and Judge what is Right to be done relative thereto & Report their opinion.

pound. Voted that Ebenʳ Johnson have Liberty to build a pound at his own Cost near his house & be key keeper thereof.

[Highway.] Whereas the Proprietors have appointed a Committee to State the width of the highway Conveyed to Capᵗ Miles and Capᵗ Trowbridge before their homelots by the Propʳˢ Committee and also to view the Bank & Shore from Grenoughs Point to the ferry point, Draw a plan of the Same and thereon point out the grants that have been made this Town being Sensable yᵗ *[it]* is an affar of very great Importance yᵗ the highways be kept open and proper Places for landing be kept for Publick use, Do therefore appoint yᵉ Selectmen to Joyne with the sᵈ Propʳˢ Committee to do the business particularly mentioned in yᵉ Propʳˢ vote of the 3ᵈ of october 1769 and make report of their doings unto the Town at another meeting.[3]

[APRIL 8, 1771]

[p. 14] AT A TOWN MEETING HELD IN NEW HAVEN UPON THE 8ᵀᴴ DAY OF APRIL 1771.

[Moderator.] Voted that Mʳ James Pierpoint[4] be moderator.

Survveyer. Voted that Noah Ives be Surveyer of highways in the room of Joshua Chandler Esqʳ.*Highway.* Voted that the Selectmen lay out a highway across the Govʳˢ quarter where it will best accomodate yᵉ Publick.

Mr. Martin. Voted that yᵉ Selectmen Lease unto Mʳ *[...]* Martin a Small piece of

---

1. Clay deposits in the New Haven area extended from North Haven across what were then marshy meadows to the Montowese section of town.
2. Jonathan Mansfield (1685/6 - 1775).
3. The highway mentioned was likely West Water Street, located near the deepest waters of the harbor.
4. James Pierpont (1699 - 1776) was the son of the Reverend James Pierpont.

Land in Mount Carmel near where he Dwells to Set a Shop upon During the Pleasure of the Town.[1]

[Committee Report.] The ~~Committee~~ Selectmen appointed the Last meeting to Joyn with the Prop^{rs} Committee about the Shore and flatts &c made the following report which was read and Considered by the Town and was by vote accepted and ordered to be Recorded.

We the Subscribers being a Committee appointed by the Prop^{rs} of ye Common and undivided Lands in New Haven and also being appointed by s^d Town of New Haven to State ye width of that highway which the Prop^{rs} Committee Conveyed unto Capt Miles and Capt Trowbridge in Lieu of the highway they Conveyed to ye Prop^{rs} before their Houses — And also to view the bank on Shore from Grenoughs Point to the ferry Point, See what grants have been made and draw a plan of ye bank & point out thereon the grants that have been made and report to ye Prop^{rs} and Town ye true State and Circumstances of the bank or Shore with their opinion what is needfull and best that the Prop^{rs} Should do relative thereto. *[p. 15]* Agreeable to the Trust in us reposed we have viewed the State & Circumstances of the highway Conveyed as aforesaid to s^d Miles & Trowbridge and are of the opinion that the old original highway is four rods wide and they ye s^d Miles and Trowbridge lines ought to hold four rods wide against each of their s^d Lots and have accordingly Stated out the Same in Lieu of the highway Conveyed as aforesaid, we then went to Granoughs point and found y^t Mr Grunough Supposed y^t he had a Legall right on ye South and west of his Late homestead to the Creek Save a needfull highway — and on that Principle Conveyed the Same in pc *[?]* with a warrentee to Mr James Rice and y^t Mr Rice & others have Expended Large Sums of money in building a Dike and highway from s^d Grunoughs Point to the oysterpoint which we Suppose will be of great Publick advantage not only for passing and repassing but for a Landing and watering all which have been made very Beneficial at the Cost of s^d Rice and his associates in building s^d Dike. In Consideration thereof we Humbly give it as our opinion that ye prop^{rs} Grant to s^d Mr Grunough all ye Land that Lyes North from the Southwest Corner of Mr Richard Rosewells Lot to a Stake on the Edge of ye Creek the west side being in length Ten rods and Seven Tenths of a rod the Course is west 29 Degrees South from s^d Southwest Corner as also the Lands y^t Lye South of s^d homestead beginning at the west Corner of the old ware

1. Likely Samuel Martin of Hamden, who served as Connecticut militiaman in Col. Mosley's Regiment in 1779. See, Henry Phelps Johnson, *Record of Service of Connecticut Men in the War of the Revolution* (1889), I: 615. See also, 1790 United States Federal Census. [database on-line]. Provo, UT, USA.

house and from thence running west 40 Degrees South Eight rods to a Stake and from thence five rods and a half South 20 Degrees East and from *[there]* in a Strait Line to ye Southwestern most Corner of Capt Trowbridges Pier untill it Comes within 60 feet of the Easternmost part of the highway y^t of the highway that Leads between the houses of Capt Thos Rice and Capt Trowbridges heirs, we also give it as *[p. 16]* our opinion that there Shall be a Slip of Sixty feet wide Extending in a Strait Line of the s^d Street untill it Comes to Low water mark. We also find that Capt Trowbridge in his Life Time and heirs Since have made Incroachment against the whole width of s^d Trowbridges home lot south of the highway Stated as aforesaid. We also find y^t Mr Enos Alling hath also Incroached the Whole width of his lot South of said highway Stated or aforesaid.

We also find that Mr Hudson formerly had a grant form the proprietors for Liberty to build a ware house which was Placed in Such a Form y^t it will project a Little into the Street y^t leads to the Harbour between the houses of Danl Lyman Esqr and James Peck which he is willing to quit Claim to ye prop^rs provided he is Quieted in his Incroachment with respect to the Incroachment made by the s^d Alling and the Trowbridges, we give it as our opinion y^t Some Disinterested and Judicious men be Chosen to Settle and adjust that matter which the s^d Alling and Trowbridges are willing to agree to.

Mr James Rice Lyes between s^d Alling and ye Trowbridges, and is Desireous that ye Same men may be Desired to Say what he ought to give to have his Lot extend as far as s^d Alling and Trowbridge, we also report it as our opinion that there Should be a slip running in a Strait Line with ye west side of ye Street y^t runs by Deacon Lymans to ye Chanel and to Extend on the East Line after it passes Capt Pecks grant Six rods wide to the Chanel as aforesaid. We also find that the Prop^rs granted to Bates 50 or 60 feet wide running towards ye Channel South 29 Degrees East. We also find y^t ye Prop^rs granted to Capt James Peck a Certain part of the flatts which grant was made in Feby 1744 *[p. 17]* And was on the East Side of the Claim of the Proprietors of Bates Wharf not to interfer with s^d Prop^rs Claim, and not to Exceed five rods in width and to begin as far Southerly as ye end of the then present wharff and to continue to the Chanel. We also find that there hath been many Incroachments on the west Side of the s^d wharff grants viz. Michael Todd one rod and Six Tenths of a rod ye Length of his grant*[,]* Jacob Pinto one rod*[,]* Jonathan Osborn one rod: Capt Joseph Munson 4 rods*[,]* Capt Stephen Mansfield two rods and a half*[,]* Capt Camp two rods and a half*[.]* These Incroachments are the whole Length of the grants made by the union

Wharff Company[1] and also we find that Thomas Trowbridge had a grant of
Twenty two feet wide and 30 feet Long above highwater mark and two or three
rods into the flatts Eastward of Mr Bates Grant Since which M^{essrs} Howell and
Alling have got the fie[?] and possision and have incroached on the East Side
thirty four feet wide & five rods Long, we also find y^t the Prop^{rs} Committee
Conveyed to Deacon Lyman by Deed of warrentee a part of the flats bounded
north on the above Grant west of the wharff grant Extending South four rods
and East 3 rods.

We also find that there is a report of a Committee which was Accepted by the
proprietors wherein Capt Munson has a grant of a piece of flatts which he is to
have on Certain Conditions which will Extend to the Channel if those Conditions are Complyed with — There is a Large Slip of Land not yet granted on the
East Side of s^d Munsons Grant and South of Sabins Dike. The next grant we
find is a grant to Mr Jeremiah Atwater of the Place whereon the house Stands
y^t was built by Mr Eliot[,] then another slip untill it Comes to a grant made to
the Revd Mr Pierpoint, then a Slip of Ten feet[,] then another grant to Jeremiah
[p. 18] Atwater[,] then a Slip of one rod[,] then another grant to John Morris[,]
then another grant to Moses Mansfield[,] then a Slit between Moses Mansfields
grant where Sabins Still house now Stands and Browns grant — Then a grant to
Francis Browne[2][,] then a Slip[,] then a grant to John Munson[,] then a Slip of
Twenty Feet[,] then a grant where Mr Shermans house now stands. On all these
grants there is Incroachments Save the two ~~Last~~ first.

Then there is a Large Slip[,] the next grant we find is to John Todd, then another grant to Francis Browne[,] then we find an Incroachment made by Abram
Tuttle, and another Incroachment where Capt Ray now Lives[,] then we find a
grant to Ele^z Browne, then we find an Incroachment made by Mr Isaacs.

We also Give it as our opinion that a wise and Judicious Committee Consisting
of two or three men be Chosen to Settle with all those that have Incroached
upon the prop^{rs} Interest in the most prai[s]able and Equitable Manner they Can

1. The original wharf was constructed in 1717 and was gradually expanded over the years. Maintenance costs were high, leading its owners to seek public incorporation in 1760 as the Union Wharf
Company. Although vital to New Haven's maritime enterprise, the wharf's upkeep always proved
problematic.
2. Francis Brown (1610-1668) was originally from Ratcliffe, York, England. He lived in East Haven and was a tailor by trade. He also ran a ferry across the Quinnipiac River to New Haven.
See, "Francis Brown," Devin Family Association, 2018, http://www.devintimber.org/getperson.
php?personID=I6240/..

So that those who have Incroached may be Quited in their possession, That the Same Committee be Impowered to Lay out all needfull Slips and also Convenient Building yards.

New Haven april 8, 1771

Jonathan Mansfield
James Pierpoint
Willm Grunough
Danl Lyman
Phin^s Bradly
Ben^j Woodin
Saml Bishop J^r
J. Chandler
Andrew Bradly
Step^n Ball
Jeremiah Atwater

[DECEMBER 9, 1771]

AT A TOWN MEETING HELD IN NEW HAVEN UPON Y^E 9TH DAY OF DECEMBER 1771.

Town Clerk. Samuel Bishop J^r Chosen Town Clerk.

Mod^r. John Hubbard Esqr Chosen moderator.

Selectmen. Voted that M^essrs Stephen Ball, Jeremiah Atwater, John Woodward, Joshua Chandler, Andrew Bradly, Phenias Bradly and Benjamin Douglass[1] be Selectmen for the Town the year Ensuing.

Constables. Voted that Jonathan Mix,[2] Abram Auger & Isaac Bishop be Constables the year Ensuing.

Coll^r. Voted that Jonathan Mix be Collector of ye Country rate the year Ensuing.

Committee about a City. Whereas a motion was made to the Town that this Town

---

1. Benjamin Douglas (1739 - 1775) graduated from Yale in 1760 and established a thriving law practice in New Haven until his premature death from erysipelas at the age of 37. See, Franklin B. Dexter, *Biographical Sketches of the Graduates of Yale College,* (New York, 1896), Vol. II: 650.
2. Jonathan Mix (1753 - 1816) of Hamden served with distinction in the American Revolution as a captain of marines. He spent time aboard the British prison ship *Jersey.* Following the war he created a revolutionary wagon spring that launched New Haven as the center of the carriage industry.

might have the Priviliges of a City, and that proper measures might be taken to obtain ye Same.

It is thereupon voted y^t Roger Sherman, John Whiting, Thomas Darling, Daniel Lyman, David Wooster, Joshua Chandler, James A. Hillhouse, Simeon Bristoll, Caleb Beecher Esqr, Saml Bishop J^r & M^essrs James Peck, Benjamin Douglass, Ralph Isaacs, Adam Babcock, Thomas Howell, Joel Hotchkiss, Sam^ll Clark J^r, and John Woodward be a Committee to take ye Same into Consideration, and Judge of the motion what is best for the Town to do with regard to the Same and report thereupon thereon to the Town at another Town meeting.[1]

This meeting adjourned to ye next monday at 10" of the Clock in the forenoon.

[DECEMBER 16, 1771]

[p. 20] AT A TOWN MEETING HELD IN NEW HAVEN BY ADJOURN-MENT UPON THE 16TH DAY OF DECEMBER 1771.

Mod^r. Voted y^t Col: David Wooster be moderator in the room of Col: Hubbard who is absent.

Constable. Voted y^t John White J^r be Constable in the room of Isaac Bishop who is released.

Constables. Voted that John Gilbert, Amos Thomas J^r, Stephen Sanford J^r, Lemuel Bradley, Lamberton Painter and John Denison be Constables the year Ensuing.

Surveyers of highways. Voted that Jacob Pardee, Jonathan Roberts, Gaskill Woodward, Job Smith, Joseph Holt, Saml^l Thompson Ju^r, Joseph Merwin J^r, Nathl Downs J^r, Nehemiah Smith, Joseph Bradly J^r, Seth Blackslee, Hez^r Pierpoint, Jonathan Heaton, James Smith, Obed Johnson, Nathl Sperry, Titus Smith, Solomon Gilbert, Lazarus Toles, Edward Perkins, Tim° Brown, Isaac Beecher,[2] Eben^r Bishop J^r, Ralph Isaacs, James Thompson, Benjn Douglass, David Wooster, Phillip Rexford, Saml Beecher, John Woodin 3^d, Willm Denslee, Moses Gilbert, Theop^s Goodyear[3]

---

1. The committee apparently voted against the idea as there is no record of the General Assembly receiving such a petition. New Haven did finally incorporate as a city in January 21, 1784.
2. Isaac Beecher (1716 - 1801) of Amity. The other contemporary Isaac (1726/7 - 1814) was called Jr., and was a West Haven resident.
3. Theophilus Goodyear (1731 - 1793) of Hamden responded to the Lexington alarm of 1775 and compiled a distinguished military record during the Revolution. As one of Hamden's first selectmen,

and Samuel Dickerman[1] be Surveyers of highways the year Ensuing.

Districts. Voted that ye Selectmen give the Surveyers their Districts.

Key Keepers. Voted that John Thompson E.H. *[East Haven]*, Joseph Munson, Noah Potter, James Thompson, Joseph Gilbert, Aaron Gilbert, Joel Tuttle, Samuel Candee J^r, James Bishop, Enos Granis, William Adams. Elisha Bradly, Joseph Beecher J^r, Benjamin Pardee, Joseph Turner and Noah Ives be key keepers the year ensuing.

Cullers. *[p. 21]* Voted y^t John Miles, Newman Trowbridge, Robert Browne and John Beecher of W. H. *[West Haven]* be Surveyers and Cullers of Lumber.

Branders. Voted that Theop^s Munson, Elisha Booth, Simeon Bradly, Thomas Mansfield, Joseph Peck, Jonathan Ives, Roger Peck and George Smith be branders of horses ye year Ensuing.

Sealer. Voted that Theop^s Munson be Sealer of ~~dry~~ weights and measures.

Sealer. Voted that John Miles be Sealer of dry measures.

Treas^r. Voted that Samuel Bishop J^r, be Town Treasurer ye year ensuing.

viewers. Voted that John Mix, Nathan Mansfield, Obediah Hotchkiss, Ephram Humaston, Thomas Mansfield, Josiah Bradly and Sam^{ll} Thompson be fence viewers ye year Ensuing.

Grandjurymen. Voted that Elip^t Pardee,[2] David Bishop, Peter Booth, Samuel Osborn, Sam^{ll} Mallrop, Sam^{ll} Downs, Jonathan Smith, James Blackslee, Nath^{ll} Heaton Ju^r, Jesse Goodyear and John Miles be Grandjurymen the year Ensuing.

Listers. Voted y^t Peter Colt,[3] William Jones, Samuel Whittelsey, Jared Robinson,

---

he voted against the U.S. Constitution at the Hartford Convention of 1788.

1. Samuel Dickerman (1745 - 1789) also served as one of Hamden's inaugural first selectmen following the town's incorporation. See, Hartley, pp. 99, 102.

2. Eliphalet Pardee (1726 - 1804) of East Haven ran a ferry over the Quinnipiac River based at Dragon Point.

3. Peter Colt (1744 - 1824) served as Deputy Commissary General of Purchases for the Eastern Department with the rank of colonel during the Revolution. He served as Treasurer of Connecticut from 1789 - 1793 before removing to Patterson New Jersey. See, https://www.zoominfo.com/p/Peter-Colt/119201283.

Henry F. Huse, John Gills, Joseph Turner, Sam^{ll} Sacket J^r, Jesse Ford, Elihu Hotchkiss, Sam^{ll} Martin, Hez^r Smith and Oliver Smith be Listers the year ensuing.

Tythingmen. Voted y^t John Warner, Nathan Dumer, Gregson Gilbert, Charles Alling, Eben^r Brocket, Solomon Tuttle, Titus Tharpe, John Heminway, Levi Pardee, Joseph Hotchkiss, Ephram Turner be Tythingmen the year Ensuing.

Rate. Voted that there be a rate or Tax Collected of the Inhabitants of ye Town on the present List of one penny half penny on the pound to Defray ye necessary Charges of the Town the year Ensuing.

[p. 22] Voted y^t ye Town rate be paid on the first Day of march next.

Coll^r. Voted that Barnabas Baldwin, Jonathan Mix, Samuel Candee J^r, Ezra Sperry, Enos Todd, Israel Potter and Lemuel Bradly be Collectors of the Town rate .

This meeting adjourned to ye 1st monday of January next at 1 of the Clock in the afternoon.

[JANUARY 6, 1772]

AT A TOWN MEETING HELD IN NEW HAVEN BY ADJOURNMENT UPON THE SIXTH DAY OF JANUARY 1772.

D[eacon] Mansfield. Voted that ye Selectmen quit all y^e *[sic.]* ye Interest that the Town hath to pass through the Land of Deacon Mansfield North of where his Son Nathan Mansfield now Dwells Provided that Deacon Mansfield Conveys unto the Town a highway on the west side of his Land when the Same is Now fenced out .

[West River] Bridge. Voted that ye Selectmen of the Town of New Haven be Desired to view the State of the west bridge and if it is found needfull to be Rebuilt to make such agreement with the Prop^{rs} of the meadow above ye s^d Bridge towards the rebuilding of s^d Bridge as shall seem to them Just and Reasonable.[1]

Swine. Voted that swine be allowed to go upon the Commons & highways in this Town the year Ensuing and shall not be Liable to be impounded from thence — Provided they are ringed all the year and Sufficiently yoaked from the Tenth

---

1. This entry refers to the West River bridge between New Haven proper and West Haven. The original bridge was constructed in 1641. *See,* NHCR, I: *passim.*

of march to the 10th of november next.

Crows. Voted that whosoever of the Inhabitants of this Town Shall kill any
Crows within the Limits of the Town the year Ensuing, Shall have paid unto
them Six pence p^r head by ye Collectors of ye Town rate, Provided they Shew the
heads of such Crows to s^d Coll^{rs}.[1]

[p. 23] Oysters. Whereas the Catching of oysters in the Harbour of this Town in
the Summer months and with drags at any time in the year is found to be very
Prejudicial to the growth and increase of that very usefull article of subsis-
tence —Therefore voted and ordered that no person whatsoever Do Catch any
oysters in the Harbour or Cove of this Town in the months of may*[,]* June*[,]*
July*[,]* August*[,]* and Sepr Annually, Saving on the monday and Tuesday before
the Publick Commencement, nor with a Dragg at any Time in the year, and that
the waste shells taken with the oysters be Severed from the oysters at the Place
taken in the Harbour or Cove and Not Carried and Cleaned on the Shore or
Land, on Pain of forfieting Twenty Shillings Lawfull money for every offence
above mentioned, Except that of Catching with a Dragg, and for that offence y^e
Sum of forty shillings, one half to him who shall sue for and Recover the Same
and the other half to the use of the Town Treasury, Provided Nevertheless that
David Wooster, Dan^{ll} Lyman and John Whiting Esq^{rs}, Mr John Woodward and
Capt Amos Morris or anyone of them may Give Leave and Licence to Catch
oysters within the s^d five months in Cases of Sickness only the Same being Certified under their hands and not to Exceed one bushel at anyone time.

Further voted that Joseph Munson, Ralph Isaacs, Benjamin Sanford, Thomas
Mansfield, Jeremiah Osborn, John Woodward, Amos Morris and Ben^j Smith
be and they are hereby Specially Desired to take Care to Prosecute all and any
breaches of this order, this Special Request not to hinder any other of the Inhabitants from prosecuting as they may have opportunity.

Voted that the Same regulation under the Same Penalties Shall Extend to Stoney
river, Excepting ye waste shells that is taken with ye oysters being severed there from.

Also the above persons are also Desired to prosecute in s^d Stoney River, or any
other persons in Manner as above mentioned.

---

1. This law indicates that farming remained a major pursuit in the New Haven area, which could
ill-afford crop losses due to invasive crows.

[APRIL 13, 1772]

[p. 24] AT A TOWN MEETING HELD IN NEW HAVEN APRIL 13ᵀᴴ 1772.

[Moderator.] Voted that Rogʳ Sherman Esqʳ be moderator.

Oysters in Stoney river. Whereas it is found very detrementiall to the Interests of the Town of New Haven to have the Oyster beds in Stoney river broke up by peoples taking shells which arises from the Liberty Granted by the vote of the Town in the Last meeting — Therefore voted that the oyster beds in Stoney River Shall be under the Same Regulation and Penalties as they are in the Harbour and Cove and that no Shells Shall be taken in sᵈ Stoney River from first of may untill the first of october next and that the Same method Shall be Observed in Separating the Shells from the oysters as is to be Observed in the Harbour and Cove.

This meeting adjourned without Day.

[DECEMBER 14, 1772]

AT A MEETING OF THE TOWN UPON THE 14ᵀᴴ DAY OF DECEMBER 1772.

Modʳ. Cᵒˡ John Hubbard Chosen moderator.

Clerk. Samˡ Bishop Jʳ Chosen Town Clerk.

Selectmen. Mᵉˢˢʳˢ Stephen Ball, Phenias Bradly, Jeremiah Atwater, Benjamin Douglass, John Woodward, Joshua Chandler and David Perkins Chosen Selectmen the year Ensuing.

Overseers [of poor]. Voted that the above sᵈ Selectmen together with Samˡˡ Atwater, Jonathan Smith and Joel Hotchkis be overseers of the poor in this Town the year Ensuing.

[p. 25] Constables. Voted that Jonathan Mix, John White Jr., Abhram Auger, Ambros Ward, John Denison, John Gilbert, Amos Thomas Jr., Stephen Sanford Jʳ ¹ Lamberton Painter and Lemuel Bradly be Constables in this

---

1.Stephen Sanford Jr. (1740 - 1790), nephew of Capt. Stephen Sanford (1706 - 1779).

Town the year Ensuing.

Coll^r. Voted that Amos Thomas J^r be Collector of ye Country rate the year Ensuing. ~~by vote passed~~[?]

Grandjurymen. Voted that Benjamin Douglass, Amos Botisford, David Austin, Abiather Camp, Erastus Bradly, Benjn Pardee, Joseph Holt, Jesse Todd, Obed Bradly, John Benham, Lamberton Smith J^r, Stephen Sanford, Joseph Beecher, Stephen Goodyear, Jesse Bradly and Jonathan Osborn be Grandjurymen for this Town the year Ensuing.

Voted that Caleb Hotchkiss J^r, Isaac Bishop, Obediah Hotchkiss, Joseph Mansfield, Charles Prindle, James Gilbert, John Gilbert J^r, Amos Morris,[1] Isaac Chidsey, Giles Pierpoint, Jacob Hitchcock, Jotham Blackslee, Jesse Stevens, John Beecher J^r, Benjamin Smith, Solomon Gilbert, Theophilus Goodyear, Isaac Beecher and Isaac Ford *[...]*[2]

Voted that the Thanks of the Town be returned to the Civil authority for their Late Spirited address to the inhabitants of s^d Town, wisely Calculated and intended to Supress vice and Countinance and Establish virtue and good order and for their good endeavours in patronizing and Inforcing the Same by Example — also to the worthy Clergy of s^d Town for their pious endeavors to exmpelyfy *[sic.]* the s^d address by their Several discourses and Exhortations Subsequent thereto, and hereby Give to s^d authority full assurance that our approbation of s^d Measure Shall be best manifested by Supporting them all in our power for accomplishing so good an end, and that this vote be made a Record of accordingly.[3]

This meeting adj^d to the 28^h Day of Decr next.

[DECEMBER 28, 1772]

[p. 26] AT A TOWN MEETING HELD IN NEW HAVEN BY ADJOURN-

---

1. Capt. Amos Morris (1725 - 1801) first built the Morris House in 1750, then rebuilt the what is today known as the Pardee-Morris House following its destruction by British troops during the invasion of New Haven in 1779. See, https://www.findagrave.com/memorial/27033339/amos-morris; http://www.newhavenmuseum.org/visit/pardee-morris-house/.
2. The clerk neglected to write what office these individuals held.
4. Several prominent townsmen circulated a petition remonstrating "the Growing Immoralities in this Town, Especially in the Rising Generation." Especially troubling was the increase in theft in town. A copy of the address is in the Benjamin Trumbull Papers, Box 22, Yale University Manuscript Collection.

MENT UPON THE TWENTY EIGHTH DAY OF DECEMBER 1772.

Key Keepers. Voted that John Thompson of E. H. *[East Haven]*, Joel Tuttle, Saml Candee J^r, Noah Ives, James Bishop, Joseph Turner, William Adams, Seth Peck, Benj. Pardee J^r, Elisha Bradly, Eben^r Johnson, Joseph Munson, Noah Potter, James Thompson, Joseph Gilbert, Aaron Gilbert and Daniel Beecher, be key keepers in this Town the year Ensuing.

Branders. Voted that Theop^s Munson, Elisha Bradly, Simeon Bradly, Ephram Humaston, Joseph Peck, Jonathan Ives, Roger Peck and George Smith be branders of horses ye year Ensuing.

Cullers. Voted that John Miles, Newman Trowbridge, Robert Brown and John Beecher J^r, be Culers of Lumber ye year Ensuing.

Fence viewers. Voted that John Mix, Nathan Mansfield, Obediah Hotchkiss, Ephram Humaston, Thomas Mansfield, Josiah Bradly & Saml Thompson be fence viewers the year Ensuing.

Tythingmen. Voted that Capt Saml Atwater be a Tythingman the year Ensuing.

W^ts & mea^r. Voted that Theop^s Munson be Sealer of weights & measures the year Ensuing.

[Dry] measure. Voted that John Miles be Sealer of dry measures ye year Ensuing.

Treas^r. Voted y^t Samuel Bishop J^r be Town Treasurer ye year Ensuing.

Sealer. Voted y^t Stephen Bradly be Leather Sealer the year Ensuing.

[Surveyors of highways.] Voted that Col: Wooster, Jeremiah Atwater, Benjamin Douglass, James Thompson, William Sperry, John Woodin the 3^d, Charles Alling, Henry Toles, Eben^r Johnson, Jacob Bradly, Joseph Tuttle, Saml Heminway J^r, Joseph Granis, Jos^h Bradly J^r, Jonathan Heaton, Lawrence Clinton, Joseph Hull, Caleb Hitchcock J^r, Lazarus Toles, And^r Bradly, *[p. 27]* Enoch Newton, Simeon Bristoll, Noah Wolcot, Joseph Peck, Caleb Beecher, David Sanford, Nathl Tuttle, Titus Peck and Lucas Lines be Surveyers of highways the year Ensuing.
Listers. Voted that Adam Babcock, Isaac Jones, Jonathan Fitch, Asa Todd, Silas Alling, Samuel Forbs, Ichabod Russel, Nathan Smith J^r, Joshua Barns, Gideon Todd J^r, Jesse Ford, Abram Newton and David Beecher J^r be Listers for this

Town the year Ensuing.

[List.] Voted that there shall be three pounds paid of the Town Treasury to pay the making up the List.

Rate. Voted that a Rate or Tax of one penny three farthings[1] on the pound on the present List be Collected of the inhabitants of the Town to defray the necessary Charges of the Town the year Ensuing.

Voted that s^d Rate be paid by the first day of Feby next.

Coll^rs. Voted that David Atwater J^r, Isaac Chidsey, Oliver Smith, John Gilbert, Amos Thomas J^r, David Sperry J^r and Stephen Sanford J^r be Collectors of the Town Rate ye year Ensuing.

Constable. Voted that Stephen Peck be Constable the year Ensuing.

pound. Voted that Seth Heaton have Liberty to build a pound and be key keeper thereof.

[Highways and Sacketts Bridge.] Voted that the Selectmen be desired to remove all Incroachments and Incumbrances of the highways in the Town of New Haven.

Also voted that ye Selectmen afford Such Reasonable aid to the Builders of Sackits Bridge over muddy River as Shall appear to be Just and Equitable not Exceeding five pounds.[2]

[p. 28] Committee. Upon the motion of Walter Munson that there might be a bridge built over the East river[3] near his Grist mill at the East end of the blue hills. Voted that John Whiting Esqr and Mr Stephen Ball be a Committee to view the Circumstances thereof, and report their opinion to the Town at their next meeting.

Coll. Voted that Abram Auger be Collector of the Country rate the year ensuing.

This meeting adjourned to the Last monday of January Next at two of the

---

1. A farthing was equal to 1/4 of a pence, meaning the tax rate was 1^{3/4} pence on the pound.
2. The first Muddy River Bridge built was constructed in 1718. The above-mentioned bridge may refer to the East River Bridge built at Sackett's Landing.
3. Now known as the Quinnipiac River.

Clock in the afternoon.

[JANUARY 25, 1773]

AT A TOWN MEETING HOLDEN IN NEW HAVEN BY ADJOURN-MENT UPON THE 25ᵀᴴ DAY OF JANUARY ANNO DOM 1773.

Mod^r. Voted that Mr Jonathan Fitch be moderator of this meeting.

Districts. Voted that the Selectmen give the districts to the Surveyers of the highways.

Coll^r. Voted that Isaac Chidsey be released from being Coll^r of the Town rate, and Saml Davenport Chosen in his Stead.

Swine. Voted that Swine be allowed to go upon the Commons and highways in this Town the year Ensuing, and shall not be Liable to be Impounded from thence provided they are ringed all the year, and Sufficiently yoaked from the 10th of march to the 10th of December.

Coll^r. Voted y^t John Gilbert be released From being Coll^r of the Town rate, and James Bishop ye 4th Chosen in his stead.

Coll^r. Voted y^t David Atwater be released from being Coll^r of the Town rate and Jonathan Osborn Chosen Coll^r in his Stead.

[p. 29] Tythingmen. Voted that Caleb Hotchkiss J^r and Isaac Bishop be released from being Tythingrnen and Mathew Gilbert and Nicholas Peck Chosen in their Stead.

Grandjuryman. Voted y^t Jonathan Osborn be released from being Grandjuryman and Daniel Upton Chosen in his Stead.

This meeting adjourned without day.

[APRIL 12, 1773]

AT A TOWN MEETING HELD IN NEW HAVEN APRIL 12ᵀᴴ, 1773.[1]

---

1. At a Freemen's Meeting held on the same day, the Reverend Benjamin Trumbull of North Haven delivered his famous "A Discourse, Delivered at the Anniversary Meeting of the Freemen of the Town of New-Haven, April 12, 1773," in which he reasoned for American home rule. It was likely

Surveyers. Voted y^t Nehemiah Smith and Saml Smith of west Haven and Danl Bradly and Saml Maltrop be Surveyers of highways.

[Collector.] Voted y^t Sam^{ll} Tuttle of East Haven be Coll^r of the Town rate in the Room of Saml Davenport.

[Collector.] Voted y^t Peter Perkins be Collector of the Town rate in ye Room of Stephen Sanford J^r.

This meeting adjourned to the Last monday of Instant april at 4 of the Clock in the afternoon.[1]

[DECEMBER 20, 1773][2]

[p. 30] AT A TOWN MEETING HELD IN NEW HAVEN UPON THE 20TH DAY OF DECEMBER ANNO DOMINI 1773.

Clerk. Samuel Bishop J^r Chosen Town Clerk.

Mod^r. Daniel Lyman Esqr Chosen moderator.

Selectmen. Voted that M^{essrs} Stephen Ball, Jeremiah Atwater, Stephen Mansfield, Tim^o Jones J^r, John Woodward, Joshua Chandler and David Perkins be Selectmen the year Ensuing.

Overseers of the poor. Voted that the above said Selectmen together with Capt Jonathan Smith, Capt Joel Hotchkis and Capt Saml Atwater be overseers of the poor ye Ensuing year.

Constables. Voted y^t John White J^r, Jonathan Mix, Robert Brown, John Denision, Lamberton painter, John Gilbert, Lemuel Bradly, Amos Thomas J^r, Sanuel Martin and Stephen Sanford J^r be Constables the year Ensuing.

Grandjurymen. Voted y^t Ezchiel Hays, James Bradly, Elias Shipman, Samuel

the first such plea made at a public meeting in New Haven. See, https://quod.lib.umich.edu/cgi/t/text/text-idx?c=evans;cc=evans;rgn=main;view=text;idno=N10279.0001.001.

1. There is no record of this meeting being recorded.

2. While New Haveners no doubt heard that the Sons of Liberty had thrown chests of tea into Boston harbor only four days earlier in protest of the Tea Act, there is no mention of that event or their reaction to it in these public records.

Holt, Zebulon Farren, Isaac Beecher J^r, W*[est]* Haven, Saml Candee J^r, Joseph Bradly J^r, Titus Tharp, Titus Smith, Isaac Dickerman, Titus Peck, Henry Toles J^r, Barnabas Baldwin J^r, John Mix and Caleb Hitchcock J^r, be grand jurymen the year Ensuing.

Listers. Voted y^t Jonathan Fitch, Tim^o Jones J^r, Nathan Mansfield, John Miles J^r, Abiather Camp, Saml Forbes, Ichabod Russel, Nathan Smith J^r, Gideon Todd J^r, Joshua Barns, Jesse Ford, Abram Norton, David Beecher J^r, Lemuel Humpherville & Moses Gilbert be Listers the year ensuing.

[p. 31] Tythingmen. Voted that Paul Noyes, Joseph Munson, Nathl Fitch, John Hubbard, Joel Ford, Caleb Alling, Charles Prindle, Thomas Bills, Saml Sheppard, Dan Holt, George Smith, Jonathan Thompson, Thaddeus Clark, Danl Basset, Peter Eastman, Elihu Rogers, Obed Johnson, Joel Bradly, Alvan Bradly, Tim^o Lounsbury and Stephen Ives be Tythingmen the year Ensuing.

Surveyers of highways. Voted that Joshua Chandler, Ralph Isaacs, Lemuel Hotchkiss, David Wooster, Silas Alling, Stephen Ford, Elisha Booth, Caleb Alling, James Alling, Isaac Chidsey, Dan Bradly, Joseph Tuttle, Jacob Pardee, Samuel Maltop, Jacob Smith, Saml Smith, Jno Johnson, Seth Blackslee, Solomon Tuttle, Caleb Clark, Jared Hill, Danl Barns, Joel Blackslee, Elias Beech, Andrew Bradly, John Cotter, Abner Bradly J^r, John Heaton, Thomas Darling, Danl Bradly J^r, Jesse Goodyear, Israel Thomas, Ruben Sperry, Joseph Hotchkiss, Daniel Hotchkis and Jonathan Tuttle be Surveyers or highways the year ensuing.

This meeting adjourned to the Last monday of Instant December at one of the Clock in the afternoon.

[DECEMBER 27, 1773]

AT A TOWN MEETING HELD IN NEW HAVEN BY ADJOURNMENT UPON THE 27TH DAY OR DECEMBER 1773.

[Surveyor.] Voted y^t Mr Timothy Jones J^r be Surveyer of highways the year ensuing.

[Districts.] Voted y^t ye Selectmen give the Districts to the Surveyers of highway agreeable to ye Law in such case Provided.

[p. 32] Grandjurymen. Voted that Elias Shipman be released from being Grandjuryman and Daniel Bontecou Chosen in his room.

Sealer. Voted that Stephen Bradly be leather sealer.

Treas. Voted that Samuel Bishop J^r be Town Treasurer the year ensuing.

Key Keepers. Voted y^t John Thompson E.H. *[East Haven]*, Joseph Munson, Noah Potter, James Thompson, Jo^s Gilbert, Aaron Gilbert, Noah Ives, Joel Tuttle, Saml. Candee J^r, James Bishop, Enos Granis, William Adams, Elisha Bradly, Seth Peck, Benjamin Pardee and Seth Blackslee be key keepers ye year Ensuing.

Cullers. Voted that John Miles, Newman Trowbridge, Robert Brown and John Beecher W. H. *[West Haven]* be Surveyers & Cullers of Lumber the year ensuing.

Branders. Voted that Theop^s Munson, Elisha Booth, Simeon Bradly, Epheram Humaston, Joseph Peck, Jonathan Ives, Roger Peck and George Smith be Branders of horses the year Ensuing.

Pound. Voted that Jeremiah Osborn have liberty to build a pound near his house at his own Cost and be the keeper of the key ye year Ensuing.

Sealer. Voted that Theophilus Muson be Sealer of weights and measures the year Ensuing.

Sealer. Voted that John Miles be Sealer of dry measures the year Ensuing.

[Fence viewers.] Voted that John Mix, Nathan Mansfield and Obed^h Hotchkis be fence viewers the year ensuing.

[p. 33] Rate. Voted that a rate or Tax of one penny half penny on a pound be Collected of the Inhabitants of this Town upon the present list, to defray the Charges of the Town.

Voted y^t s^d rate Shall be paid upon the first day of March next.

Coll^s. Voted that John Pierpoint, John Denision, Lamberton Painter, John Gilbert, Amos Thomas J^r, Samuel Martin and Stephen Sanford J^r, be Collectors of s^d Rate.

Record books. Whereas the Two oldest books of the Town Records are so worn out that it is needfull that they be new bound. It is thereupon voted that the

Selectmen together with ye Town Clerk imploy Mr Green[1] to bind the same and also see what new alphabets are needfull to be made to the ancient books, and Cause the same to be made.[2]

This meeting adjourned to monday next at one of ye Clock in the afternoon.

[JANUARY 3, 1774]

AT A TOWN MEETING HOLDEN IN NEW HAVEN BY ADJOURN-MENT UPON THE THIRD DAY OF JANUARY 1774.

Constable. Voted that John Wise be Constable the year ensuing and also be one of the Collectors of ye Town rate.

Tythingman. Voted that Caleb Alling be released from being Tythingman and Joel Gilbert Chosen in his room.

Surveyer. Voted that John Gilbert be Surveyer of highways the year ensuing.

[p. 34] Swine. Voted that Swine going at large on ye highways and Town Commons the year ensuing Shall not be liable to be impounded from thence, Provided they are ringed all the year and Sufficiently yoaked from the first day of march next, to the 10th Day of December next.

Pound. Voted that Peter Johnson have liberty to build a pound near his house at his own Cost and be keeper of the key.

[Pound.] Voted that Joel Munson have liberty to build a pound near where he Dwells at his own Cost and be keeper of the key.

[MARCH 10, 1774]

AT A TOWN MEETING HELD IN NEW HAVEN UPON THE 10TH DAY

1.Thomas Green (1735-1812) and his brother, Samuel Green (1743 - 1799), founded the *Connecticut Journal* in 1767, which was continued by Thomas's son, Thomas Green, Jr. (1766 - 1825). Following Thomas Jr.'s death, the paper passed through many owners over the years as the New Haven *Journal Courier.* It was absorbed by *The New Haven Register* in 1987.

2. The books in question are the town records dating back to the founding of New Haven. Mr. Green is likely Samuel Green, publisher of the *Connecticut Journal,* based in New Haven. See. "Connecticut Newspaper Pioneers," *Connecticut State Library website,* https://ctstatelibrary.org/newspioneers/. These records were published and are referenced here as *NHCR* and *NHTR.*

OF MARCH ANNO DOMINI 1774.

[Moderator.] Thomas Darling Esq' Chosen moderator of this Meeting.

[Susquehanna] Committee. Voted that it is the opinion of this Town that this Colonys extending their Jurisdiction over those Lands lying west of New york on y' Susquehannah River and Challenged by M' Penn as being within his patant without first proscuiting their Claims before his majesty in Council (the only proper place of Decision) will be tedious and expensive as will probably be of dangerous Tendency.[1]

Voted that Col. Leverett Hubbard, Mess" Adam Babcock and Edward Carrinton be a Committee to repair to Middletown on the Last wednesday of march Instant and Confer with Such Gentlemen as may be appointed by other Towns & thin *[sic]* & there draw up a Suitable petition & remonstrance to be preferred to the Gen" assembly to be held at *[p. 35]* Hartford in may next on the principles and make report to this Town at their Next meeting.

This meeting to *[proxy?]* Day in april next at four of the Clock in the afternoon.

[APRIL 11, 1774]

AT A TOWN MEETING HOLDEN IN NEW HAVEN BY ADJOURN-MENT UPON THE 11ᵀᴴ DAY OF APRIL ANNO DOMINI 1774.

Committee. The Committee appointed by this Town at their meeting upon the 10ᵗʰ day of march last to repair to middletown on the last wednesday of march to infer with Such Gentlemen as may be appointed from other Towns to draw up a Suitable Petition and remonstrance to be preferr'ᵈ to the Gen" assembly in may next &c as by the votes of s'ᵈ Town may appear — made their report in the following manner*[.]*

To the Inhabitants of the Town of New Haven in Town meeting assembled Gentlemen*[:]*

---

1. This meeting was held in response to the Connecticut Assembly's decision to incorporate the township of Westmoreland, located in the Susquehanna Valley of what is now Pennsylvania, into the Colony of Connecticut. At a time when royal relations were already strained, many New Haveners worried such activities threatened Connecticut's charter. The Mr. Penn referred to here was likely Thomas Penn (1702 - 1775), who became proprietor of Pennsylvania in 1718, following the death of his father, William.

We the Subiribers appointed your be Committee to repair to Middletown on the 30th Day of march Last to Confer with Such Committees as Should be appointed by any other Towns relative to the Colonys extending their Judridiction over y[e] Lands lying west of New york & Challang[ed] by M[r] Penn as being within his Patant & to draw up Some Sutable Petition and remonstrance on the premises & make report, now beg leave to report to this meeting that they did repair to s[d] middletown on s[d] day & there meet with the Committees of Twenty two other Towns and after mature Consideration all unanimously agreed on the annexed *[p. 36]* Petition and Remonstrance to be prefered to the Honorable Gen[ll] assembly in may next.

We are your most obed[t] and Humble Servants

New Haven April 11th, 1774   Adam Babcock

Edward Carrinton

[Susquehanna Company]. To the Hon[ble] the Gen[ll] assembly of the Gov[r] & Company of the Colony of Connecticut to be holden at Hartford on the Second thursday of may Next.

We the Inhabitants of New Haven in Town meeting assembled with Hearts full of Submission and Duty and tenderly affected for the Honour interest and Peace of this Colony and the wellfare and Happiness of our Selves and our posterity Beg leave Humbly to Petition & Remonstrate against Certain acts and doings of the Last Generall assimbly of this Colony and measures taken in favour of the Susquehannah Company (So Called) whereby y[e] ~~Judis~~ Jurisdiction of this Colony is attempted to be extended to Lands west of the Province of New york measures which your remonstrants conceive to be of a dangerous tendency and pregnant with the Greatest mischief to them and their posterity and highly derogatory to the Honour & Interest and Destructive of the peace of this Colony and a Great Grievance.

Your Petitioners as British Subjects Conceive they have an undoubted right to lay their Grievances before your Honours by their Humble Petition a right vested in their ancestors from the Earlist Periods an essential Part of their Privileges, vindicated asserted and Confirmed on the most trying & glorious occassions and at the expense of blood & treasure transmitted to them the exercise of which at this and in this manner as they are Sure it ought not so they humbly hope it will not give any *[p. 37]* offence or umbrage to your Honours or their fellow Subjects your Hon[rs] remonstrants beg Leave with the freedom of Englishmen and the duty of Subjects to lay their grievances before your Honours the principal of which and from which as its Source all other Grievances are derived is that ye Proprietors of the Susquehannah Company who Claim the Lands over which Jurisdition is Extended who were members of the last assembly and Deeply interested in the Questions discussed and determined were Suffered to and did Sit &c all in s^d assembly in those very matters in which they were So Deeply interested and for which their Partners Settled on s^d Lands under their votes and for their benefit were Suitors to s^d assembly, Your remonstrants Conceive themselves warranted to assert that s^d members were interested from all the acts and transactions of s^d Company from the Parculiar Engagedness of s^d members in promoting the interest of s^d Company and from their frequent Declarations y^t they have Expended Emense Sums of money in purchasing the Native right and prosecuting measures in England & America to Compleate their Title and from their having prosecuted at their own Expence a memorial to the assembly in may Last praying or the Exercise of Jurisdiction over s^d Lands by this Colony all which they must Loose unless the General assembly would be prevailed upon to take ye Steps which ye Last assembly hath taken, but we will not take up your Hon^rs time to prove their interest and Partiality in the present Case, Since it is So apparent & notorious that not a freeman in the Colony can be ignorant of it and as to their being permitted to debate & give their *[p. 38]* voice in determining the important Questions y^t Came under the Consideration of the Last assembly in which their interest was Concerned is Contrary to all antient precedent & usuage as your remonstrants are informed*[.]* So it appears to your remonstrants unreasonable*[,]* unconstitutional & of very danarous tendency when partial and interested men not only vote to serve their own ends but are likewise admitted to narrate facts to argue - persuade in Short to be witness or Council and Judges for themselves, That full Confidence may be repossed in the Supreme Legislature is of the highest importance hence the wise care of our anccstors y^t an Equal representation Should take place y^t Election Should be that all Suspicion of Partiality predudice & Sinister or interested views in the members of that august body Should be prevented, and it is with Deep Concern and Grief y^t they are obliged to inform Your Hon^rs that the measure they Complain of not only tend to weaken and destroy y^t Confidence in their opinion but have in fact regard to the Last assembly had that unhappy Effect of which the freting of your remonstrants are to them the highest Evidence they can Confide, they ever have confided, and they Still Confide in the unbiased and impartial determiantions of their rulers but they Cannot Consider the determinations of the last assembly in the measures Complained of may of which would not have passed had not s^d proprietors voted for the Same, as unbiased and Impartial*[.]* Your remonstrants beg have to say further that it is not men but measures they urged*[?]* they have no personal dislike to the Gentlemen who are members of that Company they would think themselves warranted to Complain in any Case where men the best of men with the Same interest & prejudices were admitted to debate and decide.*[p. 39]* Your remonstrants would justly be tempted to distrust their own Judgements and quiet their fears had a Disinterested Representative of the Colony taken any measures of which they Could not discern the propriety and against they might have nosins of wright with them preforming their rulers as they were appointed to watch for their good had both the meanes and the will to determine wisely and for their best interests, but now they beg leave to Shew to your Hon^rs that they Conceive the Extension of Jursidiction to those Lands by the Last assembly was of dangerous and in their apprehension may be of fatal tendency the Title of the Colony to those Lands is Contested Should the Same on tryal be found defective we Conceive the Colony might Justly be Charged with usurping an unwarrantable misusing and abusing their Chartered powers and priviledges and thereby a pretence be punished for depriving us our dearest Rights and Priviledges & at this Time Especially impolitic when debates run high between the parent State & her Colonys, and we may purpose every opportunity will be watched & geredily Seized by administration to enlarge and Extend the power and influence of the Crown in America[.] Again our humanity is Shocked when we Consider what bloody tradgdies may ensue from the C[l]ashing of opposite Jurisdictions atually Exercised within the Same Limits[.] We apprehend great numbers of Subjects in this Colony taught as they are from their youth to place their highest Confidence in the Legesture will be by the acts of the Last assembly tempted to transport themselves & their Effects and Settle on those Lands pending the Controversey about the Title and will waste their personal Estate in Improvements of s^d Lands, and in Case the Title of the Colony Should finialy fail they would be reduced to abject wretchedness[,] dependence & poverty there *[p. 40]* Or fall back on this Colony by thousands in Extreme Penury to waste the residue of their Lives a burden to themselves and an expence and Dead wight upon the Community by which means the Support of the poor already a heavy burden will become intolerable — Your Remonstrants are Convinced by the arguments offered by the Committee appointed to treat with his Hon^r Govr Penn Contained in their reports to the Last Assembly that the possession of those Lands is So recent that it Cannot aid or affect our Title or be of any use on the tryal of the Same and therefore must be Calculated Wholly & Solely for the Benefit of the Susquehannah Company and procured by the great influence and address of their Proprietors who sat in the Last assembly.* And altho we have reason to think the Title of the Colony to those Lands Slender and precarious yet that being a matter of which we are not so Competent Judges nor perhaps furnished with Facts & documents by which a Judgement may be made, we are will and desirous that the right of the Colony

to them and the procedure and Policy of asserting that Should be Judged of and
determined by a Disinterested assembly.

We therefore Humbly pray your Hon^rs to Exclude the Prop^rs of the Susquehanna
Company from a voice on these matters and reconsider the afores^d votes and
doings of the Assembly in oct^r and January Last and as we are will*[ing]* to do
Justice to all men let ye Susquehanna Company by their Council and Council
assigned by your Hon^rs to manage ~~and~~ the opposite side of the Question be
admitted to a publick & open hearing upon the afores^d matters which we Esteem
of the highest and Last importance and we Shall be happy to abide by and ac-
quiesce in the Decision that Shall be made. In the mean time we humbly hope
that the inhabitants of the New made town of Westmoreland may be suspended
from interfering in the voting being represented or otherwise transacting in the
affair of government during Such time as the title of the Colony to the Same
is in Suspence & undecided because till then it cannot be known whether it is
this colony or not and your remonstrants as it is duty bound Shall over pay &c.

[p. 41] *The acquiescences of the Colony under the grant of Pennsylvania is
of no more force than the acquiescence of the Proprietors under ye grant to
Connecticut an*[d]* can have Little weight on either side Since till very Lately the
indians refused to give up the country to either and neither can be considered as
having Suffered their Claim to have lain Culpably Dormant under the particular
Circumstances of the Case and the Situation of the Country. Printed report of
the Committee page 30.

This Town by vote to accept and approve of the foregoing report
of the Committee
102 affirmative
99 negative[1]

Representatives. To Saml Bishop and Thomas Darling Esq^rs the freeman of the
Town of New Haven having made Choice of you for our representatives at the
Gen^ll assembly to be holden at Hartford in may next, we the inhabitants of s^d

---

1. New Haveners were nearly equally divided on the Susquehanna issue. The New Light cause to expand into Pennsylvania was championed by the Rev. Benjamin Trumbull of North Haven, cousin of
Governor Jonathan Trumbull. The conservatives in New Haven, known as Old Lights, were fearful
that the colony's continued efforts to expand into Pennsylvania would threaten the revocation of the
colony's charter and jeopardize its religious autonomy, especially during a period of increased tension
with the Britain. The issue turned violent during the Revolution with the slaughter of 150 Connecticut
settlers in what came to known as the "Wyoming Massacre." The violence continued until 1786, when
Connecticut finally relinquished its claims to what was then called "the Western Reserve."

Town in Town meeting assembled, do instruct and direct you to *[...]* The petition and remonstrance which this Town have this day voted to be preferred to Honble Gen^11 assembly and to inforce and Support the Same with your utmost Abilitys and Skill that the measures therein proposed may be adopted by Legislature of this Colony.

[Lister.] Voted that Saml Dickerman be Lister in the room of Abr^m Norton.

This meeting adjourned without day.

[MAY 23, 1774]

[p. 42] AT A LEGALL TOWN MEETING HELD IN NEW HAVEN ON THE 23^D DAY OF MAY 1774.

[Moderator.] Daniel Lyman Esqr moderator

Voted that we will to the utmost of our abilies *[sic.]* assert and defend the Libertys and immunities of British America and we will cooperate with our Sister Towns in this and the other Colonies in any Constitutional measures that may be thought most Condusive to the preservation of our invaluable rights and priviledges.[1]

Committee [of Correspondence]. Voted that Joshua Chandler Esqr, Saml Bishop J^r, Esqr, Daniel Lyman Esqr, Mr Stephen Ball, Pierpoint Edwards Esqr,John Whiting Esqr, Mr Isaac Doolittle, Mr David Austin, Capt Joseph Munson, Mr Peter Colt, Mr Jeremiah Atwater, Mr Tim^o Jones J^r, Mr. Isaac Beers, Capt Timothy Bradly, Mr Silas Kimberly, Simeon Bristoll Esqr, Mr John Woodward and Capt Joel Hotchkiss be a Standing Committee for the Salutary purpose of Keeping up a Correspondence with Towns of this and ye neighboring Colonies and in Conjunction with them pursuing in the present important Crisis Such Judicious and Constitutional measures as Shall appear to be necessary for the preservation of our Just rights thru maintenance of Publick peace and Support of Gen^ll union which at this Time is So absolutely necessary requisite to be preserved throughout this Continent, also voted that a Copy of the above Resolves Shall be transmitted to the Committee of Correspondence for the Town of Boston in answer to their Letter to this Town.

---

1. New Haveners were reacting to what was known as the Intolerable or Coercive Acts, which led to the First Continental Congress to coordinate a united colonial protest to the British Parliament's actions.

This meeting adjourned to ye 3^d ~~Tuesday~~ monday of June next at two of the Clock in the afternoon.

[JUNE 20, 1774]

AT A TOWN MEETING HOLDEN IN NEW HAVEN BY ADJOURNMENT UPON THE 20TH DAY OF JUNE 1774.

Congress. Voted that Saml Bishop Esqr be desired to inform the Honble Committee of Correspondence of this Colony that it would be very agreeable to this Town to have a general Congress as Soon as may be and that in their opinion a general annual Congress would have a great tendency to promote the wellfare and Happiness of all the amercian Colonies.

Voted that upon the request of the Committee of Correspondence the Selectmen be desired to call a Town meeting.[1]

This meeting adjourned without day.

[SEPTEMBER 20, 1774]

AT A TOWN MEETING HELD IN NEW HAVEN UPON THE 20TH DAY OF SEPTEMBER ANNO DOMNI 1774.

[Moderator.] Thomas Darling Esqr Chosen moderator.

This meeting adjourned four weeks from this day at one of the Clock in the afternoon, to be held at the brick meeting house.

[p. 44]   *[OCTOBER 18, 1774]*

AT A TOWN MEETING HELD IN NEW HAVEN BY ADJOURNMENT UPON THE 18TH DAY OF OCTOBER ANNO DOMNI 1774.

Subscription for Boston. Voted that it is the opinion of this Town that a Subscription be Sett on foot for the relief of the inhabitants of the Town of Boston that are now Suffering in the Common cause of American Freedom; And that Messrs

---

1. This meeting came in response to mounting colonial reaction to the Intolerable Acts and the New Haven Committee of Correspondence requesting the town's support for what became the First Continental Congress.

Joseph Munson, David Austin, Benj Douglass, Adam Babcock, Enos Alling, Isaac Doolittle, Henry Daggett, Jonathan Osborn, Isaac Chidsey, Azariah Bradly, Silas Kimberly, Sam¹ Candee, James Heaton Jᵣ¹ Stephen Jacobs, Timothy Bradly, Amos Perkins, Simeon Bristoll, Theopˢ Goodyear, Isaac Beecher Jᵣ, Timothy Ball and Samuel Beecher be a Committee to Receive in Subscriptions and transmit what may be Collected to the Selectmen of the Town of Boston to be by them disposed of for the Support of the inhabitants of the Town of Boston.[1]

Powder. Voted that the Selectmen build a Suteable house to put the Towns Stock of powder in of Such dimensions as they Shall Judge needfull, either upon the Land of Messʳˢ Beers, Doolittle or Meloy.

Voted that the Selectmen procure a Stock of powder agreeable to the Law in Such case Provided, as soon as may be, for the Town use.

This meeting adjourned without day.

[NOVEMBER 14, 1774]

AT A TOWN MEETING HOLDEN IN NEW HAVEN UPON THE 14ᵀᴴ DAY OF NOVᵣ ANNO DOM. 1774.

Committee. In persuance of the Resolve of the house of Representatives in october Last in New Haven to Chuse a Committee for the purpose mentioned in the 11ᵗʰ article of yᵉ association *[p. 45.]* Entered into by the Late Continental Congress held at Philadelphia.[2]

[Moderator.] Voted that Roger Sherman Esqᵣ be moderator.

Committee. Voted that this Town will Chuse a Committee for the purpose mentioned in the 11ᵗʰ article of sᵈ association agreeable to the resolve and recommendation of sᵈ house of Representatives.[3]

[Committee.] Voted that the majᵣ part of the Committee be Chosen within the

---

1. Bostonians were suffering as a result of the British port closure, which prompted the surrounding colonies to come to its aid with donations of food.
2. The Congress also passed the Articles of Association, which called on the colonies to stop importing goods from the British Isles beginning on December 1, 1774, if the Intolerable Acts were not repealed.
3. This appears to be s repetitive entry from the town clerk.

Limits of the first Society.[1]

Committee. Voted that the following persons be a Committee for the purpose aforesaid, viz. Jonathan Fitch, Michael Todd, David Atwater Jr, Saml Bird, David Austin, Timothy Jones Jr, Joseph Munson, Peter Colt, Abram Bradly, Saml Mansfield, Henry Daggett, John White Jr, James Gilbert, Robert Brown, Thomas Bills, John Miles, Thomas Green, Daniel Bontecou, Jonathan Osborn, Stephen Smith, Azariah Bradly, Jonathan Smith, John Benham, Jesse Todd, Giles Pierpoint, Timo Bradly, Enoch Newton, Isaac Beecher Jr, Joel Hotchkis, Samuel Martin and Joel Bradly Jr.

This meeting adjourned without day.

[DECEMBER 20, 1774]

AT A TOWN MEETING HELD IN NEW HAVEN BY ADJOURNMENT UPON THE 20TH DAY OF DECEMBER ANNO DOM 1774.

Clerk . Saml Bishop Jur Chosen Town Clerk.

Moderator. Thomas Darling Esqr Chosen moderator.

[Selectmen.] Voted that there be one Selectman in the first Society one in white Haven one in the Church and one in Fair Haven.[2]

[p. 46] Selectmen. Voted that Messrs Stephen Ball, Jeremiah Atwater, James Gilbert, Isaac Doolittle, John Woodward, Joshua Chandler and David Perkins be Selectmen yr year Ensuing.

This meeting *[adjourned]* to tuesday the 20th day of instant Decr at 10 of the Clock in the forenoon.

[DECEMBER 20, 1774]

AT A TOWN MEETING HELD IN NEW HAVEN BY ADJOURNMENT UPON THE 20TH DAY OF DECEMBER ANNO DOM 1774.

---

1. This resolution was likely meant to prevent "radical" New Lights and dissenters from gaining a majority in the committee's makeup.
3. The demographic selection of selectmen represented New Haven's attempt to become more inclusive of the members of the three churches that were now on the New Haven Green.

[Continential Association] Voted that this Town do approve of the association entered into by the Late Continental Congress held at Philadelphia.[1]

Committee of inspection. Whereas the inhabitants of the Town of New Haven at their Town meeting held on the 14th Day of Nov[r] Last Called for the purpose of Chusing a Committee of inspection (according to the advice of the Continental Congress and a vote of the Lower house of assembly of this Colony) to carry into execution the Resolution of s[d] Congress did nominate and appoint a Conmittee of thirty one persons Named in the Records of the proceedings of said Town; which Committee are now unanimously approved by this meeting, And whereas a number of the inhabitants of this Town are desireous to have s[d] Committee enlarged in order therefore that there may be peace & unanimity in this Town — Voted that the following persons be added to s[d] Committee viz. Mess[rs] Stephen Ball, Benj Douglass, Phinias Bradly, John Mix, Will[am] Grenough, Levi Ives, Isaac Doolittle,[2] Elias Shipman, Amos Morris, Isaac Chidsey, Lamberton Painter, Lamberton Smith J[r], Joseph Pierpoint, Joshua Barns, Amos Perkins, Sam[l] Newton, Sam[l] Atwater, Jonathan Dickerman, Tim[o] Ball, and Amos Hitchcock.

[DECEMBER 26, 1774]

[p. 47] AT A TOWN MEETING HELD IN NEW HAVEN BY ADJOURNMENT UPON THE 26[H] DAY OF DECEMBER ANNO DOM 1774.

[Moderator] Daniel Lyman E[sqr] Chosen moderator.

Constables. Voted that Jonathan Mix, John Wise, Stephen Hotchkis, John White J[r], James Blackslee, Elisha Booth, John Denison, Lamberton Painter, John Gilbert, Lemuel Bradly,   Samuel Martin and Amos Hitchcock be Constables the year Ensuing.

Coll. Voted that James Blackslee be Collector of the County rate the year ensuing.

Grandjurymen. Voted that Stephin Dickerman, Joseph Howell, Nathan Beers, Joel Atwater, John Warner, Jacob Thompson, W[m] McCracken, Elias Shipman, John

---

1. The Continental Association implemented a trade boycott with Great Britain as of 1774.
2. Isaac Doolittle (1721 - 1798) was a member of Trinity Church, who was known as New Haven's first "ingenious mechanic." He was a clock maker, manufacturer, and is credited as the builder of the first American-made printing press. An ardent patriot, he built two gunpowder mills in support of the American cause during the Revolution.

Davenport, Sam^ll Forbs, Benj. Smith, John Beecher W. H. *[West Haven]*, Enoch Ray, Saml Mix, Justus J. Fitch, Enoch Newton, Amos Sherman, Joseph Gilbert, Jason Bradly, David Beecher J^r and Stephen Ives be Grandjurymen the year ensuing.

Overseers. Voted that the Selectmen together with Capt Nehemiah Smith, Capt Samuel Atwater and Daniel Beecher be overseers of the poor the year ensuing.

Listers. Voted that Messrs Jonathan Fitch, Nathan Mansfield, Tim° Jones J^r, John White J^r, Abiather Camp, Henry Daggett, Caleb Alling, Lemuel Humphreville, James Chidsey, Jos^h Heminway, Saml Clark J^r, Ithamer Tuttle, Eben^r Barns, Jo^s Beecher J^r, Abel Atwater and Benajah Peck be Listers the year ensuing.

[p. 48] Tythingmen. Voted that Jonah Hotchkis, Nathan Oaks, Joseph Gilbert, Joseph Peck 3^d, Charles Prindle, Eben^r Chidsey, Levi Pardee, John Johnson J^r, Silas Kimberly, Lemuel Humpherville, Jonathan Heaton, Ambros Barns, Saml Alling J^r, Charles Bradly, Hez^h Basset, Charles Tuttle, Edward Perkins, Lucas Lines, Jeremiah Parmale be Tythingmen the year ensuing.

Surveyers. Voted that Ralph Isaacs, David Wooster, Benjamin Douglass, Tim° Jones J^r, Phileman Potter, Joseph Munson, Lemuel Hotchkis, Isaac Doolittle, Danl Lyman, Henry Toles, Hez^h Ball, John Ball, John Gilbert J^r, John Gorham, John Mix, Jacob Bradly, Jonathan Roberts, Ichabod Russel, Benj Bishop, John Woodward J^r, Oliver Smith, Saml Sherman, Asa Smith, Eben^r Heaton, David Bishop, Jared Hill, Elias Beech, Oliver Blackslee, Dan Barns, Stephen Ives, Titus Tuttle, Zop^r Blackslee, Thomas Darling, Benjn Bradly, Amos Thomas, Lazarus Toles, Joseph Merwin J^r, Amos Perkins J^r, Abr^m Chatterton, Jonathan Dickerman, Jonathan Tuttle, Joseph Downs, Ruben Bradly, Linas Gilbert, John Russel and Tim° Ball be Surveyers of highways the Year ensuing.

[Leather Sealer] Voted that Stephen Bradly be Leather Sealer ye year Ensuing.

Key Keepers. Voted that John Thompson E:H:*[East Haven]*, Joseph Munson, Noah Potter, James Thompson, Joseph Gilbert, Aaron Gilbert, Noah Ives, Joel Tuttle, Lamberton Smith J^r, James Bishop, Phileman Heaton, William Adams, Seth Peck, Benjn Pardee, Seth Blackslee, Peter Johnson and Jeremiah Osborn be key keepers the year Ensuing.

Cullers of Lumber. Voted that John Miles, Newman Trowbridge, Robert Brown and John Beecher of W: H:*[West Haven]* be Surveyers and Culers of Lumber the year ensuing.

[p. 49] Pound. Voted y^t John Bradly have Liberty to build a pound at his own Cost and be keeper of the key.

Branders. Voted that Theop^s Munson, Elisha Booth, Simeon Bradly, Ephram Humaston, Joseph Peck, Jonathan Ives, Roger Peck and George Smith be branders of horses ye year ensuing.

Sealer. Voted that Theop^s Munson be Sealer of weights and measures the year ensuing.

Sealer. Voted that John Miles *[be]* Sealer of dry measures the year Ensuing.

Fence viewers. Voted that John Mix, Nathan Mansfield and Obadiah Hotchkis be fence viewers the year ensuing.

[Highway] Committee report. We the Subscribers Selectmen of the Town of New Haven persuant to a Report of a Committee of the prop^s of ye Common and undivided Land made ye 21st Day of Feb: A.D. 1774 which s^d Committee reported it as their opinion that it would be Beneficial for a highway to be opened from the Dike near the Long wharff at the rear of the grants formerly made to Mr Henry Glover, Joseph Alsop and Mr Leet half a rod wide from s^d Dike to the half rod highway north of Mr Prouts old warehouse and at the request of Sundry Inhabitants of the Town of New Haven.

Proceeded to Layout s^d highway having first notified the persons who were owners of the Land thro^{gh} which the Same was to be laid out, who appeared and upon viewing the same we are of opinion that s^d proposed highway is needfull, and accordingly we Surveyed and Laid out the Same in manner following beginning at s^d Dike at the westerly Corner of s^d Elijah Forbes Land taking Eight feet and a half of the Same and so running a Strait Line through s^d Forbes Land untill it Comes to a point in s^d Forbes Land adjoyning the half rod highway North of Mr John Prouts ware house and from s^d Last mentioned highway from the point in s^d Forbes Land Extending west 8$_{1/2}$ feet into the Land of s^d Prout & thence *[p. 50]* Containing Eight feet and an half wide from s^d Line in said Forbes Land thru the Land of said Prout Joseph Munson & Hezehiah Sabin untill it Comes to s^d Dike s^d highway is about four rods in Length and 8$^{1/2}$ feet wide Bounded East on s^d Forbes Land and west on Hez^h Sabin, Joseph Munson & John Prout Esqr, their Lands. And the s^d Prout, Munson and Sabin were willing s^d highway should be laid thro^h their Lands as aforesaid and desired no recompence and we not being able to agree with s^d Forbes his recompence or Damages to be Settled as the Law Directs. The above work performed april A:D: 1774.

Stephen Ball
Tim° Jones J^r } Selectmen
John Woodward
J. Chandler

I do hereby appoint Messrs Thomas Howell, James Sherman and William Grunough as appraisers to Estimate the Damage that may be done to Elijah Forbs by
laying out the within Described highway through his Land.

Test. Thomas Darling   Jus^t of Peace

We the Subscribers Freeholders under oath appointed by Thomas Darling Esqr Just.
of Peace to appraise and Estimate the Damage done to Elijah Forbs by Laying
out the within mentioned highway do adjudge the Same to be Six pounds Lawfull
money.

William Grenough
Thomas Howell   } appraisers
James Sherman

This Town having read and duely Considered of the foregoing Survey and Laying out of the highway by the Selectmen in Manner afore^d, do by vote accept of
the Same, agreeable to the Law in Such Case Provided and order y^t the Same be
Recorded.

Highway. Voted that the Selectmen prefer a Petition to the Gen^{ll} assembly in
may next to enable this Town to tax themselves for the purpose of mending &
repairing the highways in this Town unless they Shall think fit in Such Case to
make a general Law for that purpose.

[p. 51] This meeting adjourned to fryday next at 10 of ye Clock in the forenoon.

[DECEMBER 30, 1774]

AT A TOWN MEETING HELD IN NEW HAVEN BY ADJOURNMENT
DECEMBER 30TH 1774.

Pounds. Voted that Bazel Munson, Thomas Pardee and Hezehiah Tuttle have
Liberty to build pounds and be key keepers of the Same.

Swine. Voted that Swine going at Large on the highways and Town Commons the year ensuing shall not be Liable to be impounded from thence, Provided they are ringed all the year, and sufficently yoaked from the first day of march next to 10 Day of December next.

Overseers. Voted that the Selectmen and overseers of the Poor shall Receive the excise money out of the Colony Treasury and distribute the Same according unto the Late act of the General assembly relative thereto.

Indian money.[1] Voted that there be the Sum of one Hundred Pounds or the Indian money so Called Collected in, and be disposed of to pay for a Stock of Powder which the Town is Obliged to Secure by the Late act of assembly it is also recommended to the Several School Committees in the Town to let those persons that are indebted to the Town for Indian money so Called exchange ye bonds from the Town to the School Committee Provided they give Such Security as the s^d School Committee shall approve of.[2]

Tax. *[p. 52]* Voted that there be a rate or Tax of Two pence half penny on the pound [to] be Collected of the inhabitants of this Town upon the present List to defray the necessary Charges arising within the Same.

Voted that s^d rate or Tax be paid upon the first day of March next.

Coll^{rs}. Voted that Saml Smith W: H: *[West Haven]*, Saml Mansfield J^r, Amos Thomas J^r, Samuel Davenport, Jesse Goodyear, Israel Thomas, David Atwater J^r, Caleb Gilbert, Job Potter and John Miles be Collectors of s^d rate.

Coll^r. Voted that David Atwater J^r be released from being Collector and David Atwater[3] be *[collector]* in his Stead.
Constables. Voted that John Lothrop and Hezekiah Tuttle be Constables the year ensuing.

County Congress. Voted that in Case there Should be a County Congress the Com-

1. Indian money, referred to as wampum, or shell beads, was used as currency by both Native American tribes and colonists.
2. Connecticut ordered 300 barrels of gunpowder, 15 tons of lead, and 60,000 flints for the colony on January 4 - 5, 1775 through Roger Sherman, who acquired shipments in February. See *PRCC*, XIV: 387.
3. David Atwater (1736 - 1777) was killed at the Battle of Compo Hill in Danbury. He was a member of the Connecticut Light Horse.

mittee of inspection in this Town are directed to Chuse out of their number, a Suteable number to attend the Same.[1]

Treasurer. Voted that Samuel Bishop J[r] be Town Treasurer the year ensuing.

Tythingman. Voted that Lemuel Humphervile be released from being Tythingman & Merit Clark *[be]* Chosen in his room.

This meeting adjourned to the first monday of Feb[ry] next at one of the Clock in the afternoon.

[FEBRUARY 6, 1775]

[p. 53] AT A TOWN MEETING HELD IN NEW HAVEN BY ADJOURN-MENT UPON THE 6TH DAY OF FEB[RY] ANNO DOM 1775.

Constable. Voted that Lamberton Painter be released to serve as a Constable, And Oliver Smith is Chosen Constable in his room.

Coll[r]. Voted that John Miles be released from being a Collector of the Town rate and Charles Prindle be Chosen in his Room.

Lister. Voted that Eben[r] Barns be released from being a Lister, and Joshua Barns Chosen in his room.

Committee about oysters. Voted that Lamberton Smith J[r], Azariah Bradly, John Woodward, Amos Morris, Andrew Smith J[r], Tim[o] Jones J[r], Amos Botisford, Jesse Levenworth, Dan[l] Lyman, Joshua Barns and Aaron Gilbert be a Commit-tee to draw some regulations with regard to preserving the oysters within this Town, and make some proper draught for that purpose and report their doings to the Town the next meeting.

Highway at Stony brook. Voted y[t] this Town accept of and approve of the highway laid out by the Selectmen leading from Stoney Brook near to the meeting house in West Haven parrish which s[d] Survey was made and Laid out on the 6th of april 1774, Provided that y[e] inhabitants of west Haven purchase at their own Cost and procure good and authentick Deeds of the heirs of M[r] Israel Kimberly, M[rs] Eliza-beth Painter and M[rs] Eunice Stocker and also from the owners of y[e] Land from

---

1. The Connecticut General Assembly first enacted this proposal on June 3, 1774.

the Cross Road so Called to Mr Titus Beechers Land being in Length in the whole Two Hundred & Sixty two Rods. Also Provided that s^d Road shall not be opened nor the Survey Recorded untill the first Day of January next.[1]

[p. 54] This meeting adj^d to the Last monday of this instant Feb^{ry} at 10 of the Clock in the forenoon.

[FEBRUARY 27, 1775]

AT A TOWN MEETING HELD IN NEW HAVEN BY ADJOURNMENT UPON THE 27TH DAY OF FEBRUARY ANNO DOM 1775.

Coll^r. Voted that Seth Todd be Collector of the Town rate in the room of Saml Mansfield J^r, who refused to Serve and paid 26s into the Town Treasury.

[A blank space appears here in the original records denoting that the clerk intended to record an entry that was never made. In the intervening eight months of no entries, the American Revolution was now fully underway and a number of New Haveners had already marched off to war.]

[NOVEMBER 6, 1775]

AT A TOWN MEETING HOLDEN IN NEW HAVEN UPON THE SIXTH DAY OF NOV^R ANNO DOM 1775.

[Moderator]. Voted. Voted that William Grunough Esqr be moderator

Beacon. Voted that a Beacon be forthwith erected on Indian Hill in East Haven.[2]

Committee about Beacon. Voted that Mr Phinias Bradly, Mr Doolittle and Mr James Rice be a Committee to erect ye Same according to their best Judgement.

Voted that s^d Committee as Soon as the Beacon is finished fix on a proper Day for firing the Same *[p. 55]* At the going down of the Sun and give notice thereof

---

1. Possibly South Street (now Main Street) as it approached what is now First Avenue in West Haven.
2. The beacon was completed by November 14, 1775. It was located on what is now called Beacon Hill in East Haven. The first lighting of the beacon took place on November 20, 1775 and was intended to signal neighboring militias to the defense of the town. See, John Warner Barber, *History and Antiquities of New Haven...* (1870), pp. 133-134.

by advertisement in the paper requesting the ministers in the neighbouring Towns and Parrishes to Communicate the Same to their people which notice is recommended to be given on Thanksgiving day.

Voted that in every Case of an alarm the beacon be fired by order in writing from Col Fitch in his absence by order in writing from Cap[t] Thompson or Cap[t] Brown or Cap[t] Alling and by no other order and authority.

Lyme Com[tee.] Voted that the Committee of inspection of Lyme be desired to appoint one or more mert*[ious]* person*[s]* by express to give Col Fitch the earliest intelligence of the arrival of any fleet or any Hostile appearance in the Sound.[1]

[Captain Sears]. Voted that Cap[t] Sears be desired to Establish a mode of Intelligence in Case of any Danger by way of New york.[2]

Artillery Comp[y]. Voted that a Company of artillary to Consist of 40 men be inlisted to take Care of the Carriage guns, they to Chuse their officers and be under the Direction of Col Fitch.

House holders. Voted that the Town approve of the method the house holders have taken in forming themselves into two Companies and of their drawing half pound of Powder for each man deficient.

Officers. Voted that the officers of s[d] Two Companies of house holders draw a List of Such as have joyned to said Companies and notify them to meet and form themselves into a third Company or into a fire Company, and Chuse their officers &c.

Householders in the parishes. Voted that the house holders of the respective parrishes form themselves into Companies as Soon as may be and Chuse officers who are directed to view their Companies, and draw their Powder half pound to each man who has arms and is Dificient for which the Cap[t] or Lieu[t] to give a Receipt to the Selectmen to Deliver the Same to each Difficient man taking his Receipt to return the Same if not used in the Service of his Country.

[p. 56 Captain Jones] Voted that Cap[t] Jones furnish his independent Company

---

1. Fears were already high that the British would evacuate Boston in favor of New York and the possible use of Long Island as a base of British naval operations.
2. Isaac Sears (1730 - 1786), a Massachusetts native and transplanted New Yorker, Sears was an ardent patriot, privateer, and member of the Sons of Liberty.

by ye Same rule.

Col. Fitch.[1] Voted that each and every of said Companies on appearance of danger be under the command and direction of Col. Fitch and Such as he Shall appoint who is directed to assign an alarm post or posts.

Companies meeting. Voted that each Company meet at Least once every week untill ordered to the Contrary by Col. Fitch and that ye officers view at meeting the arms and Cartridges that no Powder be wasted.

Capt Thompson Company. Voted that the Town approve of Capt Thompsons Companies drawing thirty Pounds or Powder for his men.

Powder. Voted that each man of the militia dificient draw half pound of Powder in the Same manner the s^d volluntary Companies are Enabled to do.

Stands of Arms. Voted that the Govr be disired to permit one Hundred Stands of arms to be Lodged in the Library for the use of a Company in Yale College.

College Company. Voted that should a Company in College be Formed and accounted they draw in like manner half a pound of Powder to each man.[2]

Voluntary Company. Voted that the officers of each voluntary Company afore^{sd} return the Names of such as neglect to attend appointments and Such as refuse to Joyn to any Company to the next Town meeting.

firing of guns. Voted that if any person in this Township discharge a Gun wantonly or at any kind of game for the space of two months Complaint thereof be made to the respective officers of the militia or of s^d voluntary Companies, who at their discretion may return the Names of Such offenders to the next Town meeting.

[Black Rock Fort] Committee. Voted that five persons to wit Messrs Adam Babcock, Joseph Thompson, Isaac Sears, Saml Broom & Amos Morris *[p. 57]* be a Committee according to the Letter rec^d from the Govr and Committee of Safety to direct and Super intend the building [of] a fort at Black Rock, to aply to the

---

1. Jonathan Fitch (1727 - 1793) served as colonel of the Second Militia Regiment until 1775. He then became Commissary of Connecticut's militia as of April 1775 and served throughout the war.
2. The Connecticut Assembly voted to supply 100 stands of arms and gunpowder to be stored at Yale's library for use by the student company. The students drilled before General Washington when he visited New Haven later that year.

Committee of New york for Cannon and to aply for and procure Shot, to make application to the Neighbouring Towns to Come in upon an alarm & to request the Gov[r] to lengthen out the term for Cap[t] Thompsons Company Service if thought requisite.[1]

Agents. Voted y[t] Two persons to wit Mess[rs] Adam Babcock and Ben[j] Douglas be agents to apply to the assembly in behalf of this Town for 6 Row galleys and 3 Floating Batteries and whatever Else the said Committee of five Shall think proper for the Defence & Safety of the Town & to Solicit and Obtain the 100 arms for the Colluge.[2]

Beacon. Voted that the afores[d] Committee appointed to Erect a Beacon, do build a watch box near the Same and that Cap[t] Thompson order a watch to be Kept there Constantly.

[Loyalists] Committee. Voted that every person who Looks upon himself bound either from Conscience or Choice to give intelligence to our Enemies of our Situation or otherwise take an active part against us or to yield obedience to any Commands of his Majesty George the 3[d] so far as to take up arms against this Town or the united Colonies, every Such person be desired peacefully to depart from the Town.

[Loyalists] Voted that a Committee of 15 to be appointed for that purpose be Desired to morrow or as Soon as may be to Call before them every person Suspected of Harbouring the Sentiments above mentioned and on Conviction they be desired to depart the Town as Soon as may be in a peaceable way.

The Committee appointed for the purpose aforesaid are Sam[l] Bishop J[r], Dan[l] Lyman, Adam Babcock, Phin[s] Bradly, Michael Todd, Pierpoint Edwards, Tim[o] Jones J[r], John Lothrop, Henry Daggett, Jeremiah Platt, Lamberton Smith J[r], Joel Hotchkis, Isaac Chidsey & Step[n] Goodyear.[3] This meeting adjourned without day.

---

1. The General Assembly appointed Joseph Thompson a lieutenant in the militia on March 14, 1776 and authorized him to enlist 30 men to complete and garrison the fort.

2. The first of the row galleys for New Haven was called the *Whiting,* named in honor of Col. Nathan Whiting of New Haven, a hero of the Seven Years' War. John McCleave was appointed captain. The galley was later captured by the British on the Hudson River..

3. The committee was composed of leading patriots, who interrogated suspected Loyalists in town. Following those interrogations, Ralph Isaacs and Abiathar Camp were both ordered to Glastonbury to live under surveillance. Isaacs, however, was too ill to travel.

[DECEMBER 11, 1775]

[p. 58] AT A TOWN MEETING IN NEW HAVEN UPON THE 11TH DAY OF DECEMBER ANNO DOM 1775.

Clerk. Voted that Sam¹ Bishop Jᵣ be Town Clerk

Modᵣ. Voted that Daniel Lyman Esqᵣ be moderator.

Selectmen. Voted that Messʳˢ Jonathan Fitch, Timothy Jones Jᵣ, Isaac Doolittle, James Gilbert, Amos Morris, Thomas Mansfield and Timothy Bradly be Selectmen the year ensuing.

Overseers [of Poor]. Voted that the Selectmen together with Nehemiah Smith, Samuel Atwater and Isaac Beecher Jᵣ be overseers of the Poor the year ensuing.

Committee [of Inspection]. Voted that there be a Committee of inspection Chosen, and that there Shall be four persons Chosen in each Society within the Limits of the First Society, and two persons in each of the other parrishes in the Town.

Conmittee of inspection. Voted that Messʳˢ Jonathan Fitch, Michael Todd, Enos Munson, Adam Babcock, Peter Colt, Tim° Jones Jᵣ, David Austin, John McChive, Isaac Doolittle, Joseph Trowbridge, Thomas Bills, Dan¹ Bontyou, James Gilbert, Mark Leavenworth, Abram Auger, Joel Gllbert, Joshua Austin, Stephen Smith, Lamberton Painter, Silas Kimberly, Jesse Todd, Noah lves, Tim° Bradly, Amos Perkins, Joel Bradly Jᵣ, Bazel Munson, Isaac Beecher Jᵣ, & Joel Hotchkis be a Committee of inspection in this Town the year Ensuing.

Committee to procure Powder. Voted that Daniel Basset, Adam Babcock, Joseph Munson, Michael Todd, Phinias Bradly, Caleb Beecher, Lamberton Smith Jᵣ, Simeon Bristoll, Amos Morris & Timothy Ball, be a Committee to Consider of the best method to procure Powder & arms for the use of the Town and report their opinion to the Town at their next meeting.[1]

Voted that this meeting be adjourned to monday Next at 10 of the Clock in the forenoon.

---

1. The committee's recommendations led to the construction of a powder mill owned in part by Adam Babcock.

[DECEMBER 18, 1775]

[p. 59] AT A TOWN MEETING HELD IN NEW HAVEN BY ADJOURN-
MENT ON Y^E 18th DAY OF DECEMBER 1775

Constables. Voted y^t John Lothrop, Elisha Booth, John Mix, Joel Gilbert, John
Wise, Abram Auger, John Denison, Jesse Stevens, Amos Thomas J^r, Samuel
Martin, Amos Hitchcock, Joseph Bradly Ju^r, and Stephen Jacobs be Constables
the year ensuing.

Grandjurymen. Voted that Saml Forbs, Samuel Townsend, Saml Sherman, Zach-
eus Candee, Zopher Blackslee, Levi Cooper, Job Blackslee, Stephen Ives,
Lazarus Toles, Obed Johnson, Jason Bradly, Edward Perkins, Stephen Sanford
J^r, Jacob Thompson, Joseph Peck J^r, James Prescott, Thomas Bills, Abram
Thompson, Stephen Dickerman and Stephen Hotchkis be grandjurymen the
year ensuing.

Listers. Voted that Joel Gilbert, Henry Daggett, Timothy Thompson, Israel
Potter, Azel Kimberly, Charles Chauncy, Jonathan Ingersoll, Dan Todd, Peter
Eastman, Joseph Beecher J^r, Joseph Gilbert J^r, Benajah Peck, Benjamin Sanford, Peter Colt, Nathl Woodin, Philemon Potter & Henry Toles be Listers the
year ensuing.

L[eather] Sealer. Voted that Stephen Bradly be Leather Sealer the ensuing year.

Key Keepers. Voted that John Thompson E. H. *[East Haven]*, Joseph Munson,
Noah Potter, James Thompson, Joseph Gilbert, Aaron Gilbert, Noah Ives, Joel
Tuttle, Lamberton *[Smith]]^r*, James Bishop 4th, Phileman Heaton, William Ad-
ams, Saml Horton, Seth Peck, Seth Blackslee, Peter Johnson, Jeremiah Osborn,
John Bradly, Bazel Munson and Eli Bradly be Key Keepers the year ensuing.

Voted that Isaac Blackslee be *[...]* [1]

[p. 60] Agents. Voted that Samuel Bishop J^r, and Jonathan Fitch Esq^rs be agents
for the Town, to make application to the present Gen^ll assembly that this Town
may be allowed to Chuse a Number of Selectmen, not exceeding thirteen.

Adjourned to the Last wednesday of Instant December at one of the Clock

---

1. The clerk failed to complete this entry.

in the afternoon.

[DECEMBER 26, 1775]

AT A MEETING OF THE INHABITANTS OF THE TOWN OF NEW HA-
VEN HOLDEN BY ADJOURNMENT UPON THE 26ᵀᴴ DAY OF DECᴿ 1775.

Moderator. Mʳ Phineas Bradly Chosen moderator.

Surveyers. Voted that John Mix, Obediah Hotchkis, Isaac Bishop, James Basset, Job Potter, Silas Alling, John Miles, Ralph Isaacs, Silas Kimberly, John Platt, Samuel Davenport, Daniel Smith, Benjamin Pierpoint, Jonathan Dayton, Jesse Ford, Seth Downs, Joel Bradly, Eli Bradly, Ezra Sperry, John Smith, Stephen Ives, Thomas Darling, Joseph Gilbert and Jonathan Heaton be Surveyers of highways in this Town the year Ensuing.

Constable. Voted yᵗ John Austin be Constable & Collʳ of the Country rate the year ensuing.

Collector. Voted yᵗ Elisha Booth be Collector of the Country rate in the room of Capᵗ John Mix and John Austin who refused.

Constable. Voted yᵗ Samˡ Humaston Jʳ be Constable the year ensuing, and also be Collector of the Country Rate the Ensuing year - & Sworn.

Constable. Voted yᵗ Joseph Bradly Jʳ be released from being Constable and Lemuel Bradly Chosen in his room.

[p. 61] Constable. Voted yᵗ Stephen Jacobs be released from being Constable and John Gilbert Chosen in his room.

Treasʳ. Voted yᵗ Samuel Bishop Jʳ be Town Treasurer the year Ensuing.

Tax. Voted yᵗ there be a Tax or rate Collected of the Inhabitants of this Town on the present List, to defray the necessary Charges of the Town.

Collectors. Voted that Titus Bradly, Amos Thomas Jʳ, Jeremiah Ives, David Beecher Jʳ, Jesse Stevens, Stephen Hotchkis, Danˡ Bontecou, John Austin, Phileman Potter and Samˡ Forbs be Collectors of the Town rate the year ensuing.

Tythingmen. Voted that Charles Bishop, John Davenport, Grixson Gilbert, Israel Bishop, Jonah Bradly, Phin⁵ Bradly J', Richard Cutler, Job Perrit, Azel Kimberly, George Smith, Nehemiah Smith, Phileman Smith, Stephen Thompson, Jacob Bradly, Abraham Alling, Jospeh Gilbert, Amos Bradly, David Sperry, Benjamin Brocket, Gideon Todd J', Jonathan Barns J' & David Barns be Tythingmen the year Ensuing.

This meeting adjourned to monday next at two of the Clock in the afternoon.

[JANUARY 1, 1776]

AT A TOWN MEETING IN NEW HAVEN HELD BY ADJOURNMENT UPON THE FIRST DAY OF JANUARY 1776.

Grandjurymen. Voted that Phinias Bradly & Pierpoint Edwards be Grandjurymen in the room of James Prescott and Abraham Thompson.

[p. 62] Grandjuryman. Voted yᵗ Lieuᵗ Jonathan Dickerman[1] be Grandjuryman in the room of Jason Bradly.

Grandjuryman. Voted yᵗ Mʳ Charles Chauncy be Grandjuryman in the room of Stephen Dickerman.

Grandjuryman. Voted yᵗ Mʳ Stephen Peck be Grandjuryman in the room of Charles Chauncy.

Grandjuryman. Voted yᵗ Capᵗ John Gilbert be Grandjuryman in the room of Jacob Thompson.

Collector. Voted that Charles Bradly be Collector of the Town rate in the room of Amos Thomas.

Collʳ. Voted that ~~Charles Bradley~~ Gold Sherman be Collector of the Town rate in the room of John Austin.

Collector. Voted yᵗ Jacob Thompson be one of the Collʳˢ of the Town rate in the room of Phileman Potter.

---

1. Jonathan Dickerman (1719 - 1795), a Mt. Carmel resident, was a veteran of the Revolutionary War, member of the Committee of Inspection in 1777 as well as an Inspector of Provisions in 1780. See, https://www.wikitree.com/wiki/Dickerman-115#_note-2.

Swine. Voted y^t Swine going at Large upon the high ways and Town Commons Shall not be Liable to be impounded from thence, Provided they are ringed all the year and Sufficiently yoked from the 10th Day of march to the 10th Day of December next.

Coll^r. Voted y^t Samuel Humaston J^r be Collector of the Country rate y^t James Blackslee was Chosen to Collect.

[DECEMBER 9, 1776]

[*p. 63*] AT A TOWN MEETING HELD IN NEW HAVEN UPON THE 9TH DAY OF DECEMBER ANNO DOMINI 1776.[1]

Clerk. Voted y^t Samuel Bishop J^r be Town Clerk.

Moderator. Voted y^t Mr Phineas Bradly be moderator of this meeting.

Selectmen. Voted that Messrs Jonathan Fitch, Tim° Jones J^r, Isaac Doolittle, James Gilbert, Thomas Howell, Hez^h Sabin, Abr^m Auger, Amos Morris, Nehemiah Smith, Thomas Mansfield, Tim° Bradly, Samuel Atwater and Isaac Beecher J^r be Selectmen the year Ensuing.

Committee of inspection. Voted y^t the above named Selectmen be the Committee of inspection the year ensuing.

Constables. Voted y^t Elisha Booth, Samuel Humaston J^r, John Wise, John Denison, Phileman Smith, Justus J. Fitch, Amos Thomas J^r, Saml Dickerman, Amos Hitchcock and John Austin be Constables the year ensuing.

Collector. Voted y^t Elisha Booth be Collector of ye Country rate the year ensuing.

---

1. The fact that Samuel Bishop, Jr. did not record a town meeting for 11 months may be the result of several factors, from the Revolution's impact on the town's normal functions to Bishop's own possible inability to record meetings due to his additional duties as a Deputy in the Connecticut General Assembly representing New Haven, his continued role as the town treasurer, judge, in addition to a prolonged illness. During this period, several momentous events occurred, including Captain Benedict Arnold's demand for the powderhouse keys on April 22, 1775 following New Haven receiving news of the Battles of Lexington and Concord. Three months later, New Haveners read the Declaration of Independence for the first time in New Haven's *The Connecticut Journal* on July 17, 1776. That event was soon followed by more ominous news of several British victories against American troops in New York, including the loss of Forts Lee and Washington along the Hudson River.

Said Booth refused to Collect s^d Rate, thereupon Voted y^t s^d Samuel Humaston J^r be Collector of the Country rate the year ensuing.

Listers. Voted y^t James Hillhouse, Charles Chauncy, Elias Beers, Nathl Wood-in, Henry Daggett, Phileman Potter, Elias Shipman, Benjamin Sanford, James Thompson, Saml Heminway J^r, Azael Kimberly, Henry Toles, Eli Sacket, Abel Bishop, Benj. Peck, Lucas Lines, Joseph Gilbert J^r, Jona^n Gilbert and Joel Gilbert be Listers the year ensuing.

[p. 64] Grandjurymen. Voted y^t John Pierpoint, William Lyon, Robert Dawson, Joseph Heminway, Gamaliel Benham, Thomas Cooper J^r, Titus Tuttle, Amos Perkins J^r, Saml Alling J^r, Jos. Hotchkis of Bethany, Nathl Tuttle J^r, Jason Bradly & Abel Burrett be Grandjurymen the year Ensuing.

Committee to procure Small arms. Voted y^t Samuel Bishop J^r, Charles Chauncy, Henry Daggett, Timothy Jones J^r, and Joseph Thompson be a Committee to make application to his Hon^r the Govr and his Council of Safety to request them to direct that a number of Small arms might be procured and carried to this Town for the use of Such as we are destitute of the Same. That a number of field pieces might be Provided for the defence of the Town — and y^t a barge might be Provided as occasion Shall offer to obtain intelligence and watch the motions of those that may attempt to Land and annoy the Town.

This meeting adjourned to monday next at 10 of the Clock in the forenoon.

[DECEMBER 16, 1776]

AT A TOWN MEETING HELD IN NEW HAVEN BY ADJOURNMENT UPON THE 16TH DAY OF DECEMBER 1776.

Key Keepers. Voted y^t John Thompson of East Haven, Joseph Munson, Noah Potter, Joseph Gilbert, Aaron Gilbert, Noah Ives, Joel Tuttle, Lamberton Smith J^r, James Bishop 4th, Phileman Heaton, William Adams, Saml Horton, Seth Peck, Seth Blackslee, Peter Johnson Jur, John Bradly, Bazel Munson & Eli Bradly be key keepers the year ensuing.

[p. 65] Sealer of Leather. Voted that Stephen Bradly be leather Sealer the year ensuing.

Sealer of Weights. Voted y^t Theop^s Munson be sealer of weights and measures, the year ensuing.

Sealer of dry measures. Voted y^t John Miles be sealer of dry measures the year ensuing.

Fenceviewers. Voted y^t Capt John Mix, Nathan Mansfield and Obediah Hotchkis be fence viewers the year ensuing.

Tythingmen. Voted y^t Isaac Thompson, Jonathan Brigden, Nathan Howell, Jonah Hotchkis, Mark Levenworth, John Warner, Richard Cutler, Abner Bow, Isaac Malthrop, Saml Smith, Nathan Catlin, John Smith, Jotham Blackslee, Giles Pierpoint, Reuben Beecher, Saml Alling J^r, Amos Bradly, Job Todd, Roger Peck and David French be Tythingmen the year ensuing.

Tythingman. Voted that Hez^h Smith be tythingman in the room of Reuben Beecher released.

Tythingman. Voted that Caleb Alling be tythingman in the room of Mark Levenworth released.

Constable. Voted that John Austin be released from being Constable.

Constables. Voted y^t John Lothrop, Saml Thacher and John White J^r be Constables the year ensuing.

Cullers of Lumber. Voted y^t John Miles, Newman Trowbridge, Robert Brown and John Beecher of West Haven be Surveyors and Cullers of Lumber the year Ensuing.

[p. 66] Branders of horses. Voted y^t Theop^s Munson, Elisha Booth, Simeon Bradly, Epheram Humaston, Joseph Peck, Jonathan Ives, Roger Peck and George Smith be branders of horses the year ensuing.

Swine. Voted y^t Swine going at large on ye Town Commons the ensuing year shall not be Liable to be impounded from thence Provided they are ringed all ye year and Sufficiently yoaked from the 10th of March to the 10th Day of December next.

Surveyers of highways. Voted y^t Amos Botisford, James Hillhouse, John Beecher, Obidiah Hotchkis, Nathl Woodin, John Mix, John Gills, Nathan Beers, Abr^m Heminway, Stephen Tuttle, Joseph Russel, Silas Kimberly, Oliver Smith, Jonathan Barns, Deacon Cooper, Solomon Tuttle, Eben^r Blackslee, Enos Brocket,

Joseph Bradly Jr, Noadiah Carrinton, Danl Perkins, Ebenr Sperry, Jesse Ford, Reuben Beecher, Alexr Booth, Ebenr Beech, Jacob Atwater, Peter Perkins, John Lounsbury, Jesse Beecher, Joel Wheeler, David Hull and Elnathan Toles be Surveyers of highways the year Ensuing, sd Peter Perkins[1] is Chosen with Special Refference to the repairing *[of]* Waterbury road.

Treasurer. Voted that Samuel Bishop Jr be Town Treasurer the year ensuing.

Tax. Voted yt there be a rate or Tax of three pence on the pound to be Collected on the present List for defraying the necessary Charges of the Town the Ensuing *[year]*.

Voted that sd rate be paid on the first of march next.

Selectmen to give Districts. Voted yt the Selectmen give ye districts to the Surveyers of highways according to Law.

[p. 67] Collr. Voted yt Samuel Humaston Jr be Collector of Town rate.

S Humaston. Voted yt sd Humaston be allowed the Sum of fifteen pounds out of the Town Treasury for taking said rate.

Constable. Voted yt Lemuel Bradly be Constable the year Ensuing.

Grandjurymen. Voted yt Capt James Peck, James Gilbert and Benj Sanford be grandjurymen the year ensuing.

Committee about Boston donation. Voted yt Messrs Amos Botsford, Phine Bradly and Abram Bradly be a Committee to Settle with the Committee who was appointed by this Town to Receive donations for the poor in ye Town of Boston, and report make to the Town of the State of that matter, at some future meeting[2]

Tents. Whereas the Publick Charges of this Town is greatly inhand by the present distresses and by a Law of this State passed at the Sessions of the Gen11 assembly in Octr Last the Several Towns are ordered to procure one tent for every £1000 on the List and other articles for the use of the militia and whereas ye

---

1. Peter Perkins, III (1741 - 1799) was a resident of Bethany, CT. See, https://www.geni.com/people/Peter-Perkins-III/6000000003938484924.
2. This is in reference to the town meeting of October 18, 1774 in which a subscription for the poor of Boston was initiated.

Gen[ll] assembly have favoured this Town by allowing them the militia to remain for y[e] defence of this Town and not liable to be Called forth whereby they Suppose s[d] Tents &c are not necessary for y[e] militia —Voted by this Town y[t] our representatives return the Humble Thanks of this Town to the Gen[ll] assembly for their kindness in that exemption as well as their particular attention to the Safeguard and wellfare of this Town in other Instances, And also apply to the Gen[ll] assembly by memorial to have the Inhabitants exempted from being out of y[e] Charge of procuring Tents &c as the militia of this [town] are not ordered to march forth.

This meeting adjourned without Day.

[JANUARY 30, 1777]

[p. 68] AT A TOWN MEETING HOLDEN IN NEW HAVEN UPON Y[E] 30TH DAY OF JANUARY 1777

Moderator. Voted y[t] M[r] Phin[s] Bradly be moderator of this meeting.

Grandjuryman. Voted y[t] Eben[r] Chittenden be Grandjuryman in y[e] room of Benjamin Sanford who refused to serve.

Grandjuryman. Voted that Michael Baldwin be Grandjuryman in the Room of William Lyon who refused to serve.

Grandjuryman. Voted y[t] John Mix be Grandjuryman in the room of John Pierpoint who refused to serve.

Voted y[t] Sam[l] Woodin be Grandjuryman in the room of James Gilbert who refused to serve.

Tythingman. Voted y[t] adonijah Sherman be ~~Grandjuryman~~ Tythingman in the room of Nathan Howell who refused & Henry Toles be Tythingman in the room of Jonah Hotchkis who refused.

Selectman. Voted y[t] M[r] Caleb Hotchkis J[r] be Selectman in the room of Deacon Howell who refused to Serve.

Rate. Voted that in addition to the Town rate of three pence on the pound Granted in December Last, There be three pence more upon the pound added, to pay for the Tents &c ordered by an act of the Gen[ll] Assembly all to be Collected together upon y[e] first Day of march Next.[1]

Allowance to Collector. Voted y[t] Twenty Pounds be paid out of the Town treasury to the person who shall Collect the Town rate.

[Collector.] Voted that M[r] Phin[s] Bradly *[be collector]* of the Town rate.

[p. 69] Act of Assembly to regulate prices of articles. Whereas the Gen[ll] assembly of this State at their Sessions in Middletown on the 18th Day of December last past by an act did regulate the prices of a Number of articles in s[d] act enumerated. - and whereas it appears to this Town that it is of the utmost Consequence to the Community in General, and to this Town in particular y[t] s[d] act should be immediately carried into Execution. Voted therefore that this Town will by every Legal Measure endeavour to have the Directions of s[d] act Strictly complied with.[2]

Committee of inspection. This Town being fully Sensible that it is the duty of Every Friend to his Country to sell and dispose of the articles enumerated in the act of assembly fixing the prices of Labour &c at the prices at which they are therein Stated — Therefore voted y[t] those of us who have any of them beyond what we want for our own Consumption will readily and Chearfully sell them either for money or produce at the prices in s[d] act Stated, and that we will esteem all persons who Shall not do the Same enimies to this Country and treat them accordingly — Provided Such person is properly Convicted thereof before the Committee of inspection of this Town whom we impower to take Congnzence of Such offense.[3]

Civil Authority &c. to fix the price of articles. Whereas the Gen[ll] assembly in their act regulating the prices of Sundry articles therein enumerated and have Left the prices of Sundry other articles to be fixed by y[e] Civil authority &c. in every respective town.

---

1. In *The Republic of New Haven: A History of Municipal Evolution,* Charles Levermore argued that New Haven's efforts to avoid paying this tent tax evidenced the town's war weariness and the continued demands for more money.

2. The General Assembly actually met in Hartfortd on November 19th and set the price of tea not to exceed 4 s 6p per pound.

3. Known for its autocratic actions, the New Haven Committee of Inspection judged local merchant William Glen guilty of selling tea at an exorbitant price in March of 1776. The Committee ordered that Glen be ostracized by the community, leading to the merchant pleading guilty and pledging allegiance to the American cause.

Voted y^t Messrs Elisha Booth, John Mix, John Gilbert, John Sherman, Azariah Bradly, Charles Chauncy, Pierpoint Edwards, Joshua Chandler, Thomas Bills, Thomas Darling, Jonathan Dickerman, David Beecher J^r, *[p. 70]* Thomas Hazard, Isaac Beers, Joel Gilbert & Obediah Hotchkis, be and they are hereby appointed a Committee to Consult and Confer upon the prices of s^d non enumerated articles and at what price the Same may be Sold and make report to the proper board to fix the Same and prices being so affixed by the proper board the vendors of Such articles and Sale of the Same shall be under the Same regulations agreed on, and voted by the Town meeting this Day.

Col. Douglass reg^t. Voted y^t the Selectmen make needfull prepartions for Col: Douglas's Regiment, which is ordered into this Town.

This meeting adjourned without Day.

[APRIL 2, 1777]

AT A TOWN MEETING HELD IN NEW HAVEN UPON THE SECOND DAY OF APRIL A.D. 1777.

Moderator. Voted y^t Mr. Phineas Bradly be moderator of this meeting.

Town proportion of men for the Continental [army]. Whereas his Hon^r the Govr and Council of Safety have informed this Town that the Number of men to be raised for this Town to Compleat the Battelions for the Continental army is 275 men, and that this Town is difficient with regard to the Number of men, and requiring them to raise their full proportion — Therefore voted that this Town will Tax themselves to raise the remainder of the men that belongs to this Town to make up their full number.

Tax. Voted that a rate or Tax of one Shilling on the pound be Collected of the inhabitants of the Town upon the present List to raise a Sufficient Sum of money to Encourage men to inlist into the Service and for Cloathing of them.

[p. 71 Rate]. Voted that s^d Rate be forthwith paid.

Collector. Voted y^t Mr Phineas Bradly be Collector of s^d rate.

[Rate]. Voted that s^d Bradly Shall have Twenty pounds for Collecting said rate.

Soldiers. Voted y^t each Solider who shall hereafter inlist into the Contenential Army that shall be reckoned to the proportion of this Town to fill up the battalions, who shall pass muster shall Receive Ten pounds each man to be paid to them by the Committee hereafter mentioned.[1]

Also voted y^t each Solider y^t shall be inlisted hereafter together with those who have already inlisted into the said Contenental Battalions reckoned as part of this Towns proportion Shall receive annually from s^d Committee one pair of good strong shoes, one pair of good yearn stockings and one Shirt to be delivered to the Soldiers in the month of oct^r or Novr for the Term of three years if they Continue in the army so Long.[2]

[Soldiers.] Voted that in persuance of his Hon^r the Govr and the Council of Safetys recommendation this Town do appoint the Selectmen to be the Town Committee to Carry the s^d matters Recommended into Execution to provide Necessary Support for the Families of Such Soldiers Saving the Expenses of Collecting and delivering out Such Support which shall be at the Charge of this Town, also the s^d Committee to Receive the rate above voted and pay the Same out in money and Cloathes, as above directed.

Voted that the Committee above appointed do take into Consideration the advantages y^t Such Soldiers have already Received who have heretofore inlisted into the Contenental Battalions and taking into Consideration all the Circumstances of Such Soldiers the s^d Committee be ordered to make them Such further Gratuity as Shall appear to them Equal and Just.

Committee to borrow money. Voted y^t ye s^d Committee be requested to borrow money Sufficient be disbursed in bounties as are above voted and repay the Same out of the rate as soon as a Sum Sufficient Shall be Collected.

[p. 72] Small Pox. Voted that this Town do approve of the measures taken by the authority and Selectmen of this Town to prevent the Spreading of the Small pox

---

1. New Haven's one shilling per pound tax was used for sign-on bonuses of 10 pounds per man for each recruit into the Continental Army. The need was meant to meet the urgent requests of General Washington. According to William S. Wells, "List of Men from the territory embraced in the Town of New Haven, Connecticut, who are known to have Served in the Continental Army and Militia and Connecticut State and Continental Vessels and Privateers," in *Revolutionary Characters of New Haven* (1911), some 998 New Haveners eventually served as American soldiers and sailors in the Revolution.

2. Local militia needed to provide their own clothing and equipment, Eventually, state funds were allocated to buy clothing for state and Continental troops.

by inoculation or otherways and that they be requested¹ Still to persue Such further measures as they Judge expedient and necessary to obtain the end aforesaid.

[Pesthouse] Voted yᵗ yᵉ Selectmen be requested to remove to the pest houses in this Town as fast as they Shall be Sufficiently empty of Soldiers to Receive them all Such persons that Shall Receive the Small pox voluntarily after this Day.

This meeting adjourned without day.

[SEPTEMBER 23, 1777]

AT A TOWN MEETING HOLDEN IN NEW HAVEN UPON THE 23ᴰ DAY OF SEPTEMBER 1777.

Moderator. Voted that Daniel Lyman Esqʳ be moderator of this meeting.

Continental Soliders. This Town taking into Consideration the Resolves of yᵉ Govʳ and Council of Safety for Supplying the Continental Soldiers with Cloathing by the Several Towns in this State — It is thereupon Voted yᵗ this Town will Comply with the sᵈ Resolves — And as it is necessary that the Soldiers be immediately Cloathed to endure the fatague of a winter Campaign.²

[Clothing] Committee. Voted that Messʳˢ Hezʰ Sabin Jʳ and Michael Todd be a Committee to provide sᵈ articles of Cloathing as Soon as may be and deliver yᵉ Same to the Selectmen with the price of each article that they may render an account thereof to the Genˡˡ assembly in october next agreeable to the Requistion of sᵈ Govʳ and Council of Safety — And in order yᵗ sᵈ articles may be purchased as soon as possable.

[p. 73] Selectmen to procure money. Voted yᵗ the Selectmen procure a Sum of money Sufficient for the purpose aforsᵈ and deliver the Same to yᵉ Committee and in Case they Shall be obliged to borrow on the Credit of the Town for the purpose aforesaid the Town will pay yᵉ Interest of Sum or Sums untill yᵉ Same is repaid.

This meeting adjourned without Day.

---

1. The Connecticut Council of Safety's first mention of smallpox was in January 1777. In that same month, Gen. Washington ordered that all American troops passing through Philadelphia to be inoculated. A month later, he ordered mass inoculations of the troops.
2. American troops were engaged in New York as well as Pennsylvania. By December, Washington's army was suffering severe shortages at Valley Forge, Pennsylvania.

[DECEMBER 8, 1777]

AT A TOWN MEETING HELD IN NEW HAVEN UPON THE 8ᵀᴴ DAY
OF DECEMBER 1777.

Moderator. Roger Sherman Esqʳ Chosen moderator of this meeting.

Clerk. Samˡ Bishop Jʳ Chosen Town Clerk.

Selectmen. Voted yᵗ Messʳˢ Jonathan Fitch, Caleb Hotchkis Jʳ, Tim° Jones Jʳ, Hezʰ
Sabin, James Gilbert, Abrᵐ Auger, Isaac Doolittle, Amos Morris, Nehemiah
Smith, Jesse Todd, Samˡ Osborn, Samuel Atwater and Isaac Beecher Jʳ be Select-
men the year ensuing.

Commᵉ of inspection. Voted that the Selectmen be the Committee of inspection.

Constables. Voted yᵗ Samˡ Thacher, Samˡ Humaston Jʳ, John Wise, John Austin,
Henry Toles, Elisha Booth, John Denison, Phileman Smith, Phillip Daggett,
Danˡ Doolittle, Seth Peck, George Dudly and Amos Hitchcock be Constables
the year ensuing.

Collʳ. Voted that Samuel Humaston Jʳ be Collector of the Country rates the year
ensuing.

Treasʳ. Voted that Samˡ Bishop Jʳ be Town Treasurer the year Ensuing.

Grandjurymen. Voted yᵗ Ezehiel Hays, Abrᵐ Thompson, Mark Levenworth, John
Gilbert, Jacob Bradly, Samˡ Davenport, Willᵐ Trowbridge, Jotham Williams, Joel
Bassett, Levi Ray, Epheram Turner, David French, Amos Sherman, Solomon
Gilbert and David Sperry Mʳ C *[Mt. Carmel]*, be Grandjurymen the year ensuing.

[p.74] Assessors. Voted yᵗ Isaac Beers, Joel Gilbert, Jonathan Fitch, John Miles,
Stephen Smith, Samˡ Candee, Joshua Barns, Jesse Ford, Jonathan Dickerman &
Tim° Ball be assesers the year ensuing.

Listers. Voted yᵗ James Bradly, Peter Johnson, James Hillhouse, Henry Daggett,
Henry Toles, Phileman Potter, Elias Beers, Joseph Granis, Jacob Smith, Elias Shipman, Lamberton Painter, Peter Eastman, Oliver Smith, Samˡ Alling Jʳ, Tim° Ball Jʳ
and Elisha Alling be Listers yᵉ year ensuing.

Surveyers of highways. Voted y' John Mix, Michael Baldwin, Levi Ives, Lemuel Hotchkis, David Atwater, John Miles, Jabez Munson J', Nath' Woodin, John Bradly, Sam' Humphervile, Jared Bradly, Isaac Smith, Jehiel Forbs, Joseph Holt, John Davenport, Tho' Cooper J', David Sperry, Silas Kimberly, Gamaliel Benham, Eben' Blackslee, Giles Dayton, Hez' Pierpoint, Enos Brocket, Stephen Ives, Stephen Bristoll, Isaac Ford, Hez. Sperry, John Horton J', Joseph Beecher, John Lounsbury, Dan' Lounsbury, Jesse Beecher, Asa Goodyear, Bazel Munson and Jared Sherman be Surveyers of highways y' Ensuing year.

Key Keepers. Voted y' Joseph Munson, Noah Potter, Joseph Gilbert, Noah Ives, John Thompson, Joel Tuttle, Lamberton Smith Jr., David Thorp, Phileman Heaton, Will'' Adams, Sam' Horton, Seth Peck, Seth Blackslee, Peter Johnson, John Bradly, Bazel Munson, Eli Bradly and Aaron Gilbert be key keepers the year ensuing.

Constable. Voted that George Dudly be released from being Constable and Sam' Bellamy be Constable in his room the year ensuing.

[p. 75] Districts. Voted y' the Selectmen give the Surveyers of highways their districts.

Selectman. Voted y' Hez' Sabin be released from being Selectman and Jeremiah Atwater be Selectman in his room.

Leather sealer. Voted y' Stephen Bradly be Leather Sealer the year ensuing.

Sealer of W'' &c. Voted that Theop' Munson be Sealer of weights & measures the year ensuing.

Sealer of dry measures. Voted y' John Miles be Sealer of dry measures.

Voted y' this meeting be adjourned untill the Last monday of Instant Dec' at 10 of y' Clock in the forenoon.

[DECEMBER 29, 1777]

AT A TOWN MEETING IN NEW HAVEN BY ADJOURNMENT UPON THE 29TH DAY OF DECEMBER 1777.

Modʳ. Voted yᵗ John Whiting Esqʳ be moderator of this meeting.[1]

Fence Viewers. Voted that John Mix, Nathan Mansfield and Obediah Hotchkis be fence viewers the year ensuing.

Swine. Voted yᵗ Swine going at Large on the Commons and highways the Ensuing year Shall not be Liable to be impounded from thence, Provided they are ringed all the year & Sufficiently yoaked from the 10th of March to the 10th of December next.

S. Humaston allowance for Collecting rates. Voted that Samˡ Humaston Jʳ,[2] who was appointed Constable the last Town meeting and Collector of the Country rates Shall be Considered and treated by the Town as the first Constable, and that he Shall have paid unto him out of the Town Treasury one Hundred pounds, to pay him for Collecting the Country rates the two years past and the rates the ensuing year.

Salt.[3] Whereas there is 133 bushels of Salt brᵗ into this Town it being the proportion due to the Town from the State and in order that the Same may be disposed off, Therefore voted *[p. 76]* that 100 bushels of the Salt be by the Selectmen Divided to each Family according to their List and be delivered to the Societies Committees so yᵗ yᵉ Same may be divided to the members of the Societies in Such way as they Shall agree upon, Provided that no person who hath not taken the oath of fidelity be benefited thereby — And the remaining Quanity of Salt be left in the hands of the Selectmen to be Dealt out to the Families of the Soldiers, and to Such others where they Judge it most needed.

Fort at tho black rock. Voted yᵗ the Selectmen Cause Six men to be hired to take Care of the fort at the black rock and four men to take Care of the Guns &c in the Town platt, to be paid out of the Town Treasury untill the assembly Shall order men into this Town to guard the Same.[4]

Committee abᵗ Confederation. The articles of Confederation of the united States

---

1. John Whiting (1721 - 1786) was the son of Col. Joseph Whiting, Esq.(1680 - 1748).
2. Samuel Humiston (1743 - 1800) resided in Hamden.
3. Salt was in great demand due to the war as both a seasoning and food preserver. Rationing became commonplace. To help offset salt shortages, Amos Morris of East Haven established a saltworks using sea water. The works were destroyed by the British during the Invasion of New Haven in 1779.
4. The General Assembly first ordered Capt. Thomson's company to be stationed at the fort in October of 1776. By December, the cannon were removed to the New Haven Green.

of America being Laid before this Town, for their Consideration —Thereupon voted that John Whiting, John Trumbull, Eneas Munson, Sam¹ Bishop J⁻, Tim° Jones J⁻, David Austin, Henry Daggett, Mark Levenworth, Levi Ives, Isaac Doolittle, Charles Chauncy, John Miles, Newman Trowbridge, Amos Morris, Stephen Smith, Joshua Austin, Pierpoint Edwards, Lamberton Smith, Nemiah Smith, Silas Kimberly, Jonathan Dayton, Jesse Todd, Noah Ives, Thomas Mansfield, Caleb Beecher, Sam¹ Osborn, Amos Perkins, Sam¹ Atwater, Bazel Munson, Stephen Goodyear, Isaac Beecher, Tim° Peck and Timothy Ball be a Committee to take into Consideration sᵈ articles, and make their report to the Town the next meeting with their opinion relative thereto.[1]

[p. 77] Tax. Voted that there be a rate or Tax of Six pence on the pound be Collected of the inhabitants of the Town on yᵉ present List, to pay the Charges of the Town the year Ensuing.

Voted that sᵈ Rate shall be paid on yᵉ first of march next.

Collʳ. Voted that Capt. Abrᵐ Bradly be Collʳ of sᵈ rate.

Selectmen. Voted that the Selectmen be released from being a Committee of inspection.

Committee of inspection. Voted yᵗ Isaac Beers, Peter Johnson, Levi Ives, John Miles, Isaac Chidsey, Silas Kimberly, Stephen Ives, Jesse Ford, Stephen Goodyear & Jared Sherman be the Committee of inspection the year ensuing.

This meeting adjourned untill monday next at two of the Clock in the afternoon.

[JANUARY 5, 1778]

AT A TOWN MEETING HELD IN NEW HAVEN BY ADJOURNMENT UPON THE 5TH DAY OF JANUARY 1778

Moderator. Mʳ Phinias Bradly Chosen moderator.

Committees report on the Confederation. The Committee appointed the Last meeting to take into Consideration the articles of Confederation of the united States of America, made their report to this meeting in the following manner viz.

---

1. The report was submitted and read in public on January 7, 1788.

To the inhabitants of the Town of New Haven in town meeting assembled —
We the Committee appointed to Consider the articles of Confederation beg
Leave to report that we have examined them, and notwithstanding they appear
to have been drawn with much Care and attention. Still [p. 78] There are a few
expressions we could wish had been otherwise, of this Nature is that Clause
in the fourth article prohibiting any State from Laying any Duty imposition or
Restriction on the property of any of the States — We conceive it altogether
proper y^t no State Should have power to Lay any Embargo Duty or Ristraint on
any property of the united States, but we See no reason why the property of
one of the States whilst in any other Should be priviledged otherwise than the
property of an Individual, and tho we do not think ye Danger very Considerable. Still we fear y^t by this Clause a door might be opened for totally removing
in time of Scarity Some much Demanded article if in a future period of Corruption a Sister State Should Conduct so Dishonorably as to employ agents to
purchase up Such article in a Neighbouring State and then have a right by virtue
of this Clause to Remove it notwithstanding any embargo and free from any
duty or restraint.

In this article it is also provided that no State Shall have power to prevent ye re-
movel of property imported into any State to another State of which the owner
is an inhabitant, we presume y^t in this Clause by owner was meant importer and
we only wish it had been so expressed of the Same Nature is our objection to
furnishing Troops in proportion to the white inhabitants only as we hope the
Time may be when a black may be a [p. 79] Freeman and the owner of property
and then he ought to Contribute his proportion toward furnishing troops.[1] But
Considering the dangers y^t may attend ye delay of Ratifying ye Confederation
and the other Considerations laid before the States by Congress, we Should by
no means have mentioned those Lesser objections if we had not found much
greater Difficulty in agreeing to that part of ye Eighth article which directs y^t y^e
Common Treasury Shall be Supplyed by the States in proportion to the value
of ye Lands and improvements within each State merchandise[,] manufactures[,]
and improvements which employ numbers of Labourers and many other Circumstances may be Such y^t one State may be affluent and wealthy on ground of
Smaller value whilst another is poor on Lands of much greater price.

But the inequallity of ye Tax is not a greater objection against this mode of aser-

---

1. This is the first instance of New Haveners officially desiring eventual freedom for African Americans held in slavery. In reality, the Connecticut Assembly rejected emancipation bills in 1777, 1779,
and 1780. In 1774, slave importation was banned and by 1784 gradual emancipation was adopted in
Connecticut. It was not until 1848, however, that slavery was entirely abolished in the state.

taining the Quota than the Difficulties that attend puting it in practice. We fear that this may be a Source of endless Jealousies, discontents and Controversies different appraisment when most faithfully made may very greatly differ from each other and the Lands in many States Continually altering in value must occassion frequent appraisments and those depending altogether on the opinion of appraisers if different may occasion perpetual uneasiness — We think y^t ye only eligible mode of asertaining the proportion is Such as is reducable to a Certainty and depends not at all on opinions.[1]

New Haven Jany All which is Submitted by your Humble Servants
5th 1778   Signed p^r order
                             Saml Bishop J^r Chairman

[p. 80] Committee report accepted. Voted y^t ye forgoing Report of ye Com^{ttee} be accepted, and that the Representatives of this Town be desired to Comunicate the Same to the Gen^{ll} assembly as ye Sentiments of this Town.

Lister. Voted y^t Henry Daggett be released from being Lister and Joseph Peck is Chosen in his room.

Coll^r released. Voted y^t Abr^m Bradly be released from Collecting ye Town Rate.

Coll^r. Voted y^t John Hubbard be Collector of the Town rate the year ensuing.

Coll^{rs} allowance. Voted that the Coll^r of the Town rate be allowed the Sum of thirty pounds for Collecting s^d rate.

Salt. Voted y^t Messrs Jeremiah Atwater & Bazel Munson Sell the Salt belonging to this Town according to their discretion for the benefit of the Town, Selling not more than one peck to any one family and only to those persons Inhabitants of this Town who have taken the oath of fidelity till after the first Day of February next — and y^t the vote of the last Town meeting relating to s^d Salt be rescinded.

Selectmen to Supply Off^s &c with provisions. Voted y^t the Selectmen be desired to Supply the Commissioned officers with provisions for their familys at the Same rate of non Commissioned officers and Soldiers.

---

1. Despite the New Haven committee's reservations, the Connecticut Assembly ratified the Articles of Confederation on February 12, 1778.

Highway. Upon the motion of Capt John Mix conserning a highway to be purchased from the Little bridge (so Called) Eastward to the highway — Thereupon voted that Mr Hez^h Sabin, Capt Amos Morris and Capt Samuel Atwater be a Committee to view the Land and report on what Terms the Same may be purchased.

Selectmen to remove incroachm^ts. Voted the Selectmen be ordered to remove ye incroachments on the highway back of the Shop of Mr Adonijah Sherman, made by Capt Elijah Forbs.

[p. 81] Grandjurymen. Voted y^t Isaac Bishop, Jacob Brocket and Gideon Todd J^r be Grandjurymen in ye room of Joel Bassett, Levi Ray and Ezehiel Hays.

This meeting adjourned without day.

[JANUARY 16, 1778]

AT A TOWN MEETING HELD IN NEW HAVEN UPON THE 16TH DAY OF JANUARY 1778.

Mod^r. Voted y^t Daniel Lyman Esqr be moderator.

Surveyer. Voted y^t Joseph Peck be Surveyer of highways in the room of Michael Baldwin.

Constable and Collector. Whereas Samuel Humaston J^r was Chosen Constable and Collector of the Country rates for the present year having refused to Serve on account of his bad State of health — Thereupon voted y^t Capt Jesse Ford[1] be Constable and Coll^r of the Country rates the present year in the room of s^d Humaston.

agents. Voted that Roger Sherman and Saml Bishop J^r Esq^rs be agents in behalf of this Town to make application to the Gen^ll assembly Now Sitting at Hartford that s^d Ford may be Established Constable & Coll^r as afores^d in the room of s^d Humaston.

Coll^rs allowance. Voted that Capt Jesse Ford Shall have ye Sum of Eighty pounds paid out of the Town Treasury for Collecting the above Rates.

2. Capt. Jesse Ford (1736 - 1812) was a Woodbridge resident and member of the First Congregational Church in New Haven. The title captain referred to his seafaring status. As a member of the Connecticut General Assembly, Ford joined Captain Henry Daggett in making a successful case for the incorporation of New Haven as a city in January 1784.

Coll^s allowance. Also voted that Sam^{ll} Humaston J^r Shall have ye Sum of Twenty pounds paid out of the Town Treasury for Collecting the Country rates ye two years past.

Surveyer. Voted y^t Eben^r Townsend be Surveyer in Jn° Miles room.

This meeting adj^d without Day.

[MARCH 16, 1778]

[p. 82] AT A TOWN MEETING HELD IN NEW HAVEN UPON THE 16TH DAY OF MARCH 1778.

Mod^r. Voted that Daniel Lyman Esqr be moderator.

Committee to procure Cloathing for the army. The act of the Gen^{ll} assembly made at Hartford on the Second Thursday of January Last for Supplying the army with Cloathing being Laid before this meeting, Thereupon voted that Elisha Booth, Abel Burret, Levi Ives, John Miles, Saml Davenport, Joshua Austin, Nehemiah Smith, Nathan Smith J^r, Gideon Todd J^r, Thos Cooper J^r, Samuel Osborn, William Adams, Abner Todd, Stephen Goodyear, Peter Perkins and Isaac Beecher J^r be a Committee to procure Cloathing for the army agreeable to the afors^d act of assembly.

Further voted that in Case s^d Committee Shall want money to procure the above Cloathing they are hereby directed to apply to the Selectmen for so much money as Shall be wanted for the purpose afores^d and s^d Selectmen are hereby directed to procure the Same in the most prudent manner they can.

Committee of inspection. Voted that Messrs James Hillhouse, Abel Burret, Tim° Atwater, Newman Trowbridge and Hez^h. Sabin Ju^r be added to the Committee of inspection that was Chosen the Last meeting.

Defence of the Town. A motion being made, that Some further Measures might be taken for the defence of the Town — Thereupon voted y^t Messrs Jesse Levenworth,[1] James Hillhouse, Isaac Doolittle, Peter Johnson, Ben-

---

1. Jesse Leavenworth (1740 - 1824) was a a lieutenant in the 2nd Company of the Governor's Foot Guard who marched to Massachusetts with Captain Benedict Arnold following news of the Battle of Lexington in 1775. He later served as a captain at Fort Ticonderoga.

jamin Trumble,[1] Hez[h] Sabin J[r], Amos Morris, Joshua Austin, Lamberton Smith, Silas Kimberly, Joshua Barns, Caleb Beecher, Sam[l] Osborn, Bazel Munson, Joel Bradly, Peter Perkins, Amos Hitchcock and Samuel Willmot be a Committee to view the Town, Judge what is needfull to be done for the defence of the Town, and make their report of their opinion to the next meeting.

This meeting adj[d] to monday next at two of y[e] Clock in the afternoon.

[MARCH 23, 1778]

[p. 83] AT A TOWN MEETING HELD IN NEW HAVEN BY ADJOURN-MENT UPON THE 23[D] DAY OF MARCH 1778.

Committees report about the defence of the Town. The Committee appointed the Last meeting to view y[e] Town and See what is needfull to be done for the defence of y[e] Same made their report, which is accepted, approved & ordered to be Recorded, a Letter being prepared agreeable to s[d] Report ~~to s[d] report~~ to Lay before his Excellency the Gov[r] and Council of Safety is Considered and approved of, Thereupon voted y[t] Dan[l] Lyman Esq[r] the moderator of this meeting be desired to Sign y[e] Same, which report is in the following words viz.

To the Inhabitants of the Town of New Haven in Town meeting assembled — Gentlemen —

In pusuance of our appointment we took the earliest opportunity of viewing the Grounds round s[d] Town and the Several passes by which an enemy would most probably take their rout[e] were they to make a Decent upon it, particularly those by which it might be most easily Surprised and are unanimously of the opinion y[t] the Town is well Situated for defence and y[t] many things may be done which by the blessings of Providence, would greatly lend to protection of it — with Submission to your wisdom we beg leave to propose & recommend the following measures as immediately necessary viz. That two small works Should be erected at the west Bridge Capable of Receiving four pieces of ordnance which we are of the opinion would with a Sufficient Number of men to defend

---

1. The Reverend Benjamin Trumbull (1735 - 1820) graduated from Yale in 1759 and was appointed pastor of the North Haven Congregational Church in 1760, a position he led until his death. A prolific author, Trumbull, was cousin to Gov. Jonathan Trumbull, was the leading proponent of the colony's Susquehanna claim, land served with distinction in the Revolution as a chaplain. He later authored the first history of Connecticut.

and Serve them well, very Effectually Secure y^t pass.[1] These works we Judge would [p. 84] Cost Two Days work with a good Team and about Seventy days of other Labour. The other only pass into Town from the westward is on the Roads by or near the paper mill, the ground there is very advantageous for defence, the whole of it by which the enemy Could pass between the west Rock and any part of the River which is fordable being easily Commanded by Cannon. We are of the opinion that a Small work or Redoubt on the East side of the west River hill on the road leading to amity Capable of Receiving two or three field pieces is necessary in order to Secure y^t pass, this probably would Cost about half the Labour of the work proposed at the west bridge. As to West Haven and East Haven these are so many high Grounds upon which a post may be taken with nearly equal advantage and So many places where the enemy may Land y^t we can See no Special advantage in fortifying any particular post, but recommend the furnishing of each of s^d Parrishes with a fieldpiece as Soon as a Sufficient Number of men Can be procured for that purpose. We think it also very Necessary in order to defend the Town y^t a Number of men with a Director or Captain of the Gun, be Settled and assigned to each field piece whose business upon an attack Shall be to Carry on and Serve the pieces as occasion may require. Further we think it Necessary that a Number of intrenching Tools Should be immediately provided and ready for use as occasion might require upon any Invasion.

And as all precautions will not be Sufficient without a body of men to guard the out Skirts of the Town & [p. 85] Give Notice of the first approaches of an enemy & to Obstruct and Harass them till the inhabitants can be ~~Called~~ Collected, we recommend it to the Town to write a pressing Letter to his Excellency the Govr and his Council of Safety representing the State of the Town and exhibiting the Sentiments which plead for its defence and Earnestly Soliciting that two or three Hundred of the New Recruits now raising in this State may be Stationed here immediately for y^t purpose till the Campaign Shall open or Some further intelligence may be obtained with regard to Designs of ye Enemy, and y^t till Such time as those men are raised they would order in two or three Hundred of the militia. We are Gentlemen your most obedient and Humble Servants.

New Haven March 23^d 1778.   Joseph Thompson
                                                Isaac Doolittle
                                                Lamberton Smith
                                                Hez^h Sabin J^r
                                                Ben^j Trumbull

1. During the British invasion of July 5 - 6, 1779, this defensive position forced the British to abandon plans of entering into New Haven via the West River Bridge, which was taken up by the defenders. Today, the Defenders Monument stands in proximity of the original defensive works.

Agent. Further voted that Revd Benj Trumbull be agent in behalf of this Town forthwith to take a Copy of s^d Report and s^d Letter and apply to his Excellency the Govr and Council of Safety and endeavor to obtain if possible all the men &c mentioned in s^d Report and Letter.[1]

Committee. Voted y^t Col: Thompson, Capt Saml Willmot, Capt Peter Johnson, Mr Doolittle, Mr Stephen Thompson, Capt Silas Kimberly, Capt Jacob Brocket, Capt Osborn, Capt Stephen *[p. 86]* Goodyear and Capt Amos Hitchcock be a Committee to Lay out the works and git Same done in a vollentary way by the Inhabitants of the Town, and Such person as Shall be appointed to oversee ye work to have a reasonable Reward.

This meeting adj^d without Day.

[DECEMBER 14, 1778]

AT A TOWN MEETING HOLDEN IN NEW HAVEN UPON THE 14TH DAY OF DECEMBER 1778.

Clerk. Voted that Samuel Bishop J^r be Town Clerk.

Mod^r. Voted that Dan^ll Lyman Esqr be moderator.

Selectmen. Voted that Messrs Jonathan Fitch, Caleb Hotchkis 2^d, Timothy Jones J^r, Jeremiah Atwater, James Gilbert, Abr^m Auger, Isaac Doolittle, Amos Morris, Nehemiah Smith, Jesse Todd, Samuel Atwater, Saml Osborn and Isaac Beecher J^r be Selectmen the year ensuing.

Selectman. Voted y^t Jesse Todd be released from being Selectman and Epheram Humaston be Selectman in his room.

Constable & Collector. Voted that Capt Jesse Ford be Constable and Collector of the Country rates the year ensuing.

Allowance to Capt Ford about Collecting rates. The Town having granted to Capt Jesse Ford the Sum of Eighty pounds at a Town meeting on the 16th Day of January last, to induce him to Collect the Country rates the Last year, he now requested

1. Selecting the Reverend Trumbull was a coy move. He was a veteran of the early New York campaign as well as the failed march on Quebec. He was also Governor Trumbull's cousin.

of the Town that he might be made good on account of the monies being of equal in value to what it was when s^d sum was granted. Thereupon voted that s^d Ford be made good with regard to s^d money.

[Committee to consider Allowance.] Voted y^t Messrs John Whiting, Pierpoint Edwards, Caleb Beecher, Phin^s Bradly and David Austin be a Committee to take into Consideration what *[p. 87]* allowance ought to be made to Capt Ford for Collecting the Country rates the year past in addition to what was granted him and make report to the Town at their next meeting.

Constables & Collector. Voted y^t Joel Atwater be Constable and Collector of the county rates the year ensuing.

Constable. Voted that John Hubbard, John Austin, Abr^m Alling, Samuel Humaston J^r. John Denison, Phileman Smith, Danl Doolittle, Seth Peck, Saml Bellamy & Amos Hitchcock be Constables the year ensuing.

Grandjurymen. Voted that Munson, Isaac Thompson, Henry Daggett, Elias Shipman, Newman Trowbridge, Jesse Denison, Eben^r Chidsey, Levi Ray, James Ives J^r, Ben^j Downs, Nathan Catlin, David Perkins, David Sperry of Mr Carmel, Eben^r Perkins, Hezehiah Sperry, James Hillhouse, Isaac Townsend & William Scott be Grandjurymen the year ensuing.

Surveyers. Voted that Peter Johnson be Surveyer of highways the year ensuing.

This meeting adjourned to the Last Monday of Instant December at 10 of ye Clock in the forenoon.

[DECEMBER 28, 1778]

AT A TOWN MEETING HELD IN NEW HAVEN BY ADJOURNMENT UPON THE 28TH DAY OF DECEMBER 1778.

Committees report about Capt Ford. The Committee appointed the Last ~~year~~ meeting to take into Consideration what allowance ought to be made to Capt Ford for Collecting the Country rates — made their report that in their opinion the Town ought to Grant him Twenty pounds in addition to the Eighty pounds Granted the Last year, and y^t in Case he Shall Collect the Two Shilling rate now Due he Shall have Twenty pounds more, which Report being Considered is by vote accepted. *[p. 88] Listers.* Voted y^t John Mix, David Austin, Peter Johnson, James Rice, Ben^j·

Woodin, Henry Daggett, Elias Shipman, Sam[ll] Humphervile, Phileman Potter, John Miles, Amos Morris J[r], John Davenport, Lamberton Painter, Silas Kimberly, Noah Ives, Dan[l] Basset, Seth Downs, Jesse Ford, Elisha Alling, Joel Bradly M[t] C [Mt. Carmel], & Tim[o] Ball be Listers the year ensuing.

Tythingmen. Voted that Isaac Hubbard, Medad Atwater, Stephen Ford, Aner Bradly, Hez[h] Auger, Dan[l] Tallmadge J[r], Newman Trowbridge, Jonathan Perkins, Sam[l] Sheppard, Moses Heminway, Jeremiah Smith, Titus Beecher, Eben[r] Brocket, Giles Dayton, Caleb Clark, Jonathan Dickerman, Jabez Hotchkis, Lamberton Toles & Abel Ives be Tythingmen the year ensuing.

Voted that Eben[r] Townsend, Levi Basset, Job Potter, David Munson J[r], Noah Potter, David Osborn, Titus Mansfield, Jonathan Booth, Barnabas Baldwin J[r], Sam[l] Osborn, John Thomas, Henry Toles, Timothy Sperry [...].[1]

Rate. Voted that there be a rate of one Shilling on the pound upon the present List Collected of the inhabitants of the Town to defray the necessary Charges of the Town the year ensuing, and to be paid upon the first Day of January Next.[2]

Collector. Voted y[t] Joel Atwater be Collector of s[d] Rate and to have Such Sum for Collecting y[e] Same as the Town hereafter Shall Judge Just and Reasonable. [p. 89] *Constable.* Voted that Henry Peck be Constable the year ensuing.

Fenceviewers. Voted that John Mix, Nathan Mansfield and Obediah Hotchkis be fence viewers the year ensuing.

Leather Sealer. Voted y[t] Stephen Bradley be Leather Sealer the year ensuing.

Sealer of w[ts]. Voted that Theop[s] Munson be Sealer of weights and measures the year Ensuing.

Sealer of Mea[s]. Voted that John Miles be Sealer of dry measures the year Ensuing.

Key Keepers. Voted that Joseph Munson, Noah Potter, Joseph Gilbert, Noah Ives,

---

1. The clerk failed to identify what office these individuals held and left a a blank space in the records..
2. The British pound was the primary form of accepted currency in America until the passage of the Coinage Act of 1792. The pound, valued the same as a pound of silver, was composed of 20 shillings. Each shilling had twelve pence or pennies. See, David Walbert's "The Value of Money in Colonial America," North Carolina Digital History, http://www.history.org/foundation/journal/summer02/money2.cfm,

John Thompson, Joel Tuttle, Lamberton Smith J^r, David Tharp, Phileman Heaton, William Adams, Saml Horton, Seth Peck, Seth Blackslee, Peter Johnson, John Bradly, Bazel Munson and Aaron Gilbert be Key Keepers the year ensuing.

Branders. Voted that Theop^s Munson, Elisha Booth, Simein Bradly, Epheram Humaston, Joseph Peck, Jonathan Ives, Roger Alling and George Smith be branders of horses the year ensuing.

This meeting adjourned to monday Next at two of the Clock in the afternoon.

[JANUARY 4, 1779]

AT A TOWN MEETING HOLDEN IN NEW HAVEN BY ADJOURNMENT UPON THE FOURTH DAY OF JANUARY 1779.

pound. Voted that Tim^o Potter have Liberty to build a pound at his own expense and be keeper of the key.

Pound. Voted that Joseph Dorman have Liberty to build a pound at his own expense and be the keeper of ye key.

Surveyer. Voted that Seth Blackslee be Surveyer of highways in the room of Joel Basset.

[p. 90] Constable. Voted that John Wise be Constable ye year ensuing in ye room of John Hubbard who refused to Serve.

Constable. Voted that John Peck be Constable ye year ensuing in the room of Abr^m Alling who refused to Serve.

Constable. Voted that Abner Austin be Constable ye year ensuing in the room of John Austin who refused to Serve.

Constable. Voted that Saml Sherman be Constable ye year ensuing in the room of Phileman Smith who refused to Serve.

Swine. Voted that Swine going *[at]* large on the highways and Commons Shall not be Liable to be impounded from thence provided they are ringed all the year and Sufficiently yoked from the 10th Day of march to the 10 Day of December next.

Rate for highways. Voted y^t the Town will repair and maintain the highways the year Ensuing agreeable to a Late act of the Gen^ll assembly, ~~agreeable~~ enabling this Town to maintain the highways by a rate or Tax. Therefore Voted that there Shall be a rate or Tax of three pence on the pound on the present List, to be Collected, for repairing the highways within this Town the year Ensuing — agreeable to s^d act of s^d Assembly.

Voted that the above rate or Tax Shall be Collected the first Day of march next.

Districts. Voted that the Selectmen Shall divide out the districts unto the Surveyers of the highways.

Highway. Upon the application of Capt Elijah Forbs praying y^t a Committee be appointed to examine into the Reasonables and propriety of Laying out a highway through his Land back of Capt Munsons & Mr Prouts Stores which has already been Laid out.

Voted that John Dibble & Epheram Strong Esq^rs and Capt John Harpin of Milford be a Committee for he purpose afores^d to Consider the reasonableness of Laying out s^d highway and make report within one month.

[p. 91] Agents. Voted that Roger Sherman, Saml Bishop J^r, Munson Esq^rs be agents in behalf of this Town to make application to the Gen^ll assembly to git reimbursement of s^d Charges accrued to s^d Town in Consequence of s^d Towns being obliged to have Guards from the first of Jany 1778 at different Seasons to the first day of January 1779 which hath been at the Cost of s^d Town.[1]

Agents. Voted y^t Roger Sherman, Saml Bishop J^r, and Munson be agents in the Name and behalf of the inhabitants of the Town to procure for the use of s^d Inhabitants the advantages of a ferry at East Haven River at the ferry point so Called.[2]

Selectmen. Voted y^t the Selectmen prepare the accounts of the Guards that have been employed the year past.

---

1. There is no record of New Haven's request for reimbursement being answered. It was not until May of 1779 that the Connecticut Assembly ordered that journals be kept of every session.
2. Ferry service across the Quinnipiac River began as early as the 1640's. Ferry Point is located at the mouth of the river at what is now Bridge Street. The British made full use of the ferry during their invasion of New Haven seven months after this entry.

[JANUARY 18, 1779]

AT A TOWN MEETING HELD IN NEW HAVEN UPON THE 18TH DAY OF JANUARY 1779.

Mod[r]. Voted that Daniel Lyman be moderator.

Clerk. Voted that Timothy Jones Ju[r] be Clerk Pro Tem.[1]

Grandjurymen. Voted that Isaac Bradly, Eldad Atwater, Nath[ll] Mix, Nath[ll] Fitch, Lemuel Hotchkis, Thomas Burrel and David Bishop be Grandjurymen the year Ensuing, in the room of Isaac Thompson, Munson, Henry Daggett, Isaac Townsend, Newman Trowbridge, Elias Shipman and James Ives J[r].

Small Pox. On the motion of Cap[t] Peter Johnson and others to have innoculation Set up in this Town under Certain restrictions and regulations which motion the Town took under Consideration who after hearing the Petitioners and Considering the motion.[2]

[p. 92] Inoculation not allowed. Voted this Town will not allow inoculation to be set up in this Town under any restrictions or regulations whatever.
This meeting adjourned without Day.

Test. Tim° Jones J[r] Clerk

[FEBRUARY 8, 1779]

At a Town *[meeting]* in New Haven held by adjournment upon the 8th Day of February 1779.

Mod[r]. Voted that Sam[l] Bishop J[r] be moderator.

Selectman. Voted that Sam[l] Atwater be released from being Selectman and Cap[t] Stephen Goodyear be Selectman in his room.

Selectman. M[r] Jeremiah Atwater refused to Serve as a Selectman thereupon voted

---

1.Timothy Jones, Jr. (1737 - 1800) graduated Yale College in 1757 and served as rector of the Hopkins Grammar School before becoming a merchant. See, Dexter, *Biographical Sketches of the Graduates of Yale College: May 1745 - May 1763*, II: 476.
2. It was not until December of 1792 that New Haveners voted in public meeting to allow Drs. Levi Ives and Munson to set up a smallpox inoculation hospital.

that Col Sabin be Selectman in his room.

Constable & Coll. Voted yᵗ Mʳ Joel Atwater be released from being Collector of the Country rates the year ensuing and Samˡ Humaston Jʳ Chosen in his room.

Surveyer. Voted yᵗ Capᵗ Samˡ Osborn be released from being Surveyer and Capᵗ Titus Smith Chosen in his Stead.

Families of Officers &c. Voted as the Sense of this meeting that the vote for Supplying Officers Families was to determine and end if the Genˡˡ assembly of this State took up the way of their Supply and acted thereon.[1]

Constables. Voted that Elisha Booth be Constable in the Room of Henry Peck.

[JUNE 22, 1779]

[p. 93] AT A TOWN MEETING HELD IN NEW HAVEN UPON THE 22ᴰ DAY OF JUNE 1779.

Modʳ. Voted that Mr. Tim° Jones Jʳ be moderator.

Tax. Voted that there be a Tax of Two Shillings on the pound be forthwith Collected of the inhabitants of this Town, to procure Cloathing for the Soldiers according to the vote of the Town, and for defraying the remainder of the Charges of the Town the present year.

Collector. Voted that Joel Atwater who was Chosen in Decʳ Last Collʳ of the Town rate then laid — Shall Collect the above rate.

Cloathing for the army. Voted yᵗ John Austin, Hezʰ Tuttle, Elias Shipman, Jonas Prentice, John Woodward Jʳ, Jesse Stevens, Amos Thomas, Thoˢ Mansfield and Stephen Lounsbury be a Committee to procure Cloathing for the Contenental army for this Town agreeable to a Late act of the Genˡˡ assembly.[2]

Committeeman. Voted yᵗ Abrᵐ Bradly be a Committeeman in the Room of the

---

1. The Governor, Council, and state representatives voted for fixed amounts for the support of officers' and enlisted men's families based on their rank.

2. The General Assembly voted that each town was to provide funds to clothe each soldier from their respective town as well as provide for his family. Charles Hoadley, ed., *The Public Records of the State of Connecticut ... May, 1778 to April 1780* (1895), pp. 134-5; 152, 277, 382.

above said Elias Shipman.

Rate. Voted y^t the Sum due from Mr Phin^s Bradly with regard to the rate he Collected which was to have been paid to the Selectman, what remains now due is hereby ordered to be paid into the Town Treasury.

Listers. Voted that the Selectmen give orders on the Town Treasurer, to the Listers to pay them for making up the List the Last Year & for making the List the present year.

[p. 94] Lister. Voted that Capt Abel Burrett be Lister in the Room of David Austin Esqr.

Lister. Voted that Henry Toles be Lister in the room of Saml Humphrevile.

Constable. Voted that Jotham Williams be Constable in the Room of Saml Sherman.

Guard by order of Selectmen. Voted that the Selectmen order out a guard for the Security of the Town as occasion may require.

Lister. Voted that Chauncey Dickerman be Lister in the Room of Elisha Alling.

Selectmen. Voted that the Selectmen together with Capt Phin^s Bradly be desired forthwith to take ye most Effectual and *[illegible crossout]* Spirited measures to prevent if possable the present Trade y^t is Carried onto Long Island.[1]

Adjourned without Day.

[AUGUST 6, 1779]

AT A TOWN MEETING HELD IN NEW HAVEN ON THE 6TH DAY OF AUGUST 1779.

Mod^r. Voted that Mr Timothy Jones J^r be moderator.

Clerk. Voted that Charles Chauncey be Town Clerk in the absence of Saml Bishop J^r the Town Clerk.

---

1. Despite various measures, illicit trade along the Connecticut shoreline continued to pose a problem for authorities throughout the Revolution.

Coll[r]. Voted that Abraham Alling be Collector of a Rate of Two Shillings upon (the pound) Laid at a former meeting for defraying the incident Charges of the Town and for procuring Cloaths for the Soldiers.

[p. 95] [British Invasion.] The Question was put whether the Town do resent and disapprove the Conduct of those inhabitants who remained in the Town with the enemy in their late incursion and while in possession of the Town without Sufficient reasons to Justify them.[1]

Voted in the affirmative.

Persons y[t] Stayed in Town when the Enemy Came. Whereas the inhabitants of the Town Platt in New Haven Lately held a meeting in s[d] Town and being Dissatisfied with a number of persons in remaining in Town with the Enemy did appoint Cap[t] Thomas Wooster, Cap[t] Peter Johnson, M[r] Henry Daggett and Pierpoint Edwards Esq[r] a Committee to hear the Reasons s[d] persons had to offer to Justify themselves and s[d] Committee having desired a number of them to attend for that purpose and Several of said persons having appeared before said Committee and given their reasons and s[d] Committee having taken down their reasons as given in writing and Laid them before this meeting. Voted y[t] this meeting approve of the Doings of s[d] Committee.

Whereas a number of the inhabitants y[t] Staid in Town with the enemy while they were in possession of the Town have been Called upon by the Committee appointed by the inhabitants of the Town Platt to give their reasons for so doing and have neglected to appear before s[d] Committee and others have not been notified.

Voted that Cap[t] Tho[s] Wooster, Cap[t] Jonas Prentice, Cap[t] Peter Johnson, M[r] Henry Daggett, Pierpoint Edwards Esq[r], Doct[r] Levi Ives, Phin[s] Bradly, Phileman Potter and Cap[t] Caleb Mix be a Committee to Call before them Such of s[d] Inhabitants who remained in Town with the Enemy and have not heretofore appeared before the Committee appointed by the inhabitants of the Town Platt and take their Reasons *[p. 96]* for their Conduct in that Particular and report the Same with their opinion thereon together with their opinion on the Reasons assigned by the inhabitants who have appeared before s[d] Committee to the Town at their next meeting.

Vote about rum.[2] Whereas Complaint hath been made to this meeting y[t] Some per-

1. British Maj. Gen. William Tryon and approximately 2,500 troops invaded New Haven on July 5 - 6, 1779.

2. Historical accounts of the invasion mention that British and Hessian troops, as well as American

sons have Lately sold rum at an exorbitant price and that others have withheld and refused to sell. Voted that this Town doth disapprove of any persons asking and receiving a greater Price for good West India rum than thirty two Doll^{rs} p^r Gallon by retail and for New England rum in proportion and also of any persons withholding the Same, and that this Town will treat with proper Contempt all persons who Shall refuse to Sell their rum or Sell the Same at more than the aforementioned price. And that Capt Abel Burret, Capt Moses Gilbert, Doct^r Levi Ives and Capt Peter Johnson be a Committee to Communicate this vote to Capt Elisah Forbes.

Committee ab^t exchange of prisoners. Voted that Mr. Tim^o Jones J^r and Charles Chauncey be a Committee to write to his Excellency the Govr to procure the Exchange of the Prisoners taken from this Town in the Late incursion of the Enemy.[1]

Commission officers. Voted that the Commission officers in the parrishes Call upon those persons who Neglected to appear and oppose the Enemy and to defend ye Town in the Late invasion and know their reasons for their neglect and the Same report to the Town.

Voted that this meeting be adjourned to the monday after next at two of the Clock in the afternoon then to meet at the State house.

The above and foregoing are the proceedings and votes of s^d Town meeting.

Test. Charles Chauncey[2] Town Clerk Pro. Tem.

[AUGUST 16, 1779]

[p. 97] AT A TOWN MEETING HELD IN NEW HAVEN BY ADJOURN-MENT UPON THE 16TH DAY OF AUGUST 1779.

Committee. Voted y^t Capt Peter Johnson and Capt Jonas Prentice be a Committee to wait upon Mr Jared Ingersoll and know the reasons why he entertained the pris-

---

militiamen, depleted New Haven's rum supply after residents placed barrels of rum within easy reach in an effort to reduce the potential of looting.

1. Reports vary on the number of prisoners taken by the British. They range from 12 to 22. Some, however, were Loyalist families who left willingly. Prisoner exchanges from the raid began as early as August 8, 1779.

2. Charles Chauncey (1747 - 1823) was a lawyer, served as Secretary of State, and Judge of the Superior Court.

oners who were Lately in this Town, and make their report to the next meeting.[1]

Vote about rum resinded. Whereas this Town did at a Legall meeting held Aug[t] 6th 1779 vote y[t] this Town disapprove of any persons asking and Receiving a greater price for good west India Rum than thirty two Dollars per Gallon by retail and for New England rum in proportion this meeting upon Second Consideration of the matter Resind the vote of the meeting aforesaid.

A Committee appointed the Last Town meeting made the following report viz.

Committees report. The Committee appointed by this Town at a Legall Town meeting holden on the 6th Day of Instant aug*[ust]* to examine into the reasons of the Conduct of those persons who Continued in Town at the Time s[d] Town was in possession of the Enemy have attended on the business for which they was appointed.

And beg leave to report that Mess[rs] Eben[r] Lines, Stephen Munson, Martin Gatler, Eben[r] Chittendon, Abr[m] Bradly, John Chandler, Theop[s] Munson, James Rice, Eli Beecher, Richard Eld, Abel Buel, Jo[s] Bradly, Ben[j] Sanford, Steph[n] Bradly, Tho[s] Davis, Freeman Huse,[2] Joseph Munson, James Lane, Sam[l] Nisbet, Eliz[r] Brown, James Sherman, James Gilbert, Elias Shipman, Newman Trowbridge, Zep[h] Hatch, Thomas Wilmot, Edward Bark, Jehiel Forbs, Eli *[p. 98]* Forbs, William Day, Enos Hotchkis, Jesse Upson, Thadd[s] Perrit, John Miles J[r], Nemiah Hotchkis, Noah Tucker and Patrick O'Collely — have waited on s[d] Committee and given their reasons for Tarrying in Town during the Time afores[d] which Reasons appear to the Committee Sufficient to Justify their Conduct in tarrying in Town then at s[d] Time. The Committee Likewise report that Nathan Mansfield, William MacCracken, Ambros Ward, Jared Mansfield and Archibald Blackslee have attended on the Committee and Given their reasons for not Leaving the Town when the Enemy took possession of it which reasons appear to the Committee intirely Insufficent to Justify themselves for putting themselves in the power and under the protection of the Enemies of the united States of America.

The Committee further report that Mess[rs] Stephen Ball, Thadd[s] Beecher, John

1. The prisoners mentioned were likely captured by the Americans during the invasion of New Haven on July 5 - 6, 1779. They were originally held on the New Haven Green and then moved to North Haven.
2. Henry Freeman Huse or Hughes (1723 - 1791) allegedly deserted the English Navy in the 1740's and moved to New Haven, where he ran a ferry across the Quinnipiac River. To save his farm during the British invasion he claimed his loyalty to the king. His son, Freeman, and his family left with the British, and Henry was then held liable for his son's considerable debts.

Townsend, Richard Cutler, Leverrt Hubbard J^r, Eben^r Huggins, Joel Beech, Josiah Roberts, Gad Wells, Charles Prindle, Edmund French, Isaac Beers, Elias Beers, Thos Rice, Saml Chatterton, Nathan Howel, Step^n Trowbridge, Wm Lyon, Jerimiah Atwater, George Cook, Asa Austin, Miles Gorham, Leveret Hubbard, John Whiting, Thos Howell, David Bonticou, Wm Mansfield, Jos^h Adams, Jerimiah Townsend J^r, Benoni Pardee, James Thompson and Henry Gibbs have waited on the Committee and given their reasons for tarrying in Town at ye Time afores^d, which reasons do not appear to the Commi^{tee} fully Sufficient to Justify their Conduct in tarrying in Town at s^d Time but the Committee taking in to their Serious Consideration the particular situation s^d persons were in at that Time that the alarm was sudden and the Time too Short for them to move their families and Effects and that many of them were kept from their own Concerns by lending their usefull aid and assistance to repell the Common enemy and the most of them being persons who have ever been accounted good members of the Community, the Committee think it their reasonable duty to recommend them to the *[p. 99]* good will and Candor of the inhabitants of the Town hoping they will pass over in Silence what ever was wrong in their Conduct at that Time as it fully appears to the Committee an error in Judging what was best for them to do in the hurry and Confusion they were then in, rather than from any design or predetermination to tarry in Town and Submitt and put themselves under the protection of the Enemies of the united States of America, the Committee make ye foregoing report in favour of s^d persons on Condition that they associate themselves with the rest of the good people of this Town to repell our merciless enemy if they Should ever invade us again.

The Committee further report that they have notified Messrs Enos Alling^1, Bela Hubbard^2, Richard Woodhall, John Alling, David Cook, Edward Carrinton, Benjn Pardee *[and]* Daniel Upson of their appointment and the time when and place where the Committee would wait on them, but they have either refused or neglected to appear and give their reasons, which refusal or neglect of s^d persons the Committee Judge to be in Contempt of the authority of this Town.

The Committee find that Messrs Elijah Forbs, William Ward, Oliver Burr, Abr^m Bradly J^r, Saml Goodwin, Zina Denison, Amos Dootlittle, Willm Brintnal, John Mix, Thos Burret, Adjon^h Sherman, William Drake, Benj Osborn, Jonah Baldwin, Saml Tuttle *[and]* John Baldwin were in Town when the enemy took possession

1. Enos Alling (1719 - 1779) was a 1746 graduate of Yale College, a prosperous merchant, and founding member of the original Trinity Church on the Green, having donated the land for its construction.
2. The Reverend Bela Hubbard (1739 - 1812) graduated Yale College in 1758 and served as Anglican missionary to West Haven and New Haven until his death.

but they were either taken off by the enemy or have Since moved out, or have otherwise been out of the way and have never been notified of the apointmen[t] of the Committee for the purpose afors[d].

The Committee would likewise acquaint the Town that they have made up the foregoing report upon the reasons which those persons gave themselves without Calling on any evidences to Contradict them which method of taking their reasons appears to the Committee very partial.

Moreover the Committee are very Confident that there are Evidences which if Called would Contradict the account that hath been given by Some of the s[d] persons, all which the Committee humbly Submit

by order of s[d] Committee.[1] Phin[s] Bradly[2] Chairman

[p. 100] Committee report accepted. Voted that the Report of the Committee be accepted and that any person who Shall be desireous to have a rehearing Shall have an opportunity to be heard before the Committee and that any person who Shall have any knowledge of the Conduct of any of s[d] persons on making Complaint to the Committee they Shall be heard and that the Committee Shall examine those persons whose reasons have been taken and make report of what they Shall do to the Town at their next meeting.[3]

This meeting adjourned unto the 30th Day of Instant August at two of the Clock in the afternoon.

[AUGUST 30, 1779]

AT A TOWN MEETING HELD IN NEW HAVEN BY ADJOURNMENT UPON THE 30TH DAY OF AUGUST 1779.

Committee of inspection. Voted that Cap[t] Thomas Wooster, Cap[t] John Mix, Cap[t] Jonas Prentice, Cap[t] Peter Johnson, M[r] Mark Levenworth, M[r] Phin[s] Bradly, Philemon Potter, Abijah Bradly and Sam[l] Candee be a Committee of inspection the

---

1. Of the 69 men questioned by the committee, 32 were found negligent and eight others refused to be interviewed. During the invasion, Americans lost 27 killed and 19 wounded. Several others were taken prisoner and four families left with the British.
2. Phineas Bradley (1745 - 1797), son of Phineas (1714 - 1779), served as Captain of the 20th Regiment of Connecticut Militia from 1779 - 1791 and played a major role in the defense of New Haven. In civilian life, Bradley was a silversmith.
3. There is no record of any subsequent actions taken as a result of these interviews.

remainder of the present year.[1]

[DECEMBER 13, 1779]

[p. 102] AT A TOWN MEETING HELD IN NEW HAVEN DEC^R 13TH 1779.

Clerk. Saml Bishop Chosen Town Clerk.

Mod^r. Mr Phin^s Bradly Chosen moderator.

Selectmen. Voted that Messrs Jonathan Fitch, Tim° Jones J^r, James Gilbert, Abram Auger, Isaac Doolittle, Amos Morris, Nehemiah Smith, Epheram Humaston, Saml Osborn, Stephen Goodyear and Isaac Beecher J^r, Charles Chauncey and Pierpont *[Edwards]* be Selectmen the year Ensuing.

Selectnan. Voted that Amos Morris be released from being Selectman and Capt Stephen Smith be Selectman in his room.

Selectman. Voted that Isaac Doolittle be released from being Selectman and Capt Joseph Trowbridge Chosen in his room.

Constable. Voted that Abr^m Alling be Constable and Collector of the Country rates the year ensuing.

Constables. Voted that Abel Burrit, Stephen Hotchkis, Benjn English, Henry Toles, John Denison, Silas Kimberly, Danl Doolittle, Job Munson, Hez^h Sperry and Seth Peck be Constables the year Ensuing.

Grandjurymen. Voted that Jonah Hotchkis, Aner Bradley, John Pierpooint, John Hubbard, Thomas Punderson, Medad Osborn, Tim° Andrews, Levi Pardee, Jeremiah Smith, John Benham, Job Blakeslee, Jonathan Barns, Saml Dickerman, Jesse Beecher, David Thomas and Benjamin Peck be grandjurymen the year ensuing.

Tythingmen. Voted that Nathl Heaton J^r, Ezra Ford, David Munson J^r, John Miles, John Heminway, Azel Kimberly, Zac^s Candee, Giles Dayton, Levi Cooper, Caleb

---

1. Following this entry the remaining half of p. 100 and the facing page are blank except for the scripted name R G Terry, written three times as if someone was practicing his penmanship. One of the signatures bears the date Dec. 3 1852. The R.G. was Robert G. Terry (1838 - 1878) whose father Alfred was a New Haven attorney who transcribed a portion of the New Haven records between 1849 - 1852. See, Powers, *NHTR*, III: i.

Clark, Jotham Blakeslee, Stephen Thompson, Charles Bradley, Samuel Atwater J[r], Jotham Tuttle, Reuben Perkins, John Russel and David Smith be Tythingmen the year ensuing.

[p. 103] Listers. Voted that Peter Johnson, James Rice, John Austin, Isaac Beecher J[r], Mark Levenworth, Henry Daggett, John Miles, James Chidsey, Isaac Forbs, Noah Ives, Dan[l] Basset, Jesse Stevens, Obed Johnson, Joel Bradly J[r], Jonathan Dickerman, Lamberton Toles, Elisha Booth and John Gills be Listers the year ensuing.

This meeting adjourned untill the Last monday of Instant Dec[r] at 10 of the Clock in the forenoon.

[DECEMBER 27, 1779]

AT A TOWN MEETING HELD IN NEW HAVEN BY ADJOURNMENT UPON THE 27TH DAY OF DECEMBER 1779

Surveyers. Voted that Joseph Munson, John Mix, Jared Bradly, Lemuel Humphervile, Levi Basset, Jesse Levenworth, Michael Baldwin, Medad Atwater, Stephen Bristoll, Jonathan Booth, Abr[m] Auger, David Hull, Caleb Alling, Stephen Thompson, Stephen Pardee, Sam[l] Heminway, Stephen Smith, Sam[l] Candee, Philemon Smith, Sam[l] Mansfield, Jotham Blackslee, Jacob Hitchcock, Thomas Cooper, Job Blackslee, James Humaston J[r], John Smith, Eliakim Mallery, Hez[h] Warner, Peter Perkins, Ezra Sperry, Reuben Sperry, David Perkins, Lucas Lines, Epheram Turner, Lemuel Alling, Seth Downs & Enoch Newton be Surveyers of highways the year Ensuing.

Fence Viewers. Voted that John Mix, Nathan Mansfield and Obediah Hotchkis be fence viewers the year ensuing.

Leather Sealer. Voted that Stephen Bradly be Leather Sealer the year ensuing.

Sealer of W[ts]. Voted that Theop[s] Munson be Sealer of w[ts] and measures the year ensuing.

Sealer of Meas. Voted that John Miles be Sealer of Dry measures the year ensuing.

[p. 104] Key Keepers. Voted that Joseph Munson, Noah Potter, Phebe Dorman,[1] John Thompson E.H. *[East Haven]*, Joel Tuttle, Lamberton Smith J^r, David Thorp, Phileman Heaton, William Adams, Saml Horton, Seth Peck, Seth Blackslee, Peter Johnson, Medad Osborn, Bazel Munson and Tim° Potter be key keepers the year ensuing.

Branders. Voted that Theop^s Munson, Elisha Booth, Simeon Bradly, Epheram Humaston, Joseph Peck, Jonathan Ives, Roger Peck and George Smith be branders of horses the year Ensuing.

Swine. Voted that Swine going at Large on the Town Commons and highways the year ensuing Shall not be Liable to be impounded from thence, Provided they are ringed all the year and Sufficiently yoaked from the 10th Day of march to the 10th Day of Decr next.

Rate. Voted that there be a rate or Tax of Six Shillings upon the pound, upon the present List to be Collected upon the 10th Day of January next, to defray the necessary Charges of ye Town the year ensuing.

Coll^r. Voted that Mr Michael Baldwin be Collector of s^d Rate.

Constable. Voted that Abram Alling be released from being Constable and Coll^r of the Country rates, and Mr Jesse Ford to be Constable and Coll^r in his room.

Collector. Voted that Michael Baldwin be released from being Collector of the above Town rate, and Mr John Hubbard Chosen in his room.

Voted that this meeting be adjourned untill monday next at two of the Clock in the afternoon.

[JANUARY 3, 1780]

[p. 105] AT A TOWN MEETING HELD IN NEW HAVEN BY ADJOURN-MENT UPON THE 3RD DAY OF JANUARY 1780

Mod^r. Col. Jonathan Fitch Chosen moderator.

Voted that this meeting be adjourned untill monday Next at two of the Clock

---

1. Phoebe Dorman of Hamden assumed the role of key keeper after her husband Joseph was killed by the British during the invasion of New Haven. She then married Matthew Gilbert (1721 - 1795).

in the afternoon.[1]

[JANUARY 10, 1780]

AT A TOWN MEETING HELD IN NEW HAVEN BY ADJOURNMENT UPON THE 10ᵀᴴ DAY OF JANUARY 1780.

Constable. Voted that Capᵗ Abel Burret be released from being Constable and Tilley Blackslee be Constable in his room the year ensuing.

Selectman. Voted that James Gilbert be released from being Selectman and Joel Gilbert Chosen in his room the year Ensuing.

Lister. Voted that Mᵗ Isaac Beers be Lister the year Ensuing.

Lister. Voted that Mᵗ Henry Daggett be released from being Lister and Levi Ives Chosen Lister in his room.

Constable. Voted that Stephen Hotchkis be released from being Constable and Samˡˡ Wilmont be Constable in his room.

Constable. Voted that Capᵗ Benʲ English be released from being Constable and Mr. John Lothrop be Constable in his room the year Ensuing.

Selectman. Voted that Joseph Trowbridge be released from being Selectman and Mᵗ Henry Daggett Chosen Selectman in his room the year ensuing.

Grandjuryman. Voted that Samˡ Dickerman be released from being Grandjury-man and Gamaliel Bradly be Grandjuryman in his room.

[p. 106] allowance to Town Collᵗ. Whereas John Hubbard is Chosen Collᵗ of the Town rate and the Town hearing voted that he Should have 1-3/4 per Cent for Collecting, and he having represented to this meeting that he is unwilling to Collect the Same for the allowances as above, Thereupon voted that the Civil authority and Selectmen at the audit in Decᵗ next, Shall allow to said Hubbard such futher Sum as they Shall Judge Just and Reasonable for his Trouble in Collecting said Rate.

---

1. The meeting was likely cancelled due to lack of attendance caused by severe weather. The winter of 1779 - 1780 in the region was known as "the Hard Winter."

Coll. Voted that Capt Jesse Ford be released from being Coll^r of the Country Rates, and Mr John Lothrop be Coll^r of the Country rates in this Town the year ensuing.

allowance to Collector. Voted that this Town will pay to s^d Lothrop one half per Cent, on which Sum or Sums he Shall Collect, in addition to what he Shall Receive of the State.

Agents. Voted that Saml Bishop and Munson^1 Esqr^s be agents for this Town to make application to the Gen^{ll} Assembly now Sitting at Hartford that Mr John Lothrop who is Chosen Coll^r of the Country rates the present year might be impowered to Collect the Six Shillings Tax Laid by the assembly in October Last, to be paid this instant January, which Saml Humaston J^r, who was Coll^r of the Country rates the Last year was to have Collected, and Sickness in his family, he declined to Collect the Same.

Highway. Voted that the Selectmen Settle with Capt Mix about tbe highway laid out through his Land near the Little bridge and allow him what is Just and Reasonable.^{2}

Selectmen to Settle with Coll. Voted that the Selectmen Settle with Joel Atwater about his Collecting the Town rate the year past, and allow him what they Judge Chidsey, Saml Candee, Simeon Bristoll, Thomas Cooper and John Hubbard be Treas^r. Voted that David Austin Esqr be Town Treas^r the year ensuing.

Key Keepers. Voted that Joseph Munson, Noah Potter, Caleb Alling, Nathan Dumer,^{3} Tim^o Potter, John Martin, John Culver, Nathl Barns J^r, Danl Tuttle, Nathl Smith, Azel Kimberly, Seth Blakeslee, Thomas Cooper J^r, Ebn^r Beech and Benjn Gaylor J^r be key keepers the year ensuing.

pound. Voted that Joel Blackslee have Liberty to build a pound and be key keeper of ye Same.

Leather Sealer. Voted y^t Stephen Bradly be Leather Sealer the year ensuing.

---

1. Eneas Munson (1734 -1826), graduated Yale in 1753, served as a army chaplain during the French and Indian War and as a surgeon's mate during the Revolution. He also served as the president of the Medical Society of Connecticut as well as a legislator.

2. This highway was located in what is now the Quinnipiac River Historic District.

3. Nathan Dummer (ca. 1730 - 1813). Possibly known as Nathaniel, who was wounded during the British invasion of New Haven in 1779.

[MARCH 13, 1780]

[p. 107] AT A LEGALL TOWN MEETING HELD IN NEW HAVEN IN
THE STATE HOUSE FOR THE PURPOSE OF CHOOSING INSPECTORS
OF PROVISIONS &C AND OR REBUILDING MORRISES BRIDGE SO
CALLED AND FOR TRANSACTING OTHER MATTERS AS SHALL BE
THOUGHT NECESSARY THE 13TH DAY OF MARCH A D 1780.

Mod^r. Timothy Jones J^r was Chosen moderator.

Clerk. Charles Chauncey was Chosen Town Clerk in the absence of Saml
Bishop Esqr

Inspectors [of Provisions]. Tilley Blackslee, Capt Peter Johnson, John Wise, James
Gilbert, Col. Joseph Thompson, Michael Todd, John Austin, Levi Ives, Caleb
Mix, Richard Woodward, Isaac Doolittle, John Miles, Medad Osborn, Eldad At-
water, David Munson, Daniel Talmadge J^r, Adonijah Sherman, Lemuel Hotch-
kis, Isaac Beers, Jared Bradly, Saml Heminway, Joshua Austin, Capt Josiah Bradly,
Joseph Tuttle, Lemuel Humphervile, Oliver Smith, Saml Candee, Phileman
Smith, Capt Noah Ives, Enos Todd, Dan^{ll} Basset, Joshua Barnes, Thomas
Cooper, Capt Jesse Ford, Barn^s Baldwin, Laz^s Toles, Jonathan Dickerman,
Abner Todd, Capt Jesse Goodyear, Capt Peter Perkins, Joel Hotchkis, Capt Is-
sac Chidsey, *[and]* Amos Perkins were Chosen inspectors of Provisions &c.

Lottery. Voted that application be made to the Honble Gen^{ll} assembly to be
holden at Hartford in May next in behalf of the Town of New Haven for a
grant of such Sum of money (to be raised by Lottery or otherwise as to s^d assembly Shall sum meet) as will enable s^d Town to build a bridge across the East
River in s^d New Haven where the bridge called morrises bridge Lately Stood and
that Messrs Tim^o Jones J^r, Charles Chauncey *[and]* Pierpoint Edwards be a Committee to prefer a memorial for y^t Purpose.[1]

[p. 108] Grandjuryman. Pierpoint Edwards Esqr was Chosen Grandjuror in the
room of John Pierpoint.

1.The East River is now known as the Quinnipiac River. The General Assembly authorized New
Haven to hold a lottery to raise not more than £1,000 to replace the old structure and causeway
apparently damaged during the British invasion of July 5 - 6, 1779. Charles Hoadley, ed., *The Public
Records of the State of Connecticut... May, 1780 to December 27, 1781* (1922), p. 81.

Grandjuryman. Ensign Tho[s] Cooper[1] Chosen Grandjuror in the room of Jonathan Barns.

Grandjuryman. Adonijah Sherman[2] was Chosen Grandjuror in the room of Jonah Hotchkis.

Grandjuryman. Doc[tr] Levi Ives was Chosen Grandjuror in the room of Mark Levenworth Esq[r].

Collector. Voted that Michael Baldwin be Collector for the Town of New Haven to Collect the State Taxes that Shall be Collected after those Taxes Shall be Collected by M[r] John Lothrop.

Voted that this meeting be adjourned to Tuesday the 21st Day of Instant march, at two of the Clock [*in the*] afternoon then to meet at the State house.

> Charles Chauncy T Clerk in the Absence
> of Sam[l] Bishop Esq[r]

[MARCH 21, 1780]

AT A TOWN MEETING HELD IN NEW HAVEN BY ADJOURNMENT UPON THE 21ST DAY OF MARCH 1780.

Vote On an act for Establishing bills of Cred[t]. Voted by this Town that they are Satisfied with and do approve of the act of the General assembly of this State made and Enacted at the Last Session of s[d] Assembly Entitled an act for Supporting the Credit and Currency of bills of Credit Emitted and made Currant by the Congress of the united States of America and the bills of Publick Credit of this state and the promoting and futherance [*of*] Cumulative Justice, and herby Signify our approbation thereof.

[*p. 109*] *Selectmen to Settle with Coll[r].* Voted y[t] the Selectmen Settle with Sam[l] Humaston J[r] about his Collecting the County rates, and allow him therefor such Sums as they Judge Just and Reasonable.

---

1. Thomas Cooper (1737 - 1808) of North Haven, first served as a corporal in the 1st Connecticut Regiment during the Revolution, then as an ensign. He drowned in New Haven harbor during a storm at the age of 71.

2. Adonijah Sherman (1734/5 - 1786) of New Haven was taken prisoner by the British during the 1779 invasion of New Haven. After the war he moved to Catskill, New York.

[Grandjuryman]. Voted that Thomas Cooper J[r] be released from being Grand Juryman and Nath[ll] Beech Chosen in his room.

Grandjuryman. Voted that Adonijah Sherman be released from being Grandjuryman, and John Mix J[r] Chosen in his room.

[Key Keeper] Voted that Medad Osborn be released from being Key keeper and John Culver Chosen in his room.

[May 8, 1780]

AT A TOWN MEETING HELD IN NEW HAVEN UPON THE 8th DAY OF MAY 1780.

Key keeper. Voted that Sam[l] Bradly be key keeper in East Haven in the Room of John Thompson Dec[d.1]

Committeeman. Voted that James Rice be one of the Committee of inspection.

Amity & Bethany. Whereas the inhabitants of the Societies of Amity & Bethany have Cited this Town to appear before the Gen[ll] assembly of the State of Connecticut to be holden at Hartford on the 2[d] Thursday of instant may to Show their reason if any they have why they Should not be incorporated into a Town with all Town priviledges as by their petition and Citation being laid before this meeting fully appears. Thereupon Voted y[t] Pierpoint Edwards & Charles Chauncey Esq[rs] be agents to Oppose the Granting of s[d] Petition by the assembly.[2]

[p. 110] Key Keeper. Voted that Capt. Peter Johnson be released from being key keeper and John Peasj[r] Chosen in his room.

Key Keeper. Voted that Cap[t] Caleb Alling be key keeper in room of the wid[o] Dorman.[3]

---

1. John Thompson (1754 - 1780) who drowned at sea.
2. Outlying parishes of New Haven clamored for independence for some time. It was not until 1784 - 1785, however that the State Legislature approved the creation of East Haven, Hamden, North Haven, and Woodbridge, which was known as the parish of Amity. Leonard Labaree, ed., *The Public Records of the State of Connecticut From May, 1785 through January, 1789* (1945), Vol. 7.
3. Phebe Dorman (1731 - 1820) was the widow of Joseph Dorman (1723 - 1779) of Hamden. He was a member of the 17th Company, 2nd Regiment of Connecticut Militia who was killed during the British invasion of New Haven in 1779.

This meeting adj^d without Day.

[JUNE 28, 1780]

AT A TOWN MEETING HELD IN NEW HAVEN JUNE 28, 1780.

Mod^r. Voted that Mr Tim° Jones J^r be moderator of this meeting.

Lottery. Voted that five men be Chosen managers of the Lottery Granted by the assembly.

managers. Voted that Messrs David Austin, Michael Todd, Mark Levenworth, Henry Daggett and Jonas Prentice be the managers of the Lottery and to proceed therein agreeable to the act of the Gen^{ll} assembly.

Committee. Voted that Mr Hillhouse, Mr Mark Levenworth, Eneas Munson Esqr and Doct^r Levi Ives be a Committee forthwith to draw an association with regard to the Illicit Trade and report the Same to this meeting.[1]

Bills of Cred^t. Voted that we will receive the New Continental money and bills of Credit Lately emitted by this State equal to gold and Silver in all payments and that we will freely Sell all Such articles as we have to dispose of for Such money.[2]

Voted that Mr Edwards and Mr Chauncy Shall take the Names of the persons who voted for and who against the above vote, who reported there was 264 for the vote and 8 against as appears by the names of the persons on file.

Com^{ee}. Voted that Capt Peter Johnson, Capt Abel Burret, Doct^r Levi Ives, Mr John Miles, Mr Joshua Austin, Lam^b Smith Esqr, Deacon Jesse Todd, Capt Tim° Bradly, Capt Saml Atwater & Capt Peter Perkins be a Committee to see if the inhabitants of this Town who are not present will Sign to the foregoing Vote [p. 111] and make report who hath signed for, and who against s^d Vote.

---

1. New Haveners and most Americans along the coast had a long tradition of smuggling. As the war progressed, that tradition only continued, driven by profits, necessity, and a time-worn tolerance of illicit trade.
2. In an effort to restore the nascent government's credit, the Continental Congress required each state to levy a $15 million tax, monthly, for 13 months. Connecticut's share was over $22,000,000, of which she actually paid $9,151,484 in bills. Despite the effort, it did little to restore public faith in credit, despite the veiled threat of taking the names of those voting against the measure might lead to prosecution. Wyman W. Parker, *Connecticut's Colonial and Continental Money* (1976), pp. 41 - 49.

rate. Voted that a rate be laid upon the inhabitants of the Town upon the present List of one Shilling upon the pound for defraying the incident Charges of the Town and other Extraordinary Charges of the Town that may arise in the Course of ye present year to be paid in Connecticut money of the New Emissions or Gold and Silver. Provided Nevertheless that s^d Tax may be paid in Continental money at Such an exchange as the Selectmen Shall from Time to Time affix, and that the s^d Rate be forthwith Collected and paid.

Coll^r. Voted that Messrs Peter Johnson, Pierp^t Edwards, Levi Ives, Benjn English, Jacob Bradly, Tim^o Andrews J^r, Lamberton Smith, Enoch Newton, Elisha Chapman and Hez^h Sperry be Collectors of the above rate.

association. The Committee appointed to draw an association reported one in the following words viz. We the Subscribers Inhabitants of the Town of New Haven Sensible of the Great importance of Supporting and Establishing the Credit of the paper Currency emited by this State Since January List for the purpose of Carrying on the present war and Establishing us in the Enjoyment of Independence and Liberty — and Considering the pernicious Tendency & Dangerous Consequence of an Illicit Trade Carried on with our Enemies as having a direct Tendency to depreciate & ruin the Credit of our s^d Currency and to inervate and Contravene all our warlike Efforts and Enterprises — Do therefore associate and Solemnly pledge our faith and Hon^r that we will neither directly or indirectly have any Connection with s^d Elicit trade nor purchase any goods, wares or merchandise we believe or are Suspicious were imported from Long Island or any other place Contrary to the Laws of this State against Elicit trade and y^t we will not have any trade or Commerce with any persons we have reason to Suspect are Concerned in or have any Connection with s^d trade.[1]

Resolved y^t the association drawn by order of this meeting be tendered by Capt Peter Johnson, Capt Abel Burret, Doct^r Levi Ives, Mr John Miles, Mr Joshua Austin, Lamb^t Smith Esqr, *[p. 112]* Deacon Jesse Todd, Capt Tim^o Bradley, Capt Saml Atwater, and Capt Peter Perkins.

[Following half-page is blank.]

Selectmen. Voted that the Selectmen pay to the militia now ordered to march Such Sum as they Shall Judge Just & reasonable.

---

1. Anyone wishing to travel to areas under enemy control needed to acquire a licence from the selectmen of the town from which he or she departed. By 1780, the General Assembly rescinded those licences entirely due to the level of illicit trade. *PRSC,* Vol 7, p. 234 - 235.

This meeting adjourned to the 6th Day of July next at 2 of the Clock in the afternoon.

[JULY 6, 1780]

AT A TOWN MEETING HELD IN NEW HAVEN BY ADJOURNMENT UPON THE 6TH DAY OF JULY 1780.

Committee about Soldiers. Voted y^t Col. Sabin, Saml Austin, John Mix, Pierpoint Edwards, Stephen Smith, Jesse Todd, Isaac Ford, Simeon Bristoll, Lamberton Smith, Eneas Munson & Abr^m Auger be a Committee to Consider what ought to be given to the Soliders now ordered to be detached into the Service of State, and report their opinion thereon to this meeting.[1]

[p. 113] Bounty to Soldiers. The Committee having made their report —thereupon — Voted that a bounty of £4-10 be given to every Able bodied effective man who Shall engage in the Service of this State from this Town and Serve three months as part of ye Quota of men ordered by the Gen^{ll} assembly to march ye 15th of instant July to be under the Command of his Excellency Gen^{ll} Washington.[2]

Bounty. Also Voted a bounty of £12-0-0 be given to every able bodied man &c who Shall Engage for Six months to Serve in the Continental Army.

Also voted that upon proper Certificates the Selectmen be desired to pay the Several bounties from the Town Treasury.[3]

[NOVEMBER 13, 1780]

[p. 114] AT A TOWN MEETING HELD IN NEW HAVEN UPON THE 13TH DAY OF NOVEMBER 1780.

Mod^r. Voted that Mr Tim° Jones be moderator of this meeting.

---

1. In June of 1780, the General Assembly ordered the raising of two new battalions to serve for a two-month period and be stationed on what it called the southwestern frontier of the state. According to Mark V. Kwasny's *Washington's Partisan War, 1776 - 1783*, the order was was meant to check the activities of partisan troops that had driven American supporters from southwestern Connecticut. *PRSC,* Vol. 3: 119 - 120. 248 - 249.
2. Quotas for new, able-bodied recruits were falling so short by 1780 that towns were offering additional sign-on bounties In addition, the state exempted those who found adequate replacements from military service for the term of heir replacement's service. *PRSC,* Vol 3: 175.
3 Remainder of page 113 and first half of p. 114 are blank.

Tax. Voted a Tax be laid upon the rates and rateable Estates of the inhabitants of this Town upon the List of 1779 of Six pence upon the pound payable in beef of the first Quality, to be Computed at 5^d p^r pound and that of an inferior Quality being Good and marketable at four pence half penny p^r pound, or pork not exceeding five Score weight p^r hog at five pence p^r pound between five and 8 Score five pence half penny p^r pound, and all above 8 Score at Six pence p^r pound or in wheat flour at Twenty four Shilling p^r Hundred gross weight; and those who shall neglect or refuse to pay the provisions at ye Rate aforesaid by the 15th Day of January next shall *[p. 115]* Forfiet and pay Double the value thereof — Provided nevertheless that no beef Shall be received in upon s^d Tax after the 15th Day of Decr next and that the Coll^{rs} to be appointed are hereby impowered and Directed to Collect s^d Tax and forfieture accordingly.[1]

Provisions. Voted that Capt Peter Johnson, Isaac Forbs, Capt Nathan Smith, Enos Todd, Enoch Newton, David Grannis and Isaac Beecher Shall Receive the Salt necessary for Salting the provisions agreeable to ye foregoing vote to procure Casks to Contain s^d provisions, to Receive and inspect the Same*[,]* See that it is good and marketable and put up the Same well, and that they Shall Conform themselves to the Late act of the assembly relating to said provision. And they are also appointed Collectors of the foregoing rate agreeable to the above vote.

Managers of the Lottery. The managers of the Lottery requested of this meeting to give their advice whether they had best to draw the Lottery agreeable to their advertisment.

Voted the managers be directed to draw the Lottery agreeable to their advertisment.

Voted this Town reconsider the above Vote, and postpone advertising the managers till next Town meeting.

Committee. Voted that Messrs Tim^o Jones, Hez^h Sabin J^r and James Hillhouse be a Committee to ascertain the Number of Soldiers in the Continental Army belonging to this Town.[2]

---

1. A tax payable in beef and pork indicates the town's need to raise its share of adequate provisions for Connecticut troops as mandated by the General Assembly in October of 1780, *PRSC*, Vol 3: 176.
2. No such report has been located. According to William S. Wells, compiler, "List of Men from the territory embraced in the Town of New Haven, Connecticut, who are known to have Served in the Continental Army and Militia and Connecticut State and Continental Vessels and Privateers," *Revolutionary Characters of New Haven* (1911), some 998 men served.

This meeting adjourned to thursday next at two of the Clock in the afternoon.

There was no meeting opened at the Time to which it was adjourned.[1]

[DECEMBER 11, 1780]

[p. 116] AT A TOWN MEETING HELD IN NEW HAVEN UPON THE 11TH DAY OF DECEMBER 1780.

Clerk. Sam[l] Bishop Chosen Town Clerk.

Mod[r]. Dan[l] Lyman Esq[r] Chosen moderator.

Selectmen. Voted that Mess[rs] Tim[o] Jones, Joel Gilbert, John Hubbard, Joseph Peck J[r], Peter Johnson, Obed[h] Hotchkis, Newman Trowbridge, Stephen Smith, Nehemiah Smith, Jesse Todd, Stephen Goodyear, Jesse Ford and Peter Perkins be Selectmen the year ensuing.

Collector. Voted that Eliada Sanford[2] be a Receiver of the Provisions and Collector of the Town rate which was Granted the last Town meeting and to have y[e] Same power and authority as the Receivers and Coll[rs] had at s[d] meeting.

Lottery. Voted that the managers of the Lottery be directed forthwith *[to]* proceed to drawing the first Class.

Constable. Voted y[t] M[r] Michael Baldwin be Constable and Collector of the Country rates in this Town the year ensuing.

Constables. Voted that Tiley Blackslee, John Wise, John Mix J[r], Elisha Booth, John Denison, Justus Smith, Dan[l] Doolittle, Job Munson, Hez[h] Sperry and Reuben Beecher be Constables the year Ensuing.

Grandjurymen. Voted that Isaac Hubbard, Nathan Oaks, Simeon Jocelin, Tho[s] Punderson J[r], Levi Basset, Sam[l] Townsend, Sam[l] Holt, John Benham, Jeremiah Smith, Nath[ll] Beech, Peter Eastman, Giles Dayton, Tim[o] Goodyear, Elip[t] John-

---

1. The following Thursday was November 23. The notation suggests that Samuel Bishop made this entry after the fact.
1. Eliada Sanford (1755? - 1820) served in the 1776 New York campaign under Captain Jacob Brockett, fought against the British in the invasion of New Haven, and later served as Deacon the North Haven Congregational Church.

son, David French, Joseph Beecher, Amos Thomas, Job Blackslee, Levi Ray, Jason Bradly, Ezra Ives, Lamberton Toles, Amos Perkins J^r be Grandjurymen the year ensuing.

[p. 117] Listers. Voted y^t John Austin, William Lyon, Joseph Gilbert, Moses Gilbert, Levi Ives, James Rice, Azariah Bradly, Jared Robinson, Philemon Smith, Job Blackslee, Levi Ray, Jason Bradly, Ezra Ives, Lamberton Toles and Amos Perkins J^r be Listers the year ensuing.

This meeting adjourned to monday next at 1 of ye Clock in the afternoon.

[DECEMBER 18, 1780]

AT A TOWN MEETING HELD IN NEW HAVEN BY ADJOURNMENT ON THE 18TH DAY OF DECEMBER 1780.

Treas^r. Voted that Saml Bishop be Town Treasurer the year ensuing.

Surveyers. Voted that Michael Baldwin, John Mix, Joseph Munson, Philemon Potter, Medad Atwater, Isaac Bradly, Levi Basset, Richard Woodward, Saml Cooper J^r, John Gorham, Stephen Thompson, Saml Goodsell, Jos^h Russel, Sam^{ll} Thompson J^r, Nathan Smith J^r, Sam^{ll} Smith, Sam^{ll} Candee, Joel Basset, Oliver Smith, William Sanford J^r, Jotham Blackslee, Saml Basset J^r, Saml Hitchcock J^r, Jonathan Dickerman, Eben^r Beech, Elijah Sperry, Roger Peck, Amos Hitchcock, Saml Downs, Ury Tuttle, Daniel Lounsbury, Tim^o Lounsbury, Isaac Ford, Edward Carrinton, Solomon Gilbert, Jonathan Barns, Eben^r Beecher and Noah Peck J^r be Surveyers of highways the year ensuing.

Key Keepers. Voted that Joseph Munson, Noah Potter, Caleb Alling, Saml Bradly, Lamberton Smith, David Tharp, Thomas Cooper, William Adams, Dan Peck, Seth Blackslee, John Peas J^r, John Culver, Job Munson, Tim^o [?], Ben^j Gaylor J^r, Joel Tuttle, Tim^o Ball J^r, be key keepers the year ensuing.

Branders. Voted that Theop^s Munson, Elisha Booth, Abr^m Chidsey, Gregson Gilbert, Ephraim Humaston, Joseph Peck, Jonathan Ives, Roger Peck and George Smith be branders of horses the year ensuing.

Fence viewers. Voted that John Mix, Nathan Mansfield and Obediah Hotchkis be fence viewers the year ensuing.

Leather Sealer. Voted that Stephen Bradly be leather Sealer the year ensuing.

Sealer of W^ts. Voted that Theop^s Munson be Sealer of weights and measures the year ensuing.

[p. 118] Sealer. Voted that John Miles be Sealer of dry measures.

Swine. Voted that Swine going at large on the Town Commons and highways the year Ensuing Shall not be liable to be impounded from thence — Provided they are ringed all the year and Sufficiently yoaked from the 10th Day of March to the 10th Day of December next.

Tythingmen. Voted that Moses Gilbert, Eli Beecher, Job Potter, Job Parrit, Josiah Bradly, Abr^m Chidsey, Elihu Sperry, John Sanford, Eben^r Todd J^r, Levi Cooper, Jesse Stevens, Jotham Williams, Jesse Dickerman, Jotham Tuttle, John Russel, Reuben Perkins, Reuben Beecher, Dan Peck and Gregson Gilbert be Tything-men the year ensuing.

Allowance to Coll^r. Voted that Michael Baldwin who was Chosen Coll^r of the Country rates the Last meeting, be allowed out of the Town Treasury Ten Shillings on the £100 pounds for each £100 he Shall Collect.

Selectman. Voted that Capt Peter Johnson be released from being Selectman and Col Jonathan Fitch be Selectman in his Stead.

Selectman. Voted that Newman Trowbridge be released from being Selectman and Chas Chauncey Esqr be Selectman in his Stead.

Selectmen. Voted that the Selectmen together with Col Sabin be desired forthwith to write to his Excellency the Govr to give orders that no man Should be taken from this Town to go to horse neck agreeable to the Late orders for Draughting men for that purpose.[1]

This meeting adjourned to monday next at two of the Clock in the afternoon.

---

1. In November of 1780, the Connecticut General Assembly ordered that a new regiment of militia be raised for the defense of Horseneck. Horseneck was a portion of Greenwich, located on the west side of the Mianus River that was plagued by internecine warfare between the Loyalists and Patriots. New Haven, meanwhile, continued to fear a return by British troops. *PRSC*, Vol 3: 175 - 176.

[JANUARY 1, 1781]

[p. 119] AT A TOWN MEETING HELD IN NEW HAVEN BY ADJOURN-
MENT UPON THE OF FIRST JANUARY 1781

Guard. Whereas the Time that Cap[t] Bradlys Company was inlisted for is Now
out therefore voted that the Selectmen do forthwith hire Such Number of men
as they Judge needfull to keep the fort for the present and that they be Desired
to appoint Some person or persons to inlist the number of men proposed by the
assembly the Last Session. Voted the Civil authority and Selectmen be desired
to furnish a guard to patrole the Streets of the Town till next Town meeting.

Lottery. Voted that David Austin Esq[r] be released from being one of the managers of the Lottery for the bridge over the East River and M[r] Isaac Beers
Chosen in his room.

Voted that this meeting be adjourned to monday next at one of the Clock in
the afternoon.

[JANUARY 8, 1781]

AT A TOWN MEETING HELD IN NEW HAVEN BY ADJOURNMENT
UPON THE 8TH DAY OF JANUARY 1781.

Tax. Voted this Town Tax themselves one penny half penny on the Grand List
of the year 1779 payable in provision at the following prices[:] wheat flour at
24/ p[r] Hundred gross weight, Rye flour 16/ p[r] Hund[d], Indian Corn 4/ a bushel agreeable to a Late act of the Gen[ll] assembly ordering the Several Towns in
this State to Tax themselves &c and that Hez[h] Tuttle, Isaac Forbes, Philemon
Smith, David Tharp, Tim[o] Bradly, Sam[l] Bellamy and Joel Hotchkis be the Collectors of s[d] Tax[,] Receivers of the Provisions and Conform themselves to s[d]
act, and Settle s[d] Tax with the Selectmen of s[d] Town.

[p. 120] Soldiers families. Voted that Cap[t] Joseph Munson, John Miles & Philemon Potter be a Committee to procure the provisions for the Soliders families
in this Town for the future in the room of the Selectmen agreeable to the acts
of the Gen[ll] assembly.[1]

---

1. In its October session, the General Assembly enacted legislation that mandated towns to provide
for the families of men on active duty., *PRSC*, Vol 3: 311 - 312.

Grandjuryman. Voted that Isaac Hubbard be released from being Grandjuryman.

Grandjuryrnan. Voted that Levi Basset be released from *[being]* Grandjuryman and that M[r] Jonathan Ingersol be Grandjuryman in his room.

This meeting adjourned to the 2[d] monday of Feb next at 2 of the Clock in the afternoon.

[FEBRUARY 12, 1781]

AT A TOWN MEETING HELD IN NEW HAVEN BY ADJOURNMENT ON THE 12TH DAY OF FEB 1781.

Coll[r]. Voted that Cap[t] Tim° Bradly be released from being Col[lr] of the Town rate for flour &c and that Dan Peck be Collector in his room.

Amity and Bethany. Voted this Town are willing that the Societies of Amity and Bethany should agreeable to their Petition to the Gen[ll] assembly be made into a Distinct Town with the priviledges Enjoyed by the rest of the Towns in this State, they abiding by a Determination of a Disinterested Committee who Shall say what is Just & right for s[d] Societies to pay with regards to the poor, bridges and that part they Shall Receive of the Town Stock.[1]

North Haven & Mt. Carmel. Voted this Town Consent to a petition from the inhabitants of the parishes of North Haven and mount Carmel to be made into a Distinct Town with all the priviledges Enjoyed *[p. 121]* by the rest of y[e] Towns in this State, they Complying with the determination of a disinterested Committee who Shall say what part of the burden of the poor and bridges they Shall *[blank]* and what part they Shall Receive of the Town Stock.[2]

Memorial. Voted the Representatives of this Town by memorial to the Gen[ll] assembly represent the Exposed Situation of this Town the *[...]* of having our men to defend the Town, and the great hardship *[intentionally blank]* taking our men from us by draft or otherwise especially when our Number is so Great in the Continental Army.

1. Amity (subsequently known as Woodbridge) was allowed town status in 1784. Bethany was then part of Woodbridge and did not gain its independence until May 1832.
2. North Haven and Mount Carmel (Hamden) were allowed town status in 1786.

Coll. Voted that Samuel Bellamy be released from being Coll[r] of the Tax to be Collected in flour and Job Munson Chosen in his room.

Lister. Voted that Cap[t] Abr[m] Bradly be Lister in the room of John Austin released.

Civil Authority &c to Collect the poor. Voted that the Civil authority and Selectmen are hereby desired to Collect the Sick and those poor maintained, together, *[and?]* take the best method to Support and provide for them whilest together.[1]

[JUNE 28, 1781]

[p. 122] AT A TOWN MEETING HOLDEN IN NEW HAVEN UPON THE 28TH DAY OF JUNE 1781.

Mod[r]. Voted that Dan[l] Lyman Esq[r] be moderator.

Clerk. Henry Daggett Chosen Town Clerk Pro Tem (in room of Sam[l] Bishop who is absent,) and Sworn.[2]

Listers. Voted that Thomas Howel, Jacob Daggett and Elias Shipman be Listers in the room of Abr[m] Bradly, Levi Ives and John Miles who were released.

Tax. Voted that this Town do Tax themselves four pence on the pound on the List for the year 1780 to be paid in Silver and Gold or beef Cattle agreeable to an act of the Gen[ll] assembly passed in may Last for raising Supplies for the use of the State and the Continental Army untill the first Day of January next.

Coll[r] Voted that Peter Johnson, John Heminway, Oliver Smith, Titus Bradly, Barn[s] Baldwin, Jonathan Dickerman J[r] and Jesse Beecher be Collectors of s[d] Rate.

Districts. Voted that the Selectmen divide out proper districts to the Surveyers of this Town.

Petition to the Gov[r] by Committee. Voted that Mess[rs] David Austin, John Whiting,

---

1. New Haven's care of its sick and poor dated back to the town's founding. Extended families were expected to care for their own. In lieu of that, almshouses housed the poor and orphaned minors while hospital care at the time took place in private houses. The first official hospital in New Haven opened in 1792 for the treatment of smallpox victims.
2. Bishop at this time was serving in the state legislature and as Justice of the Peace for New Haven County, among other positions.

Tim° Jones, Hez^h Sabin J^r, Henry Daggett, Mark Levenworth and Danl Lyman are appointed a Committee to prepare a Petition to his Excellency the Govr and his Council of Safety Shewing that the Safety of this Town is much endangered by the Late great requisition of men to be taken from it and praying for releif.[1]

Voted that Tim° Jones Esqr and Mr Henry Daggett are appointed to present to his Excellency the Govr the Petition of this Town prepared by s^d Committee.

[p. 123] Voted to adjourn this meeting to Next Thursday *[at]* two of the Clock in the afternoon.

Test. Henry Daggett[2] Clerk P.T.

[JULY 5, 1781]

AT A TOWN MEETING HELD IN NEW HAVEN BY ADJOURNMENT UPON THE 5^H DAY OF JULY 1781

Coll^r. Voted that Philemon Potter be Collector of the rate Granted the Last meeting for the Society of Fair Haven.

Coll^r. Voted that Josiah Burr be Collector of the rate Granted the Last meeting for the Church.[3]

Coll^r. Voted that Tiley Blackslee be Collector of the rate granted as afores^d for the Society of Fair Haven.

Coll^r. Voted that Barnabas Baldwin be released from being Collector of the rate Granted the Last meeting, and that Reuben Beecher be Coll^r in his room.

Committee ab^t Soldiers. Voted that Maj^r Levenworth, Capt Daggett, Capt Burret and Col. Sabin be a Committee to See on what Terms the men Can be disposed of which this Town has in the Continental ~~Service~~ army over their

---

1. To appease the fears of New Haven the General Assembly provided the town with 300 French muskets to be used by Yale students in case of another invasion. *PRSC,* Vol 3: 512.
2. Likely Henry Daggett (1758 - 1843), son of former Yale President Naphtali Daggett and himself a Yale graduate in 1775. He served as a Lieutenant in the 7th Connecticut Regiment as of 1780.
3. Josiah Burr (1753 - 1795) married Mary Burr in United Church in New Haven on September 7, 1780.

Quota either for Six months or three years or during the war and whether they Can be disposed of with Safety to the Town, and likewise to See how men Can be ~~disposed of~~ hired to Serve in the State battilions till next March, and report make [sic.] to the Town at their next meeting.

This meeting adjourned to Tuesday next at two of the Clock in the afternoon.

[JULY 10, 1781]

[p. 124] AT A TOWN MEETING HELD IN NEW HAVEN BY ADJOURN-MENT UPON THE 10ᵀᴴ DAY OF JULY 1781

*Mod*ʳ. Voted that Tim° Jones Esqʳ be moderator.

Comᵉ to hire Soldiers. Voted that a Committee be appointed to hire for this Town Twenty one men to Serve in the State battlions untill the first Day of march next and sᵈ Committee are desired to give their personal Security to the men they Shall hire and the Town will endemnify them. Messʳˢ Peter Johnson, Eli Levenworth, Henry Daggett, Elias Shipman, Josiah Bradly, Enos Todd, Nehemiah Smith, Samˡ Osborn, Stephen Goodyear and Ebenʳ Dayton¹ are appointed for sᵈ Commᵗᵗᵉᵉ.

Tax resinded. Voted that this Town resind the Vote they passed laying a Tax of four pence on the pound on the List for 1780 in Silver, Gold or Beef Cattle.

Tax. Voted that the Town Tax themselves four pence on the pound on sᵈ list in Silver or Gold payable by the First Day of Augᵗ next.

Collʳ. Voted that Tilley Blackslee Collect sᵈ rate.

pᵗ of Tax to be paid in Beef. Voted that one fourth part of sᵈ Tax may be paid in beaf Cattle if delivered to the Town agent on or before the 20ᵗʰ Day of July instant.

agent. Voted that Beef Cattle Shall be recᵈ by sᵈ agent untill the 10ᵗʰ Day of Augᵗ

---

1. Captain Ebenezer Dayton of Coram, NY, moved to Bethany from Coram, NY in 1776 and became a renowned privateer based out of New Haven. By the war's end, New Haven residents suspected Dayton of playing both sides in the war for personal profit, a charge he vehemently denied. Dayton disappeared mysteriously in 1786 after swimming in the Housatonic River in 1786, and was presumed drowned. He was later said to have moved to New Orleans. See, Harvey Garret Smith, "Ebenezer Dayton Patriot Peddler...," http://www.longislandgenealogy.com/patped.htm.

for one Quarter of s^d Tax.

[Agent.] Voted that s^d agent receive Beef Cattle untill the 10th Day of Sepr next for one fourth part of s^d Rate.

[Agent.] Voted that s^d agent receive Beef Cattle untill the 10th Day of Octr next for the Last Quarter of s^d Tax.

Adj^d without day — Test. Henry Daggett, Town Clerk P.T.[1]

[SEPTEMBER 24, 1781]

[p. 125] AT A TOWN MEETING HELD IN NEW HAVEN ON THE 18TH DAY OF SEP^R ANNO DOM. 1781.

Mod^r. Voted that Timothy Jones Esqr be moderator.

Voted that this meeting be adjourned to monday next at two of the Clock in the afternoon.

[SEPTEMBER 24, 1781]

AT A TOWN MEETING HOLDEN IN NEW HAVEN BY ADJOURN-MENT UPON THE 24TH DAY OF SEP^R 1781.

persons appointed to receive part of 2/6 Tax. Voted that the following persons be Receivers of those articles mentioned in the act of the Gen^ll assembly relative to the 2/6 rate viz — Henry Daggett, Isaac Chidsey, Nathan Smith J^r, Justus J. Fitch, Amos Perkins, Elisha Chapman and Tim° Ball.[1]

Selectmen. Voted that the Selectmen be desired to see y^t ye Collectors of the Last Town rate forthwith Settle their rates and the Consideration of what sum they ought to Receive (if any be) be reffer^d to the Consideration of the Next meeting.

This meeting adj^d to monday the 8th Day of oct^r next at two of the Clock in the afternoon.

---

1. Governor Trumbull and the Council of Safety recently levied new taxes to pay Connecticut troops on the Continental Line. See https://catalog.hathitrust.org/Record/010471398, *PRSC*, Vol, 3: 512.

[OCTOBER 8, 1781]

AT A TOWN MEETING HOLDEN IN NEW HAVEN UPON THE 8TH
DAY OF OCTOBER 1781 — BY ADJOURNMENT.

Surveyer. Voted that Michael Baldwin be released from being Surveyer of highways, and that Col Thompson be Surveyer in his Stead.

This meeting adjourned without Day.

[DECEMBER 10, 1781]

[p. 126] AT A TOWN MEETING HOLDEN IN NEW HAVEN UPON THE
10TH DAY OF DECEMBER 1781.

Clerk. Voted that Sam¹ Bishop *[be Town]* Clerk.

Modʳ. Voted that Danˡ Lyman Esqʳ be moderator.

Selectmen. Voted that Messʳˢ John Hubbard, Joseph Munson, Abel Burret, Henry
Daggett, Stephen Smith, Nehemiah Smith, Enos Todd, Jesse Ford, Asa Goodyear and Peter Perkins be Selectmen the year ensuing.

This meeting adjᵈ to monday next at 10 of the Clock in the forenoon.

[DECEMBER 17, 1781]

AT A TOWN MEETING HOLDEN IN NEW HAVEN UPON THE 17TH
DAY OF DECEMBER BY ADJOURNMENT ANNO DOM 1781.

Constables. Voted that Tilley Blacksle, John Mix, John Wise, John Mix Jʳ, John Denison, Peter Eastman, Danˡ Doolittle, Reuben Beecher, Job Munson, David Thomas
and Gilead Kimberly be Constables the year ensuing.

Grandjurymen. Voted that Ebenʳ Alling, Pierpoint Edwards, Mark Levenworth,
John Woodward Jʳ, Abrᵐ Chidsey, Nathˡ Stacy, Joshua Barns Jʳ, Oliver Smith,
Aze1 Kimberly, David Smith, Hezʰ Smith, Hezʰ Warner, David French, E1ipᵗ
Johnson, Tim° Atwater and Isaac Thompson be Grandjurymen the year ensuing.

Tythingmen. Voted that Levi Basset, Joshua Atwater, Abrᵐ Thompson, Samˡ

Sheppard, Sam¹ Bradly, Nath¹ Dayton, Elihu Sperry, John Barns, Enos Brocket Jʳ, Jacob Thompson, Jeremiah Smith, Jesse Stevens, Thoˢ Baldwin, David Hotchkis, Sam¹ Hitchcock Jʳ· Joel Todd, John Russel, Reuben Perkins and Newman Trowbridge be Tythingmen the year ensuing.

Grandjuryman. Voted that Mark Levenworth be released from being Grandjuryman and Jacob Daggett be Grandjuryman in his Stead.

[p. 127] Surveyers. Voted that James Hillhouse, John Mix, Joseph Thompson, Josʰ Peck, David Atwater, Erastus Bradly, Benʲ Woodin Jʳ, Abel Potter, Peter Johnson, Stephen Thompson, Sam¹ Thompson, Tim° Thompson, Joseph Holt, Silas Kimberly, Sam¹ Candee, Gideon Todd, Stephen Ives, Eliada Sanford, Oliver Smith, Jonathan Barns, Dan Todd, Sam¹ Basset Jʳ, Enoch Newton, Abner Bradly, Obed Johnson, Asa Sperry, Wilmot Bradly, Seth Downs, Ebenʳ Beech, Noah Walcot Jʳ, Caleb Doolittle, Tim° Lounsbury, Joseph Hotchtkis, Ebeʳ Lines, Hezʰ Beecher, Caleb Andrews Jʳ, Reuben Bradly, Sam¹ Atwater, Jonathan Dickerman, Caleb Alling, John Ball and Sam¹ Davenport be Surveyers of highways the year Ensuing.

Listers. Voted that Thomas Howel, James Rice, David Austin, Moses Gilbert, Joel Gilbert, Joseph Peck, Elias Shipman, Joseph Gilbert, Phileman Potter, Joseph Russel, Abrᵐ Barns, Phiⁿ Smith, Levi Ray, Job Blackslee, David Ford, Barnabas Baldwin, Jason Bradly, Ezra Ives and Sam¹ Perkins be listers the year ensuing.

Selectmen. Voted that Nehemiah Smith be released from being Selectman and Lamberton *[Smith?]*¹ be Selectman in his room.

Committee appointed to divide the Town. Voted that Messʳˢ Charles Chauncy, James Hillhouse, David Austin, Sam¹ Bishop, Henry Daggett, Caleb Alling, Isaac Beers, Isaac Doolittle, Joshua Austin, Isaac Chidsey, Nehemiah Smith, Silas Kimberly, Jonathan Dayton, Nathaniel Beech, Timothy Bradly, Jesse Ford, Sam¹ Atwater, Baszel Munson, Benajah Peck and Isaac Beecher be and they are hereby appointed a Committee to report a plan for a Division of this Town into Distinct and Separate Towns and a distribution of the Town Estate Stock & burdens and report to this on the next meeting.

This meeting adjᵈ to the 31ˢᵗ Day of Instant Decʳ at one of the Clock in the afternoon.

---

1. Lamberton Smith, Jr. (1734 - 1791) was a West Haven native and veteran of the French and Indian War. He was also a local leader in the Sons of Liberty. See, Malia, *op. cit.*

[DECEMBER 31, 1781]

[p. 128] AT A TOWN MEETING HOLDEN IN NEW HAVEN BY AD-
JOURNMENT UPON THE 31ST DAY OF DECEMBER 1781.

Tythingmen. Voted that Jesse Goodyear and Isaac Dickerman be Tythingmen the
year ensuing.

fence viewers. Voted that John Mix and Nathan Mansfield and Obediah Hotchkis
be fence viewers the year ensuing.

Leather sealer. Voted that Stephen Bradly be leather sealer the year ensuing.

Sealer [of Weights & Masures.] Voted that Theopˢ Munson be sealer of wᵗˢ & measures
the year ensuing.

Sealer [of dry measures]. Voted that John Miles be sealer of dry measures yᵉ year
ensuing.

Key Keepers. Voted that Joseph Munson, Noah Potter, Caleb Alling, John Peas
Jʳ, Timᵒ Potter, John Martin, John Culver, Joel Tuttle, Samˡ Bradly, Nathˡ Smith,
Seth Blackslee, Philemon Heaton, Dan Peck and Isaac Munson be ~~branders~~ key
keepers the year ensuing.

Branders. Voted that Theopˢ Munson, Grigson Gilbert, Abrᵐ Childsey, Ephraim
Humaston, Dan Peck, Jonathan Ives, Roger Peck and George Smith be branders
of horses yᵉ year ensuing.

Treasʳ. Voted that Samuel Bishop be Town Treasurer the year ensuing.

Surveyers. Voted that Jonathan Heaton and David Atwater Jʳ be Surveyers of
highways the year ensuing.

Tax. Voted yᵗ there be a Tax of four pence on the pound two pence of which to
be paid on the List of the year 1780 forthwith, and the other two pence on the
pound on the List of the year 1781 on the first Day of May Next, to defray yᵉ
necessary Charges of the Town.

Collʳ. Voted that John Austin be Collʳ of the foregoing Tax.

This meeting adj^d to monday next at 2 of the Clock in ye afternoon.

[JANUARY 7, 1782]

[129] AT A TOWN MEETING HOLDEN IN IN NE HAVEN BY AD-
JOURNMENT UPON THE SEVENTH DAY OF JANUARY 1782.

Selectmen about Guards. Voted that the Selectmen Supply ye Town with such
Guards as they shall find necessary, and immediately make application to the
Govr and Council of Safety or the Gen^{ll} assembly for Such a number of Guards
as will be Sufficient for this Town, in the Town Platt and the out posts. Also that
the Selectmen make Suteable application to the Govr and Council of Safety or
to the Gen^{ll} assembly to refund the money the*[y]* Shall be necessarily obliged to
pay for hiring the Guards.[1]

Coll^r. Voted that Phileman Potter be Coll^r of the Tax granted the last meeting in
the room of John Austin who refused to Serve.

Coll^r. Voted that Joel Atwater be Coll^r of s^d Tax in the room of said Phileman
Potter who refused to Serve.

Grandjuryman. Voted that Nath^{ll} Downs be Grandjuryman in the room of Azel
Kimberly who refused to Serve.

Lottery. Voted that Col Sabin, Simeon Bristoll, and Tim^o Jones Esqr be a Committee to Settle with the managers of the Lottery and report to the Town make
of their doings therein.

Bridge. Voted that Eneas Munson and James Hillhouse Esq^{rs} in behalf of this
Town Petition the Gen^{ll} assembly to appoint a Committee to fix the place to
build the bridge over East Haven River according to their resolve in may 1780
for the building of which bridge they were pleased to grant a Lottery to raise
the Sum of one Thousand pounds Lawfull money a part of which sum has
been raised.

[p. 130] Committee Town Divided. The Committee appointed the Last meeting to

1. The General Assembly granted New Haven the sum of £960 out of a total of £9,190 allocated
for the defense of coastal towns in January of 1782. It also authorized that a company of 25 men
be raised for New Haven's defense. *PRSC*, Vol. 4: 11.

report a plan for a Division of s^d Town &c made their report to this meeting in the following words viz.

We the Subscribers being appointed a Committee by the Town of New Haven at a meeting of s^d Town held by adjournment upon the 17th Day of December 1781, To report a plan for a Division of s^d Town and distribution of the Stock and burdens of s^d Town report as follows viz. That the Society of East Haven be made into a distinct and Separate Town — That the Societies of North Haven and Mount Carmell be made into a distinct & Separate Town — and y^t the Societies of Amity and Bethany be made into a distinct and Separate Town. And y^t the Estate, stock, soldiers, in the Continental Army[,] Town poor[,] bridges and other burdens of s^d Town of New Haven, (exclusive of the two lowar bridges over the East river or Such other bridge as shall be ordered by the Gen^ll assembly in Lieu thereof, which is to remain a Common burden upon s^d Town of New Haven and said New proposed Towns) be distributed to and among the s^d four towns according to the Several parts and proportion of the Grand List of s^d Town of New Haven at ye Time when the three distinct and Separate Towns or either of them Shall be made and Constituted by the Gen^ll assembly of this State, which s^d distribution Shall be made according to s^d Rate by those Judicious, Disinterested men to be appointed for y^t purpose by the Gen^ll assembly at the Time of sitting and of making s^d Separate and distinct Towns.

New Haven December 31, 1781   Signed p^r ord^r of the Committee
                                     David Austin Chairman

The foregoing report of the Committee having been duely considered, is by the Town accepted and approved and ordered to be recorded.

This meeting adj^d to monday next at 2 of the Clock *[in the]* afternoon.

[JANUARY 14, 1782]

[p. 131] AT A TOWN MEETING HOLDEN IN NEW HAVEN BY ADJOURNMENT ON THE 14TH DAY OF JANUARY 1782.

Districts. Voted that the Selectmen give the districts to ye Surveyers of highways.

Coll^r. Voted that Barnabus Baldwin be Coll^r of the Town rate in the room of Joel Atwater who refused to Serve.

Coll'. Voted that Joel Atwater be Coll[r] of the Town rate in the room of Barn[s] Baldwin who refused.

allowance to Coll'. Voted that the above[sd] Joel Atwater shall have y[e] Sum of third pounds for Collecting the Town rate, which was laid at a former meeting, s[d] Atwater agreed to take s[d] rate.

List. Voted that the Selectmen be desired to examine into the lists of this Town in y[e] years 1779 & 1780 as to the interest of those lists, and do what is needfull and proper to be done thereon.

[Remainder of p. 131 and all of p. 132 are blank.[1]]

[DECEMBER 9, 1782]

[p. 133] AT A TOWN MEETING HOLDEN IN NEW HAVEN UPON THE 9TH DAY OF DECEMBER 1782.

Clerk. Samuel Bishop Chosen Town Clerk.

Mod'. Timothy Jones Esq[r] Chosen moderator.

Selectmen. Voted that Mess[rs] John Hubbard, Joseph Munson, Abel Burret, Henry Dagget, Joseph Howel, John Austin, Isaac Beers, and Stephen Smith be Selectmen the year ensuing.

Selectman. Voted that Henry Dagget be released from being Selectman and that and Joel Gilbert be Selectman in his room.

Selectman. Voted y[t] John Hubbard be released from being Selectman and that Deacon Tho[s] Howel be Selectman in his room.

Selectman. Voted that Stephen Smith be released from being Selectman and that Isaac Chidsey be Selectman in his room.

Selectman. Voted that Lamberton Painter & Enos Todd be Selectmen the year ensuing.

---

1. There were no entries made in the town records for a 10-month period from January 14, 1782 to December 9. 1782. As noted later in the records, Samuel Bishop, the clerk, was ill.

Selectman. Voted that Enos Todd be released from being Selectmen and that Noah Ives be Selectman in his room.

Selectman. Voted that Jesse Ford, Asa Goodyear and Peter Perkins be Selectmen the year ensuing.

Selectman. Voted that Asa Goodyear be released from being Selectman and that Jonathan Dickerman be Selectman in his room.

Selectman. Voted that ~~Jeremiah Atwater~~ Abel Burret be released from being Selectman and that Jeremiah Atwater be Selectman in his room.

Constables. Voted that Tiley Blackslee, Joseph Peck, Samuel Humaston Jr, Jacob Bradly, Justus Smith, Peter Eastman, Eliada Sanford, George Dudley, Reuben Beecher, David Thomas, [p. 134] Medad Atwater and Benjn English be Constables the year ensuing.

Constable. Voted that Jacob Bradly be released from being Constable and that Jared Bradly be Constable in his room.

Collr. Voted that Samuel Humaston Jr be Collector of the State Taxes the year ensuing.

allowance to Collr. Voted that said Samuel Humaston Shall have paid unto him Ten Shillings out of the Town Treasury for each hundred pound[s] which he Shall Collect of the State Taxes.

Selectmen to call on Collrs. Voted that the Selectmen be desired to call on the Several Collrs of the State Taxes in this Town and know the State of their accts and make report to the next meeting, and also between this and the next find a Suteable person to take the Country Rate the year ensuing.

Committee about Town poor. Voted that Messrs Charles Chauncy, Peter Johnson, Abel Burret, Saml Bishop, Henry Dagget, James Gilbert, Joseph Bradly, Enos Shipman, Stephen Smith, Azariah Bradly, Lamberton Painter, Silas Kimberly, Jonathan Dayton, Nathll Beech, Thomas Darling, Caleb Beecher, Simeon Bristoll, Samuel Atwater, Timo Ball, Isaac Beecher, John Whiting and John Mix be a Committee for forming a plan for the Supporting this Towns Poor, and also a plan for making a house for their reception and for the Idle and Strouting who make it their practice to Spend their Time from door to door when their Time might be Spent for better purpose, and make report to the Next meeting.[1]

Grandjurymen. Voted that John Goodrich, John Alling J[r], Hez[h] Bradly, David Beecher, Abr[m] Alling. Phileman Potter, Josiah Burr, Elias Shipman, Joshua Austin, Amos Morris Ju[r], Joseph Merwin, Nathan Smith, Will[am] Day, Titus Tharp, John Sanford, David Hotchkis, Sam[l] Johnson J[r], Ezra Ives, Isaac Gilbert, Ury Tuttle, be Grandjurymen the ensuing year.

[p. 135] Surveyers. Voted that Russel Clark, Co[l] Hubbard, Robert Fairchild, Phileman Potter, Caleb Mix, John Mix, Medad Beecher, Stephen Brintall, Charles Alling, Benj[n] Woodin J[r], Erastus Bradly, Ichabod Page, Isaac Dickerman J[r], Stephen Thompson, Joseph Holt, Sam[l] Thompson J[r], Lamberton Painter, Ben[j] Downs, Joel Tuttle, Calvin Heaton, Caleb Clark, Enoch Jacobs, Sam[l] Basset J[r], Dan Todd, Abner Bradly, Willmot Bradly, Amos Thomas, Stephen Peck, John Horton J[r], Jabez Bradly, Joseph Johnson, Jeremiah Ives, Enos Atwater, David French, Caleb Peck, Lamberton Toles, Elias Hotchkis, John Woodin, Jesse Johnson, James Hillhouse be Surveyers of highways the year ensuing.

This meeting adj[d] to the Last monday of instant Dec[r] at 10 °Clock in the forenoon.

[DECEMBER 30, 1782]

AT A TOWN MEETING HOLDEN BY ADJOURNMENT UPON THE 30[h] DAY OF DECEMBER 1782.

[Intentional space left for entry that was never made.]

fence viewers. Voted that John Mix, Obediah Hotchkis and Noah Potter be fence viewers the year ensuing.

Leather Sealer. Voted that Stephen Bradly be Leather sealer the year ensuing.

Sealers of W[t] &c. Voted that Theop[s] Munson be Sealer of W[ts] and measures the year ensuing.

Key keepers. Voted that Joseph Munson, Noah Potter, Caleb Alling, John Peas J[r],

---

1. New Haven first voted to build "a work house or house of Correction" in 1767 to house "the Poor and Idle." That building was never approved by the Connecticut Assembly. This new effort was also abandoned due to its cost. See, Zara Jones Powers, ed., *Ancient Town Records: New Haven Town Records, 1684 - 1769* (1962), pp. 795 - 796.

Tim° Potter, John Martin, John Culver, Joel Tuttle, Sam¹ Bradly, Nath¹¹ Smith, Seth Blackslee, Phileman Heaton, Dan Peck and Isaac Munson be key keepers the year ensuing.

[p. 136] Sealer. John Miles Sealer of dry measures.

Branders. Voted Theop⁵ Munson, Gregson Gilbert, Abrᵐ Chidsey, Ephraim Humeston, Dan Peck, Jonathan Ives, Roger Peck and George Smith be branders of horses the year ensuing.

Swine. Voted that Swine going at large on Town Commons and highways, Shall not be Liable to be impounded from thence, Provided they are ringed all the year and Sufficiently yoaked from the 10th Day of march to the 10th Day of Decʳ Next.

Listers. Voted that Job Blackslee, John Barns, Job Munson, Titus Goodyear, Roger Peck, Nath¹ Tuttle, David Smith, Amos Thomas, Gurden Bradly, Dan Holt, Philemon Smith, Thomas Howel, James Rice, David Austin, Stephen Ford, Isaac Beers, Caleb Alling and Moses Pardee be Listers the year ensuing.

Tythingmen. Voted that Elihu Sperry, Abel Bishop, Thoˢ Pierpoint, Enos Brocket Jʳ, Abner Todd, Isaac Dickerman, Enos Atwater, Moses Atwater, Archibald Perkins, Aaron Mallery, Sam¹ Clinton, Elijah Perkins, Zacˢ Candee, Azel Kimberly, Jared Atwater, Amos Basset, Thoˢ Howel Jʳ, Stephen Ford & Nathan Oaks be Tythingmen the year ensuing. Also Joel Ford, Jabez Brown, Thoˢ Davis, Thadˢ Perrit, Josh Hemingway, Jesse Denison and Joˢ Peck be Tythingmen.

Agent. Voted that Mʳ Hillhouse be agent in behalf of this Town to defend &c against the Suit now depending in the County Court in favʳ of Capᵗ Joˢ Munson against the Town.¹

Agent. Voted that Mʳ Chauncy be agent in behalf of this Town to defend &c in the County Court in an action broᵗ by Benjⁿ Smith against the Town.

This meeting adjourned to the 6th Day of January Next at 2 °Clock in the afternoon.

[p. 137] Committee of inspection. Voted that Joseph Mansfield, Tiley Blackslee, Pe-

---

1. The suit likely pertained to a property issue.

ter Johnson, Thos Cooper J^r, John Heminway, Saml Candee, Erastus Bradly and Oliver Smith — be a Committee of inspection the year ensuing.

Constable. Voted that Jared Bradly be released from being Constable and John Heminway be Constable in his room.

Treas^{er}. Saml Bishop having been Town Treasurer for many years, desired to be released, on account of his bad state of health. Thereupon voted that he be released, with the Thanks of the Town, for his long Service in s^d office.[1]

Treas^{er}. Voted that David Austin Esqr be Town Treasurer the year ensuing.

Coll^r. Voted that Samuel Humaston J^r be Collector of the State Taxes in this Town the year ensuing.

allowance to Coll^r. Voted that s^d Samuel Humaston shall have paid unto him out of the Town Treasury ten Shillings on each Hundred pounds which he shall Collect out of the Town Treasury — for the sum he shall Collect of the rates.

Selectmen. Voted that Thomas Howel, Joel Gilbert, Jeremiah Atwater and Isaac Beers be released from being Selectmen.

Selectman. Voted that Elias Shipman be Selectman ye y^r ensuing.

Selectman. Voted that Jonathan Dickerman be released from being Selectman, and Daniel Bradly be Selectman in his room.

Bridge. Voted that the Selectmen Examine the acc^{ts} of Capt John Mix that have arisen in consequence of the rebuilding the bridge over the East river, and give orders on the Town Treasurer for what Sum they shall find Justly due to him and those with him that performed the work.[2]

[JANUARY 6, 1783]

[p. 138] AT A TOWN MEETING HOLDEN IN NEW HAVEN BY AD-JOURNMENT UPON THE 6TH DAY OF JANUARY 1783.

---

1. Bishop's illness helps to explain missing entries in the town records over the course of 1782.
2. East River ran parallel to present-day State Street in a southerly direction to where the Water Street bridge crosses the railroad. See, Osterweis, p. 486.

mod'. Voted that Tim° Jones Esq' be moderator.

Clerk. Voted that Henry Daggett Esq' be Clerk Pro Tem^us

Voted that this meeting be adjourned to the 13th Day of Instant January at 2 of the Clock Pm.

[JANUARY 13, 1783]

AT A TOWN MEETING HOLDEN IN NEW HAVEN BY ADJOURN-
MENT UPON THE 13TH DAY OF JANUARY 1783.

Voted that this meeting be adjourned to the 10th Day of Feby next at 2 ^OClock PM.

[FEBRUARY 10, 1783]

*[AT A TOWN MEETING HOLDEN IN NEW HAVEN BY ADJOURN-
MENT UPON THE 10TH DAY OF FEBRUARY 1783].*

Chidsey released from a fine. Voted that Abram Chidsey be released from paying his fine for refusing to Serve as a Grandjuryman the Last year.

Woodward released from his fine. Voted that John Woodward J' be released from paying his fine for refusing to serve as a Grandjuryman the Last year.

Michael Baldwin. M' Michael Baldwin Coll' of the State Taxes having Obtained Liberty from the Gen^ll assembly to appoint some Suitable person to assist him in Collecting the Taxes that are now unpaid, and that such person Sho^d be approved of by the Selectmen or by this Town — whereupon the Town do approve of M' Dudley Baldwin being appointed as above — and in Case s^d Dudley Baldwin Shall decline to Serve that the Selectmen be desired to approve of Some other Suitable person that s^d Michael Baldwin Shall nominate.

Lister. Voted y^t Phileman Smith *[be]* released from being Lister and that Sam^ll Sherman be lister in his room.

[p. 139] This meeting adj^d to the first Day of March next at 2 ^OClock Pm.

[MARCH 1, 1783]

AT A TOWN MEETING HELD IN NEW HAVEN BY ADJOURNMENT UPON THE FIRST DAY OF MARCH 1783.

Selectmen. Voted that Daniel Bradly be released from being Selectman and that Simeon Bristoll Esqr be Selectman in his room.

Grandjuryman. Voted that Joshua Austin be released from being Grandjuryman and that Azariah Bradly be Grandjuryman in his room.

Constable. Voted that Medad Atwater be released from being Constable and Abr^m Alling be Constable in his room.

poor. Voted that the Selectmen vendue the poor of the Town which are now Supported by the Town, so that they may be Supported in the cheapest manner.[1]

Tax. Voted that there be a rate or Tax or four pence on the pound on the present List to be Collected, for the necessary Charges of the Town, the year ensuing and that the same shall be paid on the first day of april next.

Coll^r. Voted that Capt John Mix be Coll^r or the s^d Tax in the room of Joel Atwater who refused to Serve.

Allowance to Coll^r. Voted that s^d John Mix shall have Collecting s^d Tax the Sum or thirty pounds paid out or the Town Treasury.

Grandjuryman. Voted that Enos Heminway be Grandjuryman in the room of Azariah Bradly.

Grandjury. Voted that Capt Nathan Smith be released from being Grandjuryman and John Johnson be Grandjuryman in his room.

[DECEMBER 8, 1783]

[p. 140] AT A TOWN MEETING HOLDEN IN NEW HAVEN UPON THE 8TH DAY OF DECEMBER AD 1783.

---

1. Under a vendue arrangement, care of the poor was put out to the lowest private bidder.

Clerk. Voted that Sam¹ Bishop be Town Clerk.

Modʳ. Voted that Roger Sherman Esqʳ be moderator.

Selectman. Voted that Messʳˢ Joseph Howel, John Austin, Abram Auger, Joseph Bradly, Isaac Chidsey, Sam¹ Candee, Noah Ives, Jesse Ford, Simeon Bristoll and Ezra Sperry be Selectmen the year ensuing.

Selectmen. Voted that there be three more Selectmen added to yᵉ above number viz. James Rice, Thoˢ Cooper Jʳ, and Michael Todd.

Constable. Voted that Samuel Humaston Jʳ be Constable and the Collector of the Country rates the year ensuing.

Constables. Voted that Abrᵐ Auger, Tiley Blackslee, Joseph Peck, Daniel Bradly, Nath¹ Smith, Dan Todd, Reuben Beecher, Jehiel Peck and David Thomas be Constables the year ensuing.

Grandjuryman. Voted yᵗ Timᵒ Atwater, David Mix, Daniel Bishop, John Lathrop, Jacob Daggett, Benjⁿ Woodin, John Miles Jʳ, Elisha Andrews, Jared Bradly, Josʰ Prindle, Silas Kimberly, Caleb Clark, Thomas Jacobs, Thomas Darling Jʳ, Elijah Perkins, Caleb Doolittle, Isaac Gilbert and Reuben Perkins be grandjuryman the year ensuing.

Treasʳ. Voted that David Austin Esqʳ be Town Treasurer the year ensuing.

Listers. Voted that Thomas Howel, James Rice, David Austin, Nath¹ Fitch, Isaac Beers, Henry Daggett, James Gilbert, Dan Holt, Gurdon Bradly, Zachⁿˢ Candee, Justus J Fitch, John Barns, Amos Thomas, David Smith, Job Munson, Titus Goodyear, Roger Peck, John Thomas, Caleb Alling, Medad Atwater and Silas Alling be listers the year ensuing.

[p. 141] Tythingmen. Voted that Hanover Barney, Thomas Howell Jʳ, Martin Parriot, Abrᵐ Alling, William Powel, Sam¹ Sheppard, Moses Heminway, John Beecher, David Trowbridge, Merrit Clark, Eli Todd, Hezʰ Tuttle 3ᵈ, Sam¹ Johnson, Ebenʳ Beecher, Isaac Dickerman, Amos Peck, Asa Goodyear, Aron Bradly, Moses Atwater, *[and]* John A. Talmadge be tything men the year ensuing.

Surveyers. Voted Russel Clark, Leveret Hubbard, James Rice, Jeremiah Atwater, Stephen Ford, Sam Dorman Jʳ, Sam¹ Candee, Medad Osborn, Daniel Alling,

Joseph Munson, Joshua Atwater, James Basset, Lemuel Hotchkis, Stephen Bristoll, and Thos Punderson be Surveyers of highways the year ensuing.

This meeting adjourned to Monday Next at one of the Clock in the afternoon.

[DECEMBER 15, 1783]

AT A TOWN MEETING HOLDEN IN NEW HAVEN BY ADJOURN-MENT UPON THE 15th DAY OF DECEMBER 1783.

Surveyers. Voted that Stephen Smith, Jacob Bradly, Sam^{ll} Holt, Tim^o Thompson, Azel Kimberly, Elijah Prindle, Joseph Tyler, Titus Bradly, John Smith, Caleb Clark, John Heaton, Hez^h Tuttle 3^d, Abr^m Blackslee, Saml Osborn, Stephen Peck, Enoch Newton, Saml Newton, Barn^s Baldwin, Eben^r Beech, Amos Peck, Jacob Atwater, Jonathan Dickerman, Daniel Beecher, Lamberton Toles, David French, Thos Johnson, Joel Wheeler, Elip^t Johnson, Saml Downs J^r, Jesse Gilbert, John Hubbard and Samuel Heminway be Surveyers of highways the year ensuing.

Districts. Voted that the Selectmen Give the districts to ye Surveyers of highways.

fence viewers. Voted y^t John Mix, Obed^h Hotchkis and Noah Potter be fence viewers the year ensuing.

[Leather sealer.] Voted y^t Stephen Bradly[1] be leather Sealer ye year ensuing.

[p. 142] Sealer of W^{ts} and meas^{es}. Voted that Israel Munson be Sealer of weights and measures the year ensuing.

Sealers. Voted y^t John Miles and Daniel Bradly be Sealers of dry measures the year ensuing.

Key Keepers. Voted that Joseph Munson, Noah Potter, Caleb Alling, John Peas J^r, Tim^o Potter, John Martin, John Culver, Nath^{ll} Barns J^r, Joel Tuttle, Nathl Smith, Azel Kimberly, Seth Blackslee, Thos Cooper J^r, Dan Peck, Ezra Munson and Benjn Gaylord J^r be key keepers the year ensuing.

pound. Voted that Matthew Gilbert have liberty to build *[a pound?]* and be the key keeper thereof.

---

1. Stephen Bradley (1723 - 1797) of East Haven.

Branders. Voted that Theo⁵ Munson, Gregson Gilbert, Abrᵐ Chidsey, Ephraim Humaston, Dan Peck, Jonathan Ives, Roger Peck and George Smith be branders of Horses the year ensuing.

Swine. Voted that Swine going at large on the Town Commons & highways *[are]* not liable to be impounded from thence, Provided they are Sufficiently ringed all the year, and yoaked from the 10ᵗʰ Day of March top the 10ᵗʰ Day of December Next.

Rates. Voted that there be a rate or Tax of four pence on the pound to be Collected of the inhabitants of this Town upon the present List to defray the Charge of the Town.

Voted that sad Rate be Collected the first Day of march next.

Collʳ. Voted that Samuel Humaston Jʳ be Collector of sᵈ rate.

Voted yᵗ this meeting be adjourned to the first monday of January next at one of the Clock in the afternoon.

[JANUARY 5, 1784]

[p. 143] AT A TOWN MEETING HELD IN NEW HAVEN BY ADJOURN-MENT, THE FIFTH DAY OF JANUARY 1784.

agents. Voted that Daniel Lyman, David Austin Esqʳˢ, and Mʳ James Hillhouse be agents to apply to the Genˡˡ assembly to be holden in this Town upon this instant January to obtain Some relief for those persons who Suffered by means of the enemies Plundering Town on the 5ᵗʰ Day of July 1779.¹

Selectmen. Voted that Mʳ John Austin be released from being Selectman and that Capᵗ Abel Burret be Selectman in his room and Stand the year ensuing.

Collʳ. Voted that Samuel Humaston Jʳ, who is Chosen Collʳ of the State Taxes the year ensuing, be paid out of the Town Ten Shilling*[s]* upon each Hundred pounds he shall Collect.

---

1. New Haven was one of several towns seeking state tax abatements on grounds that inhabitants had not fully recovered from the effects of enemy attacks.

Allowance to Coll'. Voted that Samuel Humaston J^r, who was Chosen Coll^r of the Town rate the Last meeting, shall have paid to him out of the Town Treasury ye Sum of thirty pounds for Collecting the Same.

Selectmen to Sell Land. Voted that the Selectmen be impowered and they are hereby impowered for the present year to make Sale of any lands that now doth or hereafter shall become the property of the Town, in Such way and Manner as they shall Judge will be for the interest of ye Town.[1]

Grandjuryman. Voted y^t John Lothrop be released from being Grand juryman, and that Silas merriman be Grandjuryman in his room and Stand the year ensuing.

incorporating the part of Town. Voted that the representatives of this Town in the Gen^{ll} assembly be requested to exert themselves that the act for incorporating a part of the Town of New Haven be passed with all Convenient Speed and that they be requested to promote and forward the Same accordingly.[2]

This meeting adj^{ed} without Day.

[MARCH 3, 1784]

[p. 144] AT A TOWN MEETING HOLDEN IN NEW HAVEN UPON THE 8TH DAY OF MARCH 1784.

Mod^r. Voted that Tim^o Jones Esqr be moderator.

Bridges. Voted that the Selectmen repair the bridge over ye East river called Morrisses long bridge in Such way and manner as they Judge best.[3]

Committee ab^t admitting inhabitants. On motion of Pierpoint Edwards Esqr &c. Voted that Pierpoint Edwards, John Whiting, David Austin, David Atwater, Saml Huggins, James Hillhouse, Jonathan Ingersoll and Jonathan Dickerman, be a committee to Consider of the Propriety and Expediency of admitting as inhabitants of this Town persons who in the Course of the Late war adherd to the cause of Great Britain against the united States and are of fair Characters and will be good and usefull members of Society and faithfull Citizens of this State,

---

1. Likely granted to the selectmen as a means to sell the confiscated estates of Loyalists.
2. The Connecticut Assembly passed a bill incorporating a portion of New Haven that roughly correlates with today's city limits as "The City of New Haven" on January 8, 1784.
3. Morris's Long Bridge spanned the Quinnipiac River into Fair Haven.

that s^d Committee report to this meeting.

Committees report. To the Town of New Haven in Town meeting assembled.

We your Committee appointed to Consider of the propriety and Expediency of admitting as inhabitants of this Town persons who in the Course of the late war have adherd to the cause of Great Britain against the united States and are fair Characters and will be good and usefull members of s^d Society and faithfull Citizens of this State beg leave to report — That by the federal Constitution of the united States each State as to its internal Police is Sovereign & independent to all purposes not Specially excepted in the articles of Confederation and the power of admitting. *[p. 145]* To inhabitancy is reserved unimpeached to each State liable to no Restrictions or Limitation but by its own municiple laws*[.]* That there is no law of this State y^t forbids the persons pointed out in the vote of the Town from Coming into or Dwelling therein*[.]* That by the express provisions of the Statutes of this State each Town has the excelusive right and power of admitting its inhabitants — That by the articles of the Definitive treaty and the Recommendations of Congress founded thereon a Spirit of real peace and Philanthro*[py]* towards our Countrymen of the aforesaid discription are most strongly inculeated*[.]* That as these united States by the blessing of Heaven Established their independence and Secured their Liberties on that basis to which their wishes and exertions were directed, and as the Great national Question on which those persons differed from us in Sentiment is terminated authoritatively in favor of ye united States it is our opinion y^t point of Law & Constitution it will be proper to admit as inhabitants of this Town Such persons as are Specifi*[ed]* in s^d vote — but that no persons who Committed unauthorized Lawless Plundering and murder or have waged war against these united States Contrary to the Laws and usuages of Civil *[...]^1* nations ought on any account to be admitted, with respect to the expediency of Such a measure*[.]* We beg leave to report that in our opinion no nation however Distinquished for prowess in arms and Success in war can be Considered as truely Great unless it is also Distinguished for Justice and magnanimity and no people can with the least propriety lay Claim to the Charrector of being Just who violate their most Solemn treatys or of being magnaimous who persecute a conquered and Submitting enemy, that therefore the present and future national Glory of the united States is Deeply Concerned in their conduct relative to persons discribed in s^d vote for altho at the present moment while the Distresses and Calamities of the Late war are fresh in our Recollection we may Consider a persecuting Spirit as Justifiable we must when reason

---

1. Intentional blank space.

assumes her empire reproach such a Line of Conduct and be Convinced y^t future generations not being influenced by our passions will from their Ideas of our Charrector from these acts which a faithful Historian Shall have recorded, and not from our passions of which they can have no History, That as this Town is [p. 146] is most advantagiously Situated for Commerce having [a] Spacious and Safe Harbour Surrounded by a very extensive & fertile Country which is inhabited by an industrious and enterprizing people fully Sensable of the advantages of trade — and as the relative and essential importance and consequence of this state depend on prosperity and Extent of its agriculture and Commerce Neither of which can alone render it important and happy, we are of the opinion y^t in point of real Honor & permanent utility the measure proposed will be highly expedient.

> John Whiting
> David Austin
> Jonathan Dickerman
> David Atwater
> Jonathan Ingersoll
> Pierp^t Edwards
> James Hillhouse
> Sam Huggins

Voted that the Town accept and approve the foregoing Report of Committee and that Town will admit as inhabitants thereof all persons by s^d Report recommended to be admitted and the Selectmen are directed their conduct towards Such persons accordingly.[1]

[Remaining half page is blank]

[DECEMBER 13, 1784]

[p. 147] AT A TOWN MEETING HOLDEN IN NEW HAVEN ON THE 13TH DAY OF DECEMBER ANNO DOM 1784.

Clerk. Voted y^t Saml Bishop be Town Clerk.

Mod^r. Voted y^t Tim° Jones Esqr be moderator.

---

1. New Haven's vote to welcome former Loyalists was both an effort to move beyond the partisan animosities of the Revolution as well as an attempt to attract investors to the city and in an effort to boost New Haven's aspirations to become a major commercial seaport.

Selectmen. Voted y^t James Rice, Abel Burret, Michael Todd, Abr^m Auger, Isaac Chidsey, Saml Candee, Simeon Bristoll, Thomas Cooper and John Hubbard be Selectmen the year ensuing.

Constables. Voted that Tiley Blackslee, Joseph Peck, Hiel Peck,[1] Saml Humaston J^r, Isaac Forbs, Jared Barns, Jonathan Tuttle, Philemon Smith and George Bristoll be Constables the year ensuing.

Grand jurymen. Voted that Peter Johnson, John C Ogden, Benjn Woodin, Joel Gilbert, Henry Peck, Eliz^r Goodrich, Levi Hubbard, Philemon Potter, Nathl Barny Jr., Dan Holt, Silas Kimberly, Elijah Prindle, Tim° Andrews, Abel Bishop, Alvan Bradly and Amos Peck be Grandjurymen the Year ensuing.

Surveyers. Voted y^t Stephen Ball, James Rice, Abel Burret, Elias Stilwell, Jacob Dagget, Abram Hemingway, Medad Atwater, Isaac Beers, Levi Pardee, Danl Tuttle, Zac^s Candee, Tim° Andrews, Caleb Clark, Joel Blackslee, Saml Bellamy and Jonathan Ives Ju^r be Surveyers of highways the year ensuing.

Surveyers. Voted y^t Russel Clark, Leveret Hubbard, Thomas Rice, Jeremiah Atwater, Stephen Ford, Saml Dorman, Saml Cooper, Medad Osborn, Dan^ll Alling, Joseph *[p. 148]* Munson, Joshua Atwater, James Bassett, Lem^l Hotchkis, Thomas Punderson, Abel Potter, Dan^ll Talmadge J^r, Phileman Auger, Saml Davenport, James Chidsey, Stephen Thompson, Saml Holt, John Beecher, Oliver *[...]*, Isaiah Brocket, Joseph Bradly J^r, Bethuel Todd, Gideon Todd, Benjn Pierpoint, Titus Tharp, Joseph Tyler, Glover Ball, Chauncy Dickerman, David Granis, John Perkins, Noah Wolcot J^r be Surveyers of highways the year ensuing.

Tythingmen. Voted that Gregson Gilbert, Martin Parsit, Persons Clark, David Atwater J^r, Jabez Turner, Hez^h Auger, Job Previl, Abr^m Barns, John Morris, Justus Smith, Nathl Smith, Jonathan Tuttle, John Heaton, David Barns, Enoch Ray, Hez^h Warner, Joel Hough, Jesse Dickerman, Abr^m Blackslee J^r be Tythingmen the year ensuing.

Coll^r. Voted y^t Samuel Humaston J^r be Collector of the State Taxes the year ensuring.

Treas^r. Voted that David Austin Esqr be Town Treas^r the year ensuing.

---

1. Heil Peck of Wallingford. See, 1790 U.S. Census, M637; Roll: 1; Page: 166; Image: 232; Family History Library Film: 0568141.

Key Keepers. Voted that Joseph Munson, Noah Potter, Caleb Alling, Nathan Dumer,[1] Tim° Potter, John Martin, John Culver, Nath¹ Barns Jʳ, Dan¹ Tuttle, Nath¹ Smith, Azel Kimberly, Seth Blakeslee, Thomas Cooper Jʳ, Ebnʳ Beech and Benjⁿ Gaylor Jʳ be key keepers the year ensuing.

pound. Voted that Joel Blackslee have Liberty to build a pound and be key keeper of yᵉ Same.

Leather Sealer. Voted yᵗ Stephen Bradly be Leather Sealer the year ensuing.

[p. 149] Sealer. Vote that Theopˢ Munson be Sealer of wᵗˢ and measures.

Bridge. Voted yᵗ a Sum not exceeding thirty shillings be paid out annually for Supporting a bridge over muddy river between the mills belonging to Joseph Pierpoint Esqʳ and James Pierpoint and others.[2]

Committee abᵗ Cannon. Voted that Messʳˢ Stephen Ball, Jeremiah Atwater, Isaac Doolittle, James Gilbert and James Rice be a Committee to enquire concerning the Cannon brought to this City from New York by Thomas Ives &c and make report at the adjᵉᵈ meeting.[3]

This meeting adjourned untill the Last monday of instant Decʳ at one of the Clock in yᵉ afternoon.

[DECEMBER 27, 1784]

AT A TOWN MEETING HOLDEN IN NEW HAVEN BY ADJOURN-MENT ON THE 27ᵀᴴ DAY OF DECEMBER AD 1784.

Tax. Voted that there be a Town rate of Eight pence on the pound on the present List, to be Collected of the inhabitants of the Town for defraying the necessary Charges of the Town — and to be paid on the first Day of march next.

Collʳ. Voted that Samuel Humaston Juʳ be Collector of the above rate.

---

1. Nathan Dummer (ca. 1730 - 1813). Possibly known as Nathaniel, who was wounded during the British invasion of New Haven in 1779.
2. Muddy River feeds into the Quinnipiac River in North Haven.
3. New York loaned New Haven cannon for its defense in 1776. See, Osterweis, pp. 132 - 133.

Small pox. Voted that Doct[r] Lewis Morgan[1] of the City of New Haven have Liberty and permission is hereby granted to s[d] Lewis Morgan to Communicate the Small pox by inoculation under the Direction of the Civil authority and Selectmen of s[d] Town of New Haven.

Allowance to Coll[r]. Voted that Samuel Humaston J[r] be allowed thirty pounds out of the Town Treasury for Collecting the Town rate.

[Selectman.] Voted that Thomas Cooper be released from being Selectman and y[t] Ephraim Humaston be Selectman in his room.

[p. 150] Surveyers. Voted that David Atwater J[r] and David Munson J[r] be Surveyers of highways the year ensuing.

Surveyer. Voted that Joshua Atwater be released from being Surveyer of highways and y[t] Eben[r] Gills be Surveyer of highways the year ensuing.

Surveyers. Voted that Col Hubbard be released from being Surveyer of highways and y[t] Joseph Howel be Surveyer of hignway[s] in his room the year ensuing.

Surveyors. Voted that Sam[ll] Cooper be released from being Surveyer of highways and that Gregson Gilbert be Surveyer of highways the year ensuing.

Grandjurymen. Voted y[t] Tim[o] Andrews be released from being Grandjuryman and that Elias Beech be Grandjury man in his room the year ensuing.

Guns. Voted y[t] Mess[rs] Jeremiah Atwater, Stephen Ball, James Rice, and Hez[h] Sabin J[r], be a Committee to examine further with regard to the great guns bro[t] from New york and do what they Judge is Needfull to be done with regard to them so as to Save the Town from any Cost and Charge relative thereto.[2]

This meeting adj[d] without Day.

[FEBRUARY 28, 1785]

AT A TOWN MEETING HOLDEN IN NEW HAVEN UPON THE TWENTY EIGHTH DAY OF FEB 1785.

---

1. Possibly Dr. Lewis Morgan, who eventually settled in Woodbridge, NJ.
2. Settling payment for New York's cannon was not completed by the Connecticut Legislature until 1789. See, *PRSC, Vol.* 6, p. 511.

that part of said Town who formerly belonged to s^d Town of New Haven from all the State rates due to the State Collectors of New Haven, and unpaid at this Tine which otherwise they would be Compelled to pay Provided said Town of woodbridge shall by vote agree to pay all the State rates due from the inhabitants of s^d Town to the Several Collectors of New Haven together with 1% on every £100 for Collecting ye Same and indemnife said Town of New Haven from all Losses that may happen through non payment of said Taxes.

[p. 152] East Haven Town. Voted that the inhabitants of the parish of East Haven be made into a distin*[c]*t and Separate Town they taking their part and proportion of the benefits and burdens of the Town according to their list the Division to be made by a disinterested and Judicious Committee to be appointed by the Gen^{ll} assembly.[1]

North Haven. Voted that the inhabitants of the parish of North Haven be made into a distin*[c]*t and Seperate Town they taking their part and proportion of the Benefits and burdins of the Town according to their List, the Division to be made by a disinterested and Judicious Committee to be appointed by the Gen^{ll} Assembly.

M^{t}Carmel. Voted that the inhabitants of the parish of mount Carmel and y^t part of the inhabitants of the First Society in New Haven y^t are included within the lines of the 17th Regiment Company in the 2^d regiment be made into a Distinct and Separate Town they taking their part and proportion of the Benefits ana Burdens of the Town according to their list, the Division to be made by a disinterested Committee to be appointed by the Gen^{ll} Assembly.[2]

Small pox. Voted that Doct^r Lewis Morgan be placed in ye Same situation with regard to his Small pox hospital with Doct^r Munson if he Should pursue his inoculation and the Selectmen are directed to inform him that the Town expect a Complyance with this vote.[3]

---

1. The General Assembly voted in favor of East Haven's incorporation as a separate town in May, 1785. *PRSC,* Vol. 6: 69.
2. The General Assembly agreed to the creation of the town of Hamden in May, 1785. *PRSC,* Vol. 6: 200 - 201. In their petition to the General Assembly, Hamden inhabitants spoke for most of outlying owns that they were predominantly farmers versus New Haven's growing mercantile class who dominated town meetings. See, Rachel M. Hartley, *The History of Hamden Connecticut 1786 - 1759* (1959), pp. 89 - 90.
3. Dr. Munson finally opened such a hospital in 1792 with Dr. Levi Ives.

Woodbridge bounds. Voted that Sam[l] Bishop, David Austin, Simeon Bristoll, Tim[o] Jones and Henry Daggett Esq[rs] be a Committee to Settle fix and Establish the bounds between this Town and the Town of woodbridge, with Such Committee as s[d] Town of woodbridge shall appoint for that purpose.

[Woodbridge Committee.] Voted that Sam[l] Bishop, David Austin, Simeon Bristoll, Tim[o] Jones and Henry Daggett Esq[rs] be a Committee to Settle the accounts of this Town & ~~will~~ y[e] Town of woodbridge with such Committee as y[t] Town shall appoint for that purpose.

[p. 153.] [Top quarter page of records is blank]

[December 12, 1785]

AT A TOWN MEETING HOLDEN IN NEW HAVEN UPON THE 12TH DAY OF DECEMBER.AD 1785.

Mod[r]. Voted that Tim[o] Jones Esq[r] be moderator.

Clerk. Voted that Sam[l] Bishop be Town Clerk.

Selectmen. Voted that Mess[rs] James Rice, Abel Burrit, Abr[m] Auger, Joseph Bradly, Sam[l] Candee, Simeon Bristoll, Ephraim Humaston, John Hubbard, and Sam[l] Mix be Selectmen the year ensuing.

Constables. Voted that Jonas Prentice, Tiley Blackslee, Sam[l] Humaston J[r], Joseph Peck, Burwell Smith, Giles Brocket, Jos[h] Bradly J[r], and George Bristoll be Constables the year ensuing.

Coll[r]. Voted that Samuel Humaston J[r] be Collector of the State Taxes the year ensuing.

Grandjury men. Voted y[t] Sam[l] Darling, Will[m] Hillhouse, Phileman Potter, Levi Hubbard, Phileman Smith, John Jones, Hez[h] Tuttle, Elias Beech, Eli Sacket, and Samuel Atwater J[r] be Grandjurymen the year ensuing.

Listers. Voted that Stephen Ball, James Rice, Abel Burret, Elias Stillwell, Jacob Dagget, Medad Atwater, Will[m] Lyon, Will[m] Powel, Abram Alling, Nath[l] Smith, Elijah Prindle, Tim[o] Andrews, Joel Blackslee, Caleb Clark, Abel Bishop, Levi Ray, Sam[l] Bellamy, Jonath[n] Ives J[r] and Benjamin Gaylor J[r] be Listers the year ensuing.

[p. 154] Surveyers. Voted that Sam¹ Hurnaston Jʳ, John Hubbard, Thomas Rice, Nathˡˡ Fitch, Thomas Mix, Stephen Ball, Joel Ford, Ebenʳ Hitchcock Jʳ, Elnathan Toles, Glover Ball, John *[...]¹*, Nathˡˡ Downs, Giles Pierpoint, John Barns, Jonathan Barns, Lawrence Clinton, Seth Todd, Enoch Jacobs, Isaac Tuttle, Moses Thorpe Jʳ be Surveyers of highways.

Tythingmen. Voted that Sacket Gilbert, Adonijah Sherman, Lem¹ Hotchkis, Isaac Townsend, Daniel Talmadge Jʳ, Asa Austin, Zachaniah Reed, Justus Smith, Elijah Prindle, Oliver Smith, James Humaston, John Heaton, Caleb Blackslee, Abrᵐ Blackslee, Calvin Mallery and Elisha Atwater be Tythingmen the year ensuing.

Districts. Voted that the Selectmen give the Districts to the Surveyers of highways. *Treasʳ.* Voted that David Austin be Town Treasurer the year ensuing.

agent. Voted that David Austin Esqʳ be agent in the Name and behalf of this Town to appear and answer in all actions that are or shall be broᵗ in favor of the Town or in any action broᵗ against the Town the year ensuing.

Key Keepers. Voted that Joseph Munson, Noah Potter, Caleb Alling, Nathan Dumer, Tim° Potter, John Martin, John Culver, Nath¹ Smith, Azel Kimberly, Seth Blackslee, Thomas Cooper Jʳ, Asa Goodyear Jʳ, Ebenʳ Beech, Benʲ Gaylor Jʳ, and Joel Blackslee be key keepers the year ensuing.

Leather Sealer. Voted yᵗ Stephen Bradly be Leather sealer the year ensuing.

Sealer [of weightss & measures]. Voted that Theopˢ Munson be sealer of weights and measᵉˢ.

Poor Supported. Voted yt Sam¹ Bishop Esqʳ, Simeon Bristoll and David Austin Esqʳ, James Rice, Abel Burret, Abrᵐ Auger, John Hubbard, Joseph Bradly, Sam¹ Candee, Ephriam Humaston, Job Potter, Eneas Munson Esqʳ, Neʰ Smith Esqʳ, Giles Pierpoint, Caleb Alling, Sam¹ Mix and Jesse Todd be a Committee to enquire into yᵉ present method of Supporting yᵉ poor, their number, & expense. *[p. 155]* The propriety of Collecting them together, the best place and persons to take Charge of them, and what may be yᵉ expence and make report at the adjourned meeting.

Swine. Voted that Swine going at large on the highways and Town Commons, Shall not be liable to be impounded from thence, Provided they are ringed all the year

---

1. left blank.

and Sufficiently yoaked from the 10th of march to ye 10th Day of December next. This meeting adjourned to the last monday of instant Decr at 2 of the Clock in the afternoon.

[DECEMBER 26, 1785]

AT A TOWN MEETING HOLDEN BY ADJOURNMENT UPON THE 26^H DAY OF DECEMBER 1785.

Constable. Voted y^t John Chandler be Constable in the room of Jonas Prentice.

Grandjuryman. Voted y^t Justus Smith be Grandjuryman in the room of Phileman Smith.

Lister. Voted that Abr^m Bishop be lister in the room of Abel Burnet.

Selectman. Voted that Eben^r Townsend be Selectman in the room of Abel Burrit.

Selectman. Voted y^t Deacon Ball be Selectman in the room of James Rice.

Lister. Voted y^t Elias Shipman be lister the year ensuing.

Tax. Voted there be a rate or Tax of Six pence on the pound on the present list, Collected of the inhabitants of the Town by the 15th Day of January next for defraying the necessary Charges of the Town the year ensuing.

Coll^r. Voted that John Hubbard be Collector of s^d rate.

[p. 156] [Committee about Poor.] The Committee appointed the Last Town meeting to enquire into the present method of Supporting the poor &c made their report to this meeting in the Following words viz.

To the inhabitants of the Town of New Haven to be Conven^{ed} in Town meeting on the 26th Day of instant Decr by adjournment.

Committees report about poor. We the Subscribers being appointed a Committee at your meeting holden in New Haven Decr 12, 1785 to enquire into the present method of Supporting the poor their Number and expense the propriety of Collecting them together the best place and persons to take Care of them and what may be the Expense and report make.

On Consideration of s^d matters we beg leave to report y^t we find the Number who receive Support from the Town to be 37, and that ye expense of Supporting them amounts to about £12.0.0 a p^r week exclusive of Doct^{rs} Bills and Cloathing — That to Collect the poor and have them Supported at one place would be much Cheaper for the Town, and by examining into ye State & Circumstances of each person we are of the opinion y^t it would be best y^t ye Selectmen Should Collect the following persons to one place, to be kept viz. Ichabod Barns's Child, Sarah Humphrevile, widow Fryer and the two Childern Eben^r Wilmont, Oliver Bradlys Child, And^r Reed, Sarah Dawson, Jane Harrison, John Melone, John McKensey, Jerome Smith, Wid^w Culver, Abigail Tuttle, Eunice Mansfield, Enos Blackslee, Mercy Parker,[1] widow Kimberly, wid^w Wild, Joel Alling, Stephen Beecher and Tim^o Thomas, Provided Nevertheless if the Selectmen find y^t the persons who keep any of them or any other person will appear to keep either of them at Such price as they Shall Judge will be for the interest of the Town not to remove them in that Case they are not to be removed we having had Conversation with Simeon Bristoll Esq^{r2} about taking those persons which Shall be [p. 157] Collected together, and make provision for them he hath informed y^t he Should be willing to make ye trial for this winter y^t he hath a Convenient house about two miles west of his Dwelling house where wood is very plenty y^t he wo^d provide for them all that wo^d be needfull for their Comfortable Support and in the Spring of the year lay before the Selectmen his account of Supporting them and Receive Such allowance as they should Judge Just and reasonable, which proposals we are of the opinion is best should be Complyed with we are informed y^t Doct^r Chapman[3] of Mt Carmel would visit those persons as a Doct^r whenever it sho^d be needfull Gratis.

Signed by order

Decr 26, 1785   Saml Bishop Chairman

The foregoing report of the Committee being read and Considered — Thereupon Voted that the Same be accepted — and y^t ye Selectmen shall take the foregoing report as their rule for Supporting the poor who are maintained by the Town.

[Rate.] Voted that the Town will give Twenty pounds to the person who shall Collect the Town rate.

---

1. Possibly Mercy Parker (1731 - 1795) of North Haven. Jacobus, *Ancient Families of New Haven*, Vol. 6, No. 2, p. 1376.

2. Simeon Bristol (1738 - 1805) is buried at the Mt. Carmel Burying Ground.

3. Possibly Dr. Elisha Chapman (1750 - 1819). He lived in Hamden, North Haven, and finally New Haven before moving to Marcellus, NY in 1806.

Coll^r. Voted that Sam^{ll} Humaston Junr be Collector of the Town rate in the room of John Hubbard who refused to Serve.

west Haven. The inhabitants of the Society of West Haven with those who live in the first Society west of the West river preferred their memorial to this meeting requesting y^t this Town would shew their willingness y^t they sho^d have Town priviledges Granted to them, this meeting having taken into Consideration s^d memorial do by vote express their willingness y^t s^d memorilest sho^d have Town priviledges granted to them by ye Honble *[p. 158]* General Assembly — adj^d without day.[1]

[AUGUST 14, 1786]

AT A TOWN MEETING HOLDEN IN NEW HAVEN UPON THE 14TH DAY OF AUG^T 1786.

Mod^r. Voted that David Austin be moderator.

Selectmen to Call Coll^{rs} to account. Voted that the Selectmen be requested to examine and enquire whether the Town is in Danger of Suffering from the neglect or misconduct of any of those Collectors of State Taxes who have not Settled with the Treasurer and y^t they take the most Effectual measures to Secure the Town from Such Losses and that they lay before the Town at their next meeting an Estimate of the Sums they Suppose necessary to discharge the Taxes of Such persons as are unable to pay and are thereby in danger of bringing expences on the Town.[2]

Adjourned without day.

[DECEMBER 11, 1786]

AT A TOWN MEETING HOLDEN IN NEW HAVEN UPON THE 11TH DAY OF DECEMBER 1786.

Clerk. Saml Bishop Chosen Town Clerk.

Mod^r. Tim° Jones Esqr Chosen moderator.

---

1. West Haven's request for town status was not approved by the Connecticut General Assembly. *PRSC,* Vol 6. *passim.*
2. Concern over the payment of state taxes may have arisen from the recent division of New Haven into several towns and the ongoing negotiations concerning tax obligations among those towns.

Selectmen. Voted that Messrs Stephen Ball, Eben^r Townsend, Elizer Goodrich, Joseph Bradly, Saml Candee, Thaddeus Beecher, and Levi Ives be Selectmen the year ensuing.

Selectman. Voted that Eben^r Townsend be released from being Selectman and Elias Beers[1] be Selectman in his room.

Selectman. Voted y^t Jos^h Bradly be released from being Selectman, and Isaac Beers be Selectman in his room.

Constables. Voted y^t Tilley Blackslee, Joseph Peck, and Jonas Prentice and Sam^{ll} B. Smith be Constables the year ensuing.

[p. 159] Coll. Voted that Jonas Prentice be Collector of the State Taxes the year ensuing.

Grandjurymen. Voted that Dyar White, Jeremiah Atwater, David Dagget, Richard Cutlar, Saml Darling, David Austin J^r, Jared Thompson, Josiah Burr and Justus Smith, be Grandjurymen the year ensuing.

Tythingmen. Voted that John Peck, Lem^l Hotchkis, Peter Read, Job Perrit, Nathaniel Smith and Oliver Smith be Tythingmen the year ensuing.

Survey^{rs}. Voted that Jeremiah Atwater, Joseph Howel, Josiah Burr, Peter Johnson, Thomas Rice, Mark Levenworth, Joseph Munson, Erastus Bradly, Joseph Prindle, Nathan Smith J^r, Glover Ball, Silas Alling and William Sperry be Surveyers of highways the year ensuing.

Leather Sealer. Voted that Stephen Bradly be leather sealer the year ensuing.

Sealer. Voted that John Miles be Sealer of dry measures the year ensuing.

Listers. Voted that Stephen Ball, James Rice, William Lyon, Elias Stilwell, Abraham Bishop, Jacob Dagget, Peter Read, Elias Shipman and Nath^{ll} Smith be listers the year ensuing.

Key keepers. Voted that Joseph Munson, Nathan Dumer, Noah Potter, John Martin and John Culver be key keepers the year ensuing.

---

1. Elias Beers (1746 - 1832) was the brother of Isaac Beers (1742 - 1813).

Swine. Voted that Swine going at large on the highways and Commons Shall not be liable to be impounded from thence, Provided they are ringed all the year, and Sufficiently yoaked from the 10ᵗʰ Day of march next, to the 10ᵗʰ Day of Decʳ next.

[p. 160] Committee to Settle accᵗˢ with other Towns. Voted that Timothy Jones, Samˡ Bishop, David Austin, and Chaˢ Chauncy Esqʳˢ, and Deacon Stephen Ballˡ be a Committee to Settle with the Towns of Hamden & North Haven with regard to the public interest to divide the poor of the Town, and agree with them about the bridges, and in Case they Cannot make a full Settlement relative to the matters aforesaid and in case they do not agree in any of the particular matters above mentioned, they are directed to appear before the Committee appointed by the Genˡˡ assembly when the Above Towns were incorporated, and do what is needfull in behalf of this Town relative to the matters aforesaid.[2]

[Treasurer]. Voted that David Austin Esqʳ be Town Treasurer the year ensuing.

Committee abᵗ poor. Voted that Henry Daggett, John Goodrich, Peter Johnson, James Hillhouse, Mark Levenvworth, Josiah Burr, Elijah Austin and Jeremiah Atwater be a Committee to Consider in what manner its best to Support the poor of this Town, and report their opinion thereon to the next meeting.

This meeting adjourned to the ~~first~~ 25ᵗʰ day of Instant ~~January~~ Decʳ at 2 of the Clock in yᵉ afternoon.

[DECEMBER 28, 1786]

AT A TOWN MEETING HOLDEN IN NEW HAVEN DECEMBER 28, 1786.

Collʳ. Voted that Capᵗ Jonas Prentice be Collector of the Town rate the year ensuing.

Voted that this meeting be adjourned to the first day of January next at 2 of the Clock in the afternoon.*[3]

1. Stephen Ball (1726 - 1799) was deacon of the First Church in New Haven from 1771 - 1799.
2. The General Assembly appointed a committee to settle these issues. See, *PRSC,* Vol. VI: 264 - 265.
3. The town clerk noted on the following page that the meeting of December 28 was mistakenly recorded before the town meeting of December 25, which follows on the next page.

[JANUARY 1, 1787]

[p. 161] AT A TOWN MEETING HOLDEN IN NEW HAVEN BY AD-
JOURNMENT ON THE FIRST DAY OF JANUARY 1787.

Grandjuryman. Voted that John Atwater be Grandjuryman in the room of Jeremiah Atwater.

Lister. Voted y^t Isaac Jones be lister the year ensuing.

Coll^rs allowance. Voted that ye Selectmen be desired to make such allowance to M^r
Joseph Peck and Capt Jonas Prentice, Collectors of ye State Taxes as they Shall
Judge Just and reasonable for Collecting ye State Taxes over and above what y^e
State allows for Collecting.

allowance for Coll^r. Voted that the Selectmen make a reasonable allowance to Capt
Prentice for Collecting ye Town rate the year ensuing.

rate. Voted y^t there be a rate or Tax of Eight pence on the pound ~~on the pound~~
upon the present List Collected of the inhabitants of the Town, for defraying
the necessary Charges thereof to be paid on the First Day of Feby next.

payment of Taxes. Voted that the Selectmen of the Town of New Haven as soon
as possable call upon ye Selectmen of the Several Towns of Woodbridge[,] East
Haven[,] Hamden and North Haven and desire a meeting may be of ye s^d Selectmen to devise the best methods for the Collection and payment of the Taxes
due from s^d Towns which arrived while they all were parts of the Town of New
Haven and pursue the Speedy payment of Such Taxes.

*The votes of the following ~~votes~~ meeting ought to have been Recorded before
ye meeting of ye 28th Decr on ye other leaf See y^e *.[1]

[DECEMBER 25, 1786][1]

[p. 162] AT A TOWN MEETING OF THE TOWN OF NEW HAVEN
HOLDEN BY ADJOURNMENT AT THE STATE HOUSE IN S^D NEW
HAVEN ON THE 25^H DAY OF DEC^R AD 1786.

---

1. The December 25, 1786 meeting is out of chronological order likely due to Bishop's absence. It
should precede the December 28, 1786 meeting as noted on the previous page.

Mod[r]. Timothy Jones Esq[r] was moderator.

Clerk PT. Sam[l] Bishop Esq[r] being absent Elizer Goodrich[1] was Chosen & Sworn Town Clerk Pro Tempore.

Selectman. M[r] Jeremiah Atwater was duely appointed Selectman for the year ensuing. *Lister.* M[r] James Prescot was duely appointed one of the listers for s[d] Town for the year ensuing.

Grandjuror. Thaddeus Clark was appointed grandjuror for the year ensuing and Justus Smith was excused from the office of Grandjuryman and Jesse Stevens was appointed Grandjuryman for the year ensuing in the stead of Justus Smith.

Tythingman. Azel Kimberly was appointed Tythingman for the year ensuing in the stead of Oliver Smith who was Excused from s[d] office.

Surveyers. Nehemiah Smith and Gamaliel Benham were appointed Surveyers of highways for the year ensuing in the stead of Silas Kimberly and Joseph Prindle[2] who were by s[d] meeting excused from office.

Selectman. Cap[t] Nathan Smith[3] was duely appointed Selectman for the year ensuing in the stead of Cap[t] Samuel Candee who was by s[d] meeting excused from s[d] office.

Lister. Elijah Prindle was appointed Lister for the year ensuing.

Tythingman. Cap[t] Medad Osborn was appointed Tythingman for the year ensuing.

[p. 163] The meeting was adjourned untill the first day of Jan[ry] next to meet at the State house at 2 °Clock *[in the]* afternoon on s[d] Day.

Attest Eli[zr] Goodrich Town Clerk Pro Tempore

---

1. Elizur Goodrich (1761 - 1849) graduated from Yale in 1779, was wounded while defending the town during the British invasion of that same year, and went on to an illustrious career as a lawyer and public servant, including a stint in Sixth and Seventh U.S. Congresses. See, *Biographical Directory of the United States Congress, 1774 - Present*, http://bioguide.congress.gov/scripts/biodisplay. pl?index=G000294.
2. Joseph Prindle (1732 - 1814) was a Loyalist during the Revolution whose sons allegedly provided fresh provisions and intelligence to the British during the invasion of New Haven. See, Peter J. Malia, *Visible Saints, West Haven, Connecticut, 1648 - 1798* (2009), p 234.
3. Captain Nathan Smith (1724 - 1798) was a Revolutionary War veteran and native of Derby, CT. DAR, *Report of the Daughters of the American Revolution* (1904), p. 394.

[FEBRUARY 12, 1787]

AT A TOWN MEETING HOLDEN IN NEW HAVEN UPON THE 12TH DAY OF FEB 1787.

Mod[r]. Voted that Tim° Jones Esq[r] be moderator.

Coll[r]. Voted that Cap[t] Peter Johnson be Collector of the Town rate in the room of Cap[t] Prentice who refused to Serve.

Constable. Voted that Cap[t] Peter Johnson be Constable and Collector of the State Taxes in Stead of Cap[t] Prentice who refused to Serve.

This meeting adj[d] without day.

[SEPTEMBER 3, 1787]

AT A TOWN MEETING HOLDEN IN NEW HAVEN UPON THE 3[D] TUESDAY OF SEP[R] 1787.

Mod[r]. Voted that David Austin Esq[r] be moderator.

This meeting adjourned to the first day of oct[r] next at four of the Clock in the afternoon.

[OCTOBER 1, 1787]

AT A TOWN MEETING HOLDEN IN NEW HAVEN UPON THE FIRST DAY OF OCT[R] 1788 BY ADJOURNMENT.

Constable. Cap[t] Peter Johnson being Chosen Constable and Collector of the State Taxes the present year refused to Serve — thereupon Voted y[t] Cap[t] John R. Throop[1] be Constable and Coll[r] in the room of s[d] Johnson.

[Constitution.] Voted that this Town do request their representatives at the next Gen[ll] assembly to use their influence to obtain *[p. 164]* a Convention as Speedily as possible for the purpose of taking into Consideration the Constitution

---

1. John R. Throop (1755? - 1808) served as an officer in the Connecticut militia during the Revolution. William S. Wells, *op. cit.*, p. 109.

recommended by the Convention of the States.[1]

This meeting adj^d without day.

[NOVEMBER 2, 1787]

Delegates. At a meeting of the Town of New Haven holden in New Haven on the 2^d monday of Novr 1788 agreeable to a Resolve of the Gen^{ll} assembly in Octr Last, directing each Town in the State to make Choice of Delegates to attend at Hartford in the Convention directed by s^d assembly, to be holden on the 5th Thursday of January next, to take into Consideration the Constitution lately made by the Convention of the united States at Philadelphia, This Town by Vote made Choice of the Honble Roger Sherman & Pierpoint Edwards Esq^{rs} *[as]* delegates to attend s^d Convention for the purpose aforesaid.[2]

This meeting adj^d without day.

[DECEMBER 10, 1787]

AT A TOWN MEETING HOLDEN IN NEW HAVEN UPON THE 10TH DAY OF DECEMBER 1787.

Clerk. Voted that Saml Bishop be Town Clerk.

Mod^r. Voted that Tim^o Jones be moderator.

Selectmen. Voted y^t Messrs Stephen Ball, Elias Beers, Nathan Smith, Levi Ives, Zina Denison,[3] Isaac Beers, Nathan Smith and Erastus Bradly be Selectmen the year ensuing.

Constable. Voted that Joseph Peck, John R. Throop, Jonas Prentice, and Burrel Smith be Constables the year ensuing.

---

1. The Constitutional Convention took place on May 14 to September 17, 1787 in Philadelphia to address a series of governing issues that had developed under the Articles of Confederation. The eventual result of this meeting was the creation of the United States Constitution.
2. Connecticut's constitutional convention was held from January 3 - 9, 1788. While no official records of its proceedings are known to exist, New Haven delegates were said to have voted in favor of the U.S. Constitution, as reported in the local press. *PRSC*, VI: 550 - 573.
3. Zina Denison (1749 - 1789) of New Haven was the husband of Martha Austin (? - 1833).

[p. 165] Coll. Voted y^t John R. Throop be Collector of ye State Taxes the year ensuing.

Listers. Voted that Stephen Ball, Elias Shipman, Isaac Jones, Wm Lyon, Elizur Goodrich, Elias Stilwell, James Rice, Jeremiah Smith, Merit Clark, Elijah Austin & Jacob Dagget be Listers the year ensuing.

Tythingmen. Voted that Daniel Hubbard, John Peck, Luther Fitch, Daniel Crocker, Hartham Ramsdal,¹ Eli Hotchkis, Sam^{ll} Clark, Jared Mansfield, Thomas Smith and Elijah Alling be tythingmen the year ensuing.

Leather Sealer. Votec that Stephen Bradly be leather Sealer the year ensuing.

Sealer. Voted that John Miles be Sealer of dry measures the year ensuing.

Sealer W^{ts}. Voted that Theop^s Munson and Eben^r Chitterden² be Sealers of weights and measures the year ensuing.

Branders. Voted that Israel Munson, Stephen Osborn and Jeremiah Smith be branders of horses ye year ensuing.

Trea^r. Voted that David Austin Esqr be Town Treasurer the year ensuing.

Tax. Voted that this Town will repair their highways by Town Tax.

Tax. Voted that there be a Tax of one penny on the pound on the present List for repairing the highway the year ensuing.

Voted that s^d Tax shall be paid by the first day of april next.

Tax. Voted that there be a Tax of Eight pence on the pound on the present List for defraying the Charges of the Town.³

1. Harthan Ramsdell (1754 - 1823) was a native of Lynn, MA, and member of First Church in New Haven. He moved his family of 10 to Woodbridge by 1800. See, Jacobus, Vol VI, No. 4:1499; *1800 United States Federal Census*, https://www.ancestry.com/search/categories/35/?name=Harthan_Ramsdale&birth=1754_Lynn-MA&name_x=1_1
2. Ebenezer Chitterden (1726 - 1812) was a silversmith who had a shop in New Haven from 1770 -1812. See, Card File of American Craftspeople, 1600-1995. The Henry Francis du Pont Winterthur Museum, Inc. Winterthur, Delaware [database on-line]. Provo, UT, USA: Ancestry.com Operations, Inc., 2014.
3. Developing a comparison between modern costs to tax rates in the 18th century is fraught with

[p. 166] Coll. Voted that Dyar White, Simeon Baldwin[1], David Dagget, William Powel and Phileman Smith be Collectors of the Town rate or Tax.

Committee to repair highways. Voted y^t Mark Levenworth, Russel Clark, Joseph Howell, Hezekiah Beardsley, Nehemiah Smith, and Thadd^s Clark be a Committee to repair the highways for the year ensuing, and y^t ye Tax of one peny be appropriated to that purpose, and that they acc^t with the Selectmen and be Collectors of s^d Tax.

Bridge. Voted that the Selectmen be authorized to make Such disburstments towards partialy repairing the bridge Near the paper mill as they shall Judge Just and reasonable — Provided however y^t Nothing herein Contained or that shall be done by ye Selectmen Shall be Considered as adopting of s^d Bridge as a Town bridge by the Town.

Highway. Voted that the Selectmen be authorized to make Such disburstments as they Judge proper towards making a Survey of and Calling out the Committee for Laying out and Straitning the road to Remmon falls[2] not Exceeding £12.

Vote about Taxes. Whereas the Towns of New Haven[,] East Haven[,] Harnden and North Haven are Jointly holden and Liable for the payment of all State Taxes for which Warrents Issued against s^d New Haven before the incorporation of s^d Towns of East Haven[,] Hamden and North Haven — Voted that in Case the s^d Towns of East Haven[,] Hamden and North Haven shall respectively and Severally vote and agree to take upon themselves the payment of the State rates or Taxes which are now due from all & every person or persons who at the Time when the Treasurer issued his warrants for said Taxes and s^d rates Dwell or were inhabitants of s^d Towns of East Haven[,] Hamden or North Haven in such case this Town will and *[p. 167]* Doth take upon itself the payment of ye State rates of

---

risk. The value of the pound sterling in the 1780s varied from 240 pence in Britain to a high of 427 pence in New York. Using that last exchange rate, a 9 pence tax per pound represented a tax rate of 2%. See, Louis Jordan, "The Comparative Value of Money between Britain and the Colonies," *Colonial Currency*, University of Notre Dame, Department of Special Collections, https://coins.nd.edu/ColCurrency/CurrencyIntros/IntroValue.html.

1. Simeon Baldwin (1751 - 1851), graduated Yale in 1781, was admitted to the bar in 1786, and served as New Haven City clerk (1789-1800) and clerk of the District and Circuit Courts of the United States for the District of Connecticut, (1790-1803). He later served as a U.S. Congressman, associate judge of the Superior Court, (1806-17), and mayor of New Haven.

2. The road in question as likely Rimmon Road, which ran through Woodbridge to Seymour. In addition, Rammon Falls refers to the Rock Rimmon area of Beacon Falls, CT along the Naugatuck River.

all persons who dwell or were inhabitants within the present Limits of the Town at the Time when the Treasurer issued his warrants for s^d Taxes, and doth thereupon agree to indemnify and Save s^d Towns of East Haven[,] Hamden and North Haven harmless from the payments of said Rates so taken upon this Town together with expenses which may accrue thereon excepting however all State rates which are or may be in dispute between s^d Towns and the Town of Woodbridge.

This meeting adjourned [to] the first monday of Jan^{ry} next at 2 °Clock in the afternoon.

[JANUARY 7, 1788]

AT A TOWN MEETING HOLDEN IN NEW HAVEN BY ADJOURNMENT UPON THE 7TH DAY OF JANUARY 1788.

Grandjuryman. Voted Thomas Howell J^r be released from being Grandjuryman and Dyar White Chosen in his room.

[Rate.] Voted that the Town will resind ye vote [of] the last meeting laying a rate of 8 pence on the pound.

Tax. Voted that there be a rate or Tax of four pence on the pound for defraying ye Charges of the Town.

Selectman. Isaac Beers and Levi Ives desired to be released from being Selectmen.

Selectmen. On motion Voted that we are Contented with ye five remaining Selectmen. On reconsideration Voted the whole Number to remain as they were Elected.

This meeting adjourned to monday next at 2 of the Clock in the afternoon.

[JANUARY 14, 1788]

AT A TOWN MEETING HOLDEN IN NEW HAVEN BY ADJOURNMENT UPON THE 14TH DAY OF JANUARY 1788.

Accounts. Voted y^t ye Town are Satisfied with the accounts the Selectmen and treasurer have exhibited [p. 168] To the Town in this meeting.

rate resinded. Voted y^t ye 4^d Tax be resinded.

Tax. Voted y^t there be a Tax of Six pence on ye pound to be paid on the first Day of Feb^ry Next.

Coll^r. Voted y^t ye Same Collectors Chosen ye first meeting be Collectors of ye above Tax.

key keeper. Voted y^t Capt Joseph Munson be key keeper the year ensuing.

This meeting adj^d without day.

[SEPTEMBER 16, 1788]

AT A TOWN MEETING HOLDEN IN NEW HAVEN SEPT^R 16 1788.

Mod^r. Voted that Tim° Jones Esqr be moderator.

Surveyer. Voted y^t Joseph Howel who was Chosen Surveyer of highways and one of the Committee to Pay out the money raised by ye Tax for repairing the highways and Coll^r of the Tax, be released from Serving, and y^t William Powel be in ye room of s^d Howel and to do all ye business y^t s^d Howel was appointed to do & perform.

Voted y^t this meeting be adjourned without day.

[DECEMBER 8, 1788]

AT A TOWN MEETING HOLDEN IN NEW HAVEN ON THE 8TH DAY OF DECEMBER 1788.

Clerk. Voted y^t Samuel Bishop be Town Clerk.

[Moderator.] Voted y^t Roger Sherman Esqr be moderator.

Selectman. Voted y^t Stephen Ball, Elias Beers, Levi Ives, Zina Denison, Jeremiah Atwater *[and]* Erastus Bradly be Selectmen the year ensuing.

[p. 169] Selectmen. Voted y^t Zina Denison be released from being Selectman and

Jonathan Ingersoll Esqr be Selectmen in his room.

Constable. Voted y^t Peter Woodward, Joseph Peck, John R. Throop, Jonas Printice and Burwell Smith be Constabes the year ensuing.

Grandjuryman. Voted y^t Aaron Eliot, John Townsend, Jonathan Leavitt and Elijah Prindle be Grandjurymen the year ensuing.

Treas^r. Voted y^t David Austin Esqr be Town Treasurer the year ensuing.

Listers. Voted that Stephen Ball, Willm Lyon, James Rice, Isaac Jones, Elias Shipman, Elias Stilwell, Jacob Daggett & Jeremiah Smith be listers the year ensuing.

Survey^{rs}. Voted y^t Hez^h Beardslee, Mark Levenworth, Russel Clark, Willm Powel, Oliver Smith, Benjamin Thomas, and Elnathan Toles be Surveyers of Highways the year ensuing.

Leather Sealer. Voted y^t Stephen Bradly be leather sealer the year ensuing.

Sealer [of dry measures]. Voted y^t John Miles be Sealer of dry measures.

Key keeper. Voted y^t Joseph Munson, Noah Potter, Nathan Dumer, John Culver & Azael Kimberly be key keepers the year ensuing.

Swine. Voted y^t Swine going at large shall not be liable to be impounded from ye highways and Town Commons the year ensuing, Provided they are yoaked from the 10th Day of march to ye 10th Day of Decr and ringed all ye year.

[p. 170] Tythingmen. Voted y^t Thaddeus Alling, Samuel Hughton, John Clause, Jonathan Mix, Sam^{ll} Clark, Thomas Smith, Elijah Alling, Harthan Ramsdale, and David Bristoll be Tythingmen the year ensuing.

[Districts.] Voted y^t the Selectmen give the Surveyers of the highways their districts.

Oyster act. This Town taking into Consideration ye benefit that might arise to ye inhabitants from a preservation of the oysters and Clames in s^d Town and ye great increase they are induced to believe there would be of ye Same if proper regulations were made agreeable to the powers vested in s^d Town by ye Statute of ye State in such cases Provided are induced to make ye following rules and regulations.

Voted y^t no person or persons from and after ye first day of January next shall drive any Team of horses or Cattle with any Cart, Waggen, or wheel Carriage into or upon any flat, Harbour, Creek, or river in the Town of New Haven where oysters or Clames are Caught or where oyster shells are taken for ye purpose of taking oysters Clames or Shells or ye purpose of carrying away oysters Clames or Shells from any Such Flat, Harbour, Creek, or river upon pain of forfieting ye Sum of Twenty Shillings for every Such offence one half to him who Shall prosecute ye Same to conviction and ye other half to ye Town Treasury for the use of s^d Town.

And it is further Voted by s^d Town y^t no person or persons shall catch oysters or Long Clames in any of the Rivers[,] Creeks[,] or harbours[,] or upon any of ye flats[,] Beaches[,] or Shores of any Such Rivers[,] Creeks[,] or Harbours in the bounds of s^d Town of New Haven from & after the first day of may AD 1789 until the 15th Day of oct^r AD 1789 upon pain of forfieting ye Sum of Six Shillings Lawfull money for every Such offence Such person or persons shall be guilty of one half to him who Shall prosecute ye Same to Conviction and the other half to ye Town Treasurer of ye Town for ye use of s^d Town — Provided nevertheless any person or persons obtaining from two of ye Civil *[p. 171]* authority or two of ye Selectmen of s^d Town a permit under their hands allowing Such person or persons to Catch Clames or oysters as Shall be Specified in s^d Permit which Permitt s^d authority and Selectmen are hereby impowered to Grant provided s^d Permit be never for more than Two Bushels to one person at one Time and s^d Permit be returned to s^d authority or Selectmen granting ye Same within forty eight hours from ye Time of Granting ye Same and Such person or persons shall make it appear to ye Satisfaction of s^d authority and or Selectmen y^t he or they have not taken or Caught more Clames or Oysters than is Specified in s^d permit Such person or persons in Such Case Complying s^d requirement shall not incur said Penalty of Six Shillings afores^d — and also Provided y^t nothing in this Shall extend to prevent Catching long Clames at any Season of ye year westward of the Long Wharff in New Haven.[1]

Tax. Voted that there be a Tax or rate Collected by ye Surveyers of ye inhabitants of the Town, to be laid out by ye Surveyers of the highways for repairing ye highways, to be paid by the first Day of march next.

---

1. Overharvesting shellfish led New Haven to regulate the industry as early as 1762. See, Zara Powers, ed, *New Haven Town Records, 1684 - 1769* (1962), pp.760 - 761; see also, Doe Boyle, "Oystering in Connecticut, from Colonial Times to the 21st Century," Connecticut History.org, https://connecticuthistory.org/oystering-in-connecticut-from-colonial-times-to-today/.

This meeting adjourned untill monday next at 2 of the Clock in the afternoon.

[DECEMBER 15, 1788]

AT A TOWN MEETING HOLDEN IN THE TOWN OF NEW HAVEN BY ADJOURNMENT ON THE 15TH DAY OF DEC^R 1788.

Surveyer. Voted y^t Elnathan Toles be released from being Surveyer of highways and Amos Alling *[be]* Surveyer in his room.

Selectman. Voted y^t Jonathan Ingersoll Esqr be released from being Selectman and Capt Jos^h Bradly be Selectman in his room.

[p. 172] Poor Supported. Voted y^t David Austin Esqr, Deacon Ball, Doct^r Ives, Capt Thomas Punderson and Nehemiah Smith Esqr be a Committee to take into consideration a motion made by Mr Levenworth &c. with regard to ye poor &c and to hear any other proposalls with regard to ye Support of the poor &c and report to the next meeting.

This meeting adj^ed to Monday next at 2 °Clock Pm.[1]

[DECEMBER 22, 1788]

AT A TOWN MEETING HOLDEN IN NEW HAVEN BY ADJOURN-MENT UPON THE 22^D DAY OF DEC^R 1788.

Support of y^f poor. Voted y^t Messrs Roger Sherman, Willm Powel, Jos^h Thompson, Tim° Jones, Nathan Smith, Joseph Howell, Thaddeus Clark, Eneas Munson, Silas Alling, and Stephen Ball — be a Committee to take into Consideration such proposalls that have been or Such as Shall be made to them with regard to the Support of the poor & other Charges of the Town the year ensuing, and also y^t they Consider of ye motion made to this meeting about building a Bridge over ye river Near Dragon[2] — and report their opinion upon the whole of the matters refered to them unto ye Town at their next meeting.

---

1. It is interesting to note that the first presidential election in Connecticut took place between December 15, 1788 - January 10, 1789. Seven electors were selected by the Connecticut General Assembly who unanimously voted for George Washington. Still, no mention of this election was made in the town meetings.
2. Dragon was the name referring to the whole area east of the Quinnipiac River.

Voted y' this meeting be adjourned untill monday next at 2 °Colock PM.

[DECEMBER 29, 1788]

AT A TOWN MEETING HOLDEN IN NEW HAVEN BY ADJOURN-
MENT ON Y^E 29TH DAY OF DEC^R 1789.

mod^r. Voted that Tim° Jones Esqr be moderator in the room of Rog^r Sherman
Esqr who is absent.

Support of the poor. The Committee appointed the Last meeting to take into Consideration a plan or plans from any inhabitant or inhabitants of this Town to
Support ye poor &c, That they had rec^d Proposalls from Messrs *[p. 173]* Johnson*[,]* Hotchkis*[,]* and Capt Thos Punderson and his brother Samuel which proposalls were by s^d Committee introduced into the meeting were in the words
following viz.

New Haven Decr 29^h 1788. In order to Lessen ye increasing burden of ye rateable inhabitants of this Town — we ye Subscribers do promise and engage y^t we
will defray ye expenses of this Town for one year to Commence the first monday
of January next, Provided ye Town will in legall meeting grant ye s^d Subscribers
a Tax of Eight pence on ye pound on ye Grand list of the year 1788 in the manner and form as follows viz. To maintain and keep the whole of ye Town's poor
y^t is or may become Chargeable within ye s^d year, To widen and New build y^e
Neck bridge Sufficient and Strong to ye Satisfaction of ye Selectmen. To repair
all other Bridges now in being and keep them so during ye s^d Term of one year
except those hereafter excepted.

To lay out thirty pounds on ye Highways at ye direction of ye Selectmen and in
Labour at two Shillings and four pence for one mans days work and Teams at
five Shillings p^r Day.

To pay into the Treasury or any other person or persons as ye Town Shall
direct one Hundred and forty pounds Lawfull money or Town orders within
ye year ensuing.

And to do and pay all necessary Charges which shall or may arise during the
s^d Term — Except mending*[,]* repairing*[,]* or any other Expenses y^t may occur
on ye long bridge or any Extraordinary expenses y^t might arise from unusual or
Common Sickness or Smallpox in a degree y^t exceeds in ye ordinary Course of

Nature, old Law Suits and any old arrearages not intended in this agreement.

We also agree to Collect ye Town & State Tax at our own risk and no expense to ye Town.

We expect to have ye benefit of those poor persons work y^t are wholly Chargable to ye Town and are able to do Something.

[p. 174] And further we engage to receive in payment Town orders at their full denomination Eighteen Shillings Cash for one pound and in proportion for Lesser rates, also merchandize and country produce at the following prices[1]:

Wheat	6/		St Croix or other		
Rye	3/		Good rum	2/9 p^r gall	
Oats	14^d	p^r Bushel	Molassas 1/6		
Buck Wheat	2/		Tea...	2/3	
Indian corn .	2/9		Sugar...	6^d	
Oak wood .	11/	p^r Cord	Cheese ...	6^d	p^r lb
walnut D^o .	14		Butter ...	7^d	
Beaf	21/2^d	p^r lb	Wool ...	2s	
Pork ...	3s		Flax ...	4^d	
			Cotton ...		
			Salt ...	2/6/ p^r Bushel	

The above articles and prices to be Considered as payment for the first four months but after y^t as the articles may raise or fall at any other merchable price as may appear to us reasonable as also we will take many other articles at a price agreed by ye Parties that Cannot at present be enumerated.

NB it is hoped as the business of ye authority and Selectmen will in a great measure be but trifling y^t they will render their Services y^t may become Necessary gratis when ye Subscribers are obliged by Law to Call upon them, as also the Grandjurymen theirs as was Customary in former Times — furthermore we expect to be under the Control of ye Selectmen in all ye foregoing Supplys.

Lemuel Hotchkiss
Peter Johnson

---

1. The "/" and "s" designate shillings and the superscropt "d" represents pence. The "/-" was the symbol used for "shillings exactly", that is, shillings and zero pence, in the pre- decimal £sd British currency. For a further explanation of colonial money and demoninations, see, https://vitabrevis. americanancestors.org/2015/02/making-sense-money-colonial-america/.

Theo^s Punderson
Saml Punderson

We also agree y^t ye Selectmen Shall abate such rates as they think necessary, and fix ye prices of the articles in which ye Tax is payable after the first four months.

Lemuel Hotchkiss
Peter Johnson
Thos Punderson
Saml Punderson

[p. 175] which proposalls being read and Considered by ye Town Thereupon Voted y^t this Town will Contract with said Gentlemen agreeable to their plan for ye maintainence of the poor &c.[1]

Tax. Voted y^t there be a rate or Tax Collected of the inhabitants of this Town of Eight pence on ye pound on the present list to defray the Charges of ye Town to be paid the first of march next.

Tax. Voted y^t ye peny Tax for repairing highways be resinded.

Coll^r. Voted that Saml Punderson be the Collector of the Town and State Taxes the year ensuing.

Survey^{er}. Vote relating to Surveyers of Highways be resinded.

Surveyer. Voted y^t Capt Thomas Punderson, Mark Levenworth, Silas Kimberly and Silas Alling be Surveyers of highways the year ensuing.

Agents about Bridge. Voted y^t Elizer Goodrich and Isaac Beers Esq^{rs} be appointed agents in behalf of this Town to apply to ye Gen^{ll} assembly at their adj^d Sessions for license and Liberty for this Town or Such persons as this Town shall Contract with to build and erect a Bridge across the East river at Dragon with authority to receive and Collect a Toll of passengers in Such manner as the assembly Shall appoint.

Grandjuryman. Voted y^t Sam^{ll} Russel be Grandjuryman the year ensuing.

---

1. Privatization of specific charitable and public services was not uncommon in the early municipal history of New Haven.

This meeting adjourned without day.

[p. 176] Bounds between N. Haven & Hamden. We the Subscribers appointed by the Towns of New Haven and Hamden to run ye Line between s^d Towns and lay proper boundaries thereon Proeeded in said Business of ye 12th May 1789 and run a direct line from the west buttment of the Long bridge to ye north end of George Peckmans house which is north fifty degrees west and laid ye first bounds which is a heap of Stone on the East side of North Haven road 52 rods Southerly of Medad Atwaters house, the Second is a heap of Stones on a Rock at ye west end of the wid^w Jocelins house lot, The third is a heap of Stones on the Top of mount See all,[1] the fourth is a heap of stones on the Top of ye Neck rock towards ye South end, the fifth is a heap of stones toward ye north end of Neck Rock, ye Sixth is a heap of Stones round a Ceder pole on ye west side of the neck river Sxty rods Southeasterly of George Peckams house and from thence ye north end of s^d house we run a direct line to ye south east Corner of ye farm late the property of Col John Hubbard Dec^d, which is North 78^1/2 degrees west and the first bounds on ye line is a white oak tree with Stones round it Sixty rods from s^d house. The Second is a heap of Stones on ye Second quarter line*[,]* the third is a heap of Stones *[on the]* west side of Plainfield path, the fourth is a heap *[of]* Stones and Slate *[on the]* East side of Land belonging to the heirs of Deacon Jonathan Mansfield Dec^d, the fifth is a heap *[of]* Stones East side of Cheshire road forty rods northerly of Martins house. The Sixth is a heap *[of]* Stones East side of a highway about Twelve rods South of Zopher Atwaters house. The Seventh is a heap of Stones in ye middle of pine rock field, the 8th is a heap of Stones by a bunch of Chisnut 80 rods Easterly of s^d Hubbards farm. We then reviewed ye Southeast Corner and ye Southwest Corner of s^d Hubbards farm on ye west rock, thence Northerly on ye Top of ye west Rock thirty rods to ye Southeast Corner of the Town of Woodbridge which is a Ceder pole with Stones round it and all ye above described monuments we marked on ye Southerly Side NH & on the Northerly side H.

Stephen Ball
Erastus Bradly
Medad Atwater
John Hubbard

[APRIL 13, 1789]

[p. 177] AT A TOWN MEETING HOLDEN IN NEW HAVEN UPON THE

---

1. Mount See All, also known as Indian Head or Snake Rock, is the hill connecting with and east of East Rock extending to State Street. See, Osterweis, p. 487.

13ᵀᴴ DAY OF APRIL 1789.

Rate. The Selectmen having laid before yᵉ Town sundry Debts due from the Town to yᵉ amount of the Sum of £214-6-1¹/² and there being no provision made by the rate already laid to pay the Same. Thereupon Voted yᵗ there be a rate of three pence three farthings on the pound on yᵉ present list *[to]* be collected of the in-habitants of this Town to pay yᵉ above Sum & Such Other Charges of the Town as Shall thereafter become Due.

Voted yᵗ sᵈ rate be paid on the first of June next.

Collʳ. Voted that Capᵗ Peter Woodward be Collector of sᵈ rate.

Allowance to Collʳ. Voted yᵗ the Selectmen Settle with Capᵗ Peter Woodward[1] and allow him for Collecting the above rate what they Judge Just and reasonable. Further voted yᵗ yᵉ Selectmen allow Capᵗ Throop for Collecting yᵉ State Taxes of this year Such Sum as they Judge Just and reasonable.

This meeting adjourned without day.

[DECEMBER 14, 1789]

[p. 178] AT A TOWN MEETING HOLDEN IN NEW HAVEN UPON THE 14ᵀᴴ DAY OF DECᴿ 1789.

Clerk. Samˡˡ Bishop Chosen Town Clerk.

Modʳ. Timº Jones Esqʳ Chosen moderator.

Selectmen. Voted yᵗ Stephen Ball Esqʳ, Elias Beers, Levi Ives, Joseph Bradly, Jer-emiah Atwater, Erastus Bradly and Nathan Smith be Selectmen yᵉ year ensuing.

Treasʳ. Voted yᵗ David Austin Esqʳ be Town Treasurer the year ensuing.

Constables. Voted yᵗ Joseph Peck, Jonas Prentice, Peter Woodward, John R. Throop, Samˡˡ Punderson and Burrel Smith be Constables year ensuing.
Grandjurymen. Voted that Peter Johnson, Nathan Beers, Jeremiah Atwater, Levi

---

1. Capt. Peter Woodward (ca. 1761 - 1811). See, Connecticut State Library; Hartford, Connecticut; The Charles R. Hale Collection of Connecticut Cemetery Inscriptions.

Ives, Richard Eld, Jesse Stevens, Elijah Prindle, James Prescot, Jonas Prentice J[r] and Elijah Austin be Grandjurymen the year ensuing.

Listers. Voted y[t] Stephen Ball, James Rice, William Lyon, Isaac Jones, Elias Ship-man, Elias Stilwell, Jacob Daggett, David Daggett,[1] Jeremiah Smith & Merrit Clark be listers the year ensuing.

Contract. Voted y[t] Mark Levenworth[,] David Dagget[,] Henry Daggett[,] Nehe-miah Smith[,] and Elias Beers, be requested to prepare a report *[about a]* Con-tract with any Suitable person or persons for defraying the Charges of this Town for the ensuing year or any part thereof, and that y[e] Selectmen be requested to lay as accurate an Estimate as possable of the expenses of the ensuing year be-fore this meeting at the first opportunity.[2]

[p. 179] [Leather] Sealer. Voted y[t] Stephen Bradly be leather Sealer the year ensuing.

Sealer [of dry masures]. Voted y[t] John Miles be Sealer of dry measures.

Key Keepers. Voted that Jos[h] Munson, Noah Potter, Nathan Dumer, John Culver and Azel Kimberly be key keeper[s] y[e] year ensuing.

Swine. Voted y[t] Swine going a[t] large in this Town, without the limits of y[e] City, shall not be liable to be impounded from the highways and Town Commons the year ensuing, Provided they are yoaked from y[e] 10th of march to y[e] 10th of Dec[r] next and ringed all the year.

Surveyers. Voted y[t] Jonah Bradly, Thomas Punderson, Levi Ives, David Austin, Henry Daggett, Glover Ball, Joseph Howel, Jonas Merwin, Sam[ll] Candee, Amos Alling and Andrew Smith be Surveyers of Highways the year ensuing.

Tythingmen. Voted y[t] Jonas Hotchkiss, Nath[ll] Fitch, Jesse Upson, Jared Mansfield, Nath[ll] Beecher, David Bristoll and Israel Kirnberly be Tythingmen the year ensuing. *Com[e].* Voted y[t] Jeremah Atwater, Isaac Beers, Thomas Punderson and David Austin be a Committee to make a Computation of the expense of the bridge proposed to be built at Dragon so Called agreeable to the act of the Gen[ll] as-sembly *[and]* see if they can find persons to build y[e] Same and make report to

---

1. David Daggett (1764 - 1851) was a Yale graduate (1783), attorney, founder of Yale Law School, mayor of New Haven, and U.S. Senator.
2. The entry does not specify its purpose, but the next meeting mentioned care of the town's poor.

the next meeting.

Agents. Voted y^t Messrs Isaac Beers and Eliz^r Goodrich be agents in behalf of ye Town to apply to the next Gen^ll assembly to git a report of ye act of assembly obliging this Town to build bridges over ye East river and Little river so Called at the Great Island[1] y^t ye Same Shall take place as soon as the bridge at Dragon is Completed.[2]

[p. 180] This meeting adjourned to ye Last monday of instant Decr at two of the Clock in the afternoon.

[DECEMBER 28, 1789]

AT A TOWN MEETING HOLDEN IN NEW HAVEN BY ADJOURN-
MENT ON THE 28TH DAY OF DECEMBER 1789.

Selectmen. Capt Jo^s Bradly, Step^n Ball, Esqr, Elias Beers, Levi Ives, Jeremiah Atwa-
ter, Erastus Bradly & Nathan Smith who were Selectmen the Last year requested to be released from Serving as Selectmen this year. Thereupon voted y^t they be released agreeable to their request.

Selectmen. Voted y^t Thomas Punderson, Joseph Howel, Levi Ives, Azel Kimerly, and Mark Levenworth be Selectmen the year ensuing.

Highway. Voted y^t ye vote relating to repairing the highways the last meeting be resinded & repealed.

Grandjuryman. Voted y^t Doct^r Ives be released from being Grandjuryman the

year ensuing and Hez^h Auger be Grandjuryman in his Stead ye year ensuing.
Tax. Voted y^t there be a rate or Tax of Six pence three farthings on the pound on the present list be collected of the inhabitants of the Town, to defray the charges of the Town ye year ensuing and to be paid on the first day of March next.

Coll^r. Voted y^t Samuel Punderson be Collector of the Town rate.

Grandjuryman. Voted y^t Jeremiah Atwater be released from being Grandjuryman and

---

1. Possibly a reference to what is now Ball Island in the Mill River.
2. The General Assembly approved the construction of a toll bridge at the cost of £1,500 over the East River in October, 1789. *PRSC*, VII: 26, 96, 144, 241, 279, 420.

~~James P~~ Piersons Clark be grandjuryman in his Stead.

[p. 181] Committee ab' Contract. The Committee appointed yᵉ Last meeting about Supporting the poor of the Town, made their report in yᵉ words following viz.

To the inhabitants of yᵉ Town of New Haven — Gentlemen —
We yᵉ Subscribers being appointed at your annual Town meeting on yᵉ Second monday of instant December a Committee to prepare and report a Contract for defraying the Expenses of this Town for yᵉ year ensuing — Beg leave to report, That having attended to yᵉ business of our appointment we offer yᵉ Contract which accompanies this as yᵉ most eligible yᵗ we can avail our Selves of and as agreed to by the Gentlemen who Contracted for yᵉ Same purpose yᵉ past year, and as yᵉ Town might wish to be informed of yᵉ principles and Calculations on which we proceeded in forming our opinion of the propriety of Contracting in *[the]* manner proposed we beg leave to observe yᵗ it is very obvious many great advantages have been derived to yᵉ Town by defraying their expenses by Contract as was done last year yᵉ management of yᵉ whole revenues of the town being in yᵉ hands of men whose interest it is to make it their business more economy has been & will be adopted than in any other mode. That the poor Should be provided for by persons who will be induced to make yᵉ provision with as little expence as possible is an object of great importance[.] to effect this we think it advisable yᵗ yᵉ Contractors Should have it in their power, to accomodate them in such place as they See fit, we also Suppose Considerable expense may be Saved yᵉ Town by enabling the Contractors to procure for the meeting of yᵉ Selectmen and Civil authority when necessary to procure yᵉ list to be made up and to perform any other incidental Service as to Calculations we would observe that the Grand list upon which yᵉ Tax will be laid will be *[p. 182]* about £18500 and off Course yᵉ proposed Tax of 6ᵈ on the pound will raise £462-10-0[.] we Estimate the provision for the poor at £270 there is to be paid into the Treasury £100 — We allow £30 for abatemᵗˢ and £45 for Collecting yᵉ State[,] County & Town Taxes and £15 for expence of Selectmen Civil Authority for warning and transporting vagrents & other Contingent Charges the whole of Sum amount to £360. The Sum for Supporting yᵉ poor is £100 and yet is very different from their former expence. The £15 for Contigent Charges &c we see Sensable is much too low — upon the best Calculation we can make we Suppose yᵉ Contract advantageous to yᵉ Town and not injurious to yᵉ Contractors united therefore recommend it to be adopted, we know yᵗ yᵉ Sum to be paid into yᵉ Treasury will not discharge yᵉ whole Debt against yᵉ Town nor could it be done without a Tax which the inhabitants would feel themselves unwilling & unable to pay, and therefore we prefer a partial payment — all which is Humbly

Submitted by y[r] most obed[t] Hum[le] Servants.

Henry Daggett
E. Beers
D[d] Daggett   } Committee
Mark Levenworth
Nehemiah Smith

The foregoing report of the Committee having been duely Considered, is by
Vote approved and accepted.

[p. 183] Contract. we the Subscribers agree to defray y[e] expences of the Town
of New Haven for y[e] year ensuing to Commence on y[e] first day of January
1790 except the expence of rebuilding or repairing y[e] long bridge the expences
which may arise from repairing y[e] highways or neglect of repairing them or for
highways, also Such increased expences for y[e] Support of the poor as Shall arise
from y[e] Small pox, fire or extraordinary Sickness to be Judged of by y[e] Selectmen We are to pay y[e] necessary expense of house*[,]* fire*[,]* and Candles for y[e]
meetings of y[e] Selectmen but at Such Convenient place as we Shall procure. We
are to pay y[e] expence of making one Grand List but to be performed by Such
proper person as we Shall procure. We are to Collect all State*[,]* County*[,]* and
one Town Tax for y[e] year and to be answerable for y[e] amount of y[e] Same to y[e]
Several Treasurers as y[e] Law directs. We agree to pay into y[e] Town Treasury one
Hundred pounds in Town orders within y[e] year unless y[e] Selectmen Shall direct
a new bridge to be built over the west river on milford road in which Case we
are to build the bridge and to be allowed fifteen pounds therefor out of s[d] one
Hundred pounds but the Selectmen to notify their directions relative to building y[e] bridge by y[e] 15th of Jan[y] next, and provided we build s[d] Bridge we expect
to have the old one. For all which we agree to accept a Tax of Six pence on y[e]
pound payable in the Same manner as the s[d] Town Tax was last year payable. We
however are not to be answerable for any Costs which may arise by Suits against
the Town unless they arise through our neglect or in the Course of our business
provided however if we Choose to pay Cash into y[e] Town Treasury *[p. 184]* we
are to pay it at y[e] Same rate as we are to receive it on y[e] Tax. We are also to maintain & provide for the poor at Such place as we Choose y[e] accomodations &c
to be under y[e] inspection and approbation of y[e] Selectmen. The fines which are
payable to y[e] Town to be off set against y[e] Costs — and it is further provided y[t]
we have all the priviledges that the Town usually have had, to defray y[e] expences
of the poor out of their Estate, provided they have any, or, relations who are by
Law holden to pay s[d] expences we agree to the above articles provided we have

Selectmen Chosen by Ballot. Dated in New Haven Decr 28, 1789.

Lemuel Hotchkis
Peter Johnson
Thomas Punderson
Sam^{ll} Punderson

The foregoing proposalls made by ye aforesaid persons having been duely considered by this meeting is by Vote accepted and approved of.

Committee about line of y^f Town. We the Subscribers Committees appointed by ye Several Towns of New Haven and Woodbridge to perambulate & Settle the line between s^d Towns — Report y^t we began in ye South part of woodbridge where New Haven and milford meet at ye South west Corner of Obed Johnsons farm at a heap of stones being a former boundary and running on ye side of s^d farm North 75^0 East 80 rods to a heap of Stones marked NHW lying ye South side of the fence in a low Spot of wood land belonging to Dan^{ll} Alling then keeping ye Same Course 80 rods to a heap of Stones lying on ye East side of ye highway by s^d Johnsons thence with s^d highway North 5^{0}E 86^r to a heap of Stones lying on the East side of s^d highway a few rods North of a small swamp against Reuben Beechers Land on the East and Job Johnsons Land on ye west — thence keeping s^d highway 80 rods to a heap of Stones lying the East side of ye highway 5 Rods South of Bull hole thence with s^d highway 12 rods to ye Northwest Corner of west field Lots thence North 59^0 East 68 rods to a heap of Stones lying on ye west side a swamp in widow Hillhouses Land. *[p. 185]* Thence keeping ye Same Course 80 rods to a heap of Stones lying in s^d Mrs Hillhouses Land thence running ye Same Course 40 rods to a heap of Stones which was a parish boundary which we renewed and lyes on ye brow of ye Great hill and 6 or 8 rods westerly of Cherekee falls *[?]^1* then N 9^0 East 23 rods to a heap of Stones lying *[on]* ye South side of Derby road thence N 20^0 East keeping ye highway which leads to Sperrys farm 60 rods to a heap of Stones lying ye East side of s^d highway, thence N 36° East 20 rods to a heap of Stones an ancient bound of morrises farm which we renewed. Thence N 22^0 East 105 rods to a heap of Stones lying on ye East side of a wide highway or Common Land at the west end of Sperrys farm and in a direction with the line of fence on ye South Side of James Sperrys (formerly Saml Baldwins) farm thence North 66^{0}East 110 rods to a heap of Stones where ye dividing fence between Wm Sperry and Thomas Sperry both on ye waterbury road. Thence keeping ye Same Course and running on ye South side of s^d Baldwins farm 140 rods to a *[illegible crossout]* Ceder pole Standing on the Top of ye west rock with stones laid at it and marked on three Sides for a

boundary between New Haven[,] Woodbridge[,] and Hamden — which foregoing marked lines and boundaries we ye afores^d Committees agree shall be ye line
and bounds between the s^d Town of New Haven and ye Town of Woodbridge.
In Testimony of our agreement thereto we have here unto Set our hands the
11th Day of Dec^r, 1789.

Samuel Bishop	Committee
David Austin	for
Simeon Bristoll	New Haven
John Dibble	Committee
Jesse Ford	for
Thos Darling	New Haven

[Collector.] Voted y^t Sam^ll Punderson be Collector of the State Taxes the year
ensuing.

[Committee.] Voted y^t James Hillhouse, Isaac Beers & Eliz^r Goodrich be a Committee [...]^1

[p. 186] Comt^tee. The Committee appointed ye Last meeting about the bridge at
Dragon, and Henry Daggett, Capt Todd and Mr Hillhouse be a Committee to
make a Contract with any person or persons to build ye Same.

Comt^tee [on oysters]. Voted y^t Mark Levenworth, Benjn Sanford, Eliz^r Goodrich and
Nehemiah Smith be a Committee to prepare Some act or resolve to be passed
by ye Town for ye preservation of Oysters &c.

Highways. Voted y^t ye Selectmen receive ye three farthings on the pound granted
ye Last meeting for repairing ye highways, and order and direct about repairing
the Same.

Lister. Voted y^t Benjn Sanford be lister in ye room of Elias Shipman ye year ensuing.

This meeting adj^d to proxsi day^2 in april next at 2 °Clock Pm.

[FEBRUARY 1, 1790]

AT A TOWN MEETING HOLDEN IN NEW HAVEN UPON THE FIRST

---

1. The clerk failed to identify this committee. However, in the next session, it is identified as the
committee for a bridge over part of the Quinnipiac River in Fair Haven, then a place called Dragon.
2. Possibly a reference to voting day for New Haven freemen.

DAY OF FEB^Y 1790.

mod^r. David Austin Esqr Chosen moderator.

State note. Voted y^t ye State note in the hands of ye Treasurer be sold and ye money raised by ye Sale there of be paid towards the Execution y^t is now against Deacon Ball & others upon ye account of the rates yt Mr Tiley Black-slee hath been Collecting.

Rate. Voted y^t a rate of Two pence on ye pound upon the list of the year 1789 to be applyed towards ye payment of the remainder of ye Sums due on s^d Execution and in Case ye rate Shall raise more than Sufficient to pay s^d Execution, the Sum remaining to be applyed towards ye Charges of the Town.

Voted y^t s^d Rate be paid on ye 10th day of instant Feb^ry.

Coll^r. Voted y^t Peter Woodward be Col^lr of s^d rate, and y^t the Selectmen agree with him for a Compensation for Collecting ye Same.

[APRIL [...] 1790]

[p. 187] AT A TOWN MEETING HOLDEN BY ADJOURNMENT UPON THE *[...]* DAY OF APRIL 1790.

oysters. This town taking into Consideration ye benefit y^t might arise to ye inhabit-ants from a preservation of the Oysters in s^d Town and ye great increase they are induced to believe there would be of the Same if proper regulations were made agreeable to ye powers vested in s^d Town by ye Statute of ye State in Such Case Provided are induced to make ye following rules & regulations.

Voted y^t no person or persons from and after ye first day of ~~January~~ may next shall drive any Team *[of]* horses or Cattle with any Cart waggon or wheel Car-riage into or upon any flatt*[,]* Harbour*[,]* Creek*[,]* or river in the Town of New Haven where oysters or Clams are caught or where oysters Shells are taken for ye purpose of taking oysters Clams or the purpose of Carrying away oysters*[,]* Clams*[,]* or Shells from any Such flat*[,]* Harbour*[,]* Creek*[,]* or river upon pain of forfieting ye Sum of Twenty Shillings for every Such offence one half to him who shall Prosecute the Same to Conviction and ye other half to ye Town Trea-surer for the use of s^d Town.

And it is further voted by s^d Town yt no person or persons shall Catch any oysters or long clams in any of the rivers[,] Creeks[,] or Harbours[,] or upon any of ye flats[,] Beaches[,] or Shores of any Such rivers[,] Creeks[,] or Harbors in ye bounds of s^d Town of New Haven ye 15th day of instant april untill ye 8th day of october next upon pain of forfieting ye Sum of Twenty Shillings Lawfull money for every such offence such person or persons shall be guilty of one half to him who shall prosecute ye Same to Conviction and ye other half to ye Town Treasury for ye use of s^d Town.

Provided nevertheless y^t any person or persons obtaining from Ebenezer Townsend or Silas Kimberly a permit [...] allowing such person or persons to catch Clams or oysters as shall be Specified in s^d permit which Permit s^d Townsend and Kimberly are hereby impowered to grant — Provided s^d Permit be never for more than two bushels to one person at one time and s^d permit to be returned to s^d [...] granting ye Same within forty eight hours from ye time of granting the Same and Such person or persons to ye Satisfaction [...] y^t he or they have not taken or caught more Clams or oysters than is Specified in s^d Permit such person or persons in [p. 188] Such Case complying s^d requirements shall not incur s^d Penalty of Twenty Shillings as aforesaid, and also Provided nothing in this vote shall extend to prevent Catching long Clams at any season of ye year westward of ye long Wharf in NewHaven.

[DECEMBER 12, 1790]

AT A TOWN MEETING HOLDEN IN NEW HAVEN UPON THE 12TH ~~1790~~ DAY OF DECEMBER 1790.

mod^r. Voted y^t Timothy Jones Esqr be moderator.

Committee [for Work House]. Voted y^t Sam^ll Bishop, Mark Levenworth, Thomas Punderson, Peter Johnson, Jos^h Howel, David Austin, Elias Shipman, Nehemiah Smith, and Jeremiah Atwater be a Committee to report their opinion of ye expedency of building a work house[,] the kind & Size of ye building[,] ye probable expence thereof[,] and a proper place to set ye Same — The probable expense of ye Town for the coming year[,] the Sum necessary for repairing ye highways[,] and ye Sum necessary to be raised for ye use of ye Town and ye proper manner for raising ye Same and to make return to this meeting at their next adjournment.

Treas^r. Voted y^t David Austin Esqr be Town Treasurer.

Constables. Voted that Joseph Peck, John R. Throop, Peter Woodward, Jonas Prentice, Abr^m Auger, Sam^ll Punderson and David Trowbridge be Constables the year ensuing.

Grandjurymen. Voted y^t John Goodrich, Stephen Osborn, Nath^ll Fitch, Peter Johnson, Dan^ll Bishop, Hez^h Hotchkiss, Silas Hotchkiss, Willm McCracken, Russel Clark, Elijah Prindle, John Johnson, and Pierson Clark be Grandjurymen the year ensuing.

The remainder of ye votes of ye above meeting are recorded on 194 page, there not being room sufficient left when ye following votes about ye bridge were recorded.[1]

carried to the 194 page.*

[MARCH 21, 1791]

[p. 189] AT A TOWN MEETING HOLDEN IN NEW HAVEN UPON THE 21ST DAY OF MARCH 1791.

Dragon Bridge. The Committee appointed ye Last meeting to take into Consideration ye grants of the Gen^ll assembly to ye inhabitants of this Town for the purpose of erecting a bridge over ye East river at a place called Dragon, and to Contract with any person or persons relative to ye building ye Same — which Committee laid before this meeting a Contract they had made with Henry Daggett Esqr and others for the approbation of this Town which Contract is in the following words viz...[2]

This Agreement made & concluded by & between the Town of New Haven by their Committee Samuel Bishop, David Austin, Isaac Beers, Levi Ives, James Hillhouse, Elizer Goodrich & David Daggett on the one part & Henry Daggett, James Prescot & Thomas Punderson all of New Haven on the Other part Witnesseth That said Town of New Haven in Consideration of the agreements & Contracts hereafter made & Expressed & to be performed by s^d Henry Daggett, James Prescott & Thomas Punderson Do hereby give grant and Assigns to them

---

1. The town clerk is referencing the original page number of the manuscript town records, which appear within brackets throughout this volume. The original manuscript was unbound and its pages encapsulated in plastic as a preservation measure. Those records now reside in the Whitney Library at The New Haven Museum.

2. This document runs from page 189 - 193 in the original manuscript and was recorded in two different hands, Samuel Bishop, the town clerk, and an unknown contributor, which accounts for the abrupt style change.

the s^d Henry Daggett, James Prescot & Thomas Punderson & their heirs & Assigns the Liberty, powers & priveleges to the s^d Town Granted by late Acts of
Assembly inabling said Town to Erect & build a bridge across the East River
at a place called Dragon & Do hereby Authorize & impower the said Henry
Daggett, James Prescott & Thomas Punderson their heirs etc. to receive and
appropriate to their own uses the Toll established in said Act of Assembly for
the Term therein Specified & to enjoy all the Benefits which said Town of New
Haven might have enjoyed thereby & said Town by this said Committee do
also contract & engage to deliver unto said Henry Daggett, James Prescot and
Thomas Punderson within one Month from the Date hereof the whole of the
money raised by lottery for the purpose of Building a Bridge at said Dragon to
be appropriated to & laid out in Building said Bridge & Immediately to layout
good & Sufficient highways in said Town of New Haven from the Neck Bridge
or at such other place as shall be adjudged most convenient to the place where s^d
proposed Bridge shall be erected & also procure good & Sufficient highways to
be laid out in East Haven as soon as the *[p. 190]* Same can be accomplished by
pursuing ye Steps of ye Law in Case s^d East Haven shall not vollentarily lay out
and open the Same, and without any other expence to s^d Henry Daggett, James
Prescot and Thomas Punderson than is herein after expressed. And as Soon as
s^d proposed bridge Shall be Compleated in such manner as to accomodate y^e
Public s^d Town do further Contract y^t s^d Henry Daggett, James Prescot and Thos
Punderson shall have ye Exclusive property in and to y^t part of ye long bridge
so Called which belongs to s^d Town of New Haven and y^t thereafter no bridge
shall be kept up or maintained where s^d Long bridge now is untill ye experation
of s^d Time for Collecting s^d Toll. And ye s^d Henry Daggett, James Prescot and
Thos Punderson in Consideration of ye afores^d Contracts and agreements made
by s^d Town of New Haven by their s^d Committee do on their part Contract and
agree with s^d Town of New Haven to erect and by the first day of January one
Thousand seven hundred and ninety three compleat a bridge across s^d East river
at s^d placed called dragon of ye following discription and dimensions (viz). There
shall be solid abutments or piers built from each shore or bank of s^d River to
extend so far across ye Same as to leave an opening or Space of Twenty six and.
a half rods only from one butment to ye other in ye most Convenient place in s^d
river for the Current or water to pass through which s^d abutments or pier shall
be built Solid with Stone & earth thirty two feet wide at bottom and not less
than Twenty Six feet at Top*[;]* ye Sides and end thereof, to be built of Stone. The
Stone work to be at least six feet thick and Solid acrosse ye ends and four feet
and an half thick at bottom and not less than one and a half feet thick at Top on
the Sides of s^d Abutments or piers and ye whole of s^d Stone work laid Compact
together and in a workmanlike manner. And for the Term of fifteen years from

the Date of January next said Henry Daggett, James Prescot & Thomas Punderson do agree to cover s^d twenty Six & a half rods with wooden Bridges of at least Twenty feet in the clear & fenced on each side with a good fence & made & kept in all respects convenient & Commodious for Travellers during said fifteen years which Bridges they *[p. 191]* are at Liberty to build & Support in such a manner as they shall think proper provided Nevertheless that if they Shall think proper they may extend said Butments or piers & fill up & make Solled a part of said opening to be done in the Same manner as is before Described & s^d Henry Daggett, James Prescot & Thomas Punderson do further contract & agree at the Expiration of s^d fifteen years (if it shall not then already have been Done) to build & erect Geometry Bridges across the s^d Space or opening that shall then be left & remaining for the water to pass through which Bridges shall be supported by Solid stone Pillars of at least twenty feet in width & Eight in length and s^d Stones on the upper Side or end to be keyed or linked together with Iron from the surface of the water & upwards so as to prevent any Injury or Damage to s^d Pillars by the Ice & there shall not be less than one such Bridge supported in manner afores^d to every four Rods of s^d Space in the Clear exclusive of what is taken up by s^d Pillars with Liberty however to vary a few feet by Lengthin Some & Shortening others if found necessary or convenient provided the whole does not exceed one Bridge to four Rods*[.]*

And said Henry Daggett, James Prescott & Thomas Punderson do further contract covenant & Agree with s^d Town that for every Rod of such Geometry Bridges as they shall leave at the Expiration of s^d Twenty years which shall exceed sixteen Rods in the Clear exclusive of said piers & abutments & Pillars they will pay unto s^d Town the Sum of twenty five pounds Lawful Money pe^r Rod & shall not upon any condition leave more Bridges than can be built over said Space of twenty six & half Rods heretofore mentioned in this Contract & s^d Henry Daggett, James Prescott & Thomas Punderson do further contract & agree with s^d Town that During the whole of s^d Term for which they are intitled to receive Tolls they will keep s^d Abutments, Piers & Bridges in good & sufficient Repair & at all times received above the Tides and Freshets so as never to eb overflowed or incommodad & Erect & keep up a good fence on each side of s^d abutments and Bridges & at the expiration of s^d Term to Deliver up to s^d Town *[p. 192]* Said Abutments*[,]* Piers*[,]* Bridges & Pillars in good Sufficient & Substantial Repair & fenced as afores^d with a decent & substantial fence from end to end.

And s^d Henry Daggett, James Prescott & Thomas Punderson do further contract and covenant & agree that s^d Bridge shall at all times during s^d Term both day & night be suitably & faithfully attended to accomodate the Public & not impede Travellers or persons wishing to pass s^d Bridge & will also pay to s^d Town of New Haven whenever the Selectmen of s^d Town shall direct the Sum of fifty pounds Lawful Money to be laid out in procuring & repairing Highways leading to & from said Bridge in s^d New Haven or in East Haven or in both as s^d Selectmen shall direct & order & also a further Sum of fifty pounds at the expiration of ten years from this Date for a like purpose & to be Disposed of in the Same manner & Paid.

Henry Daggett, James Prescott & Thomas Punderson further contract & agree that if at any Period hereafter & before the expiration of s^d Grant said Town of New Haven or the Selectmen thereof for the Time being shall deem it expedient that the s^d Henry Daggett, James Prescott & Thomas Punderson or any other person or persons claiming or holding under them shall procure sureties for the faithful performance of this Contract or agreement or any part thereof that then s^d Henry Daggett[,] James Prescott and Thomas Punderson or whoever claim under them shall within three Months after notice to them given for that purpose procure good & sufficient suretys or securities or on failure thereof s^d Bridge Abutments &c shall be immediately Forfeited to s^d Town & s^d Town or Selectmen thereof are hereby fully authorized to enter into & upon the same & to receive & appropriate to their own use & benefit the Toll ensuing there from. And s^d Town of New Haven or the Selectmen thereof Shall have the power of requiring like Security as afores^d from time to Time if they shall Judge it Necessary & on failure of procuring the same shall *[p. 193]* be entitled to a like Forfeiture in manner afores^d & s^d Henry Daggett, James Prescott & Thomas Punderson do for themselves[,] their heirs[,] and adminis^{rs} jointly & severally covenant contract & agree with s^d Town of New Haven that if they fail of erecting s^d Bridge abutments & piers in Manner afores^d, so that s^d Town are defeated of said Grants of assembly they will forfeit & pay to s^d Town the Sum of two Thousand pounds Lawful Money — & to the faithful performance of this agreement & Contract & every part & parcel thereof the s^d Henry Daggett, James Prescot & Thomas Punderson do bind themselves[,] their heirs[,] and Assignes firmly by these presents. And the Parties to this Instrument have interchanageably set their hands & seals & to an other Instrument of the same Tenor & Date one to be imscroved *[sic]* by each party this Sixteenth Day of March A.D. 1791.

Signed Sealed & Delivered
in presence of

Stephen Ball	Henry Daggett }	Seal
Peter Woodward	James Prescott ⌡	Seal

Thomas Punderson	Seal	
Samuel Bishop	Seal	
David Austin	Seal	
Isaac Beers	Seal	Committee of New Haven
James Hillhouse	Seal	
Levi Ives	Seal	
Elizar Goodrich	Seal	
David Daggett	Seal	

which Contract having been duely considered by ye Town it is thereupon Voted y^t ye Town do accept approve of, and Establish ye Same.

Voted ye Town Clerk enter upon the Records of ye Town a fair transcript of ye Contract made by ye Town respecting Dragon Bridge, and y^t ye Transcript be compared by ye contractors and Town Clerk and upon finding ye Same to be truely Transcribed That ye Town Clerk and Contractors *[p. 194]* Subscribe a Certificate upon the Town Records immediately under such transcript, y^t y^e ~~same~~ such transcript is a true Copy of the original.

We the Subscribers, being ye s^d Town Clerk & Contractors do hereby Certify y^t we have carefully compared the foregoing transcript as entered upon Record by ye Town Clerk, with ye original Contract, and find that ye Same is a true Copy thereof.

Sam^ll Bishop Town Clerk

Henry Daggett	}	Contractors
James Prescott		for Build^ing said
Thomas Punderson		Bridge

* See 188 page[1]

Listers. Voted y^t James Rice, Willm Lyon, Jonah Hotchkis, Elias Stilwell, Isaac Jones, Jacob Daggett, David Daggett, Jos^h Peck, Benjn Sanford, Joseph Bradly, Jeremiah Smith, Oliver Smith and David Bunce[2] be Listers the year ensuing.

---

1. The town clerk recorded the entries for December 27, 1790 through February 14, 1791 *after* the March 21, 1791 meeting, so the pagination of the original document is out of chronological order.

2. David Bunce (1757 - 1799) served in the Connecticut militia during the Revolution. He built the area's first paper mill in Westville in 1776. See, Wells, p. 101. See also, John Warner Barber and Lemuel S. Punderson, eds., *History and Antiquities of New Haven, Connecticut (1856), p. 58.*

Tythingmen. Voted y^t Chauncey Alling, Isaac Thompson, Eli Hotchkis, Asa Austin, Darias Stebbins and Thomas Benham be Tythingmen ye year ensuing.

Adjourned to ye Last monday of Instant Decr at 2 of the Clock in ye afternoon.

[DECEMBER 27, 1790]

AT A TOWN MEETING HOLDEN IN NEW HAVEN BY ADJOURNMENT UPON Y^E LAST MONDAY OF DEC^R 1790.[1]

Selectmen. Voted y^t Levi Ives, Thomas Punderson, Joseph Howell, Mark Levenworth and Azel Kimberly be Selectmen ye year ensuing.

Leather Sealer. Voted y^t Stephen Bradly be leather Sealer the year ensuing.

Sealer of w^ts and mea^r. Voted y^t Israel Munson be Sealer of weights and measures the year ensuing.

[p. 195] Dry Measures. Voted y^t John Miles be Sealer of dry measures the year ensuing.

key keepers. Voted y^t Joseph Munson, Noah Potter, John Culver, Nathan Dumer and Azel Kimberly be key keepers the year ensuing.

Grand Jurymen. Voted y^t Capt Fitch, Russel Clark, Peter Johnson, and Hez^h Hotchkiss be released from being grand Jurymen ye year ensuing.

Grandjuryman. Voted y^t Luther Fitch be grandjuryman the year ensuing.

[Fenceviewers.] Voted y^t John Mix and Obediah Hotchkis be fence viewers ye year ensuing.

Survey^rs. Voted y^t Jeremaih Atwater, Mark Levenworth, Eneas Munson, Thos Rice, Thomas Punderson, Oliver Smith, David Daggett, Israel Kimberly, Amos Alling and glover Ball be Surveyers of highways the year ensuing.

Committee for work house. The Committee y^t was appointed ye last meeting to report their opinion on the Expediency of building a work house &c. Reported

---

1. This entry was recorded out of chronological order by the town clerk.

to this meeting y^t in their opinion y^t it would be for the interest of ye Town to build a work house and y^t a piece of Land ought to be procured for y^t purpose, Thereupon voted y^t ye Selectmen procure a Sutiable piece of Land to set a house upon for ye purpose afores^d.[1]

This meeting adjourned to monday next at two of the Clock in the afternoon, to meet at the office of Henry Daggett Esqr.

[DECEMBER 31, 1790]

[p. 196] AT A TOWN MEETING HOLDEN IN NEW HAVEN UPON THE 31ST DAY OF DEC^R 1790.

Mod^r. Timothy Jones moderator.

Coll. Voted y^t Samuel Punderson be Collector of the State Taxes and also the Town rate ye year ensuing.

Pound. Voted y^t Lemuel Humphervile have liberty to build a pound and be key keeper of the Same.

[JANUARY 3, 1791]

AT A TOWN MEETING HOLDEN IN NEW HAVEN BY ADJOURN-MENT AT THE OFFICE OF HENRY DAGGETT ESQ^R ON THE THIRD DAY OF JANUARY 1791.

Work house. The Selectmen who were appointed by ye Town to procure a piece of Land to Set ye work house upon at a meeting of s^d Town on the 27th day of December last having made their report to this meeting that they have agreed with Jonathan Austin for a piece of his land Containing about 17 rods at the Sum of 25/ p^r rod which lyes East of the New highway y^t runs North from ye Store of Henry Daggett Esqr to Christian Heinsons house.
This meeting having Considered of the report, Thereupon Voted y^t s^d Selectmen purchase s^d Land, and in Case ye Selectmen Judge it for ye interest of the Town to make an exchange of ye Land which C^{ol} Fitch for some of his Land near where the Goal Stands for ye purpose aforesaid they are hereby impowered to do ye Same.

---

1. The first workhouse, or almshouse, was situated on College Street immediately south of the jail. See, Barber, *History and Antiquities of New Haven*, pp. 40 - 41.

[p. 197] [Contract to Manage Town.] Capt Thomas Punderson and others proposed a Contract and laid ye Same before this meeting wherein they proposed to pay ye Charges of ye Town ye year ensuing and build ye one half ye work house which Contract is in the words following viz.

We ye Subscribers agree to defray the expences of the Town of New Haven for ye year ensuing to commence on ye 5th Day of January 1791, except ye expences of rebuilding or repairing ye long bridge, or ye expences y^t may arise from ye repairing ye highways or neglect of repairing them, or for New highways[,] also Such expence which may arise from ye Small pox or Extradrinry Sickness or fire the extradoinry to be adjudged by ye Selectmen, we are to pay ye Necessary expence of house[,] fire[,] and candles for ye Selectmen, but at Such convenient place as we Shall procure. We are to pay ye expence of one Grand list, but to be performed by such proper person as we Shall procure. We are to Collect ye State Taxes and one Town Tax for ye year and to be answerable for ye amount of ye State Tax, to the Treasurer as ye Law directs. We agree to build a house in case ye Town provide a place for a work house 40 feet long by 24 wide[,] two story high[,] a celler under the whole[,] two Stacks of Chimneys[,] 12 Smokes[,] to lay 4 floors two of them Double[,] to paint ye Celler[,] to make partition doors and Stairs[,] and to lath and plaister ye first and Second Storys, we are to put Twenty five windows in s^d house 12 Squares each 7 by 9 glass[,] to make a Suteable number of out side doors, we are to cover the Rooff with boards and pine Shingles ye Sides and ends with pine boards ye Same to be plained and lapped. We are to paint ye house red the window frames and Sashes white, all which we agree to do, provided ye Town will grant us a Tax of Six pence half penny on ye pound. Provided however ye Town engage to pay us one hundred and five pounds in one year after ye house is finished with ye Lawfull interest thereon from ye Time ye house is finished till paid. The Tax to be paid in cash or Town orders. We are however not to be answerable for any cost y^t may arise by Suits against the Town unless they arise through our neglect, or in the *[p. 198]* Course of our business[.] We are also to maintain ye poor at Such place as we Chuse the accomodations &c to be under ye inspection and approbation of ye Selectmen the fines which are payable to ye Town to be off set against ye Cost. And it is further provided that we have all ye priviledges y^t ye Town usually have had to defray ye expences of ye poor out of their Estates provided they have any, or relation who by Law are holden to pay s^d expences, we are also to have ye benefit of s^d house for the present year after s^d house is erected. We will not be holden to build any new bridge neither do we expect to be at any Cost with regard to any regulating acts which may be necessary with regard to the work house.

Thomas Punderson
New Haven Jan^{ry} 3rd 1791   Lemuel Hotchkis
Sam^{ll} Punderson
Jos^h Peck

The foregoing writing being read in this meeting and the Town having Considered of ye Same, Do by Vote accept of it, and ordered ye Same to be recorded.

[Workhouse Inspection Committee.] Voted y^t Mr Jeremiah Atwater and Mr James Bradly be a Committee to inspect the aforesaid work and see y^t ye Same is Compleated according to ye foregoing agreement.

Oysters. This Town taking into Consideration ye benefit that might arise to the inhabitants from a preservation of the oyster and clams in s^d Town and ye great increase they are induced to believe there would be of ye Same if proper regulations were made agreeable to ye powers vested in s^d Town by ye Statute of ye State in such case provided are induced to make ye following rules and regulations.

Voted y^t no person or persons from and after the 15th Day of may next shall drive any team of horses or Cattle with any Cart waggon or Wheel Carriage into or upon any flat[,] Harbour[,] or Creek[,] or river in the Town of New Haven where oysters or Clams are caught or where oyster Shell are taken for ye purpose of taking oysters *[or]* Clams *[p. 199]* for y^t purpose of carrying away oysters[,] Clames[,] or Shells from any such flat[,] Habour[,] Creek[,] or river upon pain of forfieting ye Sum of Twenty Shillings for every Such offence and half to him who Shall prosecute ye Same to Conviction and ye other half to ye Treasurer for the use of s^d Town.

And it is further Voted by s^d Town y^t no person or persons Shall Catch any Oysters or long Clames in any of ye Creeks[,] Harbours[,] or upon any of the flats[,] Beeches[,] or Shorres of any such Rivers[,] Creeks[,] or Harbours in the bounds of s^d Town of New Haven from and after ye 15 Day of may anno Domini ni 1791 untill ye 8th Day of oct^r next upon pain of forfeiting Twenty Shillings Lawfull money for every Such offence Such person or persons Shall be Guilty of one half to him who Shall prosecute ye Same to Conviction and ye other half to ye Town Treasurer of ye Town for ye use of s^d Town.

Provided nevertheless y^t any person or persons obtaining from Eben^r Townshend or Silas Kimberly by a permit under their hands allowing such person or persons to Catch Clames or oysters as shall be Specified in s^d permit which

Permit s^d Townsend or Kimberly are hereby impowered to grant. Provided y^t s^d Permit be never more than Two bushels to one person at one time and s^d Permit to be returned to s^d Townsend or Kimberly granting ye Same within forty Eight hours from the Time of Granting ye Same and Such person or persons shall make it appear to ye Satisfaction of s^d Townsend or Kimberly y^t he or they have not taken or Caught more Clames & oysters [than] are Specified in s^d Permit. Such person or persons in Such case Complying with s^d requirements Shall not incur s^d Penalty of Twenty Shillings afores^d, and also Provided y^t nothing in this vote shall extend to prevent catching long Clames at any Season of ye year westward of the long Wharf in New Haven.

[p. 200] *Tax.* Voted y^t a rate of Six pence half penny be collected of ye inhabitants of this Town on the list of ye year 1790 to defray ye Charges of this Town ye year ensuing.

Voted y^t said rate be Collected by ye first day of march next.

Coll^r. Saml Punderson who was appointed to s^d rate refused to Serve, thereupon Voted y^t Aner Adee^1 be Collector of s^d Rate in his stead.

Coll^r. Samuel Punderson who was Chosen Coll^r of the State Taxes and Constable refused to serve. Thereupon Voted y^t Aner Adee be Constable and Collector of State Taxes the year ensuing in ye room of s^d Punderson.

Agents ab^t work house. Voted y^t James Hillhouse, Pierp^t Edwards & Jonathan Ingersoll Esqr be agents in behalf of this Town to apply to ye General assembly for Liberty and authority for this Town to make bye Laws from time to time to regulate a work house and house of Correction in this Town.^2

This meeting adjourned without day.

[FEBRUARY 14, 1791]

(p. 201] AT A TOWN MEETING HOLDEN IN NEW HAVEN UPON THE 14TH DAY OF FEBRUARY 1791.

---

1. Aner Adee (1759 - 1794?) was a Woodbridge native. See, www.dcnyhistory.org/pdfs/Adee-Clergyman.pdf.
2. The Assembly enacted such legislation in 1792, but reserved the right of the Superior Court to repeal any laws it judged unreasonable or unjust. See, *PRSC*, Vol. VII: 381.

Mod^r. Tim° Jones Esqr moderator.

Committee for Dragon Bridge. Voted y^t David Austin, Sam^ll Bishop, Isaac Beers, Eliz^r Goodrich, James Hillhouse, Levi Ives and David Daggett be a Committee to take into Consideration ye grants of ye General assembly to ye inhabitants of this Town for ye purpose of erecting and maintaining a bridge over ye East river a*[t]* Dragon an*[d]* also to examine whether it is advisable for this Town to build the whole or a part of s^d bridge at ye expence of ye Town or to authorize some individual or individuals to build ye Same and in case said Committee are of opinion y^t it is adviseable to procure individuals to build s^d Bridge s^d Committee are hereby authorized to Contract with any Suteable person or persons to errect a Suteable *[bridge]* at s^d place at his or their own expence and to authorize such person or persons for his or their own proper use to Collect ye Toll from s^d Bridge at ye proper Cost and expence of such person or persons contracting to build.[1]

Committee about money. Voted y^t Abr^m Bradly, Hez^h Sabin and Simeon Baldwin be a Committee to receive ye money of those persons who hold ye Same that was raised by Lottery to build a bridge at Dragon.

This meeting adjourned without day.

[MARCH 21, 1791]

[p. 202] AT A TOWN MEETING HOLDEN IN NEW HAVEN ON THE 21ST DAY OF MARCH 1791

Dragon Bridge. Voted y^t ye Selectmen of this Town be a Committee to ascertain with ye Contractors undertaken to build Dragon Bridge at what place at s^d Dragon the proposed bridge shall be erected and make report thereof to ye Town Clerk who shall record the Same.

Bridge. Voted y^t ye Town Clerk enter upon the Records of ye Town a fair transcript of the Contract by ye Town respecting Dragon Bridge.

---

1. The memorial of John Barns of East Haven argued that he and others built Long Bridge over the Quinnipiac River at Dragon some years prior and keep the existing bridge in good order and free of tolls. The Assembly resolved to allow Barns to continue offering use of Long Bridge without a toll. That decision was a major disincentive to the contractors involved n the building of the new bridge, who intended to charge a toll. *PRSC*, Vol. VII: 336.

Agents ab[t] dragon Bridge. Voted y[t] Pierp[t] Edwards and James Hillhouse Esqr[s] be agents and a Committee in behalf of this Town to apply to y[e] General assembly in may next to procure Suitable Highways in New Haven and East Haven leading to and from the bridge proposed to be erected at Dragon in Case s[d] Towns shall not Vollentarily lay out and open y[e] Same.

This meeting adj[d] without day.

[SEPTEMBER 23, 1791]

AT A TOWN MEETING HOLDEN IN NEW HAVEN UPON THE 23[D] DAY OF SEP[R] 1791.

Mod[r]. Voted y[t] Timothy Jones Esq[r] be moderator.

Oysters. Voted y[t] no person or persons excepting the inhabitants of the Town of New Haven shall hereafter Catch any oysters or long Clames in any of y[e] Rivers[,] Creeks[,] or Harbours upon any of the flats[,] beeches[,] or Shores of any such Rivers[,] Creeks[,] or Harbours in y[e] bounds of s[d] Town of New Haven upon pain of forfeting y[e] Sum of [...][1]

[p. 203] Committee ab[t] oysters. Voted y[t] David Daggett, Joseph Howell, Isaac Beers, Simeon Baldwin, Nathan Smith, Hez[h] Wetmore, Eliz[r] Goodrich and Samuel Candee be a Committee to prepare some proper act or votes for y[e] preservation of the oysters in this Town, and make report to the Town at their next meeting.

This meeting adjourned to y[r] 26th Day of instant Sep[r] 1791.

[SEPTEMBER 26, 1791]

[Clerk.] Voted y[t] Eliz[r] Goodrich be Town Clerk for this meeting the Clerk being absent.

Oyster act. Whereas an exclusive right to the fishery within the limits of the Town of New Haven by Law appertains to the inhabitants of s[d] Town and whereas it is expedient to regulate said fishery by establishing rules and ordinances for the preservation of the oysters within s[d] limits in pursuance of the

---

1. The town clerk neglected to enter the amount of the fine.

authority drerived from ye Statute of this State entiitled an act for encouraging and regulating Fisheries.

Voted y^t no person from and after ye 30th day of Sepr instant shall within ye Limits of this Town drive or cause to be driven any Team of horses or Cattle with any Cart waggon or other Carriage into or upon any flat[,] Harbour[,] Creek[,] or river where oysters or oyster shells are growing[,] caught[,] or taken upon pain of forfieting Twenty Shillings for every Such offence.

Voted y^t from and after ye 30th day of Sepr instant untill ye first day of Decr next no person shall take[,] gather[,] or Collect any oyster shells in from or upon any of the flatts[,] Beeches[,] Rivers[,] Creeks[,] or harbours[,] or waters within ye Limits of s^d Town on ye pain of forfieting Twenty Shillings for every such offence.

Voted y^t Joseph Howell, Elias Stilwell, Step^n Alling, Levi Ives, Stephen Row, Josiah Burr, Robert Brown, Azel Kimberly, Thomas Painter & Thomas Rice & each of them have authority and authority is hereby given to them and each of them from and after ye 30th day of Sepr instant untill ye 1st day of Decr next to grant a permit or permits in writing signed by them or ye person granting ye Same therein & thereby licencing ye person or persons therein Named to catch oysters at any place within y^e *[p. 204]* Limits of ye Town of New Haven in such quanty or quanties and for such a period of Time as shall be in such permit or permits specified and no person from and after ye 30th of Sepr instant untill the first day or Decr next shall catch or cause to be caught any oysters in or upon any of the flats[,] Beeches[,] rivers[,] Creeks[,] Harbour waters[,] or shores within ye Limits of ye Town of New Haven except by a permit or permits granted and Obtained as afores^d on ye pain of forfieting Twenty Shillings for every Such offence.

Voted y^t each and every penalty which may or Shall be incurred by any person or persons by a violation of ye rules and regulations this day Established by this Town relative to oysters and oyster Shells and for ye preservation of ye Same by Virtue or in Consequence of any Vote or votes this day passed by this Town Shall be in case of being said for by any private person the one half to him who sues for and recovers ye Same and ye other half to ye Treasurer of ye Town of New Haven to and for ye use of s^d Town and in case of being Sued by s^d Treasurer in behalf of s^d Town, Such penalty Shall be to and for ye use of s^d Town. And when requested by ye persons heretofore appointed to grant permits or a major part of them it shall be ye Duty of s^d Treasurer in behalf of this Town to prosecute every violation of ye rules and regulations afores^d.

The foregoing votes were passed in Meeting of the Town of New Haven this 26th Day of Sepʳ 1791.

attest Elezʳ Goodrich Town Clerk pro Tempʳᵉ

[DECEMBER 12, 1791]

[p. 205] AT A TOWN MEETING HOLDEN IN NEW HAVEN UPON THE 12ᵀᴴ DAY OF DECEMBER 1791.

Clerk. Samˡ Bishop Chosen Town Clerk.

Modʳ. Voted yᵗ Timothy Jones Esqʳ be moderator.

Selectmen. Voted yᵗ Levi Ives, Joseph Howell, Thoˢ Punderson, Simeon Baldwin and Thomas Painter be Selectmen the year ensuing.

Treasʳ. Voted yᵗ David Austin Esqʳ be Town Treasurer the year ensuing.

Constables. Voted yᵗ Jonas Prentice, Peter Woodward, John R. Throop, Joseph Peck, Aner Adee, David Trowbridge and Abrᵐ Auger be Constables the year ensuing.

Grandjurymen. Voted yᵗ John Goodrich, Luther Fitch, Silas Hotchkis, Stephen Osbourn, William Walker, David Bristoll and Thomas Benham be grand jurymen year ensuing.

Listers. Voted yᵗ James Rice, Willᵐ Lyon, Jonah Hotchis, Elias Stillwell,[1] Isaac Jones, Jacob Daggett, David Daggett, Joseph Drake, Willᵐ Powel, Jeremiah Smith, Oliver Smith, Hezʰ Hotchkiss and David Bunce be listers yᵉ year ensuing.

Tythingmen. Voted yᵗ Pember Jocelin, Bradford Hubbard, Amos Doolittle, Isaac Thompson, Merit Carrinton, Amos Hill, Asa Austin, Gold Smith and David Benham be Tythingmen yᵉ year ensuing.

Sealers of leather. Voted yᵗ Nathˡˡ Fitch and James merriman be sealers of leather yᵉ year ensuing.

---

1. Elias Stillwell (ca. 1748 - 1824) of New Haven served as a private in the Second Company of the Governor's Foot Guard in 1775. He was later commissioned a captain in the First Connecticut Regiment, serving throughout the Revolution. He was an original member of the Society of the Cincinnati. His membership certificate, signed by George Washington, resides at the New Haven Museum.

Sealer of w^{ts} & measures. Voted y^t Israel Munson be Sealer of weights and measures the year ensuing.

Sealer [of dry measures]. Voted y^t John Miles be Sealer of dry measures the year ensuing.

[p. 206] Key Keepers. Voted y^t Joseph Munson, Noah Potter, John Culver, Nathan Dumer and Azel Kimberly be key keepers ye year ensuing.

fence viewers. Voted y^t John Mix, Obediah Hotchkis and Noah Potter be fence viewers ye year ensuing.

Highways. Voted y^t ye Town the year ensuing will mend their highways by a Tax.

Contract to support the poor. Voted y^t the Town will Contract for ye Support of the poor and ye other annual expence of the Town ye year ensuing with any person or persons who will enter into such Contract as ye Town may approve.

Com^{ee} about the poor. Voted y^t Messrs Jeremiah Atwater, David Austin, Eneas Munson, Hez^h Sabin and Nehemiah Smith be a Committee to receive proposals for Contracting for ye Support of ye poor and ye other Current expence of ye Town ye year ensuing and report make *[sic.]* to ye next meeting of this Town with their opinion of ye propriety of Contracting and also report Such Contract to ye Town as s^d Committee deem expedient.

Committee ab^t oysters. Voted y^t Jonathan Ingersoll, Eliz^r Goodrich, Simeon Baldwin and David Daggett be a Committee to prepare a proper act for this Town to pass for the preservation of Oysters in the Harbour the year ensuing and report such act to ye Town at their next meeting.

Committee ab^t Lottery. The Committee appointed by the Town to adjust accounts with ye holders of the money arising from the East river lottery &c. made their report in ye following words viz.

We ye subscribers being appointed by ye Town of New Haven with others to settle and adjust accounts with ye holders of ye money arising from East river Bridge lotery and to receive and pay ye Same to ye Contractors for building s^d Bridge — Report as follows:

That we have received of Col Hez^h Sabin who held ye money paid

by Esqr Daggett Prenciple	£139 - 16 - 4
Interest accrewed in his hands	15 - 11 - 11
	155 - 8 - 3
[p. 207] Of M Levenworth Esqr (one of y^e managers)	
in State notes	78 - 0 - 0
Of Timothy Jones Esqr (who held y^e money paid in	
by Maj^{or} Prentice) Principle	189 - 19 - 9
interest accrued in his hands	27 - 17 - 1$_{1/2}$
	217 - 16 - 10 $_{1/2}$
Of Michael Todd (one of y^e managers)	
In notes and bills including In^t	30 - 0 - 3
Amounting in y^e whole to	£481 - 5 - 4 $_{1/2}$

The whole of which we received in paper ,and have paid over to y^e Contractors and have their receipt therefor.

We have further to observe y^t y^e Sum above mentioned as received of Col Sabin are in full of all demands against him.

That it has never been in our power to ascertain the Exact Sum due from Mr Levenworth as we were never able to obtain his account we believe however there is a further Sum due from him.

That there appears a difference between ye account of Maj^r Prentice who paid his money to Tim^o Jones Esqr and ye account rendered by Esqr Jones of monies in his hands, the difference is about £6 in State money, as those gentlemen did not perfectly agree in their Ideas respecting this difference we made ye Settlement with Esqr Jones upon ye receipts which Ma^{jr} Prentice produced so y^t there is about Six pounds in State money due from one of those gentlemen, with respect to Capt Todds account we have to observe y^t he has Charged ye Lottery with £13 - 0 - 0 as paid M Levenworth Esqr to answer prizes and a further Sum of £21 - 18 - 0 due from Maj^r Eli Levenworth for Tickets he took to sell – both of which Capt Todd says were done by consent of the managers and he thinks himself not answerable as we have rec^d no account from M Levenworth Esqr we know not whether he has Credited ye Sum Charged him.

New Haven June 1, 1791

Levi Ives
Simeon Baldwin

[p. 208] [Lottery.] A Statement of the avails of East river Bridge lottery as received by Levi Ives one of ye Selectmen of New Haven and Simeon Baldwin one of ye Committee of s^d Town who were appointed to receive ye Same and pay it over to the Contractors of s^d Bridge

1791 May of Col Sabin Principle	139 - 16 - 4	
Interest accrueding his hands	15 - 11 - 11	
his hands		155 - 8 - 3
of Mark Levenworth		78 -
in State note		
of Timothy Jones Esqr		
1 Rhode Island bill —	1 - 4 - 0	
1 Machusetts D^o	12 - 0	
his due bill for state notes	24 - 13 - 2	
his note against Town of New Haven	51 - 1 - 1	
State notes State money &c	140 - 6 - 7$\frac{1}{2}$	
		217 - 16 - 10$\frac{1}{2}$
Of Michael Todd		
1 Contin^l New Hampshire bill	48S	
State note note *[sic.]* and State money	£27 - 12 - 3 = 30 - 0 - 3	
		481 - 5 - 4$\frac{1}{2}$

Rec^d New Haven May 13th = 1791

Of Levi Ives and Simeon Baldwin the above numerated notes and bills amounting to four Hundred Eighty one pounds five Shillings and four pence half penny — including one forty Shilling counterfit state bill of y^e emission of June 1780 — amounting with interest to Forty Seven Shillings and 6^d.[1]

Henry Daggett   ⎱   Contractors
James Prescott   ⎰   for Building
Thomas Punderson   ⎰   s^d bridge

The foregoing report of ye Committee and ye above Receipt, being laid before this meeting, and having been duely considered, Thereupon Voted y^t the Same be accepted and ye Same be recorded.

This meeting adjourned to ye Last monday of instant December at two of y^e

---

1. In an effort to undermine the nascent American economy, the British forged Continental currency throughout the American Revolution. See, Stuart Hatfield, "Faking It: British Counterfeiting During the American Revolution, *Journal of the American Revolution*, October 7, 2015, https://allthingsliberty.com/2015/10/faking-it-british-counterfeiting-during-the-american-revolution/

Clock in ye afternoon.

[DECEMBER 26, 1791]

[p. 209] AT A TOWN MEETING HOLDEN IN NEW HAVEN BY AD-
JOURNMENT UPON THE 26 DAY OF DECEMBER 1791.

Oysters. Rules and ordinances for regulating ye fishery of Oysters.

Where as an exclusive right to ye fishery of oysters within the Limits of ye Town
of New Haven by Law appertains to ye inhabitants of s^d ye Town ~~of New Ha-
ven~~ and whereas it *[is]* expedient to regulate s^d Fishery by Establishing rules and
ordeniances for ye preservation of ye oysters within s^d Limits in persuence of
authority derived from the Statute of this State entitled an act for encourging
and regulating fisheries.

Voted y^t no person from and after ye first day of Jany next Shall within ye Limits
of this Town drive or cause to be driven any Team of horses or cattle with any
cart waggon or other carriage into or upon any flatt*[,]* Harbour*[,]* creek*[,]* or
river where oysters or oystershells are growing*[,]* caught*[,]* or taken upon pain
of forfieting Twenty Shillings for every such offence.

Voted y^t from and after ye first day of may untill the first day of December annually no person shall take*[,]* gather*[,]* or Collect any oyster Shells in from or
upon any of the flatts*[,]* beeches, rivers*[,]* Creeks*[,]* or Harbours*[,]* or waters
within ye limits of s^d Town on pain of forfieting Twenty Shilling*[s]* for every
Such offence.

Voted y^t Joseph Howell, Levi Ives, Robert Brown, Josiah Burr, Elias Stilwell,
Stephen Row, Stephen Alling, Thomas Painter, Silas Kimberly and Thomas Rice
and each of them have authority and authority is hereby given unto them and
each of them from ~~and after~~ ye first day of may annually to grant permit or
permits in writing Signed by them or the person granting ye Same therein and
there by licensing ye person or persons therein named to catch oysters at any
place within ye Limits of ye Town of New Haven in Such quantity or quantities
and for such period of Time as shall be in such permit Specified, and no person
after ye first day of may untill ye first day of December annually Shall catch or
cause to be caught any oysters in or upon any of ye flatts*[,]* beeches*[,]* Creeks*[,]*
Harbour *[p. 210]* waters, or Shores within ye Limits of ye Town of New Haven
except by Virtue of a permit or permits granted and obtained as aforesaid on y^e

pain of forfeiting Twenty Shillings for every such offence.

Voted y^t each and every penalty which may or Shall be incurred by any person or persons by a violation of ye rules and regulations this day established by this Town relative to ye oysters and oystershells and for ye preservation of ye Same or by Virtue and in consequence of any vote or votes this day passed by this Town relative to the Same Shall be if Sued for by any private person the one half to him who Shall Sue for & recover ye Same and the other half to ye Treasurer of this Town of New Haven to and for ye use of s^d Town.

And if Sued for by s^d Treasurer in behalf of s^d Town such penalty shall be to and for ye use of s^d Town.

And when requested by the persons appointed to grant permitts or a maj^r Part of them, it Shall be the duty of s^d Treasurer in behalf of this Town to prosecute every violation of ye rules and regulations aforesaid.

Lister. Voted y^t Jonah Hotchkis be released from being Lister and that John Goodrich be lister in his room.

Leather sealer. Voted y^t James Merriman be released from being Leather sealer and y^t Stephen Bradly be leather sealer in his room.

Rate. Voted y^t there be a rate of Six pence half penny on ye pound on the Grand List for ye year 1791 collected of the inhabitants of this Town to defray the Charges of this Town ye year ensuing.

Voted y^t s^d rate Shall be paid on ye first day of march next.

Coll. Voted y^t Aner Adee be Collector *[of]* ye State Taxes in this Town ye year ensuing.
Coll. Voted y^t Aner Adee be Collector of ye above Town rate.

Surveyers. Voted y^t David Benham, James B. Reynolds, Peter Johnson, Elijah Thompson and Hezekiah Sabin be Surveyers of Highways ye year ensuing.

[p. 211] Committee Dragon Bridge. Voted y^t Samuel Bishop, David Austin, James Bradly, Jeremiah Atwater, Hez^h Sabin, Joseph Drake, Nehemiah Smith, Nathan Smith, and Pierpoint Edwards be a Committee to take into Consideration ye Contract lately entered into by this Town with Henry Daggett and others for building Drag-

on Bridge the present Situation of s^d Bridge with ye Genuine Cost of building s^d Bridge and report their doings with their opinions at ye next adjourned meeting.

This meeting adjourned to ye 1st Monday of Feb^{ry} next at 2 ^{O}Clock in ye afternoon.

[FEBRUARY 6, 1792]

AT A TOWN MEETING HOLDEN BY ADJOURNMENT UPON THE 6TH DAY OF FEB 1792.

Committee about Dragon Bridge. The Committee appointed ye Last meeting to take into Consideration ye Contract lately entered into by the Town with Henry Daggett and others relative to building Dragon Bridge so Called made their report in the following words viz.

We being appoi*[n]*ted to take into Consideration the Contract lately entered into by ye Town with Henry Daggett and others for building dragon Bridge ye present Situation of s^d bridge with ye Genuine Cost of building s^d Bridge and report their doings with their opinion to the Next adjourned meeting.

Report [on Dragon Bridge]. That having seen and inspected s^d Contract and examined ye manner in which it was formed we find y^t ye Town did enter into a Contract with s^d Henry Daggett & others for building s^d Dragon Bridge which Contract we herewith lay before y̲e̲ Town, we also report y^t s^d Contract hath been so formed y^t it is Legally binding upon ye Town, and y^t therefore y^t ye Town will in Case any infraction of ye Covenants on ye part of ye Town in s^d Contract contained Shall happen, be at Law responsable to s^d Henry Daggett & others *[p. 212]* For ye Damages occasioned by Such infraction, we are however of opinion y^t no infraction on ye part of the Town hath as yet Happened.

We find y^t s^d Henry Daggett and others, have built at s^d Dragon a well Constructed Bridge Convenient for all kind of passing with Teams*[,]* horses &c but s^d Bridge is not intirely Compleated, the abutments not being filled with dirt, and ye side fences not being all erected.

We further report y^t we have not been able, to ascertain ye Genuine Cost of s^d Bridge, as we could not possess our Selves of ye documents necessary to accomplish y^t part of our Commission, ye s^d Contractors have however furnished us with an Estimate of ye cost of said bridge made by them which we herewith lay before ye Town.

We consider ye imbarresments which at present attend s^d Bridge arising from a resolve of ye general assembly passed in oct^r Last as not asinibale *[sic.]* to any fault of the Town and y^t it will be very Eligible to Save the Town from any difficultes which may hereafter arise from ye opperation of that resolve.

We therefore Submit to ye Consideration of ye Town the Expediencey of appointing an agent to apply in behalf of ye Town to ye Next assembly for a grant of a lottery in order to enable the Town to make said Dragon bridge a free Bridge.[1]

| New Haven Feb^{ry} 6th 1792 | Pierpoint Edwards Saml Bishop David Austin Neh^h Smith Nathan Smith Joseph Drake Jeremiah Atwater James Bradly | } Committee |

Whereupon voted y^t ye foregoing report of ye Comm^{tee} be accepted and y^t Pierpoint *[Edwards]* Esqr be agent in ye Name and behalf of this Town to apply to ye next Gen^{ll} assembly to git a Grant of a lottery for ye purpose mentioned in ye foregoing report of s^d Committee.

[APRIL 9, 1792]

[p. 213] AT A TOWN MEETING HOLDEN IN NEW HAVEN UPON THE 9TH DAY OF APRIL 1792.

Mod. Voted y^t Timothy Jones Esqr be moderator.

Agents ab^t work house. Voted y^t David Daggett and William Hillhouse Esq^{rs} be agents in behalf of this Town to apply to ye General assembly in may next to git an act passed enabling this Town to make such Rules and regulations as are

---

1. In October of 1791, the General Assembly voted to allow legacy families who built a bridge over the East River to continue operating that bridge with no tolls. That decision was in direct conflict with Daggett and company's contract with New Haven, which allowed for the building of a new bridge at the contractors' expense that would be paid for by virtue of a toll being charged for 20 years. Since that bridge was deemed not technically completed, the General Assembly approved New Haven's request to hold a lottery to raise £3,000 in May of 1792. Those funds would ostensibly be used to pay off the contractors and make the bridge toll free. See *PRSC,* VII: 420 - 421.

needfull for the persons who shall be Committed to s^d house.

Dragon Bridge. Voted y^t in the opinion of this Town it is expedient That Henry Daggett, James Prescot and Thomas Punderson apply to ye General assembly to be holden in may Next for an indemnification or reimbursment of the Expences of Building Dragon Bridge and that ye agent heretofore appointed to prefer a petition in behalf of ye Town assist them therein.

This meeting adjourned without day.

[JUNE 11, 1792]

AT A TOWN MEETING HOLDEN UPON THE 11TH DAY OF JUNE 1792.

Mod^r. Tim° Jones Esqr Chosen moderator.

Bye laws for work house. Voted y^t Elizur Goodrich, Simeon Baldwin, Roger Sherman Esq^{rs}, and Mr Joseph Peck prepare a code of Bye Laws to regulate ye work house in the Town of New Haven and report to the next meeting of this Town.

Dragon Bridge. Voted y^t David Austin, James Hillhouse Esq^{rs}, Capt Thomas Painter, Joseph Bradly Esqr, Mr Levi Ives and Mr Silas Alling and Mr Jos^h Howell be a Committee to Converse with ye Contractors of Dragon Bridge relative to ye Contract heretofore *[p. 214]* made by ye Town of New Haven and ye s^d Contractors and relative to a late act of assembly to reimburse them ye expence &c. of s^d Bridge and report to the Next meeting of this Town what shall be done in ye premises.

This meeting adjourned to ye 25th day of instant June at 2 of ye Clock in the afternoon.

[JUNE 25, 1792]

AT A TOWN MEETING HOLDEN BY ADJOURNMENT UPON Y^E 25TH DAY OF JUNE 1792.

Mod^r. Voted that Roger Sherman Esqr be moderator.

Committee ab^t Dragon Bridge. To ye Committee of ye Town of New Haven appointed to Confer with the Subscribers relative to the building of Dragon Bridge and to the Grants of the Gen^{ll} assembly respecting the Same and report &c.

Gentlemen — Having ever been desireous of a fair and friendly Settlement with ye Town we have heretofore made Several proposals to ye Town relative to s^d Business, and now hoping to Close ye Business we are induced to make ye following proposals viz.

We will Compleat ye fence and fill up the abutment within forty days to ye Satisfaction of ye Selectmen of ye Town, and resign ye bridge to ye Town any and every Claim we have thereto and all ye avails of ye old Lottery which has Come into our hands Except £250 Lawfull money and Convey to ye Town all our right in and to ye Lottery granted to us by ye Last Gen^ll Assembly provided ye Town will Settle our accounts being £1097 - 11 - 3[.] And after deducting from s^d account ye aforesaid Sum of £250 - 0 - 0[,] give us Notes for the residue on Interest payable in nine months. And if ye Town prefers having our Claims adjusted by proper persons we are willing to Submit our whole Claims to ye Judgement of three disinterested men [p. 215] mutually Chosen provided we are secured of ye payment of their award without Cost, and Provided ye Submitment be made and finished within one month[,] and also Provided we are released and fully discharged from any further Claim of s^d Town on account of ye Contract made and entered into on the 16th Day of march AD 1791 relative to ye building s^d Dragon Bridge, and provided they Close with ye aforesaid proposal we will receive (for the Ease and Benefit of s^d Town) to ye amount of £200 - 0 - 0 in tickets of ye Last granted Lottery in part payment of our notes, if ye Lottery is drawn in a reasonable time.

We would likewise make another proposal of Settlement to y^e Town viz — That Provided we are fully discharged from every part of s^d Contract and from all Claims of y^e Town or State of Connecticut respecting y^e keeping s^d Bridge in repair or rebuilding y^e Same, we will deliver over to y^e Town all y^e avails of the old Lottery except £250 = 0 : 0 L money and we will deliver to y^e Selectmen of New Haven fifty Doll^rs in Tickets in y^e Last granted Lottery And accept y^e grant of y^e aforesaid Last granted lottery in full of all Claimes we have against s^d Town by vertue of s^d Contract — on Condition we are Compleatly discharged from all Claimes of any kind or nature relative to s^d Dragon Bridge except ye finishing the fence and filling up ye abutments as aforesaid which we ingage to do.

Dated in New Haven   Henry Daggett
this 25^h Day of June   James Prescott
1792   Thomas Punderson

[p. 216] [Dragon Bridge.] The Committee appointed by ye Town of New Haven to Confer with ye Contractors for building Dragon Bridge and to report their

Opinion what ought to be done relative to ye Contract between s^d Town and said Contractors — Beg leave to report that they have had sundry Conferences with s^d Contractors who have Submitted to ye Consideration of ye Committee the foregoing proposals of Settlement. But the Committee do not think it adviseable for the Town to undertake ye management of s^d Lottery but it is ye opinion of ye Committee, y^t if s^d Contractors will keep s^d Bridge in repair and Rescue ye Same for three years and then deliver the Same to ye Town in good repair, or will pay ye Town one Hundred and fifty Dollars in Tickets to be lodged in ye Treasury and deliver the bridge in good repair according to ye Terms of their proposal y^t s^d Town and said Contractors Shall mutually discharge each other from s^d Contract.   New Haven June 25th 1792

> Silas Alling
> Joseph Bradly
> Joseph Howell
> James Hillhouse
> Levi Ives
> Thomas Painter

Upon ye Report of Committee aforesaid — Voted that this Town accept of ye report within mentioned with this alteration viz. excluding ye words and fifty next after ye word one Hundred in, ye s^d report and Voted also y^t upon ye s^d Daggett[,] Punderson & Prescots delivering a good Sufficient quit Claim Deed of their right to s^d Bridge abutments &c ye Same having been first Compleated by said Daggett &c in manner as stated in ye foregoing proposition that then ye Selectmen of this Town be and they are hereby authorized to execute a full discharge of ye Contract heretofore entered into by s^d Daggett &c at ye Same time receiving of s^d Daggett &c a full discharge of all contracts made [p. 217] By said Town in any way to s^d Daggett &c relative to said Bridge and receiving of them also said Tickets or Security for them.

Work house Bye Laws. Whereas the general assembly of this State at their Session in May Last past authorized ye inhabitants of ye Town of New Haven to Establish Bye Laws[,] Rules[,] and regulations for ye well ordering ye work house or house of Correction in s^d Town &c.

It is therefore Voted y^t it shall and may be Lawfull for any assistant or Justice of ye peace resident in s^d Town and they are hereby authorized and impowered, on their knowledge or upon ye Complaint or information of one of ye overseers of s^d house, and due conviction thereon, to send to s^d workhouse all persons of the following Charrector and discription, found or taken within ye Limits of s^d Town viz. all Rouges[,] vagabonds[,] Sturdy Beggers[,] and other lew^d[,] Idle[,] disolute[,] profane[,] and disorderly persons[,] all runaways[,] stubbern Servants and Childern[,] Common Drunkards[,] common night walkers[,] Pilferers and all persons who neglect their Calling, misspend what they earn and do not provide for ye Support of themselves and familes and also all persons under distraction and unfit to go at large whose relations or friends do not take Care of their Safe Confinement, and order them to be Confined in s^d house and kept to Labour under ye Rules and regulations there of, untill released by order of Law.

Voted y^t Such assistant or Justice of Peace Shall Specify in his warrant or order of Commitment ye Period of Time which Such person or persons Shall be holden in s^d house not exceeding three months on a Conviction of either of the offences or disorders aforesaid. And ye overseers of s^d house with ye advice of any assistant or Justice of Peace resident in s^d Town Shall have authority to release and discharge Such person or persons from s^d house at any time before ye experation of ye time Specified by Such assistant or Justice such warrant or order of Coromitment *[p. 218]* Notwithstanding. And all persons Committed as aforesaid shall be allowed out of their earnings two thirds thereof first deducting there form ye Cost & expence of their Commitment and Support, to be assesed by the overseers, and ye other third of their earnings shall be to ye use of this Town, unless such persons are heads of families in which case ye overseers are authorized to apply ye whole of s^d earnings or so much as they shall think necessary for ye relief and support of the families of such persons.

Voted that ye Selectmen of this Town for ye Time being be and they are hereby appointed the overseers of s^d house and shall have authority to appoint a master of s^d house, and him remove at Pleasure and shall from time to time make Such allowance to s^d master for his care and Service as they Judge Just and reasonable to be paid from ye Treasury of this Town, and Shall at ye expence of this Town furnish to s^d master from time to time materials sutiable to keep to Labour such persons as are Committed to s^d house and shall direct ye master as to ye Quatity & quality of ye Labour to be exacted from, and ye Quantity and quality of food and drink to be furnished to ye respective persons in his Custody.

Voted y^t ye master of s^d house receive all persons sent to s^d house as aforesaid and shall keep them to Labour untill released by order of Law and Shall as ye overseers shall direct punish them by puting fetters or shakles upon them or by whipping on ye naked body not exceeding ten stripes at one time and from time to time in case they be stubborn, disorderly or Idle and do not preform their

Tasks and y^t in good Condition or may hold them in Close confinement and may also with ye direction of ye overseers abridge them of their food and drink as ye Case shall require *[p. 219]* untill they be reduced to order and obedience. And ye s^d master shall keep an exact account of all materials furnished and of all ye profits and earnings that shall be made by labour of those under his custody, and shall account therefor with s^d overseers at least once in three months and oftener if required by s^d overseers, and ye master of s^d house who shall refuse to account as aforesaid or shall otherwise be neglegent in his Duty required by ye rules and regulations of this town relative to s^d house shall not only be liable to account in ye ordinary Course of Law but Shall pay a fine of Twenty shillings for every such neglect to be recovered by s^d overseers for ye use of this Town.

Voted y^t in case any person or persons Committed to s^d house shall inlawfully abscond or make his Escape thereform, he or they shall on being returned to s^d house be Corrected on ye Naked body not exceeding ten Stripes according to ye direction of ye overseers and it shall be ye duty of ye master to inflict such Correction.

Voted ye Town Clerk cause the Rules and regulations of this Town this day established for ye government of ye work house to be printed for three weeks Successively in the Newspaper of Messrs Thomas & Samuel Green, and also present a Copy thereof to ye Honble Sup^r Court to be holden in ye County of New Haven on July next for ye examination of said Court.

This meeting adjourned without Day.

[p. 220] Proposals for defraying Certain expences of the Town of New Haven.

Contract about the poor. We the Subscribers in Consideration y^t ye Town of New Haven will accept ye following proposalls and do & will grant to us the Subscribers ye avails of a Tax of Six pence half penny on ye pound on ye Last Grand list of s^d Town — do Contract & agree with s^d Town as follows viz:

1. That from ye 5th Day on Jan^{ry} AD 1792 to ye 5th Day of January 1793, we will maintain & Support ye poor in s^d Town y^t now are or that may become Chargable to said Town during s^d Time at such place or places as we shall procure with ye approbation of ye Selectmen of s^d Town, and we will Save harmless ye Town of New Haven from all Such expence.

Provided nevertheless y^t we shall have all the priviledges which ye Town usually ye use of this Town, unless such persons are heads of families in which case ye overseers are authorized to apply ye whole of s^d earnings or so much as they shall think necessary for ye relief and support of the families of such persons.

Voted that ye Selectmen of this Town for ye Time being be and they are hereby appointed the overseers of s^d house and shall have authority to appoint a master of s^d house, and him remove at Pleasure and shall from time to time make Such allowance to s^d master for his care and Service as they Judge Just and reasonable to be paid from ye Treasury of this Town, and Shall at ye expence of this Town furnish to s^d master from time to time materials sutiable to keep to Labour such persons as are Committed to s^d house and shall direct ye master as to ye Quatity & quality of ye Labour to be exacted from, and ye Quantity and quality of food and drink to be furnished to ye respective persons in his Custody.

Voted y^t ye master of s^d house receive all persons sent to s^d house as aforesaid and shall keep them to Labour untill released by order of Law and Shall as ye overseers shall direct punish them by puting fetters or shakles upon them or by whipping on ye naked body not exceeding ten stripes at one time and from time to time in case they be stubborn, disorderly or Idle and do not preform their Tasks and y^t in good Condition or may hold them in Close confinement and may also with ye direction of ye overseers abridge them of their food and drink as ye Case shall require *[p. 219]* untill they be reduced to order and obedience. And ye s^d master shall keep an exact account of all materials furnished and of all ye profits and earnings that shall be made by labour of those under his custody, and shall account therefor with s^d overseers at least once in three months and oftener if required by s^d overseers, and ye master of s^d house who shall refuse to account as aforesaid or shall otherwise be neglegent in his Duty required by ye rules and regulations of this town relative to s^d house shall not only be liable to account in ye ordinary Course of Law but Shall pay a fine of Twenty shillings for every such neglect to be recovered by s^d overseers for ye use of this Town.

Voted y^t in case any person or persons Committed to s^d house shall inlawful-ly abscond or make his Escape therefrom, he or they shall on being returned to s^d house be Corrected on ye Naked body not exceeding ten Stripes accord-ing to ye direction of ye overseers and it shall be ye duty of ye master to inflict such Correction.

Voted ye Town Clerk cause the Rules and regulations of this Town this day established for ye government of ye work house to be printed for three weeks Successively in the Newspaper of Messrs Thomas & Samuel Green, and also present a Copy thereof to ye Honble Sup^r Court to be holden in ye County of New Haven on July next for ye examination of said Court.

This meeting adjourned without Day.

[p. 220] Proposals for defraying Certain expences of the Town of New Haven.

Contract about the poor. We the Subscribers in Consideration y^t ye Town of New Haven will accept ye following proposalls and do & will grant to us the Subscribers ye avails of a Tax of Six pence half penny on ye pound on ye Last Grand list of s^d Town — do Contract & agree with s^d Town as follows viz:

1. That from ye 5th Day on Jany AD 1792 to ye 5th Day of January 1793, we will maintain & Support ye poor in s^d Town y^t now are or that may become Chargable to said Town during s^d Time at such place or places as we shall procure with ye approbation of ye Selectmen of s^d Town, and we will Save harmless ye Town of New Haven from all Such expence.

Provided nevertheless y^t we shall have all the priviledges which ye Town usually have had of defraying ye expence and of Supporting individuals out of their own Estate if they have any, or from ye Estate of such relations of such persons as are by Law bound to give them Support and y^t we shall have ye use and improvement of ye work house for ye accomodation of ye poor and others, and y^t ye Town of New Haven do apply to ye General assembly at their next session for Liberty and authority to make rules and regulations respecting such work house and the persons in it.

2. That we will pay for ye necessary expences of house fire and candles for ye accomodation of the Selectmen at their meetings, at Such convenient place as we shall procure.

3. That we will pay expence of making up one grand list for ye Town to be made by Such proper person as we shall procure.

[p. 221] 4th. That we will pay ye expences of Collecting ye State Taxes for ye year ensuing, and one Town Tax and will be answerable for ye amount of ye State Taxes as ye Law directs.

5. That we will discharge ye s^d Town from a Debt of one Hundred and five pounds ye ballance due to us for building ye work house.

6. That we will lay out and expend ye avails of one half penny of s^d Tax in repairing highways and bridges or pay the Same into ye Treasury of s^d Town as ye Selectmen Shall direct.

7. That we will also defray all ye other usual Expences of said Town during the Time for which we Contact excepting all expences which may arise from or any way respecting ye long or Dragon Bridge — so Called, excepting also all expences which may arise from an aplication to ye General assembly for liberty to regulate ye work house or that may arise for new highways or new bridges excepting also such expences as may arise from the Small pox[,] fire[,] or Extraordinary Sickness viz. such Sickness as ye Selectmen of s^d Town shall Judge to be Extraordinary — exceep[t]ing also all ~~such~~ Costs which may arise from any suit against the Town unless they arise through our neglect or in ye Course of our business.

Provided nevertheless y^t ye bills of Costs for Justices[,] Grand jurors[,] Sheriffs[,] and Constables shall be Taxed according to Law, and y^t all fines payable to ye Town Shall be appropriated towards ye defraying ye Cost of Criminal prosecutions — and all persons Convicted of Crimes shall be assigned to us in Service a reasonable time to defray ye expence in they shall be able to pay it. Provided also y^t we are not to be Chargeable with Costs in any such Cases unless ye Grandjuror making Complaint shall have first made due enquiry and found reasonable evidence for ye presentment of ye person complained of.

[DECEMBER 10, 1792]

[p. 222] AT A TOWN MEETING HOLDEN IN NEW HAVEN ON THE 10TH DAY OF DECEMBER 1792.

Clerk. Sam^ll Bishop Chosen Town Clerk.

Mod^r. Tim° Jones Esqr Chosen moderator.

Selectmen. Voted y^t Levi Ives, Simeon Baldwin, Joseph Howel, Thomas Punderson and Thomas Painter be selectmen the year ensuing.

Constables. Voted y^t Jonas Prentice, Peter Woodward, John R. Throop, Joseph Peck, Aner Adee and David Trowbridge be constables the year ensuing.

Grandjurymen. Voted y^t John Goodrich, Eldad Mix, Eli Hotchkiss, Stephen Atwater, Thomas Benham & David Bristoll be ~~Grand~~jurors for ~~the Year~~ ensuing.

Listers. Voted that Joseph Howell, Jonah Hotchkiss, Nathan Beers, Isaac Jones, David Daggett, Joseph Drake, William Powell, John Prindle, Jeremiah Smith, Hezekiah Hotchkiss and David Hull be Listers the year ensuing.

Treas[r]. Voted y[t] David Austin Esq[r] be Town Treasurer the year ensuing.

Tythingmen. Voted y[t] David Atwater, Samuel Nivens, Joseph Peck, Asa Austin, Darious Stebbins and David Bristoll Ju[r] be Tythingmen the year Ensuing.

Leather Sealers. Voted y[t] Nath[ll] Fitch and James Merriman be leather sealers y[e] year ensuing.

Sealer of w[t] &c. Voted y[t] Israel Munson be sealer of weights and measures y[e] year ensuing.

[p. 223] Sealer [of dry measures]. Voted y[t] John Miles be Sealer of dry measures the year ensuing.

Key Keepers. Voted yt Joseph Munson, Noah Potter, John Culver, Nathan Dumer and Azel Kimberly be key keepers the year ensuing.

Fence viewers. Voted y[t] John Mix, Obediah Hotchkiss and Noah Potter be fence viewers the year Ensuing.

Committee about the poor. Voted y[t] Samuel Bishop, Simeon Baldwin, David Austin, Eneas Munson and Levi Ives be a Committee to receive proposals for Contracting for y[e] Support of y[e] poor and other incident Charges of y[e] Town for the year ensuing and make report to the next Town meeting with their opinion of the Propriety of Contracting and also report such Contract to y[e] Town as said Committee Deem expedient.

Small pox. Voted y[t] Doctor Levi Ive[1]s and Eneas Munson J[r2] have Liberty and

---

1. Dr. Levi Ives (1750 - 1826) served in the Continental Army under General Montgomery during the seize of Quebec and again with General Benedict Arnold in the Battle of Saratoga. See, William Richard Cutter, *et. al.* eds., *Genealogical and Family History of the State of Connecticut, Vol. IV: 1778.*
2. Dr. Munson (1734 -1826) graduated from Yale in 1753, initially served as a minister then became a physician as of 1760, establishing his practice in New Haven. An ardent patriot, he served in the General Assembly and was a principal in the formation of the Connecticut Medical Association.

Liberty is hereby granted to set up an inoculating Hospital for yᵉ Small pox in such place and at such time as yᵉ Town shall Judge proper.

Small pox. Voted yᵗ Samuel Bishop, David Austin, Stephen Ball, Henry Daggett, Thomas Painter, Eneas Munson and Simeon Baldwin be a Committee to ascertain some proper place where to erect a Hospital for sᵈ inoculation and affix the time when such inoculation shall begin and make report to the next meeting.

This meeting adjourned to the 4ᵗʰ monday of instant December at 2 of yᵉ Clock in the afternoon.

[DECEMBER 24, 1792]

[p. 224] AT A TOWN MEETING HOLDEN IN NEW HAVEN BY ADJOURNMENT UPON Yᴱ 24ᵀᴴ DAY OF DECEMBER 1792.

[Selectmen.] Voted that Cᵒˡ Joseph Drake and Mʳ Dyer White be Selectmen yᵉ year ensuing.

[Listers.] Voted yᵗ David Bunce and John Goodrich be listers yᵉ year ensuing.

Committee abᵗ the Poor. We yᵉ Subscribers being a Committee appointed by yᵉ Town of New Haven to receive proposals for Contracting for yᵉ Support of the poor &c for the year ensuing, report as follows viz. That we have received proposals from Mʳ Joseph Peck which we lay before the Town with this report.

We are of opinion yᵗ it would be adviseable to accept yᵉ proposals made by Mʳ Peck & and yᵗ yᵉ Town grant a Tax of four pence on yᵉ pound for yᵉ purposes aforesaid.

We are further of opinion yᵗ it would be adviseable to grant a Tax of one penny on yᵉ pound, to be Collected by yᵉ Same person who shall collect yᵉ four penny Tax which shall be paid into yᵉ treasury, and be exclusively appropriated to repairing the Publick roads in this Town, which we Submit to yᵉ Consideration of yᵉ Town. New Haven Decʳ 17ᵗʰ 1792

Signed by order of yᵉ Committee
Samˡ Bishop

The Town having Considered ʸᵉ ~~above~~ the above report of yᵉ Committee, do by

Vote accept ye Same.

Proposals for defraying Certain expences of the Town of New Haven for ye year 1793.

[p. 225] Contract about the Poor.[1] We ye Subscribers Joseph Peck as principle and Peter Johnson as his Surety for faithful performance in Consideration y^t ye Town of New Haven will accept ye following proposals and do and will grant to s^d Joseph the avails of a Tax of four pence on ye pound on the grand list of s^d Town for the year 1792, do Contract and agree with s^d Town as follows viz:

1. That ye s^d Joseph will from ye 5th Day of January 1793 to ye 5th Day of January 1794 maintain & support all ye poor in s^d Town y^t now are or during said Period may become Chargable to s^d Town at such place or places as ye s^d Joseph shall procure with ye approbation of ye Selectmen of s^d Town and will save harmless ye s^d Town from all such expence.

Provided Nevertheless y^t ye s^d Joseph shall have all ye priviledges which ye Town usually have had of defraying ye expence of Supporting individuals out of their own Estate if they have any, or from the Estate of Such relations of Such persons as they are by Law bound to give them Support — and y^t ye s^d Joseph have ye use & improvement of ye work house for ye accomodation of ye poor and others.

2. That ye s^d Joseph shall pay for ye necessary expence of house[,] room fire[,] and Candles for ye accomodation of ye Selectmen at their meetings at Such Convenient place as he Shall procure with their approbation.

3. That ye s^d Joseph Shall pay ye expence of making up one grand list for ye Town to be made by Such proper person as he Shall procure with ye approbation of ye Listers of sd Town.

4. That ye s^d Joseph Shall pay ye expence of Collecting ye State Taxes for ye year ensuing, and whatever Town Taxes ye Town shall grant for ye benefit of s^d Joseph or for ye repairs of roads and will be answerable for ye amount of such Taxes.

[226] 5th. That ^{ye} s^d Joseph shall pay in ye Treasury of said Town of New Haven one Sixteenth part of the whole amount ~~Such Taxes~~   the Sum raised by

---

1. This document was likely submitted to the town clerk, who then made an exact copy. Note, for example, that Peck is referred to by first name only, a practice the town clerk never followed.

ye said four penny tax.

6th. That ye s^d Joseph will defray all ye other usual Expences of said Town during ye Time, for which he proposes to contract, exceep[t]ing all expenses which
may arise from or in any way respecting the long or Dragon Bridge, so Called,
excepting all expenses y^t may arise from new highways or new bridges, Excepting also all such expenses as may arise from ye small pox[,] fire[,] or Extraordinary Sickness viz. Such Sickness as ye Selectmen of s^d Town shall Judge to be
extraordinary.

Excepting also all Costs which may arise from any Suits against ye Town unless thy
arise through the neglect of s^d Joseph or in the Course of his business.

Provided Nevertheless y^t ye bills of Costs for Services of Justices[,] Grandjurors[,]
Sheriffs[,] and Constables shall be Taxed according to Law, and y^t all fines payable
to ye Town shall be appropriated towards defraying ye Costs of Criminal prosecutions — and y^t all persons convicted of Crimes shall be assigned to ye s^d Joseph in
service for a reasonable time to defray ye expense if they shall be unable to pay it.

Provided also y^t ye s^d Joseph is not to be Chargeable with Costs in any Such Cases unless ye Grand juror making Complaint shall have first made due inquirey
and found reasonable evidence for the presentment.

Joseph Peck
Peter Johnson[1]

[Rate.] Voted y^t there be a rate or Tax of four pence on the pound on ye List for
ye year 1792, to be Collected of the inhabitants of this Town, in order to fulfill
the Contract ye Town hath this day entered into with Joseph Peck for ye Support
of ye poor & other Charges of the Town.

[p. 227] Tax. Voted y^t there be a rate or Tax of one penny on ye pound on ye List
for ye year 1792 to be collected of ye inhabitants of this Town for repairing y^e
Publick roads and highways ye year ensuing.

Voted y^t ye Two foregoing rates shall be paid on the first day of march next.

Coll^r. Voted y^t Christian Hanson be ye Collector of ye Two foregoing rates.

---

1. Captain Peter Johnson (1745 - 1813) was a Revolutionary War veteran who served under Col.
William Douglas. He married Chloe Tuttle (1738 - 1773) in 1768 and is buried at the Grove Street
Cemetery in New Haven, Wells, *Connecticut Men in the War of the Revolution*, p. 406.

and regulating fisheries.

Voted y^t no person from and after ye first day of January next, Shall within ye Limits of this Town drive or cause to be driven any Team of horses or Cattle with any Cart*[,]* waggon*[,]* or other Carriage into or upon any flat*[,]* Harbour*[,]* Creek*[,]* or river where oysters or oyster shells are growing*[,]* caught*[,]* or taken upon pain of forfieting Twenty shillings for every Such offence.

Voted y^t from and after ye first day of may untill the first day of December annually no person shall take*[,]* gather*[,]* or Collect any oyster shells in from or upon any of the flats*[,]* Beeches*[,]* rivers*[,]* Creeks*[,]* or *[p. 228]* Harbour or waters within ye Limits of s^d Town on pain of forfieting Twenty Shillings for every Such offence.

Voted y^t Joseph Howel, Levi Ives, Robert Brown, Josiah Burr, Elias Stilwell, Stephen Row, Stephen Alling, Silas Kimberly *[intentional space]* and Thomas Rice and each of them have authority and authority is hereby given unto them and each of them from ye first day of may to ye first day of ~~may~~ Decr annually to grant a permit or permits in writing Signed by them or ye person granting ye Same therein and thereby licencing the person or persons therein Named to Catch oysters at any place within ye Limits of the Town of New Haven in Such Quantity or Quantities and for such Period of Time as shall be in such permit Specified and no person from and after the first Day of may untill ye first day of ~~may~~ Decr annually shall Catch or Cause to be Caught any oysters in or upon any of ye flats*[,]* Beeches*[,]* Creeks*[,]* Harbours*[,]* waters*[,]* or shores within ye Limits of ye Town of New Haven Except by Vertue of a permit or permits granted and obtained as aforesaid on ye pain of forfieting Twenty shillings for ever*[y]* such offence.

Voted y^t each and every penalty which may or shall be incurred by any person or persons by a violation of ye rules and regulations this day Established by this Town relating to oysters and oyster shells and for ye preservation of ye Same or by vertue or in Consequence of any vote or votes this day passed by this Town relative to ye Same shall be if Sued for by any private person the one half to him who shall Sue for and recover ye Same and the other half to ye Treasurer of ye Town of New Haven to and for ye use of s^d Town, and if Sued for by s^d Treasurer in behalf of s^d Town such penalty shall be to and for ye use of s^d Town, and when requested by ye persons appointed to grant permits or a maj^r Part of them it Shall be ye duty of s^d Treasurer in behalf of this Town to prosecute every violation of ye rules and regulations aforesaid.

[DECEMBER 9, 1793]

[p. 229] AT A TOWN MEETING HOLDEN IN NEW HAVEN UPON THE 9ᵀᴴ DAY OF DECEMBER 1793.

Clerk. Voted yᵗ Samuel Bishop be Town Clerk.

Modʳ. Voted yᵗ Stephen Ball Esqʳ be moderator. Said Ball refused to serve as moderator, was by vote released.

Modʳ. Voted yᵗ Timothy Jones Esqʳ be moderator.

Selectmen. Voted yᵗ Messʳˢ Levi Ives, Simeon Baldwin, Thᵒ Punderson, Dyar White, Joseph Drake and Thomas Painter be Selectmen yᵉ year ensuing.

Treasʳ. Voted yᵗ Joseph Bradly Esqʳ be Town Treasurer the year ensuing.

Constables. Voted yᵗ Jonas Prentice, Peter Woodward, John R. Throop, Joseph Peck, Aner Adee, Christian Hanson, and David Trowbridge be Constables yᵉ year ensuing.

Grandjurymen. Voted yᵗ John Goodrich, Rosewell Judson, Luther Fitch, Samuel Punderson, Jeremiah Smith, and David Bristoll be grandjurymen yᵉ year ensuing.

Listers. Voted yᵗ Joseph Howell, John Goodrich, Isaac Jones, Nathan Beers, David Daggett, Hezʰ Hotchkiss, David Bunce, Joseph Drake, William Powell, Justus Smith, Darias Stebbins and Jonah Hotchkiss be listers yᵉ year ensuing.

Tythingmen. Voted yᵗ Doctʳ Hotchkis¹, John Peck, Samˡˡ Nivins, John Austin, Josʰ Peck, Christian Hanson, Gold Smith, and Ezra Smith be Tythingmen yᵉ year ensuing.

[p. 230] Leather Sealer. Voted yᵗ Stephen Bradly be leather sealer yᵉ year ensuing.

Sealer of wᵗˢ & measᵉˢ. Voted yᵗ Israel Munson be Sealer of weights and measures the year ensuing.

Sealer of dry measᵉ. Voted yᵗ John Miles be Sealer of dry measures the year ensuing.

---

1. Dr. Obidiah Hotchkiss (1731 - 1805) was one of the 13 physicians who founded the New Haven Medical Association in 1803.

Dragon Bridge. Upon motion, y^t some repairs might be made upon ye eastern abut-ment of Dragon Bridge & the expence of Such repairs to be defrayed out of ye Surplus of ye Last years highway tax, Voted y^t ye Selectmen are directed to cause such repairs to be made upon s^d abutment as to them shall seem Expedient and y^t ye expence be paid out of said Surplus, unless upon application of ye Selectmen of ye Selectmen of New Haven to ye Selectmen of East Haven the s^d repairs or any part thereof shall be made at ye expence of s^d Town of East Haven.

Committee. Upon motion to appoint a Committee, to take up ye State of ye Town and ye expences of ye Current year, to receive any proposals to contract for ye Support of ye poor of ye Town and other expences. Voted y^t David Daggett, Jer-emiah Atwater, Sam^ll Bishop, Simeon Baldwin, David Austin, Jos^h Bradly, Henry Daggett and Thomas Painter, be a Committee for ye above purposes and y^t they make report at ye adjourned meeting.

[Work house]Committee. Upon motion to make a Table of fees to regulate Commit-ments to ye work house. Voted that Eliz^r Goodrich, Simeon Baldwin and Dyar White be a Committee for ye above purpose and to make report at ye adj^ed meeting.

This meeting adj^ed to ye Last monday of this month at two of ye Clock in the afternoon.

[DECEMBER 30, 1793]

[p. 231] AT A TOWN MEETING HOLDEN IN NEW HAVEN BY AD-JOURNMENT UPON THE 30TH DAY OF DECEMBER 1793.

Key Keepers. Voted y^t Elisha Munson, Noah Potter, John Culver, Nathan Dumer, and Azel Kimberly be Key Keepers ye year ensuing.

fence viewers. Voted y^t Obediah Hotchkiss, Noah Potter, John Clause and Merrit Clark be fence viewers for ye year Ensuing.

Contract about ye poor. We ye Committee appointed by ye Town of New Haven to receive proposals for Contracting for ye Support of ye poor &c for ye year ensuing. Report as follows. That we have received proposalls from Mr Joseph Peck which we lay before ye Town with this report.

We are of the opinion y^t it would be adviseable to accept the proposals made by Mr Peck, and y^t ye Town grant a Tax of five pence on ye pound, on ye List 1793 for ye proposals theirin mentioned.

We are further of opinion y^t it would be adviseable to grant a Tax of one penny on ye pound on ye Same list to be Collected by ye Same person who shall Collect ye five penny^e Tax, which shall be paid into ye Treasury and be Exclusively, appropriated to repairing ye Public Roads in this Town, with ye this expectation[,] y^t ye inhabitants of ye parrish of West Haven be exempted from the payment of ye Tax on Condition they Sufficiently repair their proportion of the Public Roads in ye antient mode prescribed by Law.[1]

We are further of opinion y^t it will be ye most aconmic *[sic.]* mode of expending ye money to be raised by ye penny Tax *[p. 232]* to hire three or four honest industrious men, by the month, to be constantly employed on the roads, under the direction of the Selectmen, or Such Surveyors, as the Town shall appoint for that Purpose.

Which we submit to the consideration of the town.
New Haven, December 24th 1793.

> Signed by order of the Committee
> Samuel Bishop

The town having considered the above report of the Committee do by Vote accept the same.[2]

Proposals for defraying certain expences of the town of New Haven, for the Year 1794.

Contract ab^t poor. We the Subscribers Joseph Peck as Principal and Peter Johnson, as his surety for faithful Performance, in consideration, that the town of New Haven will accept the following proposals, & do and will grant to the said Joseph, the avails of a tax of five pence on the pound, on the grand List of s^d town for the Year 1793, do contract and agree with said town as follows, to - wit.

1. That the s^d Joseph will, from the 4th day of January 1794, to the 5th day of January 1795, maintain and support all the poor in said town, that now are, and

---

1. Since the beginning of New Haven, male residents, ages 16- 60 , were expected to work on road crews a given number of days per year or face fines. See, Malia, *Visible Saints*, pp. 16, 213.
2. With the exception of the marginalia, entries beginning with p. 232 through half of p. 237 of the original manuscript were made by Elisha Munson. Bishop at this time was serving as mayor of New Haven, an office he held from 1793 - 1803.

that during said period, may become chargeable to s^d town, at such place or places, as the s^d Joseph shall procure, with the approbation of the Selectmen of said Town, and will save the town harmless from such expence.

Provided nevertheless, that said Joseph shall have all *[p. 233]* the priviledges, which the town usually have had of defraying the expence of supporting individuals out of their own estate (if they have any) or from the estate of such relations or such persons, as are by law bound to give them support, and that the said Joseph have the use & improvement of the work-house, for the accommodation of the poor & others.

2. That the said Joseph shall pay for the necessary expences of House - room, fire and candles & paper, and other usual expences, for the accommedation of the Selectmen, at their meetings, at such convenient place, as he shall procure with your approbation.

3dly That the s^d Joseph shall pay the expence of making one Grand List, for the year ensuing, for the town, to be made by such proper person, as he shall procure, with the approbation of the Listers of s^d Town.

4^{thly} That the s^d Joseph shall pay the expence of collecting the State taxes for the year ensuing, and whatever town taxes the town shall grant for the benefit of s^d Joseph, or for the repairs of roads, and will be answerable for the amount of such taxes.

5^{thly} That said Joseph shall pay into the Treasury of the town of New Haven, one tenth part of the whole amount of the sum raised by said five-penny-tax.

6^{thly} That the s^d Joseph will defray all the other usual expences of s^d town, during the time for which he proposes to contract, excepting all expences, which may arise from repairing roads or *[p. 234]* Bridges, or that may arise from new highways or new bridges; excepting also all expences as may arise from the small pox or extraordinary sickness, viz. Such sickness, as the Selectmen of s^d town shall judge to be extraordinary — excepting also all such expences, as shall be incurred in relieving those, who may, during said period sustain loss by fire, and all abatements, which may be made on the taxes of such persons, in consequence of such fire, excepting also all Costs, which may arise from any suits against said town, unless they arise through the neglect of said Joseph, or in the Course of his business.

Provided nevertheless, that the bills of Costs for Services of Justices, Grand-jurors, Sheriffs and Constables shall be taxed according to Law. And that all fines, payable to the town shall be appropriated towards defraying the Costs of Criminal prosecutions — and that all persons convicted of Crimes shall be assigned to the s^d Joseph in service for a reasonable time, to defray the expence, if they shall be unable to pay it. Provided also, that the said Joseph is not to be chargeable with Costs in any such cases, unless the Grandjuror making complaint shall have first made due enquiry, and found reasonable evidence for the presentment.

New Haven, Decr 23^d 1793
In presence of
S. Baldwin   Joseph Peck
John Goodrich   Peter Johnson

[p. 235] The foregoing proposals having been duly considered were accepted by the town, and thereupon it was Voted.

Tax. That a tax of five pence on the pound be laid on the List of the year 1793, collectible by the 1st day of March next and

also Voted

Coll^r. That Capt Peter Johnson be Collector of s^d 5 penny tax.

Voted

Tax. That a tax of one Penny on the pound be laid on the List of 1793, for the repairing of highways, according to the mode proposed by the Committee in their report, & also

Voted

[Collector.] That Capt Peter Johnson be Collector of s^d penny tax.

Voted

Highways. That Levi Ives, Pierpoint Edwards, Thomas Punderson, Azel Kimberly & David Bristol Ju^r, be Surveyors of Highways for the year ensuing.

Voted

Coll^r. That Christian Hanson be Collector of the State tax for the Year ensuing.

Oyster act

oyster act. Rules and Ordinances for regulating the fishery of Oysters.

Whereas the exclusive right of the fishery of oysters, within the limits of the town of New Haven, by law appertains to th*[e]* Inhabitants of said town. And whereas it is expedient to regulate said fishery, by establishing rules and Ordinances for the preservation of the Oysters within s^d limits in pursuance of authority derived from the Statute of this State, entitled, "An act for encouraging & regulating fisheries.*["]*

Voted, that no person, from and after the 1st day of January *[p. 236]* Next, shall within the limits of this town, drive, or Cause to be driven, any team of horses or Cattle, with any Cart, waggon or other carriage, into or upon any flat*[,]* creek or harbour, where oysters or oyster-shells are growing, Caught or taken, upon pain of forfeiting twenty Shillings for every such offence.

Voted, that from and after the 1st day of May, until the 1st day of December, annually, no person shall take, gather or collect any oyster-shells in or upon any of the flats, beaches, rivers, Creeks or harbours or waters within the limits of s^d town, on pain of forfeiting twenty Shillings for every such offence.

Voted, that Joseph Peck, Stephen Allen & Dyer White, Thomas Painter & Benjamin Smith and Stephen Rowe, and each of them have authority, and authority is hereby given unto them, & each of them, from the 1st day of May, to the 1st day of December, annually, to grant permit or permits in writing, signed by them, or the person granting the same therein, and thereby licensing the person or persons therein named, to catch Oysters at any place within the limits of the town of New haven, in such quantity or quantities, & for such period of time, as shall be in such permit specified.

And no person, from and after the 1st day of May, until the 1st day of December annually shall catch or cause to be caught any oysters in or upon any of the flats, beaches, creeks, harbours, waters or shores within the limits of the town of Newhaven, except by virtue of a permit or *[p. 237]* permits granted and obtained as aforesaid, on the pain of forfeiting twenty Shillings for every such offence.

Voted, that each and every penalty, which may or shall be incurred, by any person or persons, by a violation of the rules and regulations this day established by this town, relative to oysters and Oyster shells, & for the preservation of the same, or by virtue thereof, and in consequence of any Vote or Votes, this day passed by this town, relative to the Same, shall be, if sued for by any private person, the one half to him, who shall sue for and recover the same, and the other half to the Treasurer of the town of New Haven, to and for the use of said town.

And if sued for by s^d Treasurer in behalf of said town, such penalty shall be to and for the use of said town, and when requested by the persons appointed to grant permits or a major part of them, it shall be the duty of said Treasurer in behalf of this town to prosecute every Violation of the rules and regulations aforesaid.

[MARCH 7, 1794]

AT A TOWN MEETING HOLDEN IN NEW HAVEN UPON Y^E 7TH DAY OF MARCH 1794.[1]

Mod^r. Voted y^t Simeon Baldwin Esqr be moderator.

[Collector] Highways. Voted y^t Christian Hanson be Collector of ye Town rate, and rate for repairing ye highways, granted in December Last, in ye room of Capt Peter Johnson who was Chosen Collector, and hath refused to Serve.
adj^d without day.

[AUGUST 29, 1794]

[p. 238] AT A TOWN MEETING HOLDEN IN NEW HAVEN ON Y^E 29^H DAY OF AUGUST 1794 — UPON ACCOUNT OF THE SICKNESS THAT NOW PREVAILS IN THE TOWN AT THIS TIME.

Mod^r. Voted y^t Timothy Jones Esqr be moderator of this meeting.

Sickness. This meeting being informed, y^t there is a Vessel Coming up y^e Harbour, it being apprehended y^t there are persons on board who are or have been Sick on board of y^e vessel. Therefore voted that Aner Adee forthwith go to the water side, and prevent any boat from landing on y^e shore, from s^d vessel, untill further orders are given.[2]

_____

1. Beginning with this entry, Samuel Bishop resumed recording the minutes of the town meetings.
2. According to the records of the Connecticut General Assembly, New Haven was struck by epi-

Tax. Voted y^t there be a rate ~~of~~ or Tax of three pence on y^e pound, Collected of y^e inhabitants of this Town to defray ye Charges of ye Sickness y^t prevails in this Town at this Time.

Voted y^t s^d rate or Tax be forthwith Collected.

Coll^r. Voted y^t M^r. be Collector of s^d Rate or Tax.

Coll^r. Said Ives refused to serve, as a Collector of s^d rate. This meeting do appoint Napthola [sic.] Daggett to be Collector of s^d rate in the room of s^d Ives.

Health officers. Voted y^t Doct^r Levi Ives, Doctor Elijah Munson & Mr William Powell[1] be health officers for this Port.[2]

Sickness. Voted y^t this Town do approve ye proceedings and regulations of ye Selectmen, heretofore *[p. 239]* Established for ye purpose of preventing a contagious disease from Spreading among us and to request them to pursue ye most vigerous measures agreeable to ye Statute for the future.[3]

Com^{tee}. Voted y^t Messrs Russel Clark, Abel Burrett, Thadd^s Beecher, Stephen Alling, Hez^h Hotchkiss and Thomas Rice be a Committee to assist and to *[...]*[4].

Adjourned without day.

[DECEMBER 8, 1794]

AT A TOWN MEETING HOLDEN IN NEW HAVEN UPON Y^E 8TH DAY

demics of scarlet fever and then yellow fever beginning in late 1793, which continued into the summer of 1794. Yellow fever was eventually traced to a merchant vessel in New Haven that had transported yellow fever victims in the Caribbean. The diseases eventually claimed 113 lives across the state; 64 were from New Haven. See, *PRSC,* Vol. VIII: 186 and 186n. See also, Atwater, *History of the City of New Haven,* pp. 86 - 88; Fredrick Hoadley, "A Review of the History of the Epidemic of Yellow Fever in New Haven, Conn. in the Year 1794," in *Papers of the New Haven Colony Historical Society,* VI: 223 - 262.

1. Captain William Powell (1745 - 1830) was likely a sea captain added to the health committee due to his knowledge of ships and their masters dealing in the West Indies trade.

2. In response to the medical crisis in New Haven, the town authorized this committee in hopes of arresting the spread of disease. The committee led to the founding of the New Haven Board of Health in March of 1795. See, New Haven Aldermen's Meeting, 1784 - 1835, MSS, p. 81. See also, Charles Levermore, *The Republic of New Haven,* pp. 234 - 237, 236n.

3. The New Haven aldermen enacted a series of sweeping mandates, from proper drainage to placement of privies, in hopes of eradicating the potential for disease in the city. See, New Haven Aldermen's Meetings, March 30, 1795, MSS, Photocopy in possession of Peter J. Malia.

4. Town clerk never completed the entry.

OF DECEMBER 1794.

Mod^r. Voted y^t Timothy Jones Esqr be moderator.

Selectmen. Voted y^t Stephen Alling, Nathan Beers, Hez^h Hotchkiss, William Powell, Thomas Painter and Thadd^s Clark be Selectmen ye year ensuing.

Treasu^r. Voted y^t Joseph Bradly Esqr be treasurer the year ensuing.

Constables. Voted y^t Joseph Peck, John R. Throop, Christian Hanson, Eli Hotch-kiss, and David Trobridge be Constables ye year ensuing.
Coll^r. That Christian Hanson be Collector of the State tax for the Year ensuing.

Grandjurymen. Voted y^t Bradford Hubbard, Nathan Smith Esqr, Daniel Read[1], Jared Mansfield, David Bristoll and Samuel Trowbridge be grandjurymen ye year Ensuing.

Listers. Voted y^t Jonah Hotchkiss, Isaac Mills, Isaac Jones, William Hillhouse, Daniel Read, David Bunce, Thomas Rice, Russel Clark, John Smith, and Justus Smith be listers ye year Ensuing.

[p. 240] Surveyers. Voted that Hez^h Sabin, Isaac Jones, Erastus Bradly, Edward Alling, Deacon Nathan Smith, Merit Clark, Darial Stebbins and Nehemiah Smith be Surveyers of highways the year ensuing.

Tythingmen. William Trowbridge, James Merriman, Amos Hill, William Warland, James Alling, Oliver Clark and Asa Austin be tythingmen the year ensuing.

Committee ab^t poor. Voted that Elizur Goodrich, Wm Powell, Step^n Alling, Hez^h Hotchkiss and Deacon Nathan Smith, together with the Selectmen Chosen last year, be a Committee for the purpose of Consulting upon the present State of the Debts of the Town; also upon the manner in which the contract for sup-porting the poor last year was Comply^d with, as also to furnish themselves with information respecting the Condition of the poor now in town, and to make report the next meeting of what shall appear to them to be the most eligible plan for the Town to adopt for defraying the expences of the ensuing year.

---

1. Daniel Read (1757 - 1836) was a comb maker by trade, a singer, and a composer of hymns. See, http://www.hymntime.com/tch/bio/r/e/a/read_d.htm.

Sickness. Voted that the Selectmen Chosen this day be a Committee for the purpose of examining all the houses and places where the epidemic sickness has been in this Town, the year past, and to inform themselves whether they have been thoroughly cleansed, and whereon they shall find that the Cleansing has been in any respect neglected, they are to cause such houses to be throughly cleansed.

This meeting adjourned to the Last monday instant December at two of the clock in the afternoon.

[DECEMBER 29, 1794]

[p. 241] AT A TOWN MEETING HOLDEN IN NEW HAVEN BY ADJOURNMENT UPON Y^E 29TH DAY OF DECEMBER 1794

[Leather] Sealer. Voted y^t Stephen Bradly be leather Sealer ye year Ensuing.

Sealer [Weights & Measures]. Voted y^t Israel Munson be Sealer of weights and measures ye year ensuing.

Sealer [Dry Measures]. Voted y^t John Miles be Sealer of dry measures the year ensuing.

Key Keepers. Voted y^t Elisha Munson, Noah Potter, John ~~Clouse~~ Culver, Nathan Dumer and Azel Kimberly be key keepers ye year ensuing.

Fence viewers. Voted y^t Obediah Hotchkiss, Noah Potter, John Clouse and Merrit Clark be fence viewers the year Ensuing.

workhouse. The letter addressed to this Town by y^t Clerk of ye County Court, by order of s^d Court relative to ye building a workhouse, being read, voted y^t ye Sam lye for Consideration untill ye next meeting.

Tax. Voted y^t there be a rate of Six pence on ye pound upon ye List of ye year 1794, Collected of ye inhabitants of this Town to defray ye Charges of the Town.

Contract to Support the poor. Voted y^t ye report of ye Committee respecting a Contract appointed ye last meeting, be accepted, and y^t ye Same be recorded, which is ye words following viz.

To the Inhabitants of ye Town of New Haven Gentlemen — we your Committee appointed to enquire into ye manner in which a contract *[p. 242]* Entered into by Joseph Peck for ye purpose of defraying Certain expences of ye Town for ye past year hath been performed.

Report y^t on enqurey & Examination we find y^t so far as respects ye Support and maintence of ye poor ye s^d Peck hath hetherto complyed with his undertaking and y^t he ye s^d Peck hath from time to time, defrayed the other Expences of ye Town for which he was holden as they have occured or come to his knowledge that there is due from s^d Peck the Tenth part of ye five penny Tax granted to him by said Contract, and y^t he remains responsable for the Collection and discharge of ye highway Tax and State Taxes for ye past year.

Your Committee have also taken into Consideration ye Expediency of forming a Contract to defray ye expences of ye Town for ye ensuing year and an inquirey find y^t for six years past ye Expenditures of ye Town have been defrayed by Contract and y^t during that period ye rates of ye Town has been dismissed[,] a Convenient work house erected[,] and a Debt of about £400-0-0 discharged[,] your Committee are of opinion y^t ye past Contracts have been benefical for ye Town and that it is adviseable to defray ye Expences of ye Ensuing year by Contract, your Committee are however of opinion y^t ye Contractor or Contractors, should be holden by ye Contract to Support and maintain either partly or intirely all Such persons as ye Selectmen Judge proper objects of Support from ye Town and y^t Such Support & maintence should be afforded in such mode or modes for such time or times and at such place or places as ye Select men approve and direct, without any reimbursment from ye property from any person Supported. That such persons as are Supported and able to Labor Should [p. 243] at ye Direction of ye Selectmen be holden to Labor for the Contractor or Contractors, y^t Such Contractor or Contractors should have a certain deffinite sum as a Compen[s]ation from ye Town and y^t in other respects ye Contract s[h]ould be nearly Simaler to ye Contract of ye past year and y^t a Sum not exceeding £400 Should be appropriated as a compensation to such person or persons as will accept and perform a Contract formed on these principles[.] Your Committee have accordingly ~~performed~~ prepared a Contract and are of opinion y^t it is Expedient y^t a rate of Six pence on ye pound be laid on ye List of 1794 for ye expences of ye ensuing year that £400 — of such rate be appropriated to ye discharge of Such Contract and yt a half penny on ye pound on s^d rate together with ye remains of ye Last years highway Tax be appropriated to making and repairing bridges and highways that in case the inhabitants of ye parrish of West Haven Choose to repair ye highways within their Limits by Labor agreeably to ye Statute y^t in Such Case they be excused from the payment of a half penny on ye pound of s^d Six penny Rate.

Signed by order

New Haven Decr 29 1794   Levi Ives Chairman

Com^{tee}. Voted y^t ye Selectmen of this Town be and they are hereby appointed a Committee for ye purpose of making a Contract Conformably to the report of ye Committee.

Tax. Voted y^t one half penny of ye tax laid this day together with arrearges of highway Taxes for past years be appropriated, to ye repairing of highways and bridges.

[p. 244] Grandjuryman. Voted William Baldwin be grandjuror for ye year Ensuing in the room of Daniel Reed resigned.

Constable. Voted Eli Hotchkiss be excused from serving the Town in ye office of Constable for ye year ensuing.

Selectman. Voted y^t Capt Thomas Painter be excused from Serving ye Town in ye office of Selectman for the Ensuing year, and Anson Clinton is appointed in his Stead.

Grandjuror. Voted y^t Willm Baldwin be excused from being Grandjuror.

Tax. Voted y^t ye Six penny rate Tax be paid by ye 1st of March next.

Coll^r. Voted that Christian Hanson be Collector of the State and Town Tax for the year ensuing.

Packer. Voted y^t Erastus Bradly be packer of beaf in this Town for ye year ensuing.

Sickness. Resolved y^t ye 18th & 19th parragra*[p]*hs of a Certain act of this state 'entitled an act providing in case of Sickness' be published in ye News paper printed in this City each week Successively from ye first week of January Next till ye 1st week in Novr Next, and y^t ye Selectmen cause ye Same to be done at ye expence of ye Town.[1]

And it is further voted that the Treasurer of ye Town for ye time being be and he is hereby requested and directed to prosecute any and all breaches of s^d Parragraphs of s^d acts and y^t ye Town will indemnify him in Such prosecutions.[2]

---

1. Reeling from a Yellow fever epidemic, New Haven authorities wanted to publicize the state law prohibiting anyone or anything that was in contact with a major disease from entering Connecticut by land or by sea. See. *PRSC,1793 - 1796*, Vol. VIII: 244 - 245.
2. At the time it was not known that infected mosquitoes carried the yellow fever virus.

This meeting adjourned to ye 2^d monday of Feby next at Two of ye Clock in ye afternoon.

[FEBRUARY 9, 1795]

[p. 245] AT A TOWN MEETING HOLDEN IN NEW HAVEN BY AD-JOURNMENT UPON THE 9TH DAY OF FEBRUARY 1795.

Clerk. Abr^m Bishop chosen Clerk Pro-Tem & Sworn.

Oyster act. Rules and ordinances for regulating the fishery of oysters.

Whereas the exclusive right of the fishery of oysters within the Limits of the Town of New Haven, by Law appertains to the inhabitants of ye s^d Town of New Haven.

And whereas it is expedient to regulate s^d fishery, by Establishing rules & or-dinances for the preservation of the oysters within s^d Limits in persuance of authority derived from the Statute of this State entitled an act for encouraging & regulating fisheries.

Voted that no person from and after ye 1st day of Jany next shall within the limits of this Town drive or cause to be driven any team of horses or cattle with any Cart*[,]* waggon*[,]* or other Carriage into or upon any flat*[,]* Creek*[,]* or harbour, where oysters or oyster shells are growing, caught or taken upon pain of forfeiting Twenty shillings for every such offence.

Voted that from and after the 1st day *[of]* may, untill the 1st day of Decr annually no person shall take*[,]* gather*[,]* or Collect any oystershells in or upon any of the flats*[,]* beeches*[,]* Creeks*[,]* Harbours*[,]* or waters within the limits of s^d Town on pain of forfeiting Twenty shillings for every such offence.

And no person from and after said 1st day of may untill the 1st day of Sepr next shall within the Limits of this Town sell or expose to sale any oysters taken or caught in or upon any of s^d flatts*[,]* beeches*[,]* creeks*[,]* Harbours*[,]* waters*[,]* or shores on pain of forfeiting Twenty shillings for every such offence.
Voted that Elias Shipman, Thomas Rice, Anson Clinton and Stephen Row and each of them Have authority *[p. 246]* And authority is hereby given to them, and each of them from ye 1st day of May to ye first day of December annually to grant Permit or permits in writing signed by them or ye person granting y^e

Same therein & thereby licencing ye person or persons therein named to Catch oysters at any place within ye Limits of ye Town of New Haven in such quantity or quanties & for such period of time as shall be in such permit Specified. And no person from & after ye 1st day of May untill ye 1st day of Decr annually shall catch or be caught any oysters in or upon any of ye flatts[,] beeches[,] Creeks[,] Harbours[,] waters[,] or shores within ye Limits of ye Town of New Haven, exceept by vertue of a permit or permits granted & obtained as afores^d on ye pain of forfeting Twenty Shillings for every such offence. And no Permit shall be granted or given between s^d 1st of may and Sepr next unless on ye written Certificate ~~Certificate~~ of some Physician residing in said Town y^t in his opinion it is expedient for ye health of ye person applying for such Permit or some member of his family y^t Such permit be given or granted.

Voted y^t each and every penalty, which may or Shall be incurred by any person or persons by a violation of ye Rules & regulations this day Established by this town relative to oysters and oyster shells, and for ye preservation of ye Same or by vertue thereof and in consequence of any vote or votes this day passed by this Town relative to ye Same Shall be if Sued for by any private person ye one half to him who Shall sue for and recover ye Same and ye other half to ye treasurer of ye Town of New Haven, to & for ye use of s^d Town. And if sued for by said Town Treasurer in behalf of s^d Town such penalty Shall be to and for ye use of s^d Town, & when requested by ye persons appointed to grant permits or a ma^{jr} part of them it shall be ye duty of s^d Treasurer in behalf of [p. 247] This town to prosecute every violation of ye rules and regulations aforesaid.

Also voted y^t it be Especially ye duty of ye Selectmen and ye Committee this day appointed ~~that it be especially~~ and of Jacob Thompson, Benjn Smith, Justus Smith, Jehu Brainard,[1] Chritian Hanson, Stephen Row, Jos^h Thomas, David Atwater & Noah Barber to make Complaint of all breeches of y^e act passed this day relative to y^e Catching of oysters, to y^e Town Treasurer and y^t it be his duty to prosecute all such Complaints.

Voted that a tax of 2$_1$/2^d on the £ be laid to defray the expences of the town to be p^d by the 1st of March Next, & y^t Christian Hanson be Collector of the same.

Adj^d without day.

---

1. Jehu Brainard (1757 - 1815) was a 1783 Yale graduate who later served as High Sheriff of New Haven County from 1793 - 1805. He married Abigail Woodhull, then Mrs. Harriet Bowditch Smith, widow of Caleb Smith.

[AUGUST 24, 1795]

AT A TOWN MEETING HOLDEN IN NEW HAVEN UPON THE 24TH DAY OF AUG^T ANNO DOMINI 1795.

Mod^r. Voted that Timothy Jones Esqr be moderator.

Sickness. Voted y^t Laben Smith who has lately arrived from New York, into ye Harbour, with a number of passingers on board, who do not belong to this Town, liberty is hereby granted to s^d Smith to land those persons at the Neck near Osborns ferry so Called, so y^t they make off in a Stage, and not indanger ye Town by reason of ye Sickness that prevails in New york.¹

Sickness. Voted y^t this Town Considering the importance of providing in ye out skirts of s^d Town an house for ye accomodation of people coming from places infected, or labouring under inffectious disorders in s^d Town, y^t a frame, partly covered belonging to Messrs Atwater and Lyon situated on the bank of ye East River in said Town may be purchased for 100 dollars and y^t ye Same may be accomodated for ye purpose aforesaid, at ye expence of 500 Dollars, do accept said report, and voted y^t this Town will purchase s^d Building to remain *[p. 248]* Perpetually ye property of ye Town for ye purpose afores^d under the direction of ye Selectmen & y^t ye Selectmen proceed forthwith to finish s^d building, and also to procure a quantity of Land under and about s^d building sufficient for ye Convenience thereof.

Tax. Voted y^t a Tax of two pence half penny on the pound be laid to defray ye expences of s^d Land & to be Collected of ye inhabitants of this Town, on the List for ye year 1794, and to be paid on y^e ~~list for~~ 15th day of Sepr next.

Coll^r. Voted y^t Christian Hanson be Coll^r of s^d Tax.
Tax. Voted that there be a Tax of one penny on the pound be Collected of the inhabitants of this Town, on the list for the year 1794 to be laid out for repairing the highways, to be Collected by the 15th Day of September next.

Coll^r. Voted y^t Christian Hanson be Collector of said Tax.

[DECEMBER 14, 1795]

1. A Yellow fever epidemic claimed 732 lives in New York in 1795. See, James Hardie, *An Account of the Yellow Fever... (1822), p 8.*

AT A TOWN MEETING HOLDEN IN NEW HAVEN DEC^R 14TH 1796.[1]

Clerk. Voted y^t Samuel Bishop be Town Clerk.

Mod^r. Voted y^t Tim° Jones Esqr be moderator.

Selectmen. Voted y^t Peter Johnson, Nath^ll Fitch, medad Osborn, Russel Clark and Anson Clinton be Selectmen ye year ensuing.

Treas^r. Voted y^t Joseph Bradly Esqr be Town Treasurer the year Ensuing.

[p. 249] Constables. Voted that Joseph Peck, John R. Throop, Pierson Clark and David Trowbridge be Constables ye year ensuing.

Listers. Voted y^t Hanover Barney, Jonah Hotchkiss, Amos Doolittle, Luther Fitch, Elisha Munson, Sam^ll Punderson, Willm Walter, David Trowbridge, John Prinde and John Miles J^r be listers ye year ensuing.

Committee for Contract. Voted y^t Capt Thomas Punderson, Joseph Darling Esqr, Nehemiah Smith Esqr, Jehu Brainard and Hanover Barney be a Committee for ye purpose of Considering ye best method of Supporting ye poor of this Town for ye year ensuing either by Contract or otherwise and make report to ye adj^d meeting. This meeting adjourned to ye Last monday of instant December at Two of ye Clock in the afternoon.

[DECEMBER 28, 1795]

AT A TOWN MEETING HOLDEN IN NEW HAVEN BY ADJOURNMENT DEC^R 28, 1795.

Sealer. Voted y^t Stephen Bradly be leather Sealer the year ensuing.

Key Keeper. Voted y^t Elisha Munson, Noah Potter, John Culver, Nathan Dumer and Nath^ll Kimberly be key keepers ye year ensuing.

Fence viewers. Voted y^t John Miles J^r, Obediah Hotchkiss and Silas Kimberly be fence viewers ye year Ensuing.

---

2. Samuel Bishop no doubt meant to write 1795.

[p. 250] Sealer. Voted y^t Israel Munson be sealer of weights and measures ye year ensuing.

Sealer. Voted that John Miles be sealer of dry measures the year ensuing.

Tythingmen. Voted y^t John Goodrich, Willm Austin, Isaac Auger, Christian Hanson, Darias Stebbins, James Alling, and Stephen Prindle, be tythingmen the year ensuing.

Coll^r. Voted y^t Christian Hanson be Constable the year ensuing.

Grandjurymen. Voted yt Joseph Mix, Levi Ives J^r, Napthali Daggett, David Bristoll, Sam^{ll} Trowbridge, and Kneeland Townsend^1 be Grandjurymen the year Ensuing.

Lister. Voted y^t Jeremiah Townsend J^r be lister in ye room of Jonah Hotchkiss excused.

Lister. Voted y^t Thadd^s Perit be a lister ye year Ensuing.

Tax. Voted That a rate or Tax of Seven pence on ye pound, upon ye List of ye 1795 be Collected of ye inhabitants of this Town, to defray the necessary Charges of ye Town, and to be paid upon ye first day of march next.

Highways. Voted y^t one hundred pounds of ye above rate or Tax be paid into ye Treasury, to repair the highways and bridges.

[p. 251] Contract. Voted y^t there shall be a Contract made with Capt Samuel Punderson, to Support the poor, and to pay the other Charges of ye Town ye year ensuing.

[Committee about Poor.] Voted y^t David Daggett, Eleiz^r Goodrich, and Dyar White Esqr be a Committee to Compleat the Contract with Capt Punderson, and execute ye Same on the principles of ye Contract of the past year, in behalf of ye Town.

Survey. Voted y^t Capt Sam^{ll} Punderson be Surveyer of highways ye year ensuing, and layout ye afores^d £100 and account with ye Selectmen for the Same.

---

1. Possibly Kneeland Townsend (1767 - 1844), who died in Milan, OH. He married Susannah Hampton (1768 - 1842) in New Haven in 1799.

Coll^r. Voted y^t Capt. Samuel Punderson be ye Collector of ye State and Town ~~Taxes~~ and State rates ye year ensuing.

[APRIL 18, 1796]

AT A TOWN MEETING IN NEW HAVEN APRIL 18, 1796.

[Moderator.] Tim° Jones Esqr moderator.

Oyster Act. Rules and ordinances for regulating to ye fishery of Oysters.

Whereas ye exclusive right of ye fishing of Oysters within ye Limits of ye Town of New Haven by Law appertains to ye inhabitants of the Town of s^d New Haven and whereas it is expedient to regulate s^d fishery by Establishing rules and ordinences for ye preservation of ye oysters within s^d Limits. In persuance of ye authority derived from the Statute of this State entitled an act for encouraging and regulating fisheries.

Voted y^t from and after ye first day of may untill ye 1st day of Decr annually no person shall take*[,]* gather*[,]* or Collect any oystershells in or upon any of ye flatts*[,]* Beches*[,]* rivers*[,]* creeks*[,]* Harbours*[,]* or waters within the Limits of s^d Town, on pain of forfeiting Twenty Shillings for every Such offence.

And no person from and after ye 1st Day of ~~September~~ may untill the 1st day of Sepr next, shall within ye Limits of this Town sell or expose to Sale any oysters taken or Caught in or upon any of s^d flatts*[,]* beeches*[,]* *[p. 252]* Creeks*[,]* Harbours*[,]* waters*[,]* or shores on pain of forfeiting Twenty Shillings for every Such offence.

Voted y^t Stephen Alling, Elias Shipman, Thomas Rice, Anson Clinton, and Stephen Row and each of them have authority and authority is hereby given unto them and each of them from and after ye 1st day of may to ye first day of Decr annually to grant Permit or permits in writing Signed by them or ye person granting ye Same and thereby Licenising ye person or persons their in Named to Catch oysters at any place within ye Limits of ye Town of New Haven in such Quantity or quanties and for Such period of Time as Shall be in s^d permit Specified, and no person from and after ye 1st day of may untill ye 1st Day of Decr annually shall Catch or Cause to be Caught any oysters in or upon any of ye flatts, Beeches, Creeks, waters, or Shores within ye Limits of ye Town of New

Haven except by vertue of a permit or permits granted and obtained as afores^d, on pain of forfeiting Twenty Shillings for every Such offence and no permit Shall be granted or given between s^d first day of may and Sepr next unless on ye written Certificate of some Phisisan *[sic.]* residing *[sic.]* in s^d Town and y^t in his opinion it is expedient for ye health of ye person applying for Such permit, or Some member of his family y^t Such permit be given or granted.

Voted y^t each and every penalty which may or Shall be incurred by any person or persons by a violation of ye Rules and regulations this day Established by this Town relative to oysters and oystershells and for ye preservation of the Same or by vertue thereof and in Consequence of any vote or votes this day passed by this Town relative to ye Same, Shall be if Sued for by any private person ye one half to him who shall sue for or recover ye Same, and the other half to ye Treasurer of ye Town of New Haven to and for ye use ~~and when requested by y^e~~ *[of]* said Town*[.]*

[p. 253] And if Sued for by s^d Treasurer in behalf of s^d Town such penalty shall be to and for ye use of s^d Town, and when requested by ye Persons appointed to grant permits or a major part of them it shall be ye Duty of ye Treasurer in behalf of this Town to prosecute every violation of ye Rules and regulations aforesaid. Also voted y^t it be especially ye Duty of ye Selectmen and ye Committee this day appointed and of Jacob Thompson, Benjn Smith, Justus Smith, John Brainard, Christian Hanson, Stephen Row, Jos^h Thomas, David Atwater, and Noah Barber to make Complaint of all breaches of ye act passed this day relative to ye Catching of oysters to the Town Treasurer, and that it be his Duty to prosecute all such Complaints.

[Tax.] Voted y^t a tax of three pence on ye pound be laid on ye list of ye year 1795 to defray ye Debts due from the Town to be forthwith Collected, and Capt Samuel Pinderson is Chosen Coll^r of s^d Tax.

Adj^d without day.

[APRIL 26, 1796]

AT A TOWN MEETING IN NEW HAVEN APRIL 26TH 1796.
[Moderator.] Tim^o Jones Esqr mod^r.

[Town Accounts.] Voted y^t Dyar White, Simeon Baldwin & Eliz^r Goodrich Esq^{rs}, Capt Thos Painter and Levi Ives be a Committee *[to]* examine ye accounts of y^e

Town, see what Sum ye Town is in debt and make report to ye next meeting. Adj^d to ye 9th day of may next at 2 °Clock in ye afternoon.

[MAY 9, 1796]

AT A TOWN MEETING HOL[D]EN IN NEW HAVEN BY ADJOURNM^T MAY 9TH 1796.

[Agents.] Voted y^t Eliz^r Goodrich & David Daggett Esq^{rs} be agents in behalf of this Town to oppose ye Petition of ye Town of Hamden before the General assembly to be holden this instant may.[1]

[Tax Collector.] Voted y^t Capt Peter Johnson be Collector of ye Town rate granted upon the 18th of April Last in ye room of Capt Sam^{ll} Punderson who was Chosen Collector, and hath refused to Serve.

[DECEMBER 12, 1796]

[p. 254] AT A TOWN MEETING HOLDEN IN NEW HAVEN ON THE 12TH DAY OF DECEMBER 1796.

Town Clerk. Voted y^t Saml Bishop be Town Clerk.

Moderator. Voted y^t Timothy Jones Esqr be moderator.

Selectmen. Voted y^t Ebenezer Peck, Nath^{ll} Fitch, Medad Osborn, Russel Clark and Gold Smith be selectmen the year ensuing.

Constables. Voted y^t Joseph Peck, John R. Throop, Piersons Clark, Samuel Punderson and Justus Smith be Constables ye year ensuing.

Grandjurymen. Voted y^t Isaac Miles Wales[2], James Merriman, Amaziah Lucas. Alexander Langmure Jun^{r,3}, Joseph Merwin J^r, and Ezra Smith be grandjurymen ye year ensuing.

1. This petition was calling for the official recognition of the Hamden East Plains Society of Whitneyville, approved by the General Assembly in August of 1795. Many of its members were formerly associated with the First Society in New Haven, which likely protested the loss of its tithe-paying church members. See. *PRSC,* Vol. VIII: 275.
2. Isaac Mile Wales (1775 - 1825) was a Milford native.
3. Alexander Langmuir (ca. 1757 - 1823).

Treasurer. Voted y^t Jos^h Bradly Esqr be Town Treasurer the year ensuing.

Listers. Voted y^t Henry Daggett J^r, Jeremiah Townsend J^r, Elisha Munson, Amos Doolittle, Samuel Punderson, Nathan Smith J^r, Thadd^s Perrit, Naph^{ll} Daggett, David Bristoll Ju^r, and David Trowbridge be lister ye year ensuing.

Tythingmen. Voted y^t John Clause, Piersons Clark, John Peck, David Atwater, David Daggett, Isaac Jones, Simeon Baldwin, Eliz^r Goodrich, Erastus Bradly, Hez^h Auger, Willm Powell, Willm Warland, Asa Austin, Benjn Downs, Saml Trowbridge and Willard Bristoll be Tythingmen ye year ensuing.

Leather Sealer. Voted y^t Step^n Bradly be leather Sealer ye year ensuing.

[p. 255] Key Keepers. Voted y^t Elisha Munson, Naoh Potter, John Culver, Nathan Dumer, and Nath^{ll} Kimberly be key keepers the year ensuing year *[sic.]*.

Pound. Voted y^t Oliver Smith have Liberty to build a pound at his Cost, and be keeper of ye Key.

Pound. Voted y^t Jonah Bradly have Liberty to build a pound at his own Cost and be keeper of ye Key.

fence viewers. Voted y^t John Miles J^r *[,]* Obediah Hotchkiss and Silas Kimberly be fence viewers ye year ensuing.

Sealer of w^{ts} &c. Voted y^t Israel Munson be Sealer of weights and measures ye year ensuing.

Sealer of Dry measures. Voted y^t John Miles be Sealer of dry measures.

[Corn meal.] inspector. Voted y^t Robert Townsend be inspector of Corn meal ye year ensuing.

Barbery Bushes.[1] Voted y^t any person or persons is authorized by ye Town to enter into any person or persons field in this Town at any Season of ye year for the purpose of distroying Barberry bushes.

---

1. The Connecticut Assembly enacted a law promoting the eradication of Barberry bushes as early as 1769 in the belief that the thorny ornamental shrub caused grain and wheat blight.

Barberry Bushes. Voted y^t ye Selectmen be authorized to expend a Certain Sum of money to distroy barberry Bushes y^t s^d Sum be 200 Dollers.

Committee about the poor. Voted y^t a Committee be appointed to agree with some person or persons to Support ye poor by Contract and make report, Therefore voted that Jeremiah Atwater, Eliz^r Goodrich, Thos Punderson, Russel Clark, and Gold Smith be a Committee for ye purpose aforesaid.

[Beef/Pork and Lumber] inspectors. Voted y^t John Miles and Newman Trowbridge be inspectors of beaf Pork & Lumber the year ensuing.

[DECEMBER 26, 1796]

[p. 256] AT A TOWN MEETING HOLDEN IN NEW HAVEN BY AD-JOURNMENT UPON Y^E 26TH DAY OF DEC^R 1796.

Oysters. Rules and ordinances for regulating ye fishery of Oysters.

Whereas ye Exclusive right of ye fishery of oysters within ye Limits of ye Town of New Haven by Law appertains to ye inhabitants of s^d Town & whereas it is expedient to regulate s^d fishery by Establishing rules and ordinances for ye preservation of ye oysters within s^d Limits in persuance of ye authority derived from the Statute of this State entitled an act for encouraging and regulating fisherys.
Voted y^t from and after ye 1st day of may untill the 1st day of Novr annually no person Shall take[,] gether[,] or Collect any oyster shells in or upon any of ye flatts[,] beeches[,] rivers[,] Creeks[,] Harbours[,] or waters within ye Limits of s^d Town on pain of forfeiting Twenty Shillings for every Such offence.

And no person from and after ye 1st day of may untill the 1st Day of Sepr next Shall within ye Limits of this Town shall sell or expose to Sale any oysters taken or caught in or upon any of s^d flatts[,] Beeches[,] Creeks[,] Harbours[,] waters[,] or Shores on pain of forfeiting Twenty Shillings for every Such offence.

Voted y^t Stephen Alling, Thos Rice, Ezra Smith and Stephen Row and each of them have authority and authority is hereby given them and each of them from and after ye 1st day of may to ye 1st day of Novr annually to grant Permit or permits in writing signed by them or the person granting the Same therein & thereby Licensing ye person or persons therein Named to catch oysters at any place within ye Limits of ye Town of New Haven in Such quantity or quantities *[p. 257]* And for Such Period of time Shall in s^d Permit Specified. And no person from and after ye 1st Day of may untill the first day of Novr annually Shall Catch or Cause to be Caught any oysters in or upon any of ye flatts[,] Beeches[,] Creeks[,] waters[,] or shores within ye Limits of ye Town of New Haven except by virtue of a permit or permits granted and obtained as afores^d, on pain of forfeiting Twenty Shillings for every Such offence, and no permit Shall be granted or given between the 1st Day of may and Sepr Next unless on ye written Certificate of Some Phisican residing in s^d Town y^t in his opinion it is expedient for ye health of ye person applying for Such permit or some member of his family y^t such permit be given or granted.

Voted y^t each and every Penalty which may or Shall be incurred by any person or persons by a violation of ye rules and regulations this Day Established by this town relative to oysters and oyster shells, and for ye preservation of ye Same or by vertue thereof and in consequence of any vote or votes this day passed by this Town relative to ye Same shall be if Sued for by any private person the one half to him who Shall Sue for and recover ye Same, and ye other half to ye Treasurer of ye Town of New Haven to and for ye use of s^d Town of New Haven[.] And if sued by s^d Treasurer in behalf of s^d Town Such penalty shall be to & for the use of s^d town. And when requested by ye persons appointed to grant permits or a major part of them it shall be ye duty of s^d Treasurer in behalf of this Town to prosecute every violation of ye rules and regulations afores^d.

Also voted y^t it be especially ye Duty of ye Selectmen and ye Committee this *[day]* appointed and of Jacob Thompson, Justus Smith, Jehu Brainard, Noah Barber, Stephen Row and David Atwater to make Complaint of all breaches of ye act passed this day relative to ye Catching of oysters to ye Town Treasurer and y^t it be his Duty to prosecute all such Complaints.

Tax. Voted y^t three cents on ye Doll^r be laid on ye list of ye year 1796 to be paid by ye inhabitants, as a rate of for Tax, to defray ye Charges of this Town ye year ensuing. Voted y^t s^d rate or Tax shall be paid by ye 1st Day of Feby next.

[p. 258] Contract about the poor. Voted y^t the Selectmen be authorized to make a Contract in behalf of this Town with Jos^h Peck for defraying ye ordinary expences of this Town ye year Ensuing and that ye s^d Peck be allowed therefor a rate of three Cents on a Dollar on ye List of 1796, ye s^d Peck undertaking to perform ye same matters and things which were undertaken ye Last year by Samuel Punderson, and instead of paying £20 into ye Treasury that he pay £51 - 13 - 4 and give Security for the performance to the acceptance of the persons aforesaid.

Coll^r. Voted y^t Joseph Peck be Collector of ye Town ~~and state~~ Tax or rate above mentioned.

Coll^r. Voted y^t Joseph Peck be Collector of ye state Taxes ye year ensuing.

Surveyers. Voted y^t Saml Clark, Nathan Smith, Nathaniel Smith, Thomas Punderson, Medad Osborn & Eben^r Johnson be Surveyers of highways the year ensuing.

Highways. Voted y^t the inhabitants of ye parish of West Haven be exempted from paying their proportion of y^e £100 to be paid for repairing highways provided they repair all ye highways within s^d parish.

Highway. Voted y^t ye Selectmen Shall and they are hereby directed to Survey and lay out a Public road or highway from ye Courthouse in this Town to Milford line in ye most direct Course to Derby landing and at ye most Convenient place according to ye Statute Law of this State in such Case provided on condition y^t ye County Court or the Towns of Milford, Woodbridge and Derby shall layout a road or highway from s^d Landing through s^d Milford and Woodbridge or either of s^d Towns to ye line of this Town.[1]

[p. 259] AT A TOWN MEETING HOLDEN ON THE 16TH DAY OF MAY AD 1797 *[See page 225. The town clerk recorded this meeting out of sequence.]*

[DECEMBER 11, 1797]

AT A TOWN MEETING HOLDEN IN NEW HAVEN UPON THE 11TH DAY OF DECEMBER 1797.

Clerk. Voted y^t Samuel Bishop be Town Clerk.

Moderator. Voted y^t Tim° Jones Esqr be moderator.

Selectmen. Voted y^t Ebenez^r Peck, Nath^{ll} Fitch, Medad Osborn, Russel Clark and Gold Smith be Selectmen ye year ensuing.

Selectmen. Voted y^t Ebenezer Peck be excused and Isaac Mills be Selectmen in his room.

---

1. This was the beginning of the New Haven-Milford Turnpike, now known as Route 1.

Treas^r. Voted y^t Joseph Bradly Esqr be Town Treasurer.

Constables. Voted y^t Joseph Peck, Pierson Clark, John R. Throop, Thomas Hull and Justus Smith be Constables ye year ensuing.

Grandjurymen. Voted y^t Eliha Munson, Stephen Twining, Joseph Lynde, Levi Ives, Stephen Atwater, Nathan Smith and Joseph Merwin J^r be Grandjurymen ye year ensuing.

Tythingmen. Voted y^t Pierson Clark, Elijah Munson, Isaac Dickerman, Tim° Jones & Henry Daggett Esq^rs, Jeremiah Atwater J^r, Capt Abel Burret, Eben^z Townsend, Capt Thomas Punderson, Stephen Dummer, Josiah Merrick and Nathan Smith J^r of West Haven be Tythingmen ye year ensuing.

Key Keepers. Voted y^t Elisha Munson, Nathan Dummer, Noah Potter, John Culver, Jonah Bradly and Nathaniel Kimberly be key keepers ye year ensuing.

[p. 260] Fence viewers. Voted y^t Obediah Hotchkiss, John Townsend, Thos Rice, Elijah Prindle and Thomas Painter be Fenceviewers ye year ensuing.

Sealers. Voted y^t Isaac Thompson and Nathaniel Fitch be leather sealers the year ensuing.

Sealer. Voted y^t Israel Munson be sealer of w^ts & measures ye year ensuing.

Sealer. Voted y^t John Miles be sealer of dry measures the year ensuing.

Listers. Voted y^t Isaac M. Wales, Amaziah Lucus, Daniel Read, Nathan Smith of ye City of New Haven, David Bunce, Marcus Merriman, Napthala Daggett, Ambros Ward J^r, David Trowbridge and David Bristoll Ju^r be listers ye year ensuing.
Committee. Voted y^t Simeon Baldwin, Joseph Bradly, Russel Clark, Dyar White and Thaddeus Clark be a Committee to report a Contract about Supporting ye poor, at ye next meeting.

This meeting adj^d to ye Last Tuesday of instant Decr at 2 of ye Clock in ye afternoon.

[DECEMBER 26, 1797]

AT A TOWN MEETING IN NEW HAVEN HOLDEN BY ADJOURN-

MENT UPON Y^E 26 DAY OF DEC^R 1797.

Contract for ye poor. Voted y^t ye Selectmen be authorized to finish ye Contract with David Hull this day accepted and approved of two Cents upon a Dollar.

Collector. Voted that Thomas Hull be Collector of the Town and State Taxes the year ensuing.

[p. 261] [Tax.] Voted y^t a Tax of two Cents upon a Dollar be laid upon ye polls and rateable Estate to fulfull ye Contract made with David Hull.

[Tax.] Voted y^t a Tax of one & a half Cents upon a Dollar be laid upon the poles and rateable Estate of ye inhabitants of this Town for ye repairs of bridges & Roads.

[Tax.] Voted y^t ye above Tax be paid upon ye first day of march next.

[Committee.] Voted y^t Thomas Punderson, James Hillhouse, Russel Clark, Ebenezer Townsend and Gold Smith be a Committee to layout ye one and a half Cent upon roads and bridges in Such way and manner as they shall judge best for ye Town.

[Fenceviewer.] Voted y^t Jeremiah Atwater 3^d be fence viewers *[sic.]* in the room of Thomas Rice.

[Agents for school societies.] Voted y^t Eliz^r Goodrich and Simeon Baldwin be appointed agents to apply in behalf of this Town to the general assembly at their Sessions in may Next to obtain a Continuance of ye act authorizing ye Several Ecclesiastical Society *[sic.]* in this state to form themselves into school Societies with all ye priviledges thereof.[1]
Voted y^t ye oyster act for this year be the same as was passed last year, with ye alteration of ye Dates.

[MARCH 4, 1798]

AT A TOWN MEETING HOLDEN IN NEW HAVEN UPON Y^E 4TH DAY OF MARCH 1798.

---

1. In 1795, Connecticut sold off land its Western Reserves in Ohio and used the money to establish a public school system. See, Clifford J. Dudley, *The History of Public Education in Connecticut,* http://teachersinstitute.yale.edu/curriculum/units/1981/cthistory/81.ch.02.x.html.

[Moderator.] Voted y[t] Timothy Jones Esq[r] be moderator.

[p. 262] Highway. Voted y[t] y[e] vote of this Town respecting y[e] New road proposed from Derby Narrows to New Haven passed at a Town meeting on y[e] 26th Day of Dec[r] 1796, be and y[e] Same is hereby repealed, rescinded and annulled.

Oyster act. Voted y[t] y[e] oyster act so Called passed on y[e] 26th day of Dec[r] last be repealed*[,]* rescinded*[,]* and annulled.

agent. Voted y[t] y[e] Hon[ble] James Hillhouse be agent in behalf of this Town to apply to y[e] gen[ll] assembly in may Next to git an act made in addition to an act, relative to y[e] distroying barberry bushes.[1]

[APRIL 9, 1798]

AT A TOWN MEETING HOLDEN IN NEW HAVEN UPON THE 9TH DAY OF APRIL 1798

moderator. Jonathan Ingersoll Esq[r] moderator.

Highway to Derby landing. Voted y[t] this Town will lay out a road or highway from this to milford line, which highway is to be part of a highway, proposed to be laid from york Street in y[e] City of New Haven to Derby landing, Provided y[e] County Court for New Haven County shall order s[d] Road to be laid out from said milford line, through said milford to s[d] landing*[,]* and Provided y[e] gen[ll] assembly Shall grant a turnpike thereon — and Provided a turn Pike Company Shall actually be formed to make and maintain s[d] road, so y[t] this Town Shall not hereafter have any expence in making and maintaining y[e] Same.[2]

Committee. Voted y[t] y[e] Committee report, on Cap[t] [Peter] Johnson's Demand, about highways &c be accepted, the account and report being lodged on file.

[p. 263] Oyster act. Rules and ordinances for regulating the fishery of oysters and Clams.

Whereas y[e] exclusive right of y[e] fishery of oysters and Clams within y[e] Limits

---

1. As noted earlier, barberry bushes contribute to the spread of fungus spores and stem rust in wheat and barley. See, *PRCC,* VII: 10.
2. The Derby Turnpike Company was authorized to collect tolls at its Malltby Lake toll booth and was the sole turnpike road from New Haven.

of ye Town of New Haven by Law appertains to ye inhabitants of s^d Town and whereas it is expedient to regulate s^d fishery by Establishing rules and ordinances for ye preservation of ye oysters and Clams within ye s^d Limits in pursuance of the authority derived from the State *[Statute]* of this State entituled *[sic.]* an act for incouraging *[sic.]* and regulating fishery.

Voted y^t from and after ye first day of april untill ye first day of Novr annually no person Shall take*[,]* gather*[,]* or Collect any oystershells in or upon any of ye flats*[,]* Beeches*[,]* rivers*[,]* Creeks*[,]* harbours*[,]* or waters within ye Limits of s^d Town upon pain of forfeiting Seven dollars for every such offence.

Voted y^t Levi Ives, Obediah Hotchkiss, Willm Powell, Nathan Smith, Stephen Row, Ezra Smith have authority and authority is hereby granted to them from ye first day of *[May]* untill ye first day of Novr annually to grant Permit or permits in writing Signed by ye person granting ye Same, therein and thereby licensing ye person or persons theirin *[sic.]* Named to ketch long Clams at any place within ye Limits of ye Town of New Haven in Such quantity or quantities and for Such period of time as Shall be in such permit Specified.

And ye s^d person or persons before named have authority and authority is hereby given to them to grant permit or permits Signed by ye person or persons granting ye same therein *[sic.]* and thereby licensing ye person or persons Named in Such permit from ye first day of october to ye first day of November annually to Catch one bushel of oysters at anyone time within ye 1st of Octr Next.

Provided nevertheless y^t if any person or family Shall obtain more than two permits in one week they shall be Considered as void and of no effect. *[p. 264]* And no person from and after ye first day of *[...]* untill ye first day of *[...]* annually Shall Catch or Cause to be Caught any oysters or Long Clams in or upon any of the flats*[,]* beeches*[,]* Creeks*[,]* Harbours*[,]* Waters*[,]* or Shores within ye Limits of ye Town of New Haven except by vertue of a permit or permits granted or obtained as afores^d on penalty of forfeiting Seven Doll^{rs} for every Such offence and no permit Shall be granted or given to Catch any oysters between ye first day of *[...]* and ye first day of Octr next, unless by a written Certificate from a Physitian *[sic.]* resding *[sic.]* in s^d Town that in his opinion tis expedjent for ye health of ye person applying for Such permit or Some member of his family y^t Such permit, be given or Granted.

Voted y^t each and every penalty or forfeiture which shall be incurred by any person or persons by a breach of any of ye rules or ordinances this day made and Established by this Town to ye oyster Shells[,] oysters[,] and Clams, and for ye preservation thereof Shall be and belong in whole to him or them who shall sue for and prosecute ye Same to Final Judgement.

[APRIL 16, 1798]

[p. 265] AT A TOWN MEETING HOLDEN IN NEW HAVEN UPON Y^E 16TH DAY OF APRIL 1798.

[Moderator.] Voted y^t Timothy Jones Esqr be moderator.

[Highway.] Upon y^e ~~above~~ motion of Peter Johnson and others praying y^t a highway might be laid out from ye Court house in ye City of New Haven, to a place Called Chustown[1] in Derby, as by their motion in writing on file appears, This Town having taken ye above motion in Consideration do thereupon — Vote y^t ye Selectmen do lay out s^d proposed highway to Woodbridge line, but ye Same not be opened untill ye above persons and their associates procure a grant of a turn pike and a Company be actually formed who Shall put and keep ye Same in good repair for Stage and other traveling and Wholly Save ye Town harmless from all expence in doing ye Same.[2]

[Leather Sealer.] Voted y^t Stephen Bradly and Elisha Bradly be leather Sealers in ye room of Isaac Thompson.

[Barberry Bushes.] Voted y^t Eliz^r Goodrich be joined with James Hillhouse Esqr to apply to ye Gen^{ll} assembly in may next, to procure an act in addition to an act relating to ye distroying barberry bushes, more Effectually to distroy s^d bushes.

Adjourned without day.

[MAY 12, 1798]

AT A TOWN MEETING HOLDEN IN NEW HAVEN UPON Y^E 12th DAY OF MAY 1798.

---

1. "Chustown" was a section of Derby located near the Falls Bridge over the Housatonic River.
2. Interest in a highway from interior parts of the state to New Haven via Derby began in the early 1790s and led to the creation of the Derby Turnpike Company in May of 1798. See, Leonard Woods Labaree and Catherine Fennelly, compilers, *The Public Records of the State of Connecticut From May 1793 through October 1796* (1951), p. 393, 393*n*. See also, *PRSC*, IX: 204, 204*n*.

[Moderator.] Voted y^t Timothy Jones be moderator.

Agent [on Boundary]. Voted y^t Eliz^r Goodrich Esqr be agent in behalf of ye Town to appear at ye General assembly *[p. 266]* Now Sitting at Hartford and to assent in behalf of this Town to an application wherein ye City of New Haven have Signified by their vote y^t s^d City intend to make to s^d assembly for an extention for ye Limits of s^d City so as to Comprehend y^t part of the Corner of New Haven which lyes Northward of ye present Limits of s^d City & Eastward of Long lane or mount Carmel road.

Adjourned without day.

[DECEMBER 10, 1798]

AT A TOWN MEETING HOLDEN IN NEW HAVEN UPON Y^E 10TH DAY OF DECEMBER 1798.

Clerk. Voted y^t Sam^ll Bishop be Town Clerk.

Mod'. Voted y^t Tim° Jones Esqr be moderator.

Selectmen. Voted y^t Henry Daggett J^r, Thomas Punderson, Medad Osborn, Edmond French and Gold Smith be Selectmen the year ensuing.

Treasurer. Voted y^t Nathan Beers be Town Treasurer the year ensuing.

Grandjurymen. Voted y^t Peter Johnson, Stephen Twining, Isaac Gilbert, Silas Hotchkiss, Isaac Thompson, Napthala Daggett, Alex^t Longmuir, Jehu Brainard, Merit Clark and Nathaniel Smith be Grandjurymen the year ensuing.

Listers. Voted y^t Eneas Munson J^r, Stephen Twining, David Hull, William Austin, Daniel Read, Silas Hotchkiss, Elijah Munson, John Hunt J^r, Stephen Row, David Trowbridge, David Bristoll J^r, Elias Stilwell, James Merriman and Amos Alling, be listers the year ensuing.

[p. 267] Key Keepers. Voted y^t Elisha Munson, Nathan Dummer, Noah Potter, John Culver, Jonah Bradly, Nathl Kimberly be key keepers ye year ensuing.

pound. Voted y^t John Hunt have Liberty to build a pound and be keeper of ye key. *Fence viewers.* Voted y^t Oliver Smith and Hanover Barney be fence viewers ye year ensuing.

Sealer. Voted y^t Isaac Thompson be leather sealer the year Ensuing.

Committee [on Boundary]. Voted that Simeon Baldwin, Timothy Jones, Peter John-son, Thomas Punderson and Abr^m Bishop be a Committee to meet a Commit-tee who may be appointed on ye part of East Haven to ascertain ye boundary line between this Town and ye Town of East Haven.

Committee [on Poor]. Voted y^t William Powel, Simeon Baldwin, Thomas Punder-son, Nath^ll Kimberly and Hanover Barney be a Committee to receive a Contract for ye Support of ye poor, and make report to ye adjourned meeting and also to make report how ye highways Shall be Supported.

Committee [on Schools]. Voted y^t Mr Simeon Baldwin, Dyar White, Eliz^r Goodrich, Joseph Drake, Thomas ~~Punderson~~ Painter, John Prindle, Jonathan Ingersoll, Hanover Barney and Sam^ll Bishop be a Committee to [...] ye School business and make report to ye adjourned meeting.

This meeting adjourned to ye 4th monday of Instant December, at 2 °Clock in the afternoon.

[DECEMBER 24, 1798]

AT A TOWN METING HOLDEN IN NEW HAVEN BY ADJOURN-MENT UPON Y^E 24TH DAY OF DEC^R 1798.

[p. 268] Selectmen. Voted y^t Henry Daggett J^r be released from being Selectman, and Jeremiah ~~Atwater~~ Townsend J^r be Selectmen in his room.

Selectman. Voted y^t Edmond French be released from being Selectmen, and y^t Alex^r Langmuir be Selectman in his room.

Selectman. Voted y^t Jeremiah Townsend J^r be released from being Selectman, and y^t Capt Hanover Barney, be Selectmen in his room.

Committee. Voted y^t Simeon Baldwin, Stephen Twining & Elias Shipman be a Committee to make a Contract with Capt Thomas Punderson, agreeably to his proposal to the Committee.

Tax. Voted y^t a Tax of Two and a half Cents on ye Dollar be Collected upon y^e

List of ye year 1798, to defray ye Charges of ye Town ye year ensuing.

Tax. Voted y^t there be a Tax of one Cent on ye Dollar be Collected upon ye above list for repairing ye highways ye year ensuing.

Voted ye above Tax Shall be paid upon ye 14th Day of Feb^{ry} next.

Collector. Voted y^t Capt. Thomas Punderson be Collector of the Town and State Taxes ye year ensuing.

Surveyers. Voted y^t Jeremiah Atwater, Saml Punderson, Joseph Peck, Medad Osborn, David Hull, Chauncey Alling, Gilead Kimberly, David Benham & Asael Thomas be Surveyers of highways ye year ensuing.

Goose act. Voted no goose or gander shall be permitted to go at large within ye Limits of ye Town of New Haven, unless such goose or gander shall be well yoked with a *[p. 269]* yoke of least Twelve Inches long, and if any Goose or gander shall be found going at large as afores^d without such yoke such goose or gander shall be liable to be impounded, and ye fee for impounding each goose or gander, and it taken Damage fees out shall be Five Cents and be holden to pay all Damages.

[West Haven.] Voted y^t Samuel Bishop Esqr, Mr Jeremiah Atwater, Eliz^r Goodrich Esqr, Capt Thos Painter and Capt Gilead Kimberly be a Committee to ascertain ye proportion of highway, which belongs to West Haven to repair and make report to ye next meeting.

[Lister.] Voted y^t Stephen Row be excused from serving as a Lister, and y^t Evelin Pierpont, serve in his room.

This meeting adjourned without Day.

[MAY 16, 1797][1]

AT A TOWN MEETING HOLDEN IN NEW HAVEN ON THE 16TH DAY OF MAY 1797.

[Moderator.] Timothy Jones Esqr was chosen Moderator.

---

1. This entry, which continues onto the next page, was entered out of chronological order.

[Clerk.] Elisha Munson[1] Clerk pro tempore, and sworn.

[Agents.] Voted. that Elizur Goodrich and David Daggett Esqr[s] be appointed agents to oppose any proceeding of the inhabitants of the Town of Hamden for extending the bounds of their Town into the present limits of the Town of New Haven.

[Collector.] Voted that Cap[t] Peter Johnson be collector of the Town rate in the room of Joseph Peck dismissed.

Voted to adjourn without day. Attest Elisha Munson Clerk pro tempore.

N.B. The above ought to have been recorded on the 259th page.

[SPRING, 1799][2]

[p. 270] [Oyster Act] Whereas the exclusive right of the Fishery of oysters and clams within the limits of the town of New haven, by law appertains to the inhabitants of said Town of New haven, and whereas it is expedient to regulate said Fishery by establishing rules and ordinances for the preservation of the oysters and Clams within the said Limits.

In pursuance of authority derived from the Statute of this State entitled "an act for encouraging and regulating Fishery:" Voted that from and after the 1st day of may until the 1st day of November, annually, no person shall take, gather, or collect, any oyster shells,in or upon an of the flatts, Beeches, Rivers, Creeks, Harbours or waters within the Limits of said Town upon pain of forfeiting Seven dollars for every Such offence.

Voted, that Stephen Alling, Stephen Roe, Thomas Painter, Nathan Smith, Levi Ives and Ebenezer Townshend have Authority and Authority is hereby granted to them or either of them from the first day of May until the first day of October annually to grant permit or permits in writing, signed by the person granting

---

1. Elisha Munson (1761 - 1841) served as a private in the 8th Connecticut Regiment in 1778. Within three years of this date, Munson would assume the duties of the town clerk on a permanent basis. See, U.S. Revolutionary War Rolls, 1775-1783; (National Archives Microfilm Publication M246, 138 rolls); War Department Collection of Revolutionary War Records, Record Group 93; National Archives, Washington. D.C.
2. This entry carries no date and was recorded by Elihu Munson, who was filling in for Samuel Bishop.

the same, therein and thereby Licensing the person or persons therein named, to catch long clams at any place within the limits of the Town of New Haven, in such quantity or quantities, and for such period of time as shall be in such permit Specified.

And no person from and after the first day of May untill the first day of October annually, shall catch or cause to be Caught, any oysters or long Clams, in or upon any of the flats, Beeches, creeks, harbours, waters or shores, within the limits of the Town of New Haven, except by Virtue of a permit or permits granted or obtained as aforesaid, on penalty of forfeiting seven dollars for every Such offence: and no permits *[p.271]* shall be granted or given to catch any oysters between the 1st day of May and the 1ˢᵗ day of October next, unless by a written Certificate from a Physician residing in said town that in his opinion it is expedient for the health of the person applying for such permit, or some member of his family, that such permit or permits be given or granted. Voted, that all penalties or forfeitures for any Breech of these rules and regulations may be recovered by action or Complaint, in the name of said Committee or anyone of them, who are hereby impowered to prosecute the same at their or his own expence, and for their or his sole use and benefit.

[2/3rds page blank]

[DECEMBER 2, 1799]

[p. 272] AT A TOWN MEETING HOLDEN IN NEW HAVEN UPON THE 2ᴰ MONDAY OF DECEMBER 1799.

Clerk. Voted yᵗ Samuel Bishop be Town Clerk.

Mod. Voted yᵗ Mʳ Jeremiah Atwater be moderator.

Selectmen. Voted that Seven Selectmen be Chosen for yᵉ Currant year.

Voted yᵗ Ebenezar Peck, Jeremiah Atwater, Thomas Punderson, Edmond French, Gilad Kimberly, Medad Osborn, and Frances Brown be Selectmen yᵉ year ensuing.

Treasʳ. Voted yᵗ Nathan Beers be Town Treasurer yᵉ year ensuing.

Grandjury men. Voted yᵗ Seth Staples, Hezʰ How, John H. Lynde, Jonathan Atwater, Elisha Munson, Joseph Merwin, Ezra Smith, David Beecher J' and Glover Ball be grand Juryman ye year ensuing.

Tythingmen. Voted y^t Peter Johnson, Stephen Twining, Jeremiah Atwater 3^d, Jere^h Townsend J^r, Martin Pariot, Isaac Townsend, Lemuel Hotchkiss, Medad Osborn, John Mix, Asa Austin, George Todd, Nath^ll Smith, David Trowbridge, and Josiah Merick be Tythingmen ye year ensuing.

Listers. Eneas Munson J^r, Stephen Twing, David Hull, Wm Austin, Daniel Reed, Silas Hotchkiss, Elijah Munson, John Hunt J^r, Stephen Row, David Trowbridge, Saml Clark, Elias Stillwell, James Merwin, and Amos Alling be Listers ye year ensuing.

p. 273] [Pound.] Voted y^t Chauncey Alling have liberty to build a pound and be ye keeper of ye key.

[Fenceviewer.] Voted y^t Oliver Smith, Samuel Punderson, Peter Johnson and ~~Oliver Smith~~ Merit Clark be fence viewers ye year ensuing.

[Leather Sealer.] Voted y^t Isaac Thompson be leather Sealer ye year ensuing.

[Boundary between East Haven and New Haven.] We ye Subscribers a Committee appointed Decr last, to meet a Committee y^t may be appointed on ye part of East Haven to ascertain ye boundary line between New Haven and East Haven Beg leave to report y^t we have examined ye records of both Towns on ye Subject land found a great variety of votes ~~on y^e~~ respecting the village of East Haven by which it appears y^t ye Lands to be included within s^d village were generally understood, but ye precise line between this Town and East Haven was Never defined. We have met a committee on ye part of East Haven but for want of any Certain principals have been unable to ascertain any boundary Lines. We apprehend y^t Establishing ye Channel in the East river and throughout ye Harbour as the boundary line would be wrong and very prejudicial to ye this Town and y^t East Haven will not volentarily accept as their boundary line ye Shore or high water mark of ye river and Harbour. Considering the obscurity of ye business and ye valu[e] of the oyster ground, we are of the opinion y^t it is expedient to wave ye question of the boundary line, except so far as may be necessary for enforcing the Laws of ye State or the votes or bye Laws of ye two Towns. And for this purpose we propose y^t a Committee be appointed to procure at ye Expence of ye Town a Copy of all ye votes *[p. 274]* Relative to Subject, also a Copy of so much of ye Charter of this Town as may Shew y^e

Southern boundary of yᵉ Town and Harbour with the rights and immunities thereby granted to yᵉ proprietors— also a Copy of yᵉ propʳˢ votes so far as may shew to what extent yᵉ proprietors have appropriated or alniated *[sic.]* any part of yᵉ Shore of yᵉ Harbour, also a Copy of yᵉ acts of yᵉ General assembly, and of yᵉ votes of this Town so far as Shall Shew yᵉ agreement, subsisting between yᵉ proprietors of the Town and those of yᵉ Towns of East Haven*[,]* North Haven*[,]* Hamden*[,]* and Woodbridge respecting proprietors Land, and yᵉ oyster Ground. And such other copies or documents as they Shall think necessary to Enable yᵉ Town to Judge of yᵉ practicability of farming out yᵉ whole of yᵉ Harbour and yᵉ adjacent rivers so far as they can be improved in yᵉ fishing of oysters and Clams for yᵉ benefit of yᵉ Several Towns composing yᵉ antient Town of New Haven which to return all yᵉ votes aforesaid for yᵉ inspection of yᵉ Town, also their opinion of yᵉ expediency and probability of farming out yᵉ Harbor and rivers aforesaid and if they shall Judge in favor of ye measure yᵗ they report their opinion of the value of public probable annual avails of ye same together with ye ways and means by which ye may be offered—The Consequence of such report ye Committee believe will obviate all ye inconveniences resulting from ye uncertainty of record, respecting yᵉ line between New Haven and East Haven to ye great benefit of ye Public.

New Haven Decʳ 9ᵗʰ 1799

    Timᵒ Jones
    Peter Jones
    Thoˢ Punderson
    Simon Baldwin
    Abrᵐ Bishop

[p. 275] The foregoing report of yᵉ Committee being by vote accepted. Thereupon voted yᵗ Timᵒ Jones, Peter Johnson, Thomas Punderson, Simeon Baldwin and Abrᵐ Bishop be a Committee for yᵉ purposes expressed in sᵈ Report and make their report to the next meeting.

[Derby Highway.] The report of yᵉ Selectmen of their laying out the highway leading to Derby landing, from york Street, being read and Considered by the Town. Thereupon Voted yᵗ the doings of yᵉ Selectmen relative to laying out sᵈ highway be accepted, and are yᵉ Same to be Recorded.

[Church St.][1] Voted yᵗ Jeremiah Atwater, Isaac Beers, Samˡ Punderson, Nehemiah Smith and Thomas Painter be and they are hereby appointed a Committee to

---

1. The marginalia is in an unknown hand. The first entry says "Church St." Another says "Chapel St."

view yᵉ road from Thadd⁵ Beechers Corner to yᵉ market by yᵉ Creek and report what measures Shall be taken to repair it for public use & Convenience and an Estimate of yᵉ expences.

[Committee about the poor.] Voted yᵗ Jeremiah Atwater, Tho⁵ Punderson, Hezʰ Hotchkiss, Stephen Alling, Isaac Mills, Tho⁵ Painter & Simeon Baldwin be a Committee to examine yᵉ accounts of yᵉ Town to Consider Generally yᵉ expence of yᵉ Town *[for]* yᵉ Support of yᵉ poor and yᵉ expenees of yᵉ highways, and make report to yᵉ Next meeting.

Voted yᵗ this meeting be adjourned to yᵉ 4ᵗʰ monday of instant Decʳ at 2 °Clock in the afternoon.

[DECEMBER 23, 1799]

[p. 276] AT A TOWN MEETING HOLDEN IN NEW HAVEN BY ADJOURNMENT ON THE 4ᵀᴴ MONDAY OF DECEMBER 1799.

[Moderator.] Jeremiah Atwater moderator.

[Committee About Poor.] The Committee appointed yᵉ Last meeting to Consider the expence of yᵉ Town in supporting yᵉ poor &c made their report unto this meeting, which is as follows viz

To yᵉ Town of New Haven ＿＿＿＿

The Committee heretofore appointed to Estimate the Currant expences of yᵉ Town and ye best mode of defraying them, Report

That they have attended to yᵉ accounts of Thomas Punderson who was yᵉ agent of yᵉ Town last year for yᵉ Supplies to yᵉ poor and incident Expences of yᵉ Town which they find have been audited by yᵉ Selectmen and may be arranged under yᵉ following heads viz *[:]*

Supplies in Cloathing & provisions for those in poor house		227 - 8 - 10
Supplies for those who have partial Supplies in Town		238 - 10 - 6
Physicians Bills for those in & out of poor house		23 - 3 - 6
Support of Duncombs son[1] in goal	4 - 4 - 3	

---

1. According to the 1800 census, John Duncomb and his of family of seven were living in Strat-

removing him & family to Fairfield	3 - 8 -11	7 - 13 - 2
Capt. Pundersons allowance as agent		18 —
Total for Support of poor including ye		514 - 16 - 0
State poor[,] Duncomb[,] Amelia Negro &c		
for which deduct		
and it leaves ye expence of supporting ye poor of this		
Town the Last year		
[p. 277] Repairs of highways paid Surveyers		150 - 0 - 0
Incidental..................................		
Furniture of poor house and now on hand	30 - 0 - 6	
printing 58/ warning meetings 26/	4 - 4 - 0	
Grand List	6 - 12 - 6	
laying out road to milford	10 - 16 - 0	
Extra Service of Selectmen	10 - 19 - 0	
Collecting Taxes	34 - 10 - 0	
Sundry small Bills	2 - 18 - 0	
Total Expence Last year		99 - 19 - 6
Amount of Expence brought over		£ 630 - 5 - 4
in part pay of which Capt. Punderson has rec^d on		
order for the avails of ye Taxes		550 - 0 - 0
leaving a ballance Still due from ye Town —— —— ——		90 - 5 - 4

The Committee find y^t ye average Number in ye poor house has been about 25 and their average expence of Cloathing[,] provisions &c, less than 4/ p^r week, That ye Supplies out have been made at about fifty places mostly partial for wood Some total during Sickness and for funeral Expences.

That there are now about 30 at y^r house and ye Number who will require a partial Support will not probably be less than it has been, they find y^t ye actual expence of ye poor is rather more than ye Late Contracts, but ye number has increased and ye partial Supplies have been more expensive and have given better Satisfaction. As ye Committee are Satisfied ye business has been managed with economy by ye Late agent they recommend ye adoption of ye Same plan for the year ensuing in preference to a Contract if a Suitable agent Can be obtained. [p. 278] The Committee are Opinion y^t Experience has fully evinced ye economy of a house for ye resort of ye poor altho^g they do not coniese [sic] that the aid of ye Town can or

---

ford. One of his male children, Zachariah Duncomb (1783 - 1839) was 16 at the time. See https://www.wikitree.com/wiki/Duncomb-11. See also, Second Census of the United States, 1800. NARA microfilm publication M32 (52 rolls). Records of the Bureau of the Census, Record Group 29. National Archives, Washington, D.C.

ought to be Confined to it[.] Certain Classes of yᵉ poor may there be Supported Cheaper than Els[e]where will be more Comfortable and may do Something in aid of their Support as it is probable yᵉ house will soon be removed, they would recommend to the Consideration of yᵉ Town a Situation more retired and where two or three acres of Land can be procured for its accommodition [sic.] they think it also worthy yᵉ attention of yᵉ Town to Consider whether economy will not Dictate an Enlargement of yᵉ building with Such arrangements as will enable them there to releave a part of yᵉ Class of yᵉ poor who have hetherto recᵈ a partial or Total Support elsewhere.

The Committee believe yᵗ yᵉ usual Current expenees of this year cannot be Calculated at a less sum than yᵉ Last. They find yᵗ yᵉ Town is in Debt about Dollers 300[.] That yᵉ County Court have ordered extensive repairs on yᵉ milford road and yᵗ others will be ordered unless made by yᵉ Town[.] That it will of Course be prudent to Provide a larger fund than usual for yᵉ repairs of highways[.] That one cent on the Dollʳ on 73,000 yᵉ amount of yᵉ G[rand] List will raise free of abatements and Collecting fees about Dollʳˢ 640.

They are therefore of opinion yᵗ yᵉ Town ought to Tax themselves three Cents for yᵉ Current [p. 279] expences and yᵉ payment of their Debt, and one Cent & a half for repairs of Highways and bridges[.] And it will be necessary in yᵉ Course of yᵉ winter to provide for yᵉ payment of yᵉ Damages assessed in the New Road to Derby amounting to Dollʳˢ [...] all which is Submitted by your Committee.

New Haven Decʳ 23ᵈ 1799

Jeremiah Atwater Chairman

[Agent for the Poor.] Voted yᵗ Samuel Punderson be agent to Support yᵉ Towns poor for yᵉ Currant year.

[Tax.] Voted yᵗ a Tax of three Cents upon yᵉ Doller be paid on yᵉ Grand list of yᵉ year 1799, to raise money for yᵉ Support of yᵉ poor and the other Charges of yᵉ Town yᵉ year Ensuing.

[Tax.] Voted yᵗ sᵈ Tax shall be paid on yᵉ 1ˢᵗ day of January Next.

[Constable and Collector.] Voted yᵗ Thomas Punderson be Constable, & Collector of yᵉ Town Tax and also Collector of yᵉ State Taxes yᵉ year ensuing.

[Committee Report on Oysters.] The Committee appointed yᵉ last meeting, to make their report, what is needfull to be done relative to ye oysters and Clams in ye Harbor made their report in ye words following viz[:]

The Committee appointed at ye Last meeting to procure Copies of record, and to Consider the Expediency and practicability of farming out ye Harbor of their Town and ye rivers emptying into s^d Harbor for ye fishery of oysters & Clams beg leave to report, That a part of ye Necessary *[p. 280]* Copies are prepared and y^t ye whole will be fairly engrossed for ye benefit of ye Town and of any Committee which may hereafter be appointed on this Subject. By inspection of ye records it appears y^t ye Southern boundary of ye antient Town of New Haven granted to ye proprietors in 1704 extended from oyster river ye South East corner of milford, East to scotch cap which is ye South west Corner of Branford, with all ye rivers, riverlets[,] emoliments[,] priviledges[,] and appurtenances in and of the whole grant included between s^d Southern boundary and ye other boundaries of s^d Town.

It further appears y^t ye whole of ye Harbor, of Dragon river, and of Stoney river, which Divides East Haven from Branford, have been in Common & undivided by ye proprietors to ye present day.

It also appears y^t by vertue of a General Law of ye State, this Town has, from time to time exercsied over ye fishery of oysters and Clames in ye Harbor & Dragon River, and y^t East Haven has Exercised like authority.

It also appears in ye Settlement between New Haven and ye other Towns which formerly composed a part of New Haven, those Towns reserved a right in ye fishery of oysters and Clams.

Your Committee find by enquiry, y^t Stoney river and Dragon river contain oysters in great abundance[.] That ye western Shore of ye Harbor Contains oysters of a Sup^r Quality Tho less abundant. That Clams are in various parts of ye Harbor and y^t partial attempts to replace oysters in ye Cove has been Successful. That ye business of Catching oysters and Clams is not and has not been for past years profitable to ye inhabitants of New Haven, except to those who live bordering, on Dragon river. That to all others it is a detremental *[sic.]* business tending to increase ye Number of Towns poor.

[p. 281] your Committee have not thought it necessary to decide how far ye proprietary right has been by ye act of ye General assembly regulating ye fishery of oysters and Clams by ye annual votes of ye Town under that act, for as far as can

be ascertained ye proprietors willing to relinguish any Claim to Such fishery for ye benefit of ye Towns to which they belong.

Upon ye premises your Committee are of opinion y^t it is expedient & [...]^t to farm out ye Harbor and rivers aforesaid for ye fishery of oysters and Clams provided ye Same be farmed out for 30 years y^t ye probable annuals avails will be at least 1500 Doll^{rs}.

They therefore beg leave to propose y^t ye Town appoint a Committee to Confer with ye proprietors of ye antient Town of New Haven and with Committees of East Haven[,] North Haven[,] Hamden[,] and woodbridge and to make an agreement with s^d proprietors and said Committees to joyn with ye Town of New Haven in an application to ye General assembly in may Next, to impower ye Town of New Haven to farm out ye Same for such term and under Such restrictions and Conditions as Shall appear most for ye interest of the parties Concerned which Committee Should proceed and for ye increase & advantage of ye valuable fishery afores^d, which Committee Shall proceed as agents in behalf of ye Town to prefer[,] advocate[,] and Support Such application and obtain a resolve in favor thereof.

Your Committee beg leave to add y^t ye probable Consequence of Such measure carried into full Efect y^t ye oysters y^t are now caught when half grown would be Suffered to remain till they were [...] y^t ye Cove on ye Eastern shore, would be [...] That oysters and Clams might be as Cheap [p. 282] in market as they now are and of a better quality[.]

That ye poor who might wish to Labor in ye fishery might find imployment from ye Lessees of ye Harbour and [...] that ye towns of North Haven[,] Hamden[,] and woodbridge which now derive little or no benefit from this fishery might recive [sic.] an annual Sum into their Treasuries.

And y^t ye Town of New Haven which Contain a great proportion of heirs [of] ye antient proprietors and which from its local Situation can derive more advantage than all ye other towns might expect to receive into their treasury an annuell Sum, which would Considerably lighten ye expence of Supporting ye poor and other public burdens all which is Submited by ———

1. Samuel Bishop, Jr., the town clerk, apparently had difficulty deciphering some of the wording in the committee's report while copying it into the town records. He left spaces, here designated by bracketed ellipses, with the likely intention of adding the missing wording at a later date. Interestingly, Bishop's son, Abraham, was a member of this committee.

Tim° Jones
Peter Johnson
Thos Punderson
Simeon Baldwin
Abr^m Bishop

Voted y^t ~~Jeremiah~~ the foregoing report of ye Committee be accepted, and Simeon Baldwin, Abr^m Bishop and Peter Johnson are appointed a Committee for ye purposes.

[Surveyers of Highways.] Voted y^t Jeremiah Atwater, Thomas Punderson, Gould Smith and Stephen Row be Surveyers of Highways ye year ensuing.

[Constable.] Voted y^t Hez^h Clark be Constable ye year ensuing.

[Selectman.] Voted y^t Willm Brintnal be a Selectman in ye room of Ebenezer Peck.

[Lister.] Voted y^t Eli Hotchkiss be lister in ye room of Daniel Read.

[Agent for Barbury Bushes.] Voted y^t David Daggett Esqr be agent for this Town to apply to ye Gen^{ll} assemby and git a further act made relative to destroying Barbury bushes.

[p. 283] [Lister.] Voted y^t Stephen Row be Lister in room of Eveling Pierpont.

[Lister.] Voted y^t Joseph Mix J^r be lister in ye room of William Austin.

[Committee for the Poor.] Voted y^t Noah Webster,[1] Elias Shipman, Jeremiah Atwater, Thomas Painter, and Thomas Punderson be a Committee to make a general enquiry into ye State of ye poor in this Town comprehending their Number, disabilities[,] characters[,] & necesities also to devise a more Ecconomical & effectual mode of releiving *[sic]* their wants and make report to some future meeting.

[3/4 blank page follows.][2]

---

1. Noah Webster, Jr. (1758 - 1843) served in his father's West Hartford militia company militia during the revolution. He graduated from Yale in 1778, served as a teacher, trained as a lawyer, and was selected to serve in the Connecticut legislature as a Federalist He is best known as a lexicographer and his famous "Blue-Backed Speller" and later *An American Dictionary of the English Language*. He is buried in New Haven's Grove Street Cemetery. See, https://www.biography.com/people/noah-webster-9526224.
2. The town clerk obviously intended to enter the minutes of the April 15, 1799 meeting here. In-

[SEPTEMBER 15, 1800]

[p. 284] AT A TOWN MEETING HOLDEN IN NEW HAVEN UPON Y^E 15TH DAY OF SEPTEMBER 1800.

[Moderator.] Voted y^t Saml Bishop be moderator.

[Sale of Alms House.] The Committee appointed by ye Town of New Haven to Examine into ye State of ye poor and devise some plan for their Support which shall be more effectual and less expensive beg leave to report*[:]*

That having attended ye duties assigned them, they are of Opinion y^t ye present alms house is utterly insufficient to accomodate ye poor of ye Town and as ye house is not well Situated and at ye expence and risqe of money*[,]* it*[,]* in the opinion of your Committee*[,]* render it utterly inexpedient to attempt it, ye Committee take y*e* Liberty to recommend to ye Town to direct ye Sale of ye present house and Land on which it Stands either at ye appraisal of indifferent men or in Some other way *[or]* manner y^t shall be deemed most beneficial to ye Town. This Committee would inform ye Town y^t ye Corporation of yale College will purchase ye house and Land on terms y^t will probably be Satisfactory. Under these Circumstances ye Committee thinks it advisable to purchase a building lot in a part of ye Town where land is cheaper, than in ye center of ye Town and build a New House which shall better accommodate ye poor and ye Town and institute some New regulations for imploying those who can perform some Labor, for restraining ye vicious & turbulant and for lessening ye expences of ye Town your Committee are of opinion y^t with a better house and with Strict regulations ye poor may be rendered more Comfortable and ye Town relieved of a part of its annual Burdens.

New Haven Sept^r   Jeremiah Atwater
12th 1800   Thos Painter
                                                       Thos Punderson
                                                       Noah Webster

[p. 285] Voted y^t ye foregoing report of ye Committee be accepted.

[Alms house.] Voted y^t Thomas Punderson, Thomas Painter, Ebenezer Townsend, Isaac Beers, and Noah Webster J^r be a Committee with full powers & they are

---

stead, he recorded the minutes of that meeting following September 15, 1800. Part of the problem may have been the fact that Bishop was also serving as the September 15 meeting's moderator.

hereby authorized to sell ye present alms house and ye lot on which it Stands on Such Terms as they Shall Judge to be most beneficial for ye Town and for y^t purpose to execute a Deed or Deeds and all other Necessary writings[.] And ye s^d Committee are furthered impowered to purchase a New lot in Such place and on Such Terms as they Shall deem most expedient for the purpose of Erecting a new alms house & ye Committee are authorized and directed to estimate ye expence of a New building and lay it before ye Town at ye annual meeting in Decr Next.

Dragon Bridge. Voted ye Selectmen be requested to Confer and Negotiate and agree with ye Selectmen of ye Town of East Haven relative to ye expence of Suppoting ye bridge at Dragon and y^t in Case ye Town of East Haven Shall refuse to bear their part of ye expence, y^t ye Selectmen of this Town be authorized to prefer a memorial to ye assembly and Compel ye Town of East Haven to be at a proper proportion of ye expence or to obtain relief in Some other way.

[Church St. is penned in margin.] Voted y^t Abr^m Bradly, Gilead Kimberly, Eben^r Peck, James Hillhouse, and Eben^r Huggins be a Committee to Examine ye highway from Thadd^s Beechers to ye market below ye house of Mr Abr^m Bradly, report ye meanes y^t Should be adopted to repair ye Same, and ye probable expence thereof.

[APRIL 15, 1799][1]

[p. 286] AT A TOWN MEETING HOLDEN IN NEW HAVEN BY ADJOURNMENT UPON THE 15TH DAY OF APRIL 1799[2]

[Oyster Act.] Rules and ordinances for regulating ye fishery of oysters and Clams. Whereas ye exclusive right to ye fishery of oysters and Clams within ye Limits of ye Town of New Haven by Law appertains to ye inhabitants of said Town of New Haven, and whereas it is expedient to regulate said fishery by establishing rules & ordinances for ye preservation of ye oysters and Clams within ye s^d limits. In pursuance of ye authority of the authority derived from ye Statute of this State entitled an act for encouraging & regulating fishery[:]

Voted y^t from and after ye first day of May until ye first day of Novr annually no person shall take[,] gather[,] or Collect any oystershells in or upon any of y^e

---

1. Samuel Bishop recorded this entry out of chronological order.
2 This entry appeared in the original records out of sequence.

flatts[,] Beeches[,] rivers[,] Creeks[,] Harbours[,] or waters within ye limits of s^d Town upon pain of forfeiting seven dollars for every such offence.

Voted y^t Stephen Alling, Step^n Row, Thos Painter, Nathan Smith, Levi Ives and Eben^r Townsend Have authority and authority is hereby granted to them or either of them from ye first day of May until ye first day of October annually to grant permit or permits in writing, signed by ye person granting ye Same therein and thereby licensing ye person or persons therein Named to ketch long Clams at any place within ye Limits of ye Town of New Haven in such quantity or quantities and for such period of time as shall be in such permit Specified.

And no person after the first day of May until ye first day of Octr annually shall Catch or Cause to be caught any oysters or long clams in or upon any of ye flats[,] beeches[,] Creeks[,] Harbours[,] waters[,] or shores within ye limits of ye Town of New Haven [p. 287] Except by virtue of a permit or permits granted or obtained as aforesaid on penalty of forfeiting seven Doll^{rs} for every Such offence, and no permit shall be granted or given to catch any oysters between ye first day of May and ye first day of october Next unless by a written Certificate from a Physian residing in s^d Town that in his opinion it is expedient for ye health of ye person applying for such permit or some member of his family y^t such permit or permits be Given or Granted.

Voted y^t all penalties or forfeitures for any breach of these rules or regulations may be recovered by action or Complaint in ye Name of s^d Committee or anyone of them who are hereby impowered to prosecute the Same at their own expence and for his Sole use and benefit.

A True Copy of Record

Examined by Sam^{ll} Bishop Clerk

[SEPTEMBER 15, 1800][1]

AT A TOWN MEETING HOLDEN IN NEW HAVEN UPON THE 15TH DAY OF SEPTEMBER 1800.

[Oyster Act.] Voted y^t ye regulations relative to oysters which were in force in

---

1. Samuel Bishop already included an entry for this date, which appeared on page 284 of the original records book.

ye year and Summer of 1799 shall be in force and revive and continue untill ye 10th Day of Decr Next and y^t ye persons in s^d regulations authorized are hereby authorized and appointed for that purpose.

Voted y^t Evelin Pierpont, Anson Clinton[1] & Ezra Smith be a Committee to give permits relative to oysters.

adjourned without day.

[OCTOBER 7, 1800]

AT A TOWN MEETING HOLDEN IN NEW HAVEN UPON Y^E 7TH DAY OF OCTOBER 1800.

[Moderator.] Voted y^t Henry Daggett Esqr be moderator.

[p. 288] West Haven. Voted y^t this Town is willing that that part of the Town of New Haven included in ye Society of west Haven and extending northerly in ye city line to ye Derby turn Pike road *[...]* Provided ye General assembly shall Judge it expedient *[to]* be incorporated into a Seperate and distinct Town.[2]

[New Haven Agent.] Voted y^t in Case a Town shall be incorporated including ye Limits aforesaid that Mr Isaac Beers be agent in behalf of this Town to be heard on ye bill in form, for ye proper Division of ye property & burthens *[sic.]* of this Town.

adjourned without Day

[DECEMBER 8, 1800]

AT A TOWN MEETING HOLDEN IN NEW HAVEN UPON THE 8^H DAY OF DECEMBER 1800.

[Clerk.] Voted y^t Sam^ll Bishop be Town Clerk.

[Moderator.] Voted y^t Henry Daggett Esqr be moderator.

---

1. Captain Anson Clinton (1764 - 1813) was a West Haven resident and the husband of Rhoda Andrews (1773 - 1849). See, https://www.ancestry.com/family-tree/person/tree/60645519/person/48319767679/facts?_phsrc=z55-198268&_phstart=successSource.
2. There is no record of the legislature considering an independent West Haven in 1800 - 1801. See, *PRSC*, X, *passim.*

[Selectmen.] Voted y^t Jeremiah Atwater, Thomas Punderson, Edmond French, Gilead Kimberly, Medad Osborn, Francis Brown, and Wm Brintnal be Selectmen y^e year ensuing.

[Treasurer.] Voted y^t Nathan Beers be Treasurer ye year ensuing.

[Constables.] Voted y^t John R. Throop, Isaac Dickerman, Hez^h Clerk, and Justus Smith be Constables ye year ensuing.

[p. 289] *[Grandjurymen.]* Voted y^t Isaac M. Wales,[1] Seth P Staples[2], Isaac Townsend Ju^r, William Bristoll, Joseph Merwin J^r and Ezra Smith be grandjurymen ye year ensuing.

[Tythingmen.] Voted y^t Jeremiah Townsend J^r, Persons Clark, Jeremiah Atwater 3rd, Jehu Brainard, William Austin, Abr^m Bradly and Joseph Mix J^r, Tim^o Fowler, William Powel, Nath^{ll} Smith & Charles Prindle be tythingmen ye year ensuing.

[Listers.] Voted y^t Eneas Munson J^r, Seth P Staples, Oliver Sherman, James Meriman, Isaac Dickerman, Austin Denison, Elijah Munson, Hez^h Auger, Amos Alling, James B. Reynolds, Samuel Clark and Evelin Pierpont be listers ye year ensuing.

[Key Keepers.] Voted y^t Timothy Fowler, Noah Potter, John Hunt, John Culver, Chauncy Alling, Israel Kimberly and Oliver Smith be key keepers ye year ensuing.

[Fenceviewers.] Voted y^t Sam^{ll} Punderson, Peter Johnson, Nehemiah Smith, and Joseph Merwin J^r be fenceviewers ye year ensuing.

[Leather Sealers.] Voted y^t Isaac Thompson and Isaac Bishop be leather Sealers ye year ensuing.

[Committee About Poor.] Voted y^t Noah Webster, Elias Shipman, Jeremiah Atwater, Thomas Painter and Thomas Punderson be a Committee to make a general inquirey into ye State of ye poor in ye Town comprehending their Number*[,]* disabilities*[,]* Charaters and Necessities, also to devise a more economical, and effectual mode of releiving their wants and make report to some future meeting.

N.B. The above Vote is recorded on the 283^d Page, and the Report on the 284th Page.

---

1. Isaac Wales (1775 - 1825) married Lois Heaton in 1799 and died in Carroll, GA in 1825. See, https://www.geni.com/people/Isaac-Wales/6000000019560953016.
2. Seth Perkins Staples (1776 - 1861), a graduate of Yale in 1797, founded what later became Yale Law School in 1846.

[p. 290] Adjourned to yᵉ fourth monday of instant Decʳ at 2 °Clock in yᵉ afternoon.

[DECEMBER 22, 1800]

AT A TOWN MEETING HOLDEN BY ADJOURNMENT DECEMBER 22ᴰ 1800.[1]

[Tax.] Voted that a Rate of 6-1/2 Cents on the Dollar become payable on the first day of January next.

Collector. Voted that Hezekiah Clark be Collector of the above Town Rate and also Collector of the State Tax.

Agent [for Poor]. Voted that Thomas Punderson be agent to take care of the Poor.

Surveyor. Voted that Jeremiah Atwater be surveyor of highways.

West Haven. Voted. That the Parish of West Haven receive their proportion of the money raised by the Town for the repair of highways to be expended by them in such way as they shall elect provided the Roads within sᵈ Parish of West Haven be repaired to the acceptance of Jeremiah Atwater who is appointed surveyor within the limits of the Town.

Constable &Tithingmen. Voted that Elisha Frost be Constable. That Samuel Nevins, Stephen S. Twining and Jonah Bradley be Tithingmen.

[Lister.] That Stephen Rowe be Lister in the room of Evelin Pierpont.

[Surveyor.] That David Lambert be Surveyor of highways.

Agent. Voted that Jeremiah Atwater be agent in behalf of the Town in cases before the Court, wherein the Town are interested.

[Grandjuryman.] Voted. That Benoni Gilbert be Grandjuriman.

adjourned without day.

---

1. Elisha Munson began serving as town clerk at this point, as discovered by his handwriting.

[APRIL 13, 1801]

[p. 291] AT A TOWN MEETING HOLDEN IN NEW HAVEN APRIL 13TH
1801.

[Moderator.] David Daggett Esqr Moderator.

[Clerk.] Samuel Bishop Clerk.

[Oyster Act.] Rules and Ordinances for regulating the Fishery of Oysters and
Clams.

<u>Voted</u> That whereas the exclusive right of the Fishery of Oysters and Clams,
within the limits of the Town of New Haven, by law appertains to the inhabitants of said Town of New Haven. And Whereas it is expedient to regulate said
fishery by establishing rules and ordinances for the preservation of the Oysters
and Clams within the said limits.

In pursuance of Authority derived from the Statute of this State entitled "An
Act for incouraging and regulating fishery." That from and after the first day of
May untill the first day of November annually, no person shall take, gather or
collect, any Oystershells, in or upon any of the Flats[,] Beeches, Creeks, Rivers,
Harbors[,] or Waters within the limits of said Town on pain of forfeiting seven
dollars for every such offence.

<u>Voted</u>. That Anson Clinton, Ezra Smith, Nathaniel Smith, Stephen Alling,
Thaddeus Perritt, Stephen Rowe, Solomon Barns, Evelyn Pierpoint, have authority and authority is hereby granted to them or either of them, from the first
day of May untill the first day of October annually, to grant permit or permits in
writing signed by the person granting the same, therein and thereby licensing the
person or persons therein named, to catch long Clams at any place within the
limits of the Town of New Haven in such quantity or quantities and for such
period of time as shall be in such permit specified.

And no person from and after the first day of May untill the first day of October, annually, shall catch or cause to be caught, any Oysters or Long Clams,
in or upon ~~in or upon~~ any of the Flats[,] beeches, creeks, harbors, waters[,] or
shores within the limits *[p. 292]* of the Town of New Haven except by virtue
of a permit or permits granted or obtained as aforesaid on penalty of forfeiting
seven dollars for every Such offence; And no permit shall be granted or given

to catch any Oysters between the first day of May and the first day of October next, unless by a written certificate from a Phicisian residing in said Town, that in his oppinion it is expedient for the health of the person applying for such permit, or some member of his family. that such permit or permits be given or granted. Provided that long Clams may be caught any where upon the shores between high and lowwater mark.

Voted that all penalties and forfeitures for any breach of these rules or regulations, may be recovered by any action or complaint, in the name of said Committee of anyone of them, who are hereby empowered to prosecute the same at their own expence, and for their sole use and benefit.

[JUNE 22, 1801]

AT A TOWN MEETING HOLDEN IN NEW HAVEN JUNE 22^D 1801.

[Moderator.] Henry Daggett Esqr Moderator.

[Clerk.] Samuel Bishop Clerk.

Agent. Voted that Mr Jeremiah Atwater be Agent for the Town in all cases wherein the Town is concerned.

Sealers. Voted. That Israel Munson and Nathaniel Lyon be sealer of Weights and Measures.

Collector. Voted. That Justus Smith be Collector of State Taxes in this Town the current year in place of Hezekiah Clark who was not sworn seasonably.

[Small Pox.] Upon the Representation and Petition of Elijah Daviss[1] praying a relinquishment of a penalty incurred for coming into this State under the operation for the small pox being one hundred and fifty dollars.

[p. 293] Voted. That Fifty dollars of said forfeiture be relinquished and that the Selectmen give him a discharge from the whole on his payment of one hundred dollars beside the expences.

---

1. Possibly Elijah Davis (ca. 1777 - 1853), a Boston native, who came to New Haven in 1801 to marry Abigail Hull (1779 - 1847). See, *Columbian Centennial*, October 28, 1801.

Adjourned to Monday next at 5 °Clock P.M.

No record has been found of the adjourned meeting.[1]
[1/3 blank page follows]

Sam[l] Bishop continued Town Clerk till the following meeting.

[DECEMBER 14, 1801]

AT A TOWN MEETING HOLDEN IN NEW HAVEN DECEMBER 14TH 1801.

The following persons were chosen as Officers for the year ensuing.

[Moderator.] Elizur Goodrich Esq[r][,] Moderator.

[Town Clerk.] Elisha Munson[,] Clerk.[2]

[Treasurer.] Nathan Beers[,] Treasurer.

Selectmen		
	Jeremiah Atwater	
	Thomas Punderson	
	Timothy Atwater	
	Ebenezer Townsend	Selectmen
	Stephen S. Twining	
	Nathan Smith	
	Joseph Prindle	

Constables. <u>Voted.</u> Elisha Frost, Hezekiah Clark and Justus Smith to be <u>Constables,</u> and that Isaac Dickerman be Constable and <u>Collector</u> of the State tax.

[p. 294] Voted to be Grandjurors viz.
Isaac M. Wales
Levi Ives Jun[r]
Henry W. Edwards[3]

---

1. This notation and the one that immediately follows it concerning Bishop appeared in very small print in Elisha Munson's handwriting.
2. Elisha Munson (1760/1 - 1841) would serve as town clerk until his death in 1841.
3. Henry W. Edwards (1779 - 1847) graduated from Princeton in 1797, attended Litchfield Law School, and served as a U.S. Congressman, U.S. Senator, and Governor of Connecticut.

Anson Clinton
David Lambert
Doct^r John Barker[1]

Voted to be *Tythingmen*	*Tythingmen* viz. Isaac Dickerman, Parsons Clark, William Hillhouse, Jehu Brainard, Elijah Monson, Naphtali Daggett, Abraham Bradley, Amaziah Lucas, Enos Smith, Oliver Clark, and Ezra Smith.

Listers. Voted That Isaac Dickerman, Abraham Dummer, Obediah Hotchkiss Junr, John Skinner, Henry W. Edwards, Hezekiah Howe, William Baldwin, Samuel Hughes, Samuel Sacket, Edward Alling, Shadrack Brooks, James B. Reynolds, Evelyn Pierpoint be Listers.

Keykeepers. Voted, that Timothy Fowler, Noah Potter, John Hunt, John Culver, Chauncey Alling, Oliver Smith, James B. Reynolds be Keykeepers.

Fence Viewers. Samuel Punderson, Peter Johnson, Samuel Camby[2], and Joseph Prindle be Viewers of Fences.

Sealers. Voted, that Israel Munson be sealer of Weights and Measures. Voted. that Isaac Thompson, Isaac Bishop and Oliver Smith be Sealers of Leather.

[Samuel Bishop.] Voted Unanimously that the Thanks of this Town be presented to Samuel Bishop Esqr for the Faithfullness and Integrity with which he has served this Town for the Term of fifty four years in the Office of Town Clerk, *[p. 295]* to which Office he has this day declined a reelection, and that the Town Clerk communicate the same by presenting a certifyed copy of this Vote.

Tax. Voted, that a Tax of five Cents on the dollar be laid on the List 1801 for the current expences of the ensuing year, and the Tax be made payable the first day of February next.

[Tax Collector.] Voted. that Isaac Dickerman be Collector of the above Tax.

Agent. Voted, that an Agent be appointed for the year ensuing to appear[,] de-

---

1. Dr. John Barker (1754 - 1813), a Yale graduate and veteran of the Revolution, was a respected member of the Connecticut Medical Society and general practitioner in New Haven. See, https://www.connecticutsar.org/john-barker-md/.

2. The town clerk likely meant Capt. Samuel Candee, Jr. (1737 - 1821) of West Haven, CT.

fend[,] and prosecute in any Suit, Action, Controversy or question wherein this Town shall be interested. Voted that Jeremiah Atwater be appointed the above Agent.

Report [on the Poor.] The Committee of the town of New Haven, appointed to carry into effect a Vote of the town directing a house to be built for the accomodation of the Poor, and the confinement of the disorderly presented their report.

Voted that we ratify and accept the report of the Committee relative to the above Alms House (which report is lodged on file).

Voted, that the Agent of the Town be instructed to appear before the Committee, appointed by the County Court, to layout a road leading from Edan Sperrys thro' Woodbridge and use his endeavors to save the Town harmless from any expence that may arise from laying out the Road.

Agent. Voted, that an especial Agent be appointed in connection with the Town Agent and that Ebenezer Townsend be the above especial Agent be appointed in connection with the Town Agent.

Surveyers. Voted, that Surveyors be apointed for the superintendence of the highways, and that the following persons be surveyors[:]

[*p. 296*] Surveyors viz.　　　Isaac Mills
　　　　　　　　　　　　　　Medad Osborn
　　　　　　　　　　　　　　Nehemiah Smith
　　　　　　　　　　　　　　Samuel Nevins
　　　　　　　　　　　　　　Noah Barber
　　　　　　　　　　　　　　Isaac Dickerman
　　　　　　　　　　　　　　Joseph Prindle Jun[r]
　　　　　　　　　　　　　　John Meloy
　　　　　　　　　　　　　　Stephen Row
　　　　　　　　　　　　　　Edward Alling

Voted. that this meeting be adjourned till the last monday Decem[r] Inst[t], then to meet at the Court House.

[DECEMBER 28, 1801]

AT A TOWN-MEETING BY ADJOURNMENT HOLDEN IN NEW HA-

VEN THE 28TH DAY OF DECEMBER AD. 1801.

[Lister, Constable, Grand juror] Voted, that William Baldwin be excused from serving as Lister and that Isaac Dickerman be excused from serving as Constable and Collector of Town and State-taxes, and that Doctᵒʳ John Barker be excused from serving as Grand juror.

Constable, Grandjuror. Voted, that Nathan Platt be appointed Constable and Collector of the Town and State Taxes, and that Eldad Gilbert be appointed Grandjuror in the room of Doctᵒʳ John Barker.

Bonds. Voted, that the Selectmen take bonds with sureties from the Collector of the Town and State Taxes for the faithfull performance of his duty.

Districts. Voted, that the Selectmen divide the Town into Districts and apportion to the Surveyor or Surveyors the money which is *[p. 297]* to be laid out in each District, with instructions that the money be laid out to the best advantage and in the most suitable season of the year. Voted, to adjourn without day.

[JANUARY 28, 1802]

AT A TOWN MEETING HOLDEN IN NEW HAVEN THE 28TH DAY OF JANᴿʸ 1802.

[Mderator.] Henry Daggett Esqʳ was chosen Moderator.

Collector. Voted, that Nathan Platt be released from being Collector of the Town and State Taxes, and that Isaac Dickerman be appointed the Collector of Said Taxes.

Comᵗᵉᵉ respecting Oysters. Voted, that Simeon Baldwin, Nathan Smith, and Elizur Goodrich be appointed a Committee to enquire what are the most expedient means for preserving the Oysters and Oyster shells in the harbor and make report at the next meeting.

Water Street. Voted that Samuel Bishop, Stephen Alling, Isaac Beers, Jeremiah Atwater, and William Brintnall be appointed a Committee to view the highway leading from the New bridge to the head of Union Wharf and report to some future meeting whether any alterations may be made in the same and also the expence of puting the same in repair and how that expence may be defrayed and also to report as to the expediency of puting said highway in repair.

Voted, to adjourn to the first Monday of March next.

[MARCH 1, 1802]

[p. 298] AT A TOWN MEETING, HOLDEN BY ADJOURNMENT, MARCH 1ST 1802.

[Moderator.] Joseph Darling Esqʳ Moderator.

[Oyster Act.] Voted, to accept the report of the Committee with amendments, restricting the catching of Oysters, Oyster shells and Clams.

Voted, the following By-Law (viz'). Be it ordained by the Town of New Haven in legal Town meeting assembled, that no person or persons shall take, gather or collect any Oyster shells in or upon any of the flats, beaches, rivers*[,]* Creeks, harbors*[,]* or Waters with in the limits of the town of NewHaven, between the first day of April and the tenth day of November annually upon pain of forfeiting for each and every such offence the Sum of Seven dollars.

Be it further ordained, That no person or persons from and after the first day of May, untill the first day of October annually, shall take or cause to be taken any Oysters in or upon any of the flats, beaches, rivers, Creeks, harbors, ~~or~~ Waters*[,]* or shores within the limits of the town of NewHaven. or any long-clams on Draggon flats without a permit as hereafter provided on pain of forfeiting for each offence the Sum of seven dollars.

Be it further ordained, That Anson Clinton, Ezra Smith, Nathaniel Smith, Stephen Alling, Thaddeus Perrit, Stephen Rowe, Solomon Barns, Evelyn Pierpont, Abel Aspinwall, and Jonah Bradley, be a Committee to superintend the catching of Oysters and clams within the limits aforesaid, and shall have Authority, and authority is hereby granted to them or either of them, within the time limited as aforesaid to grant a permit or permits in writing thereby licensing *[p. 299]* the person therein named, to take the quantity of Oysters or long clams therein mentioned at any place in such permit specified. Provided that no such permit for oysters shall be granted between the first day of May and the first day of October annually, unless upon a certificate under the hand of a Physician certifying that Oysters will be conducive to the health of the person or whose benefit the permit shall be requested; nor Shall such permit be for more than one bushel, or be of force more than twenty four hours from its date. And if any person shall take a larger quantity than is specified in any such permit, such person shall incur the penalty as is provided for taking without a permit.

Be it further ordained, That no person shall sell or offer for sale, in said New-Haven, any oysters taken within the limits of said town of NewHaven, between the first of May and the first of October annually, on pain of forfeiting one dollar for each bushel or quantity less than a bushel so taken and sold.

Be it further ordained, That all penalties and forfeitures incurred for any breach of this by-law shall belong to the treasury of the town of NewHaven: And Jeremiah Atwater and Stephen Twining Esqr are hereby appointed agents for the town to enquire after and at their discretion to prosecute to and for the use of the Town, in their name, and at their expence all breaches of this by-law. And it is hereby declared to be the duty of said committee, to make presentment or complaint to the said agents or either of them of all breaches thereof which shall come to their knowledge.

[Vagrants.] Voted, That any two or more of the Selectmen be authorized and impowered to take up and sentence to the Workhouse of the town all Vagrant*[s]* and such like other persons as may be sentenced to said House by a Justice of the Peace.

[Tax.] Voted, That Isaac Dickerman be appointed and impowered *[p. 300]* to collect the remainder of the town tax, still due on the List A.D. 1800, in the room of Hezekiah Clark formerly appointed as Collector of said tax.

Adjourned till Monday the 12th of April 1802.

[APRIL 12, 1802]

AT A TOWN-MEETING HOLDEN BY ADJOURNMENT APRIL 12TH 1802.

[Moderator.] David Daggett Esqr was chosen Moderator.

[E Water.] The committee who were appointed, at a former meeting to make report respecting the road leading from the New-bridge to the head of Union-Wharf stated that the City had formerly laid out the abovesaid-road &c. which superseded the necessity of their making any report.

<u>Voted.</u> That the town will do nothing further upon the subject.

[New Haven-East Haven Boundary.] Voted. That Messrs Elizur Goodrich, Noah Webster and Stephen Row, be impowered to prefer such petition as they Shall think proper to the General Assembly of this State at their next Session relative to ascertaining and settleing the boundary line between the Towns of New Haven and East Haven and the maintenance of Draggon Bridge.

Voted, that Thomas Rice be excused from serving as Committee*[man]* and that John Benedict be appointed in his stead.

Adjourned without day.

[DECEMBER 13, 1802]

AT A TOWN MEETING HOLDEN AT THE COURT HOUSE IN NEW HAVEN DECEM^R 13TH, 1802.

[Moderator and Clerk.] Voted. Elizur Goodrich Esqr Moderator, & Elisha Munson Clerk.

Selectmen. Timothy Atwater, Nathaniel Kimberly, Samuel Punderson, William McCracken, and Stephen Twining Selectmen.

Constables. Lockwood Deforrest and Justus Smith, Constables.

[p. 301] *Grandjurors.* Isaac M. Wales, Levi Ives J^r, Charles Denison, Samuel Trowbridge and David Lambert Grandjurymen.

Listers. John H. Lynde, Hezekiah Howe, Charles Denison, William Powel, James B. Reynolds, Oliver Clark, Kneeland Townsend, Ebenezer Peck, James Thompson Junr, Stephen Row, William Baldwin and Edward Alling, Listers.

Tythingmen. Seth P. Staples, Parsons Clark, Abraham Bradley, Joseph Mix, John Skinner, Stephen Atwater, Naphtali Daggett, Israel Terril, Samuel Clark, Stephen Twining and Elias Stilwell Tythingman.

Surveyors of highways. Samuel Punderson, Peter Johnson, Eleazur Hotchkiss, Asahel Tuttle, Gillead Kimberly, Silas Kimberly Junr, Shadrack Brooks, Stephen Row, Enos Johnson and Samuel Nevins Surveyors of highways.

Key-keepers. Timothy Fowler, Noah Potter, James B. Reynolds, Chauncey Alling, John Culver, John Hunt, Andrew Ferril.

Fence Viewers. Joseph Munson, Thomas Rice, Timothy Fowler, Hezekiah Hotchkiss, Samuel Candee and Joseph Prindle Junr Fence Viewers.

Sealers. Israel Munson, Sealer of Weights and Measures. James Thompson and Amaziah Lucas sealers of Leather.

Treasurer. Nathan Beers, Treasurer.

Voted. That the Selectmen be appointed to investigate the claim which the Town have to a piece of Land situate in front of the house owned, formerly, by Hezekiah Howe, deceased, which land is now claimed by s^d Howes heirs. And that the Selectmen be impowered to confer with and make a final settlement with s^d heirs respecting s^d Lands.

[p. 302] West Haven. The following proposition was bro^t forward by Capt. Thomas Painter, viz. That the boundaries of West Haven as described in a Vote of the Town passed October 7th 1800 might be enlarged viz. from Derby Turnpike - road by the West River to Thompsons bridge thence Northerly to Hamden Line and that all the Land lying Westerly of the above described line might be annexed to the contemplated Town of West Haven.

Voted. That the consideration of the subject be postponed till the next Town Meeting and that the Selectmen give notice thereof by advertisement in the Newpaper.

[Committee on Town Accounts.] Voted. That Noah Webster, William Powel, Simeon Baldwin, and Thomas Painter be a committee to make out an account current and state the expenditures of the Town, (under distinct heads.) for the year past, and make report to the next Town Meeting.

Voted to adjourn till the fourth monday of December ins^t 2 OClock P.M.

[DECEMBER 27, 1802]

AT A MEETING OF THE INHABITANTS OF THE TOWN HOLDEN IN NEWHAVEN BY ADJOURNMENT, ON THE 27TH DAY OF DECEMBER 1802.

[Moderator.] Elizur Goodrich Esqʳ Moderator.

[Committee on Town Accounts.] The Committee appointed the last meeting (to examine the accounts of the Town and make out an account current of the expenditures) made their report which was accepted (and recorded on the 307 page). Voted, That the Selectmen be and are hereby authorised to borrow in behalf of the Town as sum of money not exceeding fifteen hundred dollars on legal interest and for a term not exceeding six rnonths; and the sum which they shall borrow shall be paid over to the Treasurer of the Town to be employed for the purpose of paying the Debts of the Town and for defraying any current expences of the year ensuing.

[p. 303] *[Tax.]* Voted, that a tax of five cents on a dollar be laid on the List of this Town for the year 1802, for the purpose of discharging the debts and defraying the expences of the Town for the year ensuing; which tax shall be payable on the first day of Januany next.

[Tax.] Voted. That all monies raised by taxes ,or due to the Town from any other source, shall when recieved be paid over to the Treasurer of the Town; and no money shall be paid towards answering any demand against the Town, by any person whatever, except by the Treasurer, upon orders regularly drawn upon him by the Selectmen which orders shall be filed and upon the Audit of Town accounts shall be compared with the books of the Treasurer; and it shall be the duty of the Selectmen to open and keep seperate accounts with the Alms house, the Hospital, the highways and bridges*[,]* the pensioners in private families, and miscelaneous expenditures as also an account of the purchases of junk, or other materials for employment of the poor, together with the charges and proceeds of the sales of Oakum.[1]

Voted, that the Selectmen take such measures as they shall judge expedient toward introducing a more regular and economical supply of provisions, cloathing, and fuel, for the poor and materials for their employment by purchasing by wholesail such articles as are of constant use, and by substituting Peat and Coal for wood, by new agreements with Phisicians employed to visit the sick or by such regulations and provisions as may from time to time be found expedient.

---

1. Oakum is a tarred fiber used to seal gaps primarily in shipping. It was often made by prisoners and the poor who tediously unravelled ropes and cordage. See, Hugh Chisholm, editor, "Oakum," Encyclopædia Britannica. 19 (11th ed.). Cambridge University Press, 1911, p. 935.

[Vagrants.] Voted that it be the duty of the Selectmen to enforce the laws relative to Vagabonds, Vagrants and others who are not legal inhabitants of the Town, especially with regard to <u>blacks</u> and mulattoes.[1]

[Selectman.] Voted that William McCracken be excused from serving as Selectman, and Thaddeus Perrit be appointed in his room.

[p. 304] [Tax Collector.] Voted that the Collector, shall on the first of each month, pay to the Treasurer of the Town, all money which shall be collected on the Town tax.

[Tax Collector.] Voted that Col Stephen Ball be appointed collector of the Town tax.

[Fenceviewer.] Voted to excuse Thomas Rice from being Fence Viewer and that Isaac Gilbert be appointed in his room.

[Constable.] Voted. that Isaac Dickerman be appointed Constable.

[Keykeeper.] Voted to excuse Timothy Fowler from serving as Key-keeper.

[Constable & Collector.] Voted that Col Stephen Ball be appointed Constable & Collector of the State tax.

Voted to adjourn till the 2^d Monday in Jany 1803 at 2 oClock P.M. at the Court House.

[JANUARY 10, 1803]

AT A TOWN MEETING HOLDEN, BY ADJOURNMENT, ON THE 10TH DAY OF JAN^Y, 1803.

[Moderator.] Elizur Goodrich Esqr Moderator.

[Selectman.] Voted, to excuse Thaddeus Perrit from serving as Selectman.

---

1. In 1790, New Haven's black population was about 200. That increased to 600 by 1800, giving rise to racism as evidenced in this entry. See, Jean Sutherland, "Examining the African American Role in New Haven History: Pride in the Past–Hope for the Future," Yale-New Haven Teachers Institute, http://teachersinstitute.yale.edu/curriculum/units/1992/3/92.03.08.x.html.

[Selectman.] Voted that Elijah Munson be appointed Selectman for the year ensuing.

[Lister.] Voted to excuse James Thompson from being Lister and that Punderson Hotchkiss be appointed in his room.

[Lister.] Voted, to excuse Hezekiah Howe from serving as Lister and that Henry Munson be appointed in his room.

[Lister.] Voted, that Stephen Row be excused from serving as Lister and that John Hunt 1st be appointed in his room.[1]

[Constable.] Voted, that Josiah B. Morse be appointed Constable in the room of Isaac Dickerman who is excused.

[Town Agent.] Voted that Jeremiah Atwater be appointed agent to appear and defend against all suits which may be brought against the Town.

Voted, That the Selectmen of the Town be requested to search after *[p. 305]* and look up all or any of the public lands belonging to the Town and report what lands (if any there are) and the situation they are in to some future meeting.

Boundry between E. Haven. Voted that this Town will not object to the report of the Committee who were appointed by the General Assembly to ascertain the boundary-line between this Town and East Haven, which report represent the Middle waters of the main branch of the East River as the divisional line and consider it as a boundary between New Haven and East Haven.

Voted that Elizur Goodrich, Simeon Baldwin, Timothy Atwater and Noah Webster be a Committee to examine the rights and Claims of this Town to the fishery of Oysters and Clams (within the limits of s^d Town) and make report to some future meeting.

[Lister.] Voted, that James Prescott be a Lister for the present year.

Voted to adjourn 'till January 24th 1803, 2 OClock P.M.

---

1. John Hunt (1749 - 1831) was born in London, England, and was living in the New Haven area with his wife Elizabeth Tomline Hunt as of 1772. See, Will Johnson, "Male-line Descendants of John Hunt (1749 - 1831) of New Haven, Connecticut," http://www.countyhistorian.com/knol/4hmquk6fx4gu-244-male-line-descendants-of-john-hun.html.

[JANUARY 24, 1803]

AT A TOWN MEETING HOLDEN BY ADJOURNMENT ON THE 24TH OF JANY 1803.

[Moderator.] Elizur Goodrich Esqr Moderator.

[Public Lands]Report. The Committee appointed the last Town Meeting to search after and look up all or any of the public lands belonging to the Town, made report.

Voted that the said Report be accepted and recorded which is as follows viz.

Report. The Selectmen of the Town being appointed to make search for Lands within the Town, belonging to the same, make report; that they find belonging to the Town a piece of Land by the Creek a part of which is covered by the Market; also a piece of land south of Browns market, being highway but entirely useless as such, and may be leased so long as the Market continues in its present situation. Also a piece of Land on the Northeasterly side of the highway leading from the State House to Thompson Bridge[1] and extending from Hezekiah Augers Garden to the House of Mrs Bristow. This land is highway but in a bend and where the highway is of an *[p. 306]* unnecessary width, also about half an acre of Salt Marsh south of the causeway at the Neck bridge, also a piece of land containing about one and half acres by the fresh meadow, a little North of the Milford road. Also about twenty Five acres in the Beaver ponds, also a part of the flatts lying between the Still house Wharf and Mrs Braggs[2] House.

Timothy Atwater
Samuel Punderson
Stephen Twining

Public Land. Voted, that the Selectmen be authorised to lease for a term not exceeding one year that piece of land which is claimed by the public and is situated between the market and the land belonging to the heirs of Stephen Bradley. *Land.* Voted, that the Selectmen enquire into the title that the *[town]* has to a piece of land (containing one and one half acres) by the fresh Meadow situate a

1. Thompson Bridge was located in Westville. See, Osterweis, p. 275.
2. Likely Mrs. Benjamin Bragg *(née Polly Butler)*. Benjamin died in 1802 at the age of 40.

little North of the Milford road, and if the town own it, sell the same.[1]
Highway. Voted, that the Selectmen be authorized to lease for the term of one year that piece of land (being highway and at present useless) which is situate southerly of Browns Market.

Highway. Voted, that the Selectmen be instructed to straiten the highway, Westerly of Hezekiah Augurs which, by report of the Committee, appears of an unnecessary width and to sell for the use and benefit of the Town so much of said highway as may be cut off by straitening the same.

Grist Mill &c. Voted, that the Selectmen be instructed to enquire into original grants made to the former owners of the Grist Mill,[2] and the Title which the Town or proprietors still have to about twenty five acres of Land situate in the Beaver ponds, also examine the nature and quality of the soil of said Lands and make report to the next Town Meeting.[3]

[Lister.] Voted, that John Hart Lynde[4] be excused from serving as Lister and that Luther Bradley be appointed Lister in his room.
Adjourned without day.

[p. 307] Report. To the Town of New Haven. The Committee appointed at your last meeting (see Page 302) to examine the accounts of the Town and make out an account current of the expenditures — Report. That they have attended to the duties of the appointment and tho' they are satisfied that the amounts of expenditures, payments and debts have been accurately stated by the selectmen, yet they find that the accounts of the last and current year are blended and are not so arranged under distinct heads, that they cannot without considerable time and Labor make an entire seperation of them; they have however as far as their time wou'd permit classified the sums paid during the year under several distinct heads and in that shape herewith exhibit them, noticing at the same time that expenditures of former years are included. And they recommend to the Town to adopt some mode of keeping the accounts by which the expenditures under

1. This location was near present day West River Memorial Park.
2. Possibly Levi Sperry's grist mill, which he built in 1796 along the banks of the West River. The location is now known as the Pond Lilly Nature Preserve, run by the New Haven Land Trust.
3. Beaver Pond is situated on the present-day campus of Southern Connecticut State University in the Beaver Hills section of New Haven.
4. John Hart Lynde (1778 - 1817) served a clerk of the New Haven County and Probate courts. He died of Typhiod fever. His home remains at 66 Wall Street, New Haven. See, https://www.ancestry.com/family-tree/person/tree/62670335/person/40137581760/facts?_phsrc=z55-1810548&_phstart=successSource.

each head and for each year may in future be easily and accurately Stated, and
for this purpose they have prepared sundry votes for the consideration of the
Town which we also herewith present. They are of opinion from their examination of the accounts of the last year that the current expences of the comeing
year and the payment of their debts will exceed three thousand dollars, and that
it is advisable to lay Such tax as will fully meet the demands and if possible leave
something in the Treasury[,]

all which is submitted by order.

Decem[r] 26th, 1802   Noah Webster

William Powel

N.B. The above ought to   Thomas Painter
have been recorded on the 302nd page }   Simeon Baldwin

[APRIL 11, 1803]

AT A TOWN MEETING HOLDEN IN NEW HAVEN APRIL 11TH 1803.

[Moderator.] Henry Daggett Esq[r] Moderator.

[Committee about Hospital.] Voted, that Jeremiah Atwater, Thomas Painter, Ebenezer Peck, *[p. 308]* Timothy Atwater and Nathaniel Kimberly be a Committee
to examine into the expediency of disposing of the Hospital, belonging to the
town – to ascertain at what price the same can be sold and the proper place for
errecting a new Hospital, and the probable expence of the necessary land, and
of a new building for the use of a Hospital together with a place for a Hospital
and to Report the same to some future meeting.[1]

Voted to adjourn to the 25th day of April Ins[t] 2 OClock P.M.

[APRIL 25, 1803]

AT A TOWN MEETING HOLDEN IN NEW HAVEN APRIL 25TH 1803.

[Committee about Hospital.] The Committee appointed the last town meeting to
examine into the expediency of disposing of the Hospital &c. made report,
which report was not accepted.

Voted, that the meeting be adjourned without day.

---

1. The original hospital to administer inoculations was built under the direction of Drs. Levi Ives
and Eneas Munson in 1792. By 1803, this building stood in the way of road improvements that included the continuation of Chapel Street. See, Records of the Mayor, Aldermen, Common Council
and Freemen of the City of New Haven, October 4, 1803 , mss., New Haven Museum.

[DECEMBER 12, 1803]

AT A TOWN MEETING HOLDEN, AT THE COURT HOUSE, IN NEW HAVEN ON THE 12TH DAY OF DECEMBER A.D. 1803.

[Moderator.] Voted Henry Daggett Esqr Moderator.

[Town Clerk.] Elisha Munson, Clerk.

Selectmen. Timothy Atwater, Samuel Punderson, Abraham Bradley, Samuel Sacket and Ezra Smith.

Grand jurors. Samuel Darling, Levi Ives, Abel Burritt, Nathan Beers, James Merriman, David Lambert, James Alling.

Listers. Thaddeus Beecher, Ebenezer Peck, Jeremiah Atwater, Ebenezer Townsend, Joseph Drake, Ebenezer Huggins, Charles Denison, Anson Clinton, Josiah Myrick, Elijah Thompson, Stephen Row, Levi Beecher.

[p. 309] Constables. Josiah B. Morse, Lockwood Deforest and Justus Smith.

Surveyors of highways. Thomas Punderson, Medad Osborn, William Baldwin, Gillead Kimberly, Nathan Platt and Stephen Prindle.

Fence Viewers. Thomas Rice, Timothy Fowler, Hezekiah Hotchkiss, Nath^{ll} Smith and Samuel Candee.

Tythingmen. Stephen Twining, Jeremiah Townsend, Junr, Hezekiah Howe, John Skinner, John Barker, William Powel, Joel Downs, Thaddeus Clark Junr, Laban Smith, and Chauncey Alling.

Poundkeepers. Timothy Fowler, James B. Reynolds, Silas Kimberly, Joseph Gorham, John Culver, John Hunt, Andrew Ferril, Martin Parrot and Chauncey Alling.

Sealers. Israel Munson sealer of weights and measures. James Thompson and Amaziah Lucas sealers of Leather.

Treasurer. Nathan Beers.

[Derby Road Committee.] Voted. That Thomas Punderson and Isaac Mills be

a Committee to enquire into the manner of Laying out the old Derby road, whether done by the Selectmen of the Town or otherwise.

[DECEMBER 19, 1803]

AT A TOWN MEETING, HOLDEN BY ADJOURNMENT, IN NEW HAVEN DECEMBER 19ᵀᴴ 1803.

[Moderator and Town Clerk.] Henry Daggett Esqʳ Moderator, Elisha Munson Clerk.

[Selectman.] <u>Voted.</u> That Samuel Darling be appointed a Selectman and that he be excused from serving as Grandjuryman.

[Grandjuryman.] <u>Voted.</u> That Elias Stilwell be appointed Grandjuror in the room of Samuel Darling who is excused.

[Grandjuryman.] <u>Voted.</u> That Amaziah Lucas be appointed Grandjuror in the room of Abel Burritt who is excused.

[Tax.] <u>Voted.</u> That a Town Tax of four cents on the dollar be laid *[p. 310]* on the List *[of]* 1803, and that the tax be made payable on the first day of February 1804.

[Constable and Tax Collector.] <u>Voted.</u> That Lewis Alling be Collector of the Town tax also Constable and Collector of the State Tax.

[Derby Road.] Whereas Ebenezer Townsend, Thomas Punderson, Timothy Atwater, Stephen Twining and Joseph Prindle Junʳ being Selectmen of the Town of NewHaven, by their deed dated the 20ᵗʰ day of September 1802, sold and conveyed to Peter Johnson of sᵈ Town, in consideration of a certain piece of Land conveyed by sᵈ Johnson to sᵈ Town for a highway and in consideration of Labor done and to be done in making a bridge and on certain highways, a certain piece of Land in sᵈ Town, being useless highway, that is to say a part of the highway called Derby road running through a Farm of sᵈ Johnson beginning at the place where the easterly line of sᵈ farm intersects the Old Derby road, and extending westerly to the Woodbridge line reserving for the use of sᵈ New Haven so much of sᵈ highway as is sufficient to extend the new road, Leading from the Litchfield Turnpike to the sᵈ Derby road near the Dwelling house of sᵈ Johnson on his said farm, two roads *[rods]* wide across sᵈ Derby road in the

direction of s^d new road.

Voted. That the deed, sale, and conveyance of s^d Selectmen to the s^d Johnson be approved and ratified, and the same is hereby approved and ratified. Provided that the Rimmon falls Turnpike Company,[1] do by the first day of March 1804, give bond to the Treasurer of the Town of NewHaven in the sum of One thousand dollars to save s^d town harmless from all expence that may arise in consequence of s^d sale by s^d Selectmen.

[p. 311] Voted to adjourn till Tuesday the 27th day of Decem^r ins^t at 2 oClock P.M.

[DECEMBER 27, 1803]

AT A TOWN MEETING HOLDEN IN NEW HAVEN, BY ADJOURN-MENT, DECEMBER 27TH 1803.

[Moderator and Town Clerk.] Henry Daggett Esqr Moderator, Elisha Munson Clerk.

[Granjuryman.] Voted. To excuse Nathan Beers from serving as Grandjuryman.

[Land Committee.] Voted. That Elizur Goodrich, David Daggett, Thomas Painter and Elisha Munson be a Committee to investigate the claim which the Town have to a piece of Land situate in front of the House owned by the heirs of Hez^h Howe, dec^d, and that the s^d Committee be vested with the same powers that were granted to the Selectmen by a Vote of the Town which was passed December 13th 1802.

[Selectmen.] Voted. That the Selectmen be appointed for the Town for the ensuing year and that either of them be authorized to appear sue for and defend or act as agents aforesaid.

[Oyster Committee.] Voted. That Evelyne Pierpoint, Stephen Rowe, Thomas Painter, Ebenezer Townsend and Stephen Alling be appointed a Committee to enquire after and devise the best mode of preserving the Oysters in the harbor.

---

1. The Rimmon Falls Turnpike Company was established in 1802 and was operational until at least 1838. Today, the route in question is Rte. 313 in Woodbridge and Seymour. See, http://www.kurumi.com/roads/ct/ct313.html.

[Beaver Ponds.] Voted. That Elizur Goodrich, Thomas Punderson and Elisha Munson be a Committee to examine into the right, title, interest and estate of the Town in and upon certain Lands part of the Beaver ponds and ascertain in what mode the same may be made the most productive and usefull to the town and make report.

[Grandjuryman.] Voted. That Joseph Mix be appointed Grandjuror in the room of Nathan Beers who is excused.

[Lister.] Voted. To excuse Ebenezer Peck from being Lister.

[Grandjuryman.] Voted. That Isaac Dickerman be appointed Grandjuror. Voted. To adjourn without day.

[MARCH 27, 1804]

[p. 312] AT A TOWN MEETING HOLDEN AT THE COURTHOUSE IN NEWHAVEN ON THE 27TH DAY OF MARCH 1804.

[Moderator and Town Clerk.] Elizur Goodrich Esqr Moderator. Elisha Munson Clerk.

[Oyster Act.] The Committee who were appointed the last meeting to enquire after and devise the best mode of preserving Oysters in the harbor made report which was accepted.

Voted. That no person or persons, be permitted to take, gather or collect any Oystershells in or upon any of the flats, beaches, rivers, Creeks, harbors or waters within the limits of the Town of NewHaven between the first day of April and the 10th day of November annually on pain of forfeiting for each and every such offence the sum of seven dollars.

That no person or persons from and after the first day of April untill the 10th day of October annually shall take or cause to be taken, any Oysters in or upon any of the flats, beaches, rivers, creeks, harbors[,] waters or shores within the limits of the Town of NewHaven nor any Long clams on Dragon Flats excepting as hereafter provided on pain of forfeiting seven dollars for each of offence.

That no person shall catch Oysters within the limits of the Town of New Haven, at any season of the year except in the months of December and January,

without culling out the shells and small Oysters, and the same throwing over-
board in the stream at or near the place where s^d Oysters were taken on pain of
forfeiting for each and every offence the sum of seven dollars.

That John P. Austin,[1] Seth Barnes, Evelyne Pierpoint, Ezra Smith, Anson Clinton, Samuel Sacket, Phinehas Andrews, Justus Hotchkiss and Chauncey Alling,
be a Committee to superintend the catching of Oysters and Clams within the
limits aforesaid – *[p. 313]* who shall have authority granted to them or either of
them with in the time limited aforesaid, to grant a permit or permits in writing
thereby licencing the person therein named to take the quantity of Oysters or
long Clams therein mentioned, at any place in such permit specified; provided
that no such permit for Oysters shall be granted between the first day of April
and the 10th day of October annually, unless upon a certificate under the hand
of a Physician, that Oysters will be conducive to the health of the Person, for
whose benefit the permit shall be requested, nor shall such permit be for more
than one bushel, or be of force more than twenty four hours from its date; and
if any person shall take a larger quantity than is specified in any such permit,
such person shall incur the penalty as is provided for taking without a permit.

That no person or persons shall sell or offer for sale in said NewHaven any Oysters taken within the limits of said town of NewHaven between the first day of
April and 10th day of October annually on pain of forfeiting one dollar for each
bushel or lesser quantity so taken and sold.

That no person shall drive any kind of carriage in or upon any of the Oyster
banks where Oysters are growing within the before mentioned limits at any
season of the year, on pain of forfeiting seven dollars for every such offence.
That the penalties and forfeitures incured by any breach of the above regulations shall belong to the Treasury of the Town of NewHaven and that Stephen
Twining Esqr be appointed agent for the Town to enquire after and at his discretion to prosecute to and for the Town in their name, and at their expence
all breaches of the above regulations and that it be made the duty of the said
Committee to make complaint to the said agent, of all breaches of the above
said regulations that shall come to their knowledge.

[p. 314] *[Listers.]* <u>Voted</u>. That William Walter and Kneeland Townsend be ap-

---

1. John P. Austin (1774 - 1834,) graduated Yale College in 1794. He died of cholera in Texas while
settling the estate of his son John (1793 - 1833), who also died of cholera. The senior John P. Austin's remains were brought back to New Haven where he is buried at Grove Street Cemetery. See,
https://tshaonline.org/handbook/online/articles/fau10.

pointed Listers in the room of Ebenezer Peck and Thaddeus Beecher who are excused.

[Beaver Ponds.] Whereas the Proprietors of the Beaver ponds may be desirous of draining the ponds and whereas the owners of Bradleys Mill may wish to discontinue the Mill with a view that the ponds may be drained.

Voted. That Elizur Goodrich Esq' be an agent of the Town to attend any meeting of such Proprietors or Owners and consult with them as to the best mode of effecting the general interest of all concerned in said ponds and generally to take care of the interest of the Town in said ponds, provided however that such agent shall make no contract or do any act obligatory upon the Town, but shall in all cases report any provisions in his opinion necessary to be made in behalf of the Town and take advice and instruction thereon.

[Defunct Highways.] Voted. That the Selectmen be Authorized to discontinue and sell the highways enclosed in the Beaver hill Commonfields and the discontinueations of the same to the road leading from the Ditch Corner to the Sluice.

Voted to adjourn without day.

[DECEMBER 10, 1804]

AT A TOWN MEETING HOLDEN IN NEW HAVEN DECEMBER 10ᵀᴴ 1804.

[Moderator and Town Clerk.] Abel Burrit was chosen Moderator & Elisha Munson, Clerk.

Selectmen. Voted. Abraham Bradley, Samuel Punderson, Samuel Darling, Samuel Sacket & Ezra Smith - Selectmen.

Grandjurors. Voted. James Alling, Amos Alling, DeLazun DeForest,[1] Daniel Read, David Lambert, William Austin and Timothy Dwight J[2] Grandjurors.

---

1. DeLauzon DeForest (1781 - 1815) ran a book shop in New Haven with Hezekiah Howe (1775 - 1838). See, Hezekiah Howe Papers, GEN MSS 1365, Yale University, Beinecke Rare Book and Manuscript Library.
2. Timothy Dwight (1752 - 1817), was a Yale College graduate, theologian, and poet, who served as president of Yale from 1795 - 1817. See, https://connecticuthistory.org/people/timothy-dwight/
3. William Bristol (1779 - 1836), graduated Yale College in 1798, entered the legal profession, and

Listers. Voted. Thaddeus Beecher, Ebenezer Townsend, Ebenezer Huggins, William Bristol,[3] Elijah Thompson, Anson Clinton, Josiah Myrick, William Walter, Ezra Hotchkiss, Levi Beecher and Isaac Dickerman Liste

[p. 315] Constables. Voted. Josiah B. Morse, Lewis Alling, George Munson, Samuel Clark and John P. Austin Constables.

Surveyors. Voted. William Baldwin, Thomas Punderson, Isaac Dickerman, Lewis Alling, Ebenezer Peck, Gilead Kimberly, Nathan Platt, Stephen Prindle & Stephen Rowe Surveyors.

Fence Viewers. Voted. Stephen Trowbridge Jun[r], William Brintnall, Gillead Kimberly, Joseph Prindle, Moses Umfreville[1] and Hezekiah Hotchkiss Fence Viewers.

Tythingmen. Voted. Stephen Twining, Jeremiah Atwater Jun[r], Jeremiah Atwater 3[d], John Skinner, John Barker, Samuel Sacket, William Powel, Abraham Bradley, Eliakim Kimberly, Ezra Smith and Thaddeus Clark Jr., Thythingmen.

Key Keepers. Voted. Henry Munson, Timothy Fowler, Mastin Parrot, Joseph Gorham, John Culver, Andrew Farrel, John Hunt, James B. Reynolds, Chauncey Alling, Jonathan Alling, Peter Johnson and Asa Potter Keykeepers.

Sealers. Voted. That Israel Munson be Sealer of Weights & Measures and Isaac Thomas, Amaziah Lucas and James Prescott be sealers of Leather.

Treasurer. Voted. That Nathan Beers be Treasurer.

Agents. Voted. That the Selectmen be appointed agents for the Town for the year ensuing and that either of them with the consent of the Majority be authorised to appear[,] Sue and defend or act as agents aforesaid.

Committee. Voted. That Elizur Goodrich, Henry Daggett and Eneas Monson Jun[r], be a Committee to enquire into the situation *[p. 316]* of Draggon Bridge and the propriety of applying to the General Assembly for a Toll for its support and make report.

---

served in a number of capacities, from city alder to mayor in 1827 as well as the Connecticut Supreme Court from 1819 - 1926. See, https://www.fjc.gov/history/judges/bristol-william.
1. Moses Humphreville (1763 - 1829), husband of Hannah Downs Humphreville (1766 - 1845). See, Jacobus, *Families of Ancient New Haven*, Vol. III: 576.

Collector. Voted. That Lewis Alling be Collector of the State Tax.
Adjourned without day.

[DECEMBER 24, 1804]

AT A TOWN MEETING HOLDEN IN NEWHAVEN DECEMBER 24TH
1804.

[Moderator and Town Clerk.] Abel Burritt Moderator, & Elisha Munson Clerk

[Lister.] Voted. That Ebenezer Townsend be excused from serving as a Lister
and that William Brintnal be appointed a Lister in his room.

[Grandjuryman.] Voted. That Hezekiah Hotchkiss be excused from serving as
Grand juror and that Stephen Atwater be appointed a Grand juror in his room.

[Lister.] Voted. That Elijah Thompson be excused from serving as a Lister and
that Asahel Tuttle be appointed a Lister in his room.

[Constable.] Voted. That John P. Austin be excused from serving as Constable
and that Elisha Frost be appointed a Constable in his room.

[Tax.] Voted. That a tax of four and an half cents on the dollar be laid on the List
[of] 1804 and made payable on the tenth day of June AD 1805. Voted that Lewis
Alling be Collector of the Tax and receive six per cent as a compensation for collecting the same provided he settle said Tax by the first day of December 1805.

[Dragon Bridge Toll.] The Committee who were appointed the last meeting to
enquire into the situation of Draggon bridge and with respect to the propriety
of applying to the General Assembly *[p. 317]* for a Toll for its support, made a
verbal report, whereupon

Voted. that this Town is very desirous that the Bridge at Leavenworth's ferry
may be continued and preserved as being of great importance to the Town and
being of opinion that a small Toll placed on Dragon bridge would increase the
travel over the bridge at the ferry they are therefore willing and desirous that
such Toll may be collected and such part as may be necessary applied to keep up
the Bridge at Dragon in repair and the residue applied as the General Assembly

shall see fit.[1]

[Agent.] <u>Voted</u>. that Isaac Beers be appointed an Agent to apply to the General Assembly for the above purpose.

[Grandjuryman.] Voted. That Joel Atwater be appointed a Grandjuror.

Voted. to adjourn 'till, monday, January the 14th 1805 at two oClock in the afternoon.

[JANUARY 14, 1805]

At a Town meeting holden in New Haven January 14th 1805.

[Moderator.] Doct[r] Levi Ives was chosen Moderator.

[Oysters.] Voted. That no person or persons be permitted to take*[,]* gather or collect any oystershells, in or upon any of the flats*[,]* beaches, rivers, harbors or Waters, within the limits of the Town of NewHaven, between the first day of April and the 10th day of November annually nor any oysters on Dragon flats, Northerly of a line drawn from the old Old Ferry House to the dwelling house of Job Smith, in East Haven on pain of forfeiting for each and every such offence, the sum of seven dollars. That no person or persons from and after the first day of April untill the tenth of October annually, shall take or cause to be taken any Oysters *[p. 318]* in or upon any of the flats, beaches, rivers, Creeks, harbors, waters or shores within the limits of the Town of NewHaven, nor any long clams on Dragon Flats excepting as hereafter provided on pain of forfeiting seven dollars for each offence.

That no person shall catch Oysters within the limits of the Town of NewHaven at any season of the year except in the months of December and January without culling out the shells and small oysters, and the same throwing over-board in the stream at or near the place where said oysters were taken, on pain of forfeiting for each and every such offence the sum of seven dollars.

That John P. Austin, Seth Barns, Evelyne Pierpoint, Ezra Smith, Anson Clin-

---

1. Built in 1789, the Dragon Bridge over the East River proved to be a financial albatross for its investors and New Haven. In 1806, the bridge was washed away in a flood, preventing any further need for tolls or lotteries to underwrite its debt. For a history of the bridge, see *PRSC*, XII: 353.

ton, Samuel Sacket, Phinehas Andrus, Justus Hotchkiss, Chauncey Alling, Jairus Sanfrd and Sherman Kimberly, be a Committee to superintend the catching of oysters and clams within the limits aforesaid who shall have authority granted to them, or either of them within the time limited aforesaid to grant a permit or permits, in writing thereby licensing the person therein named to take the quantity of oysters or long clams therein mentioned, at any place in such permit specified provided that no such permit for Oysters shall be granted between the first day of April and the 10th day of October annually unless upon a certificate under the hand of a Physician, that oysters will be conducive to the health of the person for whose benefit the permit shall be requested; nor shall such permit be for more than one bushel, or be in force more than twenty-four hours from its date; and if [p. 319] any person shall take a Larger quantity than is specified in any such permit such person shall incur the penalty as is provided for taking without a permit.

That no person or persons shall sell or offer for sale in said NewHaven, any oysters taken within the limits of said Town of NewHaven between the first day of April and the 10th day of October annually on pain of forfeiting one dollar for each bushel or lesser quantity so taken and sold.

That no person shall drive any kind of Carriage in or upon any of the Oyster banks where oysters are growing within the before mentioned limits, at any season of the year, on pain of forfeiting seven dollars for such offence.

That the penalties and forfeitures incured by any breach of the above regulations shall belong to the Treasury of the Town of New Haven; and that Stephen Twining Esqr be appointed agent for the Town to inquire after and at his discretion, to prosecute to and for the Town in their name and at their expence all breaches of the above regulations and that it be made the duty of the said Committee to make complaint to the said agent, of all breaches of the above regulations that shall come to their knowledge.

[Surveyor.] Voted. To excuse Ebenezer Peck from serving as Surveyor.

Voted. That the conveyance heretofore made by the Selectmen to Capt Peter Johnson of an old highway in the Town of NewHaven, Northerly and Easterly of said Johnsons Farm-house is hereby approved.

[p. 320] [Committee on Vagrants.] Voted. That John Skinner, Thomas Punderson, William Bristol, Stephen Alling and Ezra Barns be a Committee to enquire after all Vagrant persons and Negros not belonging to this State who are likely to become burdensome to the Selectmen.

Voted to adjourn without day.

[APRIL 8, 1805]

AT A TOWN MEETING HOLDEN IN NEWHAVEN APRIL 8ᵀᴴ 1805.

[Moderator.] David Daggett Esqʳ was appointed Moderator.

[Beaver Ponds.] several propositions were made respecting the Lands in the Beaver ponds &c., but no business was accomplished.

<u>Voted</u>. That the meeting be adjourned without day.

[JULY 9, 1805]

AT A TOWN MEETING HOLDEN IN NEW HAVEN JULY 9ᵀᴴ 1805.

[Moderator.] Abraham Bradley Esqʳ was chosen moderator.

[Mill River Bridge.] A petition from Wᵐ Walter and others making application for the liberty of building a bridge across the Mill River &c. was made and debated upon.

<u>Voted</u>. That the Selectmen be appointed a Committee to examine into the roads which have been already laid out and what other roads it may be expedient to layout leading from Dragon bridge into the City of New Haven, and make their report to the next Town meeting.

<u>Voted</u>. to adjourn to the first monday vizᵗ the 5ᵗʰ day of August at 4 oClock in the Afternoon.

[AUGUST 5, 1805]

[p. 321] AT A TOWN MEETING HOLDEN IN NEWHAVEN AUGUST 5ᵀᴴ 1805.

[Moderator.] David Daggett Esqʳ, was chosen Moderator.

[Dragon Bridge.] The Selectmen who were appointed a Committee to examine the state of the roads leading from Dragon bridge &c. made their report, which

was not accepted.

[Mill River Bridge.] The prayer of the petition of William Walter and others for the liberty of building a bridge across the Mill River, was not granted.

[Petition.] A Petition from Cornelius Thomas and others praying a remission of the penalty incured by them for a breach of an Act provided in case of sickness, was presented and read.

Voted. That the prayer of the petitioners, with the conditions stated in their petition be granted.

Voted, to adjourn without day.

[DECEMBER 9, 1805]

AT A TOWN MEETING HOLDEN IN NEW HAVEN DECEMBER 9TH 1805.

[Moderator.] Henry Daggett Esqr was chosen Moderator.

[Town Clerk.] Elisha Munson Clerk.

Selectmen. Samuel Punderson, Daniel Read, Henry Ward, James Merriman, and Isaac Tomlinson, Selectmen.

Grandjurors. DeLazun DeForrest, William Fitch, Joel Atwater, David Lambert, James Alling, Eleazer Foster and Alexander Longmuir, Grandjurors.

Listers. Mathew Read, John Skinner, William Bristoll, Ezra Hotchkiss, Thaddeus Beecher, Stephen Alling, Timothy Dwight Junr, Stephen Prindle, Anson Clinton, Levi Beecher, Medad Osborn and William Daggett Listers.

Constables. Josiah B. Morse, Elisha Frost, Nathan Platt, John Clark, and Lewis Alling Constables.

[p. 322] Surveyors. Thomas Punderson, William Baldwin, Ebenezer Townsend J^r, John Skinner, Theophilus Smith, Daniel Smith, Gillead Kimberly, Isaac Dickerman, and Lewis Alling surveyors of highways.

Fence Viewers. Stephen Rowe, William Brintnall, Stephen Trowbridge, Nehemiah Smith Esq', Nathan Smith, Samuel Cande, Moses Umfreville and Hezekiah Hotchkiss Fence viewers.

Tithingmen. Stephen Twining, John Skinner, Seth P. Staples, Silas Kimberly, Phlemon Smith, Thaddeus Clark Jr., John Barker, Samuel Sacket, Charles Denison, Hezekiah Hotchkiss, and Luther Bradley. Tithingmen.

Key keepers. Henry Monson, Timothy Fowler, Martin Parrot, John Culver, John Hunt, James B. Reynolds, Chauncey Alling, Nathan Platt, Peter Johnson, Phinehas Andrus, Andrew Farrell and Jonathan Alling. Key keepers.

Sealers. Israel Munson, sealer of Weights and Measures. Isaac Thomas, Amaziah Lucas, and James Prescott sealers of Leather.

Treasurer. Nathan Beers. Treasurer.

Agents. Voted. that the Selectmen be appointed Agents for the Town for the Year ensuing and that either of them with the consent of the majority be authorized to appear, sue, and defend or act as Agents aforesaid.

Voted. to adjourn till December 23ᵈ at two oClock P.M.

[DECEMBER 23, 1805]

[p. 323] AT A TOWN MEETING HOLDEN BY ADJOURNMENT AT THE COURT HOUSE IN NEWHAVEN DECEMBER 23ᴰ A.D. 1805.

[Moderator.] David Daggett Esq' was chosen Moderator.

Listers. Voted. That Samuel Sacket, and Hezekiah Howe be Listers.

Selectmen. Voted. That, James Merriman be excused from serving as Selectman, and that Isaac Dickerman, Luther Bradley and Isaac Townsend Jun' be appointed Selectmen for the year ensueing.

Tax. Voted That a tax of four and an half cents on the dollar be laid on the List of August 20ᵗʰ 1805, and that the tax be made payable on the first day of February A.D. 1806.

Collector. Voted. That Lewis Alling be Collector of the Town tax and receive six per cent for collecting s^d tax, provided he settle the same by the first day of december 1806; That he also be Collector of the State tax and receive six per cent for collecting, deducting the allowance made by the State.

Bonds. Voted. That every Collector of the Town and State Tax, before he shall receive the rate bill for collection shall give bond with surety or sureties to the satisfaction of the Selectmen of the Town for the faithfull discharge of bis duties and that this be a standing order for the Town.

Agent. Voted. That Jonathan Ingersoll Esq^{ri} be appointed an Agent for the Town to make application to the General Assembly for the purpose of obtaining a Toll to be Laid on Dragon Bridge.

Voted. to adjourn without day.

[DECEMBER 8, 1806]

[p. 324] AT A TOWN MEETING HOLDEN AT THE COURT HOUSE IN NEW HAVEN ON THE 8TH DAY OF DECEMBER AD. 1806.

[Moderator and Town Clerk.] Dyer White Esqr was chosen Moderator & Elisha Munson Clerk.

A Statement of the Town Accounts was exhibited and read.

Selectmen. Voted, that the number of Selectmen, for the ensueing year be confined to three – and that Samuel Punderson, Isaac Tomlinson and Justus Smith be Selectmen.

[Selectmen.] Voted, to reconsider the Vote confining the number of Selectmen to three.

[Selectmen.] Voted, that Luther Bradley be a Selectman.

Grandjurors. Voted, That Eleazer Foster, Jeremiah Evarts[2], Hezekiah Hotchkiss,

1. Jonathan Ingersoll (1747 - 1823), a Yale graduate in 1766, served as a judge of the Connecticut Supreme Court and as Lieutenant Governor from 1816 until at his death. He was married to Grace Issacs (1771 - 1850). See, Dexter, *Biographical Sketches of the Graduates of Yale College*, III: 187 - 188.
2. Jeremiah Evarts (1781 - 1831), was a Vermont native, 1802 Yale graduate, attorney, and philan-

Justus Hotchkiss, James Alling, Joseph Prindle Junr be Grandjurors.

Listers. Voted. That, Mathew Read, John Skinner, Hezekiah Howe, Ezra Hotchkiss, Samuel Sacket, Timothy Dwight Junr. William Daggett, William Bristol, Medad Osborn, Samuel Pardee, Stephen Prindle, Gideon Kimberly and Thomas
Townsend be Listers.

Constables. Voted, That Lewis Alling, George Monson, Elisha Frost, Nathan
Platt & Josiah B. Morse be Constables.

Surveyors. Voted, That Thomas Punderson, William Baldwin, Ebenezer
Townsend, John Skinner, Ezra Hotchkiss, Isaac Dickerman, Lewis Alling, Gilead Kimberly, Theophilus Smith and Daniel Smith be Surveyors of highways.

Tythingmen. Voted, That Stephen Twining, Seth P. Staples, _[p. 325]_ William Daggett,
John Barker, Samuel Sacket, Charles Denison, Hezekiah Hotchkiss, Luther Bradley, Phileman Smith, Horace Kimberly and Oliver Clark be Tythingmen.

Poundkeepers. Voted. That Henry Monson, Timothy Fowler, Martin Parrot, John
Culver, John Hunt, James B. Reynolds, Chauncey Alling, Nathan Platt, Jonathan
Alling and Amasa Dorman be Poundkeepers.

Sealers. Voted that Israel Munson be Sealer of Weights and Measures.

[Sealers of Leather.] Voted that Amaziah Lucas, William Daggett, and James Merriman be Sealers of Leather.

Agents. Voted That the Selectmen be appointed Agents for the Town for the
Year ensueing and that either of them with the consent of the majority be authorized to appear, sue, and defend or act as Agents aforesaid.

Treasurer. Voted, That Nathan Beers be Treasurer.

[Tax] Comt^e. Voted. That Thomas Painter, Levi Ives and Jeremiah Atwater be a
Committee with the Selectmen to make an estimate of the Tax which may be
necessary to be laid for the year ensueing.

---

thropist who worked on behalf of Native Americans. See, _Appletons' Cyclopedia of American Biography,
1600-1889_ for Jeremiah Evarts, Vol III; 384 - 385.

[Dragon Bridge] Comt. Voted. That the Honble Elizur Goodrich, Stephen Twining and William Bristoll Esqr, be a Committee to enquire into the situation of Dragon Bridge and how far the Town of NewHaven is obliged to support said Bridge, and if said Bridge must *[p. 326]* be kept up whether the Town of East Haven is liable for any part of the expence of supporting said bridge and report to the adjourned Meeting — and what will be the probable expence of repairing and supporting said bridge.[1]

Fence Viewers. Voted. that Stephen Rowe, William Brintnall, Nehemiah Smith Esqr., William Baldwin, Hezekiah Hotchkiss, Nathan Smith, Joseph Prindle and Samuel Candee *[be]* Fence Viewers.

Voted, to adjourn till December 22^d at 2 oClock P.M.

[DECEMBER 22, 1806]

AT A TOWN MEETING HOLDEN BY ADJOURNMENT, IN NEW-HAVEN ON THE 22^D DAY OF DECEMBER AD. 1806.

[Moderator.] Dyer White Esqr., being Moderator.

[Grandjuryman.] Voted. That Hez^h Hotchkiss be excused from serving as Grandjuror.

Grandjuror. Voted. That Stephen Twining be Grandjuror for the year ensueing.

Tax. Voted. That a tax of five cents on the dollar be laid on the Inhabitants of this Town for the year ensuing and become payable on the first day of February 1807.

Collector of Taxes & Constable. Voted. That Doct^r John Skinner be Collector of the above tax — That he also be Constable for the year ensueing and Collector of the State Tax.

Alms-house. Voted. That Stephen Twining, Abraham Bradley, Gillead Kimberly, Lewis Alling and Asahel Tuttle be a Committee to make a plan of the Building proposed to be erected as and addition to the alms house and contract with some person to build the same.

---

1. As noted previously, Dragon Bridge had recently washed away in a flood.

Selectman. <u>Voted</u>. That Luther Bradley be excused from serving as Selectman and that William Walter be appointed a Selectman in his room.

<u>Voted</u>. to adjourn without day. Test. Elisha Munson Clk.

[MARCH 9, 1807]

[p. 327] AT A MEETING OF THE INHABITANTS OF THE TOWN OF NEWHAVEN LEGALLY WARNED, AND HOLDEN AT THE COURT HOUSE IN SAID NEWHAVEN ON THE 9TH DAY OF MARCH AD. 1807.

[Moderator.] David Daggett Esqr was chosen Moderator.

Road. A petition from Isaac and Obed Johnson for a new highway to be laid out in Dogman[1], so called, was presented and read.

<u>Voted</u>. That the Agents for the Town be instructed to oppose the prayer of said petitioners.

Sealer. <u>Voted</u>. that Isaac Munson be appointed sealer of Weights and Measures.

<u>*Hospital.*</u> A motion was made by some of the Inhabitants of the New township[2] that the Hospital situate by the Mill River might be removed to some other place.

Whereupon <u>Voted</u>. that the Selectmen be instructed to ascertain, as near as may be, the sum which the present Hospital will sell for, and the probabe expence to the Town for obtaining another and What suitable place can be procured for that purpose, and make report to some future meeting.

<u>*Dragon bridge.*</u> The Committee appointed at a former meeting to enquire into the situation of Dragon bridge &c. made their report.

After long debate the question <u>Whether they would do anything respecting Dragon Bridge</u> was proposed to the meeting. On dividing the House one hundred & seventeen appeared in favor of doing something and one hundred and

1. An area located on the West Haven-Orange town line near the Derby Road, now part of Dogburn Road.
2. New Township was the area near present State Street, near Wooster Square.

nineteen Voters against doing any thing relative to said Bridge.

A Bye Law for regulating the fishery of Oysters and Clams.

Oysters & Clams. Voted, That no person or persons be permitted to take, gather, or Collect any oystershells in or upon any of the flats, beaches, rivers, creeks, harbours, or waters within the limits of the *[p. 328]* Town of New Haven between the first day of April and the 10th day of November annually nor, any oysters on Dragon Flats northerly of a line drawn from the old ferry House to the dwelling house of Job Smith in East Haven on pain of forfeiting for each and every such offence the sum of seven Dollars.

That no person or persons from and after the first day of April until the tenth day of October annually, shall take or cause to be taken, any oysters in or upon any of the flats*[,]* beaches, rivers, creeks, harbors, waters or Shores within the limits of the town of New Haven nor any long clams on Dragon flats, excepting as hereafter provided on pain of forfeiting seven dollars for each offence.

That no Person shall catch oysters within the limits of the town of New Haven at any season of the year, except in the months of December and January without culling out the shells and small oysters at or near the place where said oysters were taken on pain of forfeiting for each and every such offence, the sum of Seven Dollars.

That William Austin, Seth Barns, Evelyne Pierpont, Ezra Smith, Anson Clinton, Samuel Sacket, Phineas Andrus, Justus Hotchkiss, Chauncey Alling, and Jarius Sanford be a Committee to superintend the catching of oysters and Clams within the limits aforesaid, who Shall have authority granted to them or either of them within the time limited aforesaid to grant a permit or permits in writing thereby licensing the person therein named to take the quantity of oysters or long clams therein mentioned at any place in *[p. 329]* Such permit specified provided that no such permit for oysters shall be granted between the first day of April and the 10th day of October annually unless upon a certificate under the hand of a Physician that oysters will be conducive to the health of the person for whose benefit the permit shall be requested; nor shall such permit be for more than one bushel or be of force more than twenty four hours from its date; and if any person shall take a larger quantity than is specified in any such permit such person shall incur the penalty as is provided for taking without a permit.

That no person or persons shall sell or offer for sale in said New Haven any oysters taken within the limits of said town of New Haven between the first day of April and 10th Day of October annually on pain of forfeiting one dollar for each bushel or lesser quantity so taken and sold.

That no person shall drive any kind of carriage in or upon any of the oyster banks where oysters are growing within the before mentioned limits at any season of the year, on pain of forfeiting seven Dollars for such offence.

That the penalties and forfeitures incurred by any breach of the above regulations shall belong to the Treasury of the Town of New Haven and that Stephen Twining Esqʳ be appointed agent for the town, to enquire after and at his discretion to prosecute to and for the town in their name and at their expence all breaches of the above regulations and that it be made the duty of the said Committee to make *[p. 330]* Complaint to the said agent of all breaches of the above regulations that shall come to their knowledge.

Voted, to adjourn without day.

                                                        Test. Elisha Munson Clerk

[NOVEMBER 9, 1807]

AT A TOWN MEETING, LEGALLY WARNED AND HOLDEN, AT THE COURT HOUSE IN THE TOWN OF NEW HAVEN ON THE 9TH DAY OF NOVEMᴿ 1807.

[Moderator.] Jeremiah Atwater was chosen Moderator & excused.

[Moderator.] Simeon Baldwin was chosen Moderator.

Dragon Bridge. Voted. That Thomas Punderson, Samuel Punderson, Thomas Painter, Ebenezer Townsend and Abraham Bradley be a Committee with full powers to build the bridge at Dragon and to negotiate a purchase of the materials now collected if it can be advantageously done and to contract with any person or persons to complete said Bridge this season or the next as they shall find most for the interest of the Town.

[Tax.] Voted, to propose laying a Tax till some future Meeting.

Voted, to adjourn without day.

Test. Elisha Munson Clerk

[DECEMBER 14, 1807]

AT A TOWN MEETING, LEGALLY WARNED AND HOLDEN, AT THE COURT HOUSE IN THE TOWN OF NEW HAVEN ON 14TH DAY OF DECEMBER AD. 1807.

[Moderator.] Dyer White Esq[r] was chosen Moderator.

[Town Clerk.] Elisha Munson Clerk.

[Budget.] The Selectmen exibited a statement of their accounts *[p. 331]* containing the receipts and expenditures of the Town from December 1806 to December 1807.

[Audit.] Voted, that Timothy Dwight Jun[r], Jonathan E. Porter and Thomas Townsend be a Committee to audit the Town accounts.

Selectmen. Voted, that the Selectmen be chosen by ballot and that the number be limited to five. Samuel Punderson, Jeremiah Atwater 3[d], Jehiel Forbes, and William Bristoll were chosen by ballot to be Selectmen and Justus Smith, of West Haven, was chosen by nomination and lifting up of hands.

Grandjurors. Voted. that Jonathan E. Porter, Charles Sherman, John H. Jacocks, Isaac Gilbert, Joseph Prindle Junr., and James Alling be Grandjurors.

Listers. Voted, that Mathew Read, John Skinner, Eleazer Foster, Aaron Forbes, Roger Sherman Junr., Hezekiah Hotchkiss, James Merriman, Abraham Bradley, Ward Atwater, Isaac Townsend Jun[r], Samuel Sackett, Gideon Kimberly, Stephen Prindle, Medad Osborn, and Ebenezer Townsend be Listers for the ensueing year.

Surveyors. Voted. that Miles Hotchkiss, William Daggett, William Baldwin, Gillead Kimberly, Nathan Platt, Samuel Clark and Timothy Fowler *[be]* Surveyors of highways.

Tythingmen. Voted,That Stephen Twining, Benjamin W. Dwight, Jesse Alling, Isaac Gilbert, Stephen Rowe, Eleazer Foster, Joel Atwater, James Henry, Gershom Fenn, Samuel Hughes, Charles Denison, Samuel Bishop, Samuel Huggins Junr, John H. Jacocks, Pember Jocelin, Philemon Smith Junr, and Thaddeus Clark Junr be Tithingmen.

[p. 332] Constable. Voted, that George Munson, Elisha Frost, John Skinner, Josiah B. Morse, Josiah Myrick and Lewis Alling be Constables.

Poundkeepers. Voted, that Lemuel Bradley, Mastin Parrot, Amasa Dorman, Chauncey Alling, Andrew Farrel, James B. Reynolds, Nathan Platt, and Jonathan Alling be Poundkeepers.

Sealer. Voted, that Isaac Munson be appointed sealer of Weights and Measures.

Treasurer. Voted, that Nathan Beers be Treasurer

Fence Viewers. Voted, that Stephen Rowe, William Brintnall, William Baldwin, Hezekiah Hotchkiss, James B. Reynolds, Samuel Clark and Stephen Prindle be Fence Viewers.

Voted to adjourn till the 4th Monday of Ins^t Decr at 2 oClock PM.

Test Elisha Munson Clerk

Continued in New Vol.[1]

[DECEMBER 20, 1807]

[p. 1] AT A TOWN MEETING HOLDEN (BY ADJOURNMENT) AT THE COURT HOUSE IN NEW HAVEN ON THE 20TH DAY OF DECEMBER, 1807

[Moderator.] Noah Webster, Esqr was chosen Moderator.

[Town Expencess.] The following Report was accepted and approved viz.
The Committee appointed to examine certain accounts exhibited in the report

---

1. This and subsequent town meetings were recorded in a second manuscript volume that began in 1808 and concluded in 1840. The original bound manuscript volumes of the New Haven Town Records were unbound and each leaf was encapsulated in protective mylar. Prior to conservation by archivists, five pages of the original manuscript were apparently removed from the volume, followed by one-and-a-half blank pages. The remaining 30 leaves of this new volume contained freeman's meetings beginning with September 19, 1769 and dated through December 1826. They appear at the end this volume.

of the Selectmen at the last Town Meeting Respectfully report -

That in the year 1802 the expencess attending prosecutions by the Grand-
jurors amounted to $49.24
The amount of fines the same year was   56.68
Leaving a balance in favor of the Town of   7.44
That in the year 1803 the expences in the
same kind of prosecutions were   44.39
And the Amount of fines the same year was   23.96
Leaving a ballance against the Town of   20.43

That in the Year 1804 the expences were   24.24
And the Amount of fines the same year was   76.03
Leaving a balance in favor of the Town of   51.79

That in the Year 1805, the expences were   72.90
And the amount of fines the same year was   137.46
Leaving a balance in favor of the Town of   64.56

That in the Year 1806 the expencess were   64.37
And the amount of fines the same Year was   83.89
Leaving a balance in favor of the Town   19.52

That from the first of January to the 24th of
December 1807, the expences were   64.21

And the amount of fines during the same period was   73.52
Leaving a ballance in favor of the Town of   9.31

The Committee wou'd observe, that during the six years commencing at January
1802, the Grand-jury prosecutions in this Town, so far from being a burthen to
the Town Treasury have been a source of clear profit of $132 [19]

Report. The accounts current of Henry Daggett Esq[r] who has heard most of the
grandjury causes for the last six years have been examined and audited by the
Selectmen and you Committee, and a balance *[p. 2]* remains in his hands due to
the Town of $113 [49] D

Besides the ballance, there are in the possession of the Town, sundry Notes giv-
en in the same kind of causes two of which are supposed to be good, amount-

ing to about $178. —

The Committee would further report, that the account of Nathan Smith Esqr was for his professional services in the case of John Hunt   68.50

And that the residue of his account was
entirely for services in Pauper cases   36.94
That Mr Twining's bill was for professional   65.30
services in the case of John Hunt
The remainder of his account was for services
in pauper cases and in prosecutions for breaches   54.59
of the Oyster Law

None of the charges in the Attorneys bills were for services in the Dragon bridge business. The charges against the Town for opposing the rebuilding of Dragon bridge have not been rendered, and must of necessity appear in the account current of the next year; of course your Committee can say nothing relative to their amount or the propriety of the particulars of which they are composed.

Timothy Dwight Junr
Jonathan Edwards Porter[1]   Auditors
Thos Townsend

[DECEMBER 24 1807]

NewHaven December 24th 1807

Hospital. Voted, That Elizur Goodrich Esqr, Simeon Baldwin Esqr, Ebenezer Peck, Gillead Kimberly and Timothy Atwater be a Committee to ascertain the sum the present hospital in the New township will sell for and the probable expence of providing another and what suitable place can be procured for that purpose and to report to some future meeting.

[Listers.] Voted. to excuse Jeremiah Atwater and Matthew Read from serving as

---

1. Jonathan Edwards Porter (1766 - 1821) graduated from Harvard in 1786 and was a practising attorney in New Haven until his death at 55.

Listers.

Grandjuors. Voted. to excuse Charles Sherman from serving as a Grandjuror and Hezekiah Belden be appointed in his room.

Listers. Voted, that Medad Osborn be excused from serving *[p. 3]* as a Lister and Elisha Hull and Eleazer Hotchkiss be appointed Listers.
Surveyor. Voted. That Elisha Hull be appointed surveyor of highways.

Tax. Voted. That a tax of five cents on the dollar be laid on the list of *[...]* and made payable on the 1ˢᵗ day of February 1808.

Collector. Voted, that John Skinner be appointed Collector of the above tax, and also of the Collector of the State tax.

[Lister.] Voted. to excuse Hezekiah Hotchkiss from serving as Lister.

Agents. Voted. That the Selectmen be appointed Agents for the Town for the Year ensuing and that either of them with the consent of the Majority be authorized to appear, sue, and defend or act as agents aforesaid.

[Relief.] On application of John Hunt for relief or remittance of Cost in case of Mʳ Bird — Voted to take no order or *[sic.]* the subject.

[Tithingman.] Voted. that Ezra Hotchkiss be Tithingman for the ensuing Year.

Oyster Act. A Bye Law was passed regulating the fishery of Oysters and Clams within the limits of the Town of New Haven for the ensuing Year viz.

Voted.... that no person be permitted to take, gather or collect any oyster shells in or upon any of the flats, beaches*[,]* rivers*[,]* creeks*[,]* harbours*[,]* or waters within the limits of the Town of New Haven between the first day April and the 10ᵗʰ day of November annually, nor any oysters on dragon Flats, Northerly of a line drawn from the old Ferry House to the Dwelling house of Job Smith in East Haven, on pain of forfeiting for each and every such offence the sum of seven Dollars. That no person or persons from and after the first day of April untill the tenth day of October Annually shall take or cause to be taken any oysters in or upon any of the flats*[,]* beaches*[,]* rivers*[,]* creeks*[,]* harbors*[,]* waters*[,]* or shores within the limits of the Town of New Haven, no any long Clams on Dragon Flats, excepting as hereafter provided, on pain of forfeiting Seven Dollars for each offence.

That no person shall catch oysters within the limits of the town of New Haven, at any season of the year except in the months of December and January, without culling out the shells and small oysters at or near the place where Said oysters were taken, on pain of forfeiting for each and every offence the Sum of seven Dollars.

A Bye Law. That William Austin, Seth Barns, Evelyn Pierpont, Ezra Smith, Anson Clinton, Phineas Andrews, Justus Hotchkiss, Chauncy Alling, *[p. 4]* Janus Sanford, Isaac Tomlinson, John Brainard and, Arnold Cande be a Committee to superintend the catching of oysters and clams within the limits aforesaid, who shall have authority granted to them or either of them within the time limited aforesaid, to grant a permit or permits, in writing thereby licensing the person therein named to take the quantity of oysters or long Clams therein Mentioned, at any place in such permit specified provided that no Such permit for oysters shall be granted between the first day of April and the 10 day of October, annually, unless upon a Certificate under the hand of a Physician, that Oysters will be Conducive to the health of the person for whose benefit the permit shall be requested; nor shall such permit be for more than one bushell, or be of force more than Twenty four hours from its date and if any person shall take a larger quantity than is Specified in any such permit Such person Shall incur the penalty as is provided for taking without a permit. That no person or persons Sell or offer for Sale, in S^d New Haven any Oysters taken within the Limits of S^d Town of New Haven between the first day of April and 10 day of October annually, on pain of forfeiting one dollar for each bushel or lesser quantity so taken and Sold. That no person Shall drive any kind of Carraige in or upon any of the oyster banks where oysters are growing, within the before mentioned limits at any Season of the year on pain of forfeiting Seven Dollars for Such Offence. That the penalties and forfeitures incured by any Breach of the above regulations, shall belong to the Treasury of the Town of New Haven and that David Daggett Esqr be appointed agent, for the Town to enquire after & at his discretion to prosecute to and for the Town in their name and at their Expence, all breaches of the above regulations, and that it be made the duty of the S^d Committee to make Complaint to the Said agent of all breaches of the above regulations that Shall Come to their Knowledge.

Voted. to adjourn without day.

Test Elisha Munson Clerk

[MAY 9, 1808]

AT A TOWN MEETING HOLDEN AT THE COURT HOUSE IN
NEW HAVEN MAY 9TH 1808.

[Moderator.] Elizur Goodrich Esqʳ was chosen Moderator.

[Norwich Letter.] A Letter from the Selectmen of the Town of Norwich *[p. 5]* addressed to the Selectmen of the Town of New Haven (relative to attachments) was submitted to the consideration of the Meeting, the conclusion was that it was inexpedient to do any thing on the subject.[1]

Voted. to adjourn without day — Test Elisha Munson, Clerk

[AUGUST 23, 1808]

AT A TOWN MEETING LEGALLY WARNED AND HOLDEN IN NEW
HAVEN ON THE 23ᴿᴰ DAY OF AUGUST 1808.

[Moderator.] The honᵇˡᵉ Elizur Goodrich Esqʳ was chosen Moderator.

Address [to President Thomas Jefferson]. <u>Voted</u>. That Elias Shipman, Noah Webster, David Dagget, Jonathan Ingersoll and Thomas Painter Esqrs. be appointed a committee to prepare an Address to be presented to the President of the United States, praying for a modification or suspension of the Embargo Laws — After a short recess, the foregoing Committee reported as follow, viz.

To Thomas Jefferson, President of the United States, the Memorial of the inhabitants of the town of New Haven, in legal meeting assembled, respectfully represents,

That your memorialists, uniformly attached to the principles of a free republican government, and firmly persuaded of the necessity and propriety of submitting to all measures adopted in the exercise of its constitutional powers, have yielded a faithful obedience to the several laws imposing an embargo on the commerce of the United States. Although some of us may have questioned

---

1. The letter concerned the Embargo Act of 1807, which prohibited American trade in foreign ports. The embargo eventually caused widespread financial ruin along coastal Connecticut communities and ended New Haven's bid to become a major seaport. See, Osterweis, pp. 193, 201.

the necessity, the policy, and even the constitutionality of the measure, yet in confidence that the prohibition would not be of long duration, we have submitted to severe privations and numerous embarrassments, with that spirit of patience and subordination, which ever characterize good citizens. Belonging to a state whose ardent patriotism is attested by her uncommon exertions during the struggle for independence and whose public spirit has ever been manifested by a prompt compliance with all the laws and requisitions of the National Government; whose love of freedom is instinctive, and whose subordination to constitutional laws is as cheerful as it is habitual; we cannot be suspected of any in disposition to make every necessary sacrifice of private interest to vindicate the honor and maintain the independence of the United States.

But in the present condition of the United States when most distressing private sufferings are aggravated by the prospect of augmented evils and public calamities, we believe it the duty of the citizens of this country to avail themselves of their constitutional right to petition for a redress of grievances. Even admitting the policy of a temporary embargo, for the purpose of collecting the property and seamen of the United States into our own ports and apprizing the merchants of the hazards, to which their property must *[p. 6]* be exposed, under the unwarrantable decrees of France and Great Britain we are not satisfied that reasons now exist to justify a continuance of this restraint. To many parts of the world, commerce may now be carried on with as much safety as at any time within these fifteen years – a period in which the trade of the United States has been unusually profitable. It is not easy to understand, why the peculiar hazards to which our trade to some parts of Europe is exposed should operate to justify an entire restraint of our commerce with other countries, in which no such hazard is incurred – still more difficult it is to comprehend, why the protection of our seamen and property on the ocean, should be alleged as a reason for a total prohibition of our inland trade, to neighboring States,which is ended to no hazard at all.[1]

It is the unquestionable right and duty of government, to protect the property of its citizens, whenever this can be done, without a sacrifice of more important public interests, but when the risque of voyages is known, we suppose it far more expedient to leave the merchant and underwriter to estimate the risque than for the government to interfere. But whatever may be the risque, we are persuaded that the losses to be incurred by a free trade, would be an incompara-

---

1. The Embargo Act did not prohibit either coastal or inland trade. See, "Embargo Act." Dictionary of American History. Encyclopedia.com. 5 Aug. 2018 <http://www.encyclopedia.com>.

bly less publick evil than a total prohibition of foreign commerce. The business of this country was suddenly arrested during a state of prosperity. Contracts of various kinds have been made for the purchase and sale of commodities in expectation, that the customary business of our citizens would be continued and enable the contracting parties to fulfill their engagements. The sudden interruption of trade has disabled many of our citizens to perform their contracts. Numerous bankruptcies in every part of the country, the ruin of honest industrious men, the distress of families, the loss of shipping, the want of occupation among many of people, followed by idleness and immoral habits and furnishing excuses for neglecting to fulfill contracts, thus impairing the sense of moral obligation with private embarrassments too numerous to be recited in detail, contribute a mass of evils, which in our opinion, claim from government a speedy relaxation of the present restraints on commerce.

Nor can we forbear to mention the extreme rigour of the laws imposing these restraints , which not only subject our coasting trade to unusual perplexities, but expose our citizens to enormous forfeitures, for trivial violations of law and even for unintentional offences. The power vested in officers of the customs, of *[p. 7]* seizing vessels and boats on mere suspicion of being engaged in illegal trade are highly alarming to a free people; as such powers are liable to enormous abuses, and are in our opinion utterly repugnant to the spirit of a free constitution.

To all these evils which are now felt by our citizens, we may add most extensive future prejudice and losses, by a diversion of the trade of foreign nations from the usual channels. Nations accustomed to receive supplies of commodities from the United States will be compelled to open a trade with other nations, which can furnish the same articles, and in some instances, such treaties and commercial regulations will be formed with our rivals, as hereafter to deprive us of some of our best markets. In such cases the continuance of the embargo may occasion an irreparable injury to the commerce of the United States.

Nor can we, in justice to ourselves, overlook the condition of Spain, Portugal, and their dependencies, which now offer an interesting spectacle to the real friends of National Independence. Recollecting the suffering of the American people, while combatting for their rights and a free government, and comparing the perilous situation of this country in 1775 with that of Spain and Portugal at this moment, rising in mass to resist the power of the mighty conqueror of France, we feel, and we think it a duty to express a lively interest in the success of their efforts. Their struggles may check the enormous strides of that conqueror, whose gigantick grasp has already embraced the greatest portion of Europe, and may, if unrestrained, extend to other parts of the globe. It is impossible, as it would be unnatural for freemen, who duly appreciate of self government not to wish that the citizens of these countries may have the benefit of supplies from the United States. Nor can we see any reasonable objection to a restoration of our trade to Spain and Portugal, since the rescinding of the British orders, with regard to these countries, has varied the state of things, and removed a great part of the hazard, which existed when the embargo was laid.

We are disposed to foster the growth of manufactures in this country as a means of rendering our citizens less dependent on foreign nations for articles of consumption. But in a country containing immense tracts of uncultivated land, we cannot help questioning the policy of attempting to force into existence manufacturing establishments which are less congenial to the habits of our people than agricultural pursuits. As far as such establishments are necessary, and adapted to our state of society, we apprehend they will best thrive with an unrestricted commerce, which will furnish capital for the purpose, and open free channels for exhorting our surplus pro- *[p. 8]* ductions.

Another consideration in our apprehension of serious moment is that a continuance of the embargo will be inevitably followed by smuggling to an unlimited extent. A frontier of more than five thousand miles in length, a great part of which is unguarded, presents opportunities of evading the laws, which no vigilance of government can prevent, and the temptations of the high price of foreign commodities, and the power of introducing them, without the payment of duties, will, we apprehend defeat every effort of government to render the embargo, for any length of time, effectual.

We highly applaud the policy which seeks to preserve the peace of the United States, and prevent the desolating calamities of war, which the people of Europe are so frequently doomed to suffer. But the ocean is the commerce highway of nations, evidently intended for the free indiscriminate use of all who choose to occupy it for an interchange of commodities; and it becomes a question of serious importance, whether any nation ought to surrender the use of their right whenever other nations see fit to lay it under illegal restraints. The history of man evinces that a nation which does not respect itself, is never respected; and that a nation is doubled exposed to aggression, which wants the will or the power to repel them. To shrink from danger is to create or increase it; as weakness never fails to invite and timidity to encourage insults, while every improper concession of rights, offer a new incentive to further encroachments. We confidently hope that the mutual surrender of unimportant claims by governments of both *[...]¹* and a spirit of conciliation will still preserve peace between nations, which have every motive for peace, and whose interests demand an unrestrained freedom of commerce. Nor can we at present see any reason to believe that a removal of the embargo, and a consequent free trade from the United States will give a just cause of offence to any foreign nation or tend in the least to expose our country to the calamities of war.[2]

In every view of this subject, your memorialists conceive a continuance of the embargo to be distressing as it is impolitic and far more injurious to our own people than to any other nation. We therefore request that in pursuance of the powers, vested in the president of the United States by an act of congress for that purpose, the operation of the several laws imposing an embargo, may be immediately suspended*[.]*
(Signed)

> Elias Shipman
> Noah Webster
> Jonathan Ingersoll } Committee
> David Daggett
> Thomas Painter

New Haven, August 29, 1808

Voted, That the foregoing report of the Committee be approved and accepted, and the Selectmen be requested to sign the same and transmit a copy to the President of the United States.

Voted, That if the President should not see fit to suspend the operation of the laws laying an embargo, before the meeting of Congress, the Selectmen be directed to transmit a copy of the foregoing Memorial to the president of the Senate, and the speaker of the House of Representatives of the United States with such alterations of the style of address at the beginning, and of the petition at the close, as shall be suitable in a memorial to be presented to the respective houses of congress.

Voted, That the selectmen transmit a copy of the foregoing proceedings of this town to the Selectmen of the several towns in this county and to the Selectmen

---

1. Intentionally left blank.
2. The petitioners' assessment that the embargo hurt American interests more than the belligerent European counties was true. Still, it was not repealed until 1809, leading many New Haveners to turn to manufacturing instead of the sea. Anglo-American relations, meanwhile, continued to deteriorate, culminating in the War of 1812.

of all the county towns in this state, with a request that they would transmit a copy to the Selectmen of the several towns in their respective counties.
Adjourned – without day------
Test Elisha Munson Clerk

[DECEMBER 12, 1808]

AT THE ANNUAL TOWN MEETING, LEGALLY WARNED AND HOLDEN AT THE COURT HOUSE IN THE TOWN OF NEW HAVEN ON THE 12TH DAY OF DECEMBER 1808, THE FOLLOWING OFFI-CERS WERE CHOSEN – VIZ.

[Moderator.] The Honble Elizur Goodrich Moderator.

[Clerk.] Elisha Munson Clerk.

[Accounts.] The Selectmen of the Town presented and read a statement of the Town accounts which was accepted.

[p. 10] Selectmen. Voted. That Samuel Punderson, Jeremiah Atwater 3^d, William Bristoll, Justus Smith and Andrew Kidson[1] be Selectmen.

Grand-jurors. Voted. That Jonathan E. Porter, George Hoadley, Matthew Read, Enos Smith, John Meloy, Marcus Merriman and Charles Bostwick be Grand-jurors.

Listers. Voted. That Matthew Read, John Skinner, Eleazer Foster, William Fitch, Aaron Forbes, Roger Sherman,[2] Abel Denison, Benjamin Woolsey Dwight, Thaddeus Sherman, James Henry, Ashel Tuttle, Elisha Hull, Eleazer Hotchkiss, Eliakim Kimberly, Joseph Prindle Junr, Johnathan Maltbie, Isaac Townsend Junr and Ward Atwater and John Rowe be appointed Listers.

Surveyors. Voted, that Silas Kimberly, Gillead Kimberly, Josiah Pardee, William Baldwin and Miles Hotchkiss be appointed Surveyors of highways.

---

1. Andrew Kidston (1762 - 1828) was a wealthy shipping merchant who lost his fortune in the great Long Wharf fire of 1820.
2. Roger Sherman, Jr. (1768 - 1856) was the son of Roger Sherman, signer of the Declaration of Independence. See, https://www.geni.com/people/Roger-Sherman-Jr/6000000002304334907.

Tythingmen. Voted, that Philemon Smith, John Meloy, Horrace Kimberly, Stephen Twining, Elijah Monson, Gardner E. Spring¹, Jeremiah Evarts, Gersham Fenn, Asa Bradley, Joel Atwater, Archibald Rice, Dᵉ Lauzun Dᵉ Forrest, Elihu Monson, Jᵣ, John Skinner be Tything men.

Constables. Voted. That Josiah Myrick, George Munson, John Skinner, Josiah B. Morse and Elisha Frost be appointed Constables.

Fence viewers. Voted. that Stephen Prindle, Anson Clinton, Hezekiah Hotchkiss, Stephen Rowe, William Brintnall and William Baldwin be Fence viewers.

Pound keepers. Voted. That James B. Reynolds, Nathan Platt, Lemuel Bradley, John Scoll, Martin Parrot and Chauncey Alling be appointed Pound keepers.

Sealer. Voted. That Isaac Munson be Sealer of Weights & Measures.

Treasurer. Voted. That Nathan Beers be appointed Treasurer.

[Removal of] Mitchel [Family.] Voted. That the Selectmen of the Town exercise *[p. 11]* their discretion with respect to affording assistance to Mᵣ *[...]* Mitchel and family in their removal from the Town of New Haven.²

Agents. Voted. That the Selectmen be appointed Agents for the Town for the year ensueing and that either of them with the consent of the majority be authorized to appear, sue, and defend or act as Agents aforesaid.

Voted to adjourn this meeting till the 4ᵗʰ Monday of Insᵗ December – at 2 oClock P.M.

Test Elisha Munson Clerk

[DECEMBER 26, 1808]

AT A TOWN MEETING HOLDEN (BY ADJOURNMENT) AT THE COURT HOUSE IN THE TOWN OF NEWHAVEN ON THE FOURTH MONDAY OF DECEMBER 1808.

Moderator. Elizur Goodrich Esqᵣ was chosen Moderator.

---

1. Gardnier E. Spring (1785 - 1873) was a Yale graduate, lawyer, and Presbyterian minister.
2.There were a number of Mitchels living in New Haven County at this time.

Hospital. Voted. That the Selectmen of the Town be authorized to sell the Hospital which is situated in the Newtownship[1] to the best advantage and find some suitable place to erecting another Hospital and that they be instructed to report at some future meeting whether in their opinion it is expedient to build another Hospital, and if expedient, to report the price of the Land, and the size and expence of the contemplated building.

Grandjuror.] Voted. That Charles Bostwich be excused from serving as Grandjuror.
Tax. Voted. That a Tax of 4 1/2 Cents on the dollar be laid on the List *[of]* 1808, and be made payable on the first day of February 1809.

Collector. Voted. That John Skinner be appointed Collector of the Town tax. Also Collector of the State tax.

Lister. Voted to excuse Jonathan Maltbie from serving as Lister and that William Sherman Jun[r] be appointed a Lister for the year ensueing.

Lister. Voted, to excuse John Row from serving as Lister for the year ensueing and that Seth Barnes be appointed a Lister in his place.

[Grandjuror.] Voted, to excuse Matthew Read from serving as Grandjuror.

Grandjuror. Voted. that Increase Cook be appointed a Grandjuror.

[p. 12] [Grandjuror.] Voted. That William Daggett be appointed a Grandjuror.

Tythingmen. Voted. That William Sherman Jun[r] and David Ritter be appointed Tythingmen.

Oyster act. Voted. That no person or persons be permitted to take, gather, or collect any oyster shells in or upon any of the flats, beaches, rivers, creeks, harbours or water within the limits of the town of New Haven, between the first day of April and the 10th day of November, annually nor any oysters on Dragon flats, northerly of a line drawn from the old ferry-house to the dwelling house of Job Smith in East Haven, on pain of forfeiting for each and every such offense the sum of seven dollars.

---

1. The Newtownship was located east of New Haven harbor and away from the shoreline. See, Jonathan Hopkins, "How We Got Here," *New Haven Independent* (October 17, 2014).

That no person or persons from and after the first day of April, until the tenth day of October annually shall take or cause to be taken any oysters in or upon any of the flats, beaches, rivers, creeks, harbours, waters, or shores within the limits of in the town of New Haven, nor any long clams on Dragon flats, excepting as liecnced *[?]* & or provided on pain of forfeiting seven dollars for each offence.

That no person shall catch oysters within the limits of the town of NewHaven, at any season of the year except in the months of December and January, without culling out the shells and small oysters at or near the place where said oysters were taken on pain of forfeiting for each and every such offence the sum of seven dollars.

That Seth Barns, Evelyn Pierpont, Ezra Smith, Anson Clinton, Phinehas Andrews, Justus Hotchkiss, Chauncey Alling, Jarius Sanford, Isaac Tomlinson, John Brainard, and John Barker be a committee to superintend the catching of oysters and clams within the limits aforesaid, who shall have authority granted to them or either of them within the time limited aforesaid to grant a permit or permits in writing thereby licensing the person therein named to take the quantity of oysters or long clams therein mentioned at any place therein in such permit specified, provided that no such permit for oysters shall be granted between the first day of April and the tenth day of October annually unless upon a certificate under the hand of a Physician that oysters will be condusive to the health of the person for whose benefit the permit shall be requested, nor shall such permit be for more than one bushel or be of force more than 24 hours from its date, and if any person shall take a large quantity than is specified in any such permit, such person shall incur the penalty as is provided to taking without a permit.

That no person or persons shall sell or offer for sale in said New Haven any oysters taken within the limits of the town of New Haven, between the first day of April and tenth day of October annually on pain of forfeiting one dollar for each bushel or lesser quantity so taken and sold.

That no person shall drive any kind of carriage in *[p. 13]* or upon any of the oyster banks where oysters are growing within the before mentioned limits at any season of the year on pain of forfeiting seven dollars for such offence.
That the penalties and forfeitures incurred by any breach of the above regulations shall belong to the treasury of the town of New Haven and that William Bristol, Esq. be appointed agent for the town to enquire after and at his discretion to prosecute to and for the town in their name and at their expence all breaches of the above regulations and that it be made the duty of committee to

make complaint to the said agent of all breaches of the above regulations that shall come to their knowledge.

Voted to adjourn without day.

Elisha Munson Clerk

[JANUARY 28, 1809]

AT A MEETING OF THE INHABITANTS OF THE TOWN OF NEW HAVEN LEGALLY WARNED AND HELD AT THE STATE HOUSE ON THE 28TH DAY OF JANUARY 1809.

[Moderator.] Jonathan Ingersol Esqr was chosen Moderator.

[Embargo Address.] An address to the Selectmen requesting a Town Meeting to be warned – was read Adjourned to the Brick Meeting house – the following resolutions were laid before the citizens and after an animated debate adopted. viz.[1]

<u>Voted</u> and <u>resolved</u>. That the citizens of this town are sincerely disposed to submit to all the laws of the national government constitutionally enacted, which are consistent with the principles on which the several states entered into the federal compact and not repugnant to the spirit and tenor of the constitution of the United States and to the fundamental principles of a free government.

Resolved, That when the rulers of a free people transgress the limits of their authority and enact laws utterly repugnant to the principles of the constitution under which they act inconsistent with the rights of a free people and incompatible with publick safety, it is not only the right but the indispensable duty of the citizens in a peaceable and constitutional manner to manifest their sense of the injury done to their rights and to seek redress with a spirit and firmness suited to the exigency of the case.

Resolved, as the sense of this meeting, That the act of the congress of the United States to enforce and make more effectual the several acts laying an Embargo,

---

1. New Haveners were reacting to Congressional debates preceding the passage of the Non-Intercourse Act of 1809, which replaced the Embargo Act of 1807. While the new legislation ended the embargo on all but England and France, it did little to restore Connecticut's shipping industry, which was the basis of the Federalist party's strength in Connecticut and especially New Haven. See, https://newingtonnow.wordpress.com/2018/01/09/connecticut-and-the-embargo-act-of-1807/.

approved by the president on the 9th of the present *[p. 14]* month is repugnant to the constitution of the United States, highly oppressive and subversive of the unalienable rights and privileges of the people and especially in the following provisions, restrictions and requirements.

1st. By the second section of the act no owner of a coasting vessel can obtain a clearance from the custom house until he has given bonds with one or more sureties in six times the value of the vessel and cargo, conditioned to reland the cargo in the United States*[.]* Such enormous bonds must compel many owners of vessels to abandon the employment, our coasting trade must be nearly annihilated, and the transportation of the most necessary commodities even the flour which one state wants and another can spare must be embarrassed if not prevented*[.]*

To aggravate the evil the president by his secret instructions to the Collectors, and the Collectors even upon suspicion that there is an intention to violate the embargo may absolutely refuse permission to any and every person to load a vessel. By this provision either the president or the collector of the port may at pleasure put a total stop to the coasting trade of the place – their power for this purpose is unlimited – a power entirely arbitrary and dangerous – a power which raises the discretion of the president and his officers above all law and control & which may be the instrument of enormous abuses for the purposes of corruption and favouritism.

2d. By the fourth section of the act no vessel or boat employed in the navigation of rivers or bays can take in loading until a permission has been obtained from a collector and bonds are given in the enormous sum of 300 dollars for each ton of the vessel which amounts to thirty thousand dollars for a vessel of one hundred tons. But what is still more oppressive, the act vests in the president the absolute power of regulating the navigation of rivers and bays at his pleasure and even the collector if they suppose there is an intention to violate the embargo may withhold permission from any person whatever. This section therefore not only subjects the river navigation to oppressive and unreasonable restrictions but puts it in the power of the president and collector wholly to destroy it.

3d. The seventh section restrains the owners of vessels who may lose their cargoes at sea, from giving in evidence to save the penalties of their bonds many actions which may be unavoidable, and which may subject them to enormous forfeitures without the least fault on their part.

4th. The ninth section vests in the collector most tremendous *[p. 15]* powers, authorizing and enjorining *[sic.]* them to seize specie,produce or manufactures in ships, vessels, boats, carts, wagons, sleys or other carriages when they have reason to believe the articles are intended for exportation or when the articles are in any manner apparently on their way <u>towards</u> the territories of a foreign nation. This enormous power to be exercised at men*['s]* discretion places a great portion of all personal property within the control of the collectors – a power that levels all the barriers which the constitution and laws have erected to guard the possession of movable property*[.]*

5th The seventh section requires that in a trial for a breach of the act the mate and seamen of the vessel shall all be produced on trial if alive, otherwise captive, distress, or accident shall not be given in evidence. As it is often impossible for owners or masters of vessels to prevent the sickness or desertion of some of the crew in a distant port, this requirement is beyond measure unreasonable, tyrannical, and oppressive.

6th. The tenth section enables the president to give <u>private</u> <u>instructions</u> to the collectors respecting the execution of the act and gives to those instructions the effect of statutes binding on courts of justice, which instructions the collectors are bound to obey and which they may give in evidence to justify any act of their own performed in the execution of their office. This power is a direct violation of the most sacred principles of the common law and common right, which have been recognized for ages and which forbid that men should be subjected to penalties except for violations of <u>known</u>, <u>public</u> laws.

7th. But the eleventh section crowns the despotic character of this act. By this the president or any person by him empowered for the purpose may command the land & naval forces or militia of the UStates to enforce the execution of the act; and this power is to be exercised without the warrant of a magistrate or any interference of the civil authorities. This unlimited power in the hands of the president and his officers lays our civil rights at the feet of military despotism.

Resolved, That these and other prohibitions, restrictions, and requirements of the said act are directly opposed to the rights and privileges for which our citizens successfully contended during the revolution and which we cannot consent to relinquish. They are also a violation of the constitution of the United States *[p. 16]* which declares that the right of the people to be secure in their houses*[,]* papers*[,]* and effects against unreasonable searches and seizures shall not be violated, that no warrant shall issue but upon probable cause supported by oath or affirmation and particularly describing the places to be searched and the person and things to be seized and which constitution declares also that "excessive bail shall not be required nor excessive fines imposed." The said act is also repugnant to the principles recognized in the declaration of Independence which among other causes alledged to justify our separation from Great Britain expressly mentions the following – "That the king of Great Britain had affected to render the military <u>independent</u> of and superior to the <u>civil</u> power" and that he had given his assent to acts of pretended legislation for cutting off our trade to all parts of the world." Therefore

Resolved, in the words of the first congress in their address to the inhabitants of Canada – "When hardy attempts are made to deprive men of the rights bestowed on them by the Almighty; when avenues are cut through the most solemn compacts for the admission of despotism, when the plighted faith of government ceases to give security to dutiful subjects; and when the insidious stratagems of peace become more terrible than the sanguinary operations of war it is high time for them to asset those rights and with honest indignation oppose the torrent of opposition rushing in upon them."[1]

Resolved, That while we are compelled to express a want of confidence in the wisdom and impartiality of our national councils we would discountenance every attempt to disturb the public peace and to recommend to all classes of people to preserve tranquility.

And whereas we have respectfully petitioned the president and the congress of the United States for a repeal of the laws laying an embargo and our rulers instead of attending to our petition are enforcing the laws with tenfold rigor and adding to the catalogue of publick wrongs and distresses by which measures we are compelled to seek redress by application to the legislature of the state—Therefore,

Resolved, That his excellency the governour be requested to convoke the legislature of this state unless in his opinion it shall be expedient, to take into consideration the alarming state of public affairs and to adopt *[p. 17]* such measures for the protection of our rights as shall be deemed advisable.

Resolved, That we highly approve of the firm spirited and dignified opposition which the senators and representatives of this state have made in the

---

1. Drawn from "Letter to the Inhabitants of Canada, May 29, 1775," in Worthington C. Ford, editor, *Journals of the Continental Congress 1774 - 1779*, (1905), Vol. II: 68 -70.

congress of the United States to the passage of the bill for enforcing the laws imposing the embargo and boldly defending the constitution which they are sworn to support.

Resolved, That the Selectmen transmit a copy of these proceedings to his Excellency the governour of this State, and also copies to the senators and representatives of this state in the congress of the United States and that these proceedings be published.[1]

Adjourned without day.

Elisha Munson Clerk

[DECEMBER 18, 1809]

AT THE ANNUAL TOWN MEETING, LEGALLY WARNED, AND HOLDEN AT THE COURT HOUSE IN THE TOWN OF NEWHAVEN ON THE 18th DAY of DECEMBER 1809.

[Moderator.] Simeon Baldwin Esq[r] was chosen Moderator.

[Accounts.] The Selectmen of the Town exhibited a statement of the Town accounts.

The following Officers were chosen for the Year ensuing viz[t]

[Town Clerk.] Elisha Munson Clerk.

Selectmen. Jeremiah Atwater 3[d], Samuel Punderson, Andrew Kidston, Eleazer Foster and Justus Smith, Selectmen.

Grand-jurors. George Hoadley, Jonathan E. Porter, Increase Cook, Enos Smith, John Meloy, Matthew Read and Amaziah Lucas – Grand jurors.

Listers. William Fitch, Increase Cook, Abraham Bradley 3[d], George Hoadley, John Scott Jun[r], Reuben Rice, Leonard Wales, James Henry, Abel Denison, Chauncey Bunce, Eliakim Kimberly, Thaddeus Clerk Jun[r], and Levi Beecher – Listers.

---

1. New Haven and Connecticut defied what was known as Bacon's Bill No. 2 becoming the first region to declare states' rights in refusing to enforce a federal law. See, Walter W. Woodward," War of 1812–The War Connecticut Hated," *Connecticut Explored*, Summer 2012, Vol. 10, No. 3.

Surveyors of highways. William Baldwin, Aaron Forbes, William Daggett, Medad Osborn, Stephen Twining, Levi Beecher, Gillead Kimberly, Elisha Benham, Laban Smith, Henry Daggett Junr, and James Merriman, Surveyors of highways.

[p.18] Tythingmen. DeLawzun Deforest, Henry Wells, Lent Bishop, Jared Thompson, Gershom Fenn, Stephen Huggins, Henry Lines, Lucius Atwater, Philemon Smith and Thaddeus Clark Junr, Nehemiah Kimberly & Elias Gilbert Tythingmen.

Constables. John Skinner, Josiah B. Morse,[1] George Monson and Josiah Myrrick. Constables.

Fence viewers. Hezekiah Hotchkiss, Stephen Row, William Baldwin, William Brintnall, Stephen Prindle and Anson Clinton. Fence viewers.

Pound keepers. Lemuel Bradley, John Scott, Mastin Parott, Chauncey Alling, Timothy Fowler, Andrew Farrel, James B. Reynolds and Nathan Platt. Pound-keepers.

Sealer. Isaac Munson, sealer of Weights and Measures.

Treasurer. Nathan Beers. Treasurer.

Hospital. Voted. That Thomas Punderson, Stephen Twining, Jeremiah Atwater 3^d, Thomas Painter, and Samuel Punderson, be a Committee to find some suitable place for erecting a New Hospital and report to some future meeting the price of the Land and the size and probable expence of the contemplated building.

Agents. Voted. That Andrew Kidston, Eleazer Foster and Justus Smith be appointed Agents for the Town for the Year ensuing and that either of them with the consent of the majority be authorized to appear, sue, and defend or act as Agents aforesaid.

Alms-house. Voted. That Elizur Goodrich, Stephen Twining, Laban Smith and the Selectmen of the Town be a Committee to revise the Rules and Regulations

---

1. Captain Josiah Booth Morse of Wolcott. See, 1800 Census of the United States, Series: M32; Roll: 2; p: 239; Image: 260. Morse served as a 2nd lieutenant in the Governor's Foot Guard during the War of 1812, and relocated to South Carolina with his family in 1816. See, *Green's Connecticut Annual Register and United States Calendar for the Year of Our Lord 1812*, https://books.google.com/books?id=jWgGAAAAMAAJ&pg=RA3-PA88&dq=captain+Josiah+B.+Morse&hl=en&sa=X&ved=0ahUKEwjo1NL57uXcAhXDylQKHYMrBZYQ6AEIPDAE#v=onepage&q=captain%20Josiah%20B.%20Morse&f=false.

for the Alms House, make such alterations, and devise such new regulations as they may judge expedient and report their opinion to some future meeting.

Jacob Thompson & Admr. Voted, that in case the heirs or adm^{rs} of Jacob Thompson dec^d pay to this town the amount due said Town on the 14th day of February 1808, on an obligation by *[p. 19]* him executed to the Town for the payment of the annual sum of five dollars, the Selectmen be authorized to cancel said obligation and give up the same to the heirs of said Thompson[1].

<u>Voted</u> to adjourn till Thursday the 28th Ins^t Decr 2 oClock P.M.

Elisha Munson – Clerk

[DECEMBER 28, 1809]

AT A TOWN MEETING HOLDEN AT THE COURT HOUSE IN NEW HAVEN, BY ADJOURNMENT, ON THE 28TH DAY OF DEC^R 1809.

[Moderator.] Elizur Goodrich Esqr was chosen Moderator.

[Tax Collector.] <u>Voted</u>. That John Skinner be appointed Collector of the State Tax.

[Hospital] <u>Report</u>. The Committee appointed the last Town meeting to consider the subject of a New Hospital made their Report.

<u>Voted</u>. To adjourn till Thursday January 4th 1810 at two oClock P.M. and that the Selectmen give public Notice in the Newspaper that the subjects of Laying a Tax and errecting a New Hospital will be submitted to the consideration of the Meeting.

Test Elisha Munson, Clerk

[JANUARY 4, 1810]

AT A TOWN MEETING HOLDEN AT THE COURT HOUSE IN NEW HAVEN, BY ADJOURNMENT ON THE 4TH DAY OF JANR^Y 1810.

[Moderator.] Stephen Twining Esqr was chosen Moderator.

---

1. Jacob Thompson (1745 - 1808). See, The Charles R. Hale Collection. Hale Collection of Connecticut Cemetery Inscriptions. Hartford, Connecticut: Connecticut State Library. See, http://www.hale-collection.com/.

[Hospital] Report.] The report of the Committee on the subject of a new Hospital made at the last meeting, was taken into consideration, and after debate was accepted.

[Hospital.] Voted. That Samuel Punderson, Jeremiah Atwater 3^d, Eleazer Foster, Justus Smith and Andrew Kidston be a Committee to carry into effect the Report of the Committee on the subject of the Hospital, to purchase the land near the Alms house; therein mentioned and contract for and superintend the building of s^d Hospital.

Burying Grounds. Voted. That the Selectmen be authorized to appropriate & fence a competent portion of the lands of the Town near the Alms house as a Burying ground for strangers who shall die either in the Alms house or Hospital.

Tax. Voted. That a Tax of four cents and an half on the dollar be laid on the List 1809 – payable on the first day of February 1810.
Collector. Voted. That John Skinner be Collector of the above Tax.

Highways and Bridges. Voted. That the sum of five hundred dollars be *[p. 20]* appropriated for the repairs of highways and Bridges for the year ensuing and that out of that sum one hundred and fifty dollars be laid out in repair of highways and bridges in the society of West Haven.

Voted to adjourn without day.

[April 23, 1810]

AT A TOWN MEETING, LEGALLY WARNED AND HOLDEN IN NEW HAVEN ON THE 23^D DAY OF APRIL 1810.

[Oyster Act &c.] A By Law regulating the fishery of Oysters & Clams.

Voted. That no person or persons be permitted between the first day of May and the 10th day of November 1810, to take, gather or collect any Oyster shells or Oysters in or upon any of the flats, beaches, rivers, creeks, harbors or waters within the following limits in the Town of New Haven, vizt Northerly of a line drawn from the old ferry house in New-Haven, to the dwelling house of Jacob Mallery in East Haven on pain of forfeiting for each and every such offence the sum of seven dollars.

That no person or persons from and after the first day of May until the first day of October 1810, shall take or cause to be taken any Oysters in or upon any of the flats, beaches, rivers[,] creeks, harbors, waters or shores within the following limits in the Town of New Haven viz' Northeasterly of a line drawn from the end of the long Wharf across the Pier to East Haven, and Southwesterly of a line drawn from the old ferry house in New Haven to the Dwelling house of Jacob Mallery in East Haven nor any long clams on Dragon flats excepting as hereafter provided on pain of forfeiting seven dollars for reach offence.

That no person or persons shall catch Oysters within the limits of the Town of New Haven at any season of the year except in the months of December and January without culling out the shells or small Oysters at or near the place where said Oysters were taken on pain of forfeiting for each and every such offence the sum of seven dollars.

That Seth Barns, Levi Tuttle, Charles Lewis, Cheney *[p. 21]* Ames, John Row and Ambrose Ward be a Committee to superintend the catching of Oysters and Clams within the limits aforesaid; who shall have authority granted to them or either of them within the time limited aforesaid to grant permit or permits in writing thereby licencing the person therein named to take the quantity of Oysters or long clams therein mentioned at any place in such permit specified: Provided that no such permit for Oysters shall be granted between the first day of may and the first day of October 1810; unless upon a certificate under the hand of a Physician, that the Oysters will be conducive to the health of the person for whose benefit the permit shall be requested; nor shall such permit be for more than one bushel or be in force more than twenty four hours from its date; and if any person shall take a larger quantity than is specified in one such permit, such person shall incur the penalty as provided for taking without a permit.

That no person shall drive any kind of carriage in or upon any of the Oyster banks where Oysters are growing within the before mentioned limits, at any season of the year, on pain of forfeiting seven dollars for every such offence.
That the penalties and forfeitures incured by any breach of the above regulations shall belong to the Treasury of the Town of New Haven and that Ebenezer Foster Esq' be appointed Agent for the Town to enquire after and at his discretion to prosecute for the Town in their name and at their expence all breaches of the foregoing regulations; and that it be made the duty of the said Committee to make complaint to the said Agent of all breaches of said regulations which shall come to their knowledge

Adjourned without day - Certified by Elisha Munson Clerk

[p. 22]   *[DECEMBER 10, 1810]*

<u>*ANNUAL MEETING.*</u> AT THE ANNUAL TOWN MEETING, LEGALLY WARNED AND HOLDEN IN THE TOWN OF NEW HAVEN ON THE 10ᵀᴴ DAY OF DECEMBER 1810 - AT 2 ᵒCLOCK P.M.

[Moderator.] The Honᵇˡᵉ Elizur Goodrich was chosen Moderator.

[Clerk.] Elisha Munson Clerk.

Accounts. The Selectmen exhibited and read a written Statement of the Town accounts for the past year.

<u>Voted,</u> that sᵈ Statement be accepted, approved and ordered to be lodged on file.

Selectmen. <u>Voted.</u> That Samuel Punderson, Jeremiah Atwater 3ᵈ, Andrew Kidston,[1] Eleazer Foster and Justus Smith be appointed Selectmen for the year ensueing.

Grand-jurors. <u>Voted,</u> that George Hoadly, Jonathan E. Porter, Leonard E. Wales, Enos Smith, Stephen Prindle and Seth Barns be appointed Grandjurors.

Listers. <u>Voted.</u> That George Hoadly, William Fitch, Increase Cook, Abraham Bradley 3ᵈ, John Scott Junʳ, Rueben Rice, Leonard E. Wales, Zacheus Candee, Thadeus Clark Junʳ, Chauncey Bunce, John Rowe, Samuel Hughes, Amos Alling, Marcus Merriman and James Henry be appointed Listers.

Surveyors. <u>Voted,</u> That William Baldwin, Dyer White Esqʳ, Luther Bradley, Eliakim Kimberly, Elisha Benham, Charles Prindle, Elisha Hull, and Eleazer Hotchkiss be appointed Surveyors of highways.

Tithingmen. <u>Voted.</u> That DᶜLauzun Deforest, Asahel Tuttle, Henry Lines, Lent Bishop, Henry Wells, Robert Townsend, John Skinner, William H. Eliot, Ebenezer Collins, Ralph Ingersoll, Philemon Smith, Nehemiah Kimberly and Thaddeus Clark be <u>Tithingmen.</u>

---

1. Andrew Kidston (1762 - 1828) was a Scottish native and wealthy shipmaster and merchant . He was the spouse of Wealthy Parmele (1772 - 1861) and is buried in Grove Street Cemetery.

Constables. <u>Voted</u>. That John Skinner, Josiah B. Morse, George Monson, and Josiah Myrreck be <u>Constables</u>.

Fence-viewers. <u>Voted</u>. That Hezekiah Hotchkiss, Stephen Rowe, William Baldwin, William Brintnall, Samuel Hughes, Gillead Kimberly, Nathan Platt, Anson Clinton and Silas Hotchkiss be appointed Fence-Viewers for the year ensueing.
[p. 23] Fence viewers. Voted. That Hezekiah Hotchkiss, Stephen Rowe, William Baldwin, William Brintnall, Samuel Hughes, Gillead Kimberly, Nathan Platt, Anson Clinton and Silas Hotchkiss be appointed <u>Fence Viewers</u>.[1]

Poundkeepers. <u>Voted</u>. That John Scott, Samuel Hull, Mastin Parrot, Cheney Ames, James B. Reynolds, Nathan Platt, Andrew Farrell, Chauncey Alling, Thomas Peck and Timothy Fowler be appointed <u>Poundkeepers</u>.

Sealer &c. <u>Voted</u>. That Isaac Munson be Sealer of Weights & Measures.

Treasurer. <u>Voted</u>. That Nathan Beers be appointed Treasurer.

Neck Bridge. <u>Voted</u>. That Thomas Punderson, Luther Bradley, Rutherford Trowbridge, Isaac Tomlinson and Anson Clinton be a Committee to examine the <u>Neck Bridge</u>[2] and take into consideration the subject of repairing or rebuilding it. If on examination said Committee should be of opinion that it would be necessary to build a New Bridge, they are directed to devise a scheme or plan of the same, consider what materials should be used in its construction, calculate the probable expences requisite for building it, and make report to the next meeting.

West Bridge. <u>Voted</u>. That the Selectmen confer with the Com^{ee} or directors of the Milford Turnpike company respecting the West Bridge[3] &c, ascertain what proportion of the railing, abutments and causeway belong to the Town and what portion belongs to the Company — also adjust and settle their respective rights relative to the keeping of s^d Bridge &c in repair.

Alms-house. <u>Voted</u> that Stephen Twining, Timothy Atwater and Marcus Merriman be a Committee to take into consideration the present State of the Almshouse – devise some scheme for lessening its expencess, revise its rules and regulations, make such alterations, and adopt such new regulations as they may judge expedient and make report to the next adjourned Meeting.

Agents. <u>Voted</u>,

---

1. The town clerk obviously made a double entry on fence viewers.
2. The Neck Bridge allowed what is now State Street to span the Mill River. See, Osterweis, p. 488.
3. The West Bridge is now U.S. 1 that spans the West River from New Haven to West Haven.

that the Selectmen be appointed Agents for the Town.

adj^d without day.   Elisha Munson Clerk

[p. 24]   *[DECEMBER 24, 1810]*

AT A TOWN MEETING HOLDEN AT THE STATE HOUSE IN NEW HAVEN, BY ADJOURNMENT, ON THE 24TH DAY OF DECEMBER AD. 1810.

[Moderator.] The Honble Elizur Goodrich being Moderator.

Tithingmen. Voted. That Maynard Franklin and John Coverly be appointed Tithingmen.

[Alms-house] The Committee appointed at the last Meeting to devise a scheme for lessening the expences at the Alms-house &c made their Report, in writing and the same was accepted, approved and ordered to be lodged on file.

Alms-house. Voted That Stephen Twining, Timothy Atwater, and Marcus Merriman be appointed a Committee to devise a suitable, convenient, and economical mode of managing the expenditures of the Alms-house and establish a scheme of Rules and regulations for the government thereof – to which it shall be the duty of the Selectmen to conform.

Listers. Voted, to excuse James Henry from serving as Lister and that Timothy Bishop be appointed a Lister in his room. Voted to excuse Samuel Hughes from serving as Lister and that Russell Hotchkiss be appointed a Lister in his room.

Surveyor of highways. Voted to excuse Dyer White Esqr from serving as a Surveyor of highways & that Henry Daggett Junr be appointed in his stead.

Neck bridge. The Committee appointed at the last meeting to take into consideration the subject of repairing or rebuilding Neck Bridge made their report in writing; which was read in meeting. – whereupon – voted that the same be accepted, approved and ordered to be lodged on file. And that the Selectmen be instructed to form a contract or contracts to cause the Bridge to be constructed according to the Scheme reported by said Committee.

Tax. Voted. That a Tax of four cents on the dollar be laid on the List 1810, and that the same be made collectable on the first day of february – 1811.

Collector. Voted that John Skinner be Collector of said Tax. Voted, that John Skinner be Collector of the State Tax.

[p. 25] [Ox-Shovels.] Voted, that, the Selectmen be instructed to procure three Ox-shovels, at the expences, and for the use of the Inhabitants of the Town, – that the shovels be committed to the custody of the Surveyors of highways, to be used by them or under their direction for the purpose of repairing highways within the limits of the Town and for no other purpose.[1]

[Grandjuror.] Voted to excuse Seth Barns from serving as Grandjuror. — and that Stephen Rowe be appointed a Grandjuror in his stead.

[Granjuror.] Voted, to excuse Stephen Rowe from serving as Grandjuror.

[Oysters and Clams.] A By-Law — regulating the fishery of Oysters and Claims. Voted. That no persons or persons be permitted between the first Day of May and the 10th day of November 1811 to take, gather or collect any Oyster shells, or Oysters in or upon any of the flats, beaches, rivers, creeks, harbors*[,]* or waters within the following limits, in the Town of New-Haven, viz – northerly of a line drawn from the old ferry house, in New Haven to the dwelling house of Jacob Mallery in East Haven on pain of forfeiting for each and every such offence the sum of seven dollars.

That no person or persons from and after the first day of May, until the first day of October 1811 shall take or cause to be taken any Oysters in or upon any of the flats, beaches, rivers, creeks, harbors, waters*[,]* or shores, within the following limits in the town of New Haven, viz*t*: Northeasterly of a line drawn from the end of the Long-Wharf across the pier to East Haven and Southwesterly of a line drawn from the old ferry house in New Haven, to the Dwelling house of Jacob Mallery in East Haven – nor any long clams on Dragon flats excepting as hereafter provided, on pain of forfeiting seven dollars for each offence.

That no person or persons, shall catch Oysters within the limits of the town of New Haven, at any season of the year, except in the months of December and January without culling out the shells and small ousters at or near the place

1. Deriving its name from the shoulder blade of an ox, an ox-shovel was used to shovel up broken rock and soil. See, http://www.oxfordreference.com/view/10.1093/oi/authority.20110803100259291.

where s^d Oysters were taken on pain of forfeiting for each and every such offence, the sum of seven dollars.

That Seth Barns, Levi Tuttle, Charles Lewis, Cheney Ames, John Rowe, and Roswell Hughes, be a committee, to superintend the catching of Oysters and Clams, within the limits aforesaid; who shall have authority granted to them, or either of them within the line the line limited aforesaid to grant a permit or permits in writing, thereby licensing the person therein named to take the quantity of oysters or long clams therein mentioned, at any place in such permit specified. Provided, that no such permit for Oysters shall be granted between the first day of May and the first day of October 1811; unles[s] when a certifi[c] ate under the name of a physician, that [p. 26] the Oysters will be conducive to the health of the person for whose benefit the permit shall be requested; nor shall such permit be for more than one bushel or be in force more than twenty four hours from its date; and if any person shall take a larger quantity than is specified in any such permit, such person shall incur the penalty as provided for taking without a permit.

That no person shall drive any kind of carraige [sic.] in or upon any of the oyster banks where oysters are growing, within the before mentioned limits, at any season of the year, on pain of forfeiting seven dollars for every such offence.
That the penalties and forfeitures incurred by any breach of the above regulations, shall belong to the Treasury of the Town of New-Haven and that Leonard E. Wales Esqr be appointed agent for the town to enquire after and at his discretion, to prosecute for the Town in their name and at their expence, all breaches of the foregoing regulations; and that it be made the duty of the s^d Committee to make complaint to the said agent, of all breaches of said regulations that shall come to their knowledge. Adjourned without day.

Certified by Elisha Munson Clerk

[MAY 4, 1811]

[Non-importation Law.][1] On the 4th day of May 1811. the Citizens of the town of New Haven convened for the purpose of taking into consideration the embarrassment to which they are subjected by the operation of the Non-Importation Law passed at the late session of Congress and having maturely deliberated on the

---

1. As relations with Great Britain deteriorated through 1810, President James Madison declared non-intercouse against Britain beginning in March of 1811. See, http://www.manythings.org/voa/history/44.html.

subject, came to the following resolutions:

Resolved as the sense of this meeting, That permanent or durable laws prohibiting the citizens of this country from trading to foreign nations are an infraction of the Constitution of the United States.

Resolved. That prohibitions of foreign trade are partial and unjust in their operation, as they peculiarly injure the merchants who have vested their property in shipping; whose habits of business are formed and cannot be easily changed and who have engaged in a lawful occupation in confidence that they should enjoy the same freedom and protection in their employment as every other class of citizens. Equally partial and unjust are such prohibitions as they affect commercial towns and commercial states whose interest is primarily affected and most sensibly injured.

Resolved.. That laws restraining our trade to foreign countries are extremely prejudicial to the agricultural interest, as *[p. 27]* by preventing the exportation of surplus productions and circumscribing the markets they discourage industry and diminish the value of lands and of labor

Resolved.. That the Non-Importation Law is not within the legislative powers of the national government; the power of prohibiting for an unlimited time the trade of our citizens to foreign countries not being included in the power to regulate that trade and not having been surrendered by this state to the United States.

Resolved.. That the Non-Importation Law is unconstitutional and repugnant to the genius of our laws as well as to the spirit of a free government; as the bonds required and the penalties annexed to a breach of the law are unreasonable and excessive.

Resolved, That the bonds required of merchants by the non-importation act to enable them to land their goods are not only excessive in their amount; but they are calculated to operate as a pledge to bind the merchant for his good behavior to government; and by placing him in the power of the administration to make him subservient to their views.

Resolved.. That the fact assumed in justification of the Non-Importation Law appears to be unfounded; the French decrees not being rescinded. Repeated advices from France announce that those decrees are still in force and declared to be the permanent law of Europe. By the official letter of our government to General Armstrong[1] dated July 10, 1810 it was declared that "a satisfactory provision for restoring American property seized in France must be combined with a repeal of the French edicts, with a view to the non-intercourse with Great Britain," and in a letter of November 2^d it is declared that in issuing the proclamation (by the president) it was presumed that this requisition on the subject of the sequestered property will have been satisfied." Yet it appears that none of the American property seized and sequestered in France has been restored; but that the amount has been augmented by recent seizures.

Resolved, That the frequent alterations of the laws respecting trade serve to embarrass and often to ensnare the honest merchant. The embargo restrained exportation but permitted importation, the order of things is now reversed exportation is permitted and importation restrained. This versatility in the measures of government while it manifests want of system, perplexes the merchant, disturbs every *[p. 28]* regular plan of business, confounds all calculation and by rendering that unlawful to day which was yesterday lawful tends to ensnare the most cautious men and to subject them to losses and embarrassments which no wisdom can foresee or prevent.

Resolved, That a law which p _____ts exportation without the right to import, aims a fatal blow at an active commerce; as it prevents a return freight in our ships without which trade cannot be lucrative or worth prosecuting, and the present law by prohibiting the importation of property purchased before the law was passed is peculiarly injurious and oppressive and especially to the merchants of New Haven.

Resolved, That the course of measures pursued by our government for a number of years past, alarms us with the apprehension that such measures are intended to depress or destroy the active commerce of the Eastern and Middle states and thus to impair our strength and diminish their importance. Nor are we less apprehensive that this policy aims gradually to introduce into this country the system which prevails on the continent of Europe. Against such projects, it is our duty to remonstrate with firmness and to express our deliberate belief that evils of this serious magnitude will in this section of the country meet with

---

1. John Armstrong (1758 - 1843) served as aide-de-camp to General Hugh Mercer and aide to General Horatio Gates during the American Revolution. Following the Revolution, Armstrong held a number of political and diplomatic posts, including minister to France from 1804 - 1810. When the War of 1812 started, Armstrong was named Secretary of War. See, https://en.wikipedia.org/wiki/John_Armstrong_Jr.

the most determined resistance.[1]

Resolved, That a perseverance in the interdicting importations from Great Britain instead of inducing the administration of that country to revoke their orders will probably issue in measures which will subject our trade to new embarrassments, by giving rise to a circuitous trade which would make British ships the carriers of our productions and by increasing the expences of freight lessen the value of our exports. To this we may add that such a trade or any measures which should multiply the difficulties of exchanging productions would increase the practice of smuggling which not only defrauds the revenue, but begets a pernicious habit of evading the laws.

Resolved, That a commerce embarassed by too much regulation and restriction is destructive to morality to fair dealing & to that respect for law which constitutes the peace and order of society and the best security of a free government. It removes the business from the upright merchant who respects the law and his oath [p. 29] and throws it into the hands of unprincipled men who disregard both. It multiplies spies and informers, it engenders distrust among citizens, it offers a premium for the encouragement of fraud and perjury, it creates litigation, it generates contept for government.

Resolved, That a free trade to the British dominions is particularly advantageous to the United States, as those countries want many of our productions while our citizens need many of the productions and manufactures of the British dominions which they furnish in great abundance and on the best terms, some of which are essential to our own manufactures.

Resolved, That the attempt to influence the measures of foreign government by prohibiting a commercial intercourse with their subjects is both inefficacious and mischievous, inefficacious because no nation is sufficiently dependent for supplies on the trade of the United States to be compelled by the want of them to change a course of measures deemed essential to its safety or interest; mischievous because such interruption to our foreign trade, checks domestic industry and enterprise, impoverishes our own citizens, impairs our national strength and importance and dries up a copious source of revenue; while it throws into

1. New England's opposition to the non-importation laws was fueled by sectionalism and self-preservation among the Federalist merchant class. Merchants believed the federal government and the Executive branch favored Southern interests at the expences of New England. Such feelings eventually led to the ill-fated Hartford Convention and demise of the Federalist party. See, "Hartford Convention," *Enclclopedia Britannia,* https://www.britannica.com/event/Hartford-Convention.

the hands of our rivals advantages which we naturally possess and which sound policy dictates we should not abandon.

Resolved, That an interdiction of the trade of the United States to Great Britain tends directly to favour the views and second the operations of her powerful and inveterate enemy. We sincerely desire a free commerce with both belligerent nations and with other nations concerned in the war upon principles of impartial neutrality. And we still believe that our government may adjust the differences with the British Cabinet or principles compatible with our interest and with our national honor.

Resolved, That the United States have no less cause to be alarmed at the enormous power of France than to be indignant at the injuries and insults which her [...] offers to our country. Under his orders our ships have been burned and sunk on the high seas, our seamen have been imprisoned and our property seized in violation of a solemn treaty and in contempt of all the [p. 30] laws of good faith of humanity and of honor. An immense amount of American property is now held in sequestration by the Emperour as a pledge to insure our compliance with his dictates; which when stripped of a slight covering of phraseology explicitly require our government to wage war with Great Britain. Such wrongs has our government long borne with no expression of indignation, but in diplomatic murmurs — injuries and outrages to which no nation not degraded to the dust would for a moment submit. We wish for neutrality and for peace; but if compelled to relinquish neutrality, we are free to declare that we cannot consent to be the degraded instruments of forging more chains for the human race and of extending that frightful despotism which now desolates Europe. All Europe testifies that the auxiliaries of France like the allies of ancient Rome while employed in rivetting the chains of other nations are made the humble instruments of forging chains for themselves.

Resolved, As the sense of this meeting that a memorial be presented to the General Assembly at their approaching session praying them to use their influence to obtain a repeal of the non importation law and to oppose as far as their constitutional powers extend every attempt of the national government to restrain the foreign commerce of this state.[1]

Voted, That the Selectmen transmit a copy of the foregoing resolutions to the

1. New Haven's petition as well as those of other towns appears in Connecticut Archives, Trade and Maritime Affairs, Ser. 2. II: 36 - 42. New Haven's resolutions also appeared in the *Connecticut Courant* on May 15, 1811.

Selectmen of the several county towns in this state and such other towns as they may judge expedient; praying them to co-operate with this town in relation to the objects of their resolutions.

Voted, That the Selectmen in behalf of the town sign the petition to the General Assembly passed at this meeting and that the representatives from this town be requested to present the same.

Voted, That James Hillhouse, William W. Woolsey, Elias Shipman, Noah Webster jun, Issac Mills, Henry Daggett jun, and William Leffingwell,[1] Esquires be a Committee in behalf of this town to present a respectful petition to the President of the United States requesting him to convene Congress for the purpose of taking into consideration the restrictions upon the commerce of the United States and to take such measures as the *[p. 31]* wisdom of that honorable body shall suggest.[2]

The following Memorial to the General Assembly was read and approved.

To the Honorable General Assembly of the State of Connecticut to be holden at Hartford on the second Thursday of May AD. 1811 – The Memorial of the Inhabitants of the town of New Haven in town meeting legally assembled May 4, 1811 humbly sheweth –

That for many years past the Town of New Haven in its wealth and population has been regularly increasing that the source of its wealth has been foreign and inland commerce and that upon this the town is dependant for its wealth and prosperity and without it must be reduced to poverty and wretchedness that the merchants and other inhabitants of the town now find that by a system of Commercial Restrictions imposed by the General Government their Commerce is already greatly diminished and will soon be entirely destroyed, that this system will if persisted in compel the merchants and a large class of the community dependent upon Commerce to abandon their employments and to leave their Ship-

---

1. William Leffingwell (1765 - 1834) was a 1786 Yale graduate, who pursued a mercantile career. He was considered the richest man in New Haven. See, https://www.geni.com/people/William-Leffingwell/6000000007209257006
2. President Madison responded to the New Haven petition in a letter dated May 24, 1811. In his response, the President noted that, "sacrifices made for the sake of the whole, result more to some than to other districts or descriptions of Citizens, this also is an effect which tho' always to be regretted, can never be entirely avoided." See, Gallard Hunt, ed., *The Writings of James Madison*, Vol. 8: 114 - 115, The Online Library of Liberty, http://lf-oll.s3.amazonaws.com/titles/1939/Madison_1356-08_EBk_v6.0.pdf.

ping to rot at their wharves and an immense amount of other property deriving its value from Commerce must speedily become useless. Your Memorialists are alarmed to find that these restrictions and embarrassments seriously affect our country at large and particularly the Northern and Middle states and owe their existence to a system of laws passed by Congress and continued by the Non Importation laws. These laws have been published and have already commenced their operation and need not be particularly stated. But your Memorialists can not refrain from observing that they deem it a first principle in government that Commerce, Agriculture and Manufactures should be equally protected – that our government has no right to sacrifice any one of these employments to the others. That it is the first and great object of every free government to protect all classes of the community in their respective lawful employments and that a system of laws permanent and absolutely prohibiting commerce except on such terms as no prudent man can engage in it is contrary to the ancient and established habits of our countrymen to the genius and spirit of every free people and a violation of the [p. 32] Constitution of the United States.

Your memorialists do not believe that the venerable sages who formed the Constitution of the United States and gave Congress the power of regulating commerce meant thereby to give them the power of destroying it and this enable them to sacrifice one part of the Union to the real or imaginary interests of the other. This system of Commercial restrictions under which our Commerce actually labors is more universal to the fair trader and to the community at large than the odious and oppressive system of laws imposed on us while Colonies by Great Britain which roused a spirit in our countrymen and led to a contest that gave us a name and rank among the independent nations of the earth.

Your Memorialists beg leave to observe further that they are not more deeply affected by the laws themselves than alarmed at the grounds on which Congress profess to have enacted them. Congress has prohibited our Commerce with Great Britain, the only nation that carries on any considerable commerce and which is capable of extending and protecting that commerce in every quarter of the globe – and this as a measure of retaliation upon that nation for injuries received when it is apparent that the mischief must and does fall chiefly on our own citizens. It further appears from those laws that our Commerce is open with France a nation which for several years past has seized and sequestered every vessel and cargo which came within her ports whose prisons are this moment filled with our seamen and whose privateers have burned and sunk our shipping upon the high seas and which is the only nation with its dependencies in whose ports no prudent merchant would trust a cents worth of property. It further appears that the grounds on which Congress profess to have enacted these laws authorizing us to carry on Commerce with *[the]* French Empire are untrue. Whatever evidence the Emperor of France might have furnished our government that his obnoxious decrees would be revoked it is now well understood that all such evidence was false and that so far from revoking those decrees the Emperor has lately declared that they shall remain the permanent laws of Europe. Under these circumstances this system of laws is calculated not only to destroy the commerce of our country but to draw us into a war with the nation most capable of injuring us and while its operation abroad is extremely feeble, at home it is beyond measure oppressive. Your *[p. 33]* Memorialists therefore look to your honors for relief and pray your honours to take the subject into consideration and to adopt such measures as shall appear best calculated to remove this system of restrictions and embarrassments on our commerce and to restore to your memorialists and the rest of their fellow citizens the free exercise of their ordinary and lawful employments.

Adjourn'd without day   Attest – Elisha Munson Clerk

[DECEMBER 9, 1811]

AT THE ANNUAL TOWN MEETING LEGALLY WARNED AND HOLDEN AT THE COURT HOUSE IN THE TOWN OF NEWHAVEN ON THE 9ᵀᴴ DAY OF DECEMBER, AD. 1811 AT 2 OCLOCK PM.

[Moderator.] Henry Daggett Esqʳ was chosen Moderator.

[Clerk.] Elisha Munson Clerk.

[Accounts.] The Selectmen exhibited a statement of the Town accounts for the past year, which was accepted and ordered to be lodged on file.

[Selectmen.] Voted. That Samuel Punderson
Andrew Kidston
Eleazer Foster
Anson Clinton
Eli Hotchkiss be appointed Selectmen
for the ensuing year.

Grand-jurors. Voted, That George Hoadly, Jonathan E. Porter, Leonard E. Wales,

Stephen Prindle, ~~and~~ Philemon Smith and Ralph I. Ingersoll[1] be Grand-Jurors.

Listers. Voted, that George Hoadly, Truman Woodward, William A. Babcock, Walter Buddington, Timothy Bishop, Russell Hotchkiss, William McCracken, Ebenezer Johnson Junr, Hezekiah Hotchkiss, Zacheus Cande, Thaddeus Clark Junr, Joseph Punderson Hotchkiss, John Rowe, Eli Ives[2] and Edward Alling be appointed Listers.

Surveyors. Voted, that William Baldwin, David Moulthrop, Medad Osborn, William Bristoll, Anthony P. Sanford, Amos Alling, Laban Smith, Isaac Dickerman, Nathan Peck, Ebenezer Townsend, Eliakim Kimberly, Nathan Platt and Elisha Benham be appointed, Surveyors of highways.

Tythingmen. Voted, that Stephen Twining, Lent Bishop, William *[p. 34]* Leffingwell, Stephen Maltby, James Henry, Luther Bradley, James Merriman, Charles Sherman, Elihu Monson, Samuel Sackett, Ralph I. Ingersoll, Bradford Smith, Nehemiah Kimberly, Thaddeus Clark Junr, Edward Carr and Reuben Hall be appointed Tythingmen.

Constables. Voted that John Skinner, Josiah B. Morse, George Monson, Eliakim Kimberly, and Benjn R. Fowler be Constables.

Fence viewers. Voted, Hezekiah Hotchkiss, Stephen Rowe, Isaac Dickerman, William Brintnall, Gillead Kimberly, Nathan Platt and Enos Smith be appointed Fence Viewers.

Pound-keepers. Voted, John Scott, Samuel Hull, Mastin Parrott, Cheney Ames, Medad Culver, James B. Reynolds, Nathan Platt, Chauncey Alling and Orin Flagg be Pound keepers.

Sealer. Voted, that Isaac Munson be Sealer of Weights & Measures.

Treasurer. Voted, that Nathan Beers be appointed Treasurer.

---

1. Ralph I. Ingersoll (1789 - 1872) was a Yale graduate, attorney, U.S. Congressman, and U.S. Minister to the Russian Empire from 1847 - 1848. Franklin B. Dexter, *Biographical Notices of Graduates of Yale College: Including Those Graduated in Classes Later Than 1815, who are Not Commemorated in the Annual Obituary Records.* Yale College. p. 252.

2. Eli Ives (1779 - 1861) was a 1799 Yale graduate and distinguished physician who help to found Yale Medical School. See, George Bulmer, "Eli Ives—Practitioner, Teacher and Botanist," *The Yale Journal of Biology and Medicine.* 4 (5): 649.b1–663., May, 1932.

Agents. Voted that the Selectmen be appointed Agents for the Town for the year ensuing and that either of them with the consent of the majority be authorized to appear, sue & defend or act as Agents aforesaid.

Bridges &c. Voted, that Isaac Tomlinson, Samuel Punderson, Asahel Tuttle, Stephen Twining and Ebenzer Townsend be appointed a Committee to view the Neck-bridge and Cause-way, ascertain what improvement it is expedient to make thereon, and estimate the probable expence requisite for the accomplishment of the object together with the alteration of the Road on Neck-hill. And also view the situation of Dragon-bridge and the Records respecting the same and make their Report to the next Town-Meeting.

Encroachments. Voted, that Isaac Tomlinson, Henry Daggett Junr, Isaac Dickerman, Asahel Tuttle, Henry W. Edwards and Thomas Painter be appointed a Committee to remove encroachments according to the Statute. Adjourned till Decr 23^d 1811 at 2 oClock PM.

Certified by Elisha Munson Clerk

[DECEMBER 23, 1811]

[p. 35] AT A TOWN MEETING HOLDEN (BY ADJOURNMENT) AT THE COURT HOUSE IN NEWHAVEN ON THE 23^D DAY OF DECEMBER 1811.

Moderator. Henry Daggett Esqr being Moderator.

[Bridge Committee.] The Committee (appointed at the last meeting) to view the Neck-Bridge[,] the Road & Cause-way adjoining and Dragon bridge &c. made their Report which was not accepted.

Land. Voted, that the Selectmen be authorized to make an exchange of Land on the top of Neck hill – with Col. Willm Lyon for the purpose of effecting a desirable alteration of the Road at that place.

highways. Voted, that Simeon Baldwin, Thaddeus Beecher and James Merriman be appointed a Committee to make a appropriation of the monies which may be allowed for the purpose of improving and repairing highways between the Rivers.

Tax. Voted, that a Tax of five cents on the dollar be laid on the List for the year 1811 – and that seven hundred and fifty dollars be allowed for improving and repairing highways throughout the Town — and that said Tax be made payable on the 1st day of feb^{ry} 1812.

Collector. Voted that John Skinner be appointed Collector of the Town tax*[.]* Voted, that John Skinner be appointed Collector of the State Tax.

[Listers.] Voted That Hervey Sanford and John C. Bush be appointed Listers.
[Oyster and Clam] By-law. A By-law regulating the fishery of Oysters and Clams. Voted that no person or persons be permitted between the first day of May and the 10th day of November 1812, to take*[,]* gather*[,]* or collect any oyster-shells or oysters in or upon any of the flats*[,]* beaches*[,]* rivers*[,]* creeks*[,]* harbors*[,]* or waters within the following limits in the Town of New Haven viz. Northerly of a line drawn from the old ferry-house in New Haven to the dwelling house of Jacob Mallery of East Haven on pain of forfeiting for each and every such offence the sum of Seven dollars.

That no person or persons from and after the 1st day of May until the 1st day of October 1812 shall take or cause to be taken any oysters in or upon any of flats, beaches, rivers*[,]* creeks*[,]* harbors*[,]* waters*[,]* or shores within the following limits in the Town of New Haven viz NorthEasterly of a line drawn from the end of the long wharf across the Pier to East Haven and southwesterly of a line drawn *[p. 36]* from the old ferry house in New Haven to the Dwelling house of Jacob Mallery in East Haven – nor any long clams on Dragon flats excepting as hereafter provided on pain of forfeiting seen dollars for each offence.

That no person or persons shall catch Oysters within the limits of the town of New Haven at any season of the year except in the months of December and January, without culling out the shells and small oysters at or near the place where said Oysters were taken on pain of forfeiting for each and every such offence the sum of seven dollars.

That John Rowe, Charles Lewis, Orin Flagg, Seth Barnes, Stephen Rowe, and Cheny Ames, be a committee to superintend the catching of oysters and Clams within the limits aforesaid; who shall have authority granted to them or either of them within the time limited aforesaid to grant a permit or permits in writing, thereby licensing the person therein named to take the quantity of oysters or long clams therein mentioned at any place in such permit specified. Provided that no such permit for oysters shall be granted between the first day of May & the 1st day of October 1812 unless upon a certificate under the hand of a Physician that the oysters will be conducive to the health of the person for whose benefit the permit shall be requested nor shall such permit be for more than one bushel or be in force more than twenty four hours from its date and if any person shall take a larger quantity than is specified in such permit such person shall incur the penalty as provided for taking without a permit.

That no person shall drive any kind of Carriage in or upon any of the oyster banks where oysters are growing within the before mentioned limits at any season of the year on pain of forfeiting seven dollars for every such offence.

That the penalties and forfeitures incurred by any breach of the above regulations shall belong to the Treasury of the town of New Haven and that Leonard E. Wales Esq[r] be appointed agent for the town to enquire after and at his discretion, to prosecute for the town in their name and at their expence, all breaches of the foregoing [p. 37] regulations; and that it be made the duty of the said Committee to make complaint to the said Agent of all breaches of said regulations that shall come to their knowledge. Adjourned without day.

Certified by – Elisha Munson Clerk

[DECEMBER 14, 1812]

AT THE ANNUAL TOWN MEETING LEGALLY WARNED AND HOLDEN AT THE WHITE HAVEN MEETING HOUSE[2] IN THE TOWN OF NEW HAVEN ON THE 14TH DAY OF DECEMBER 1812, AT TWO oCLOCK P.M.

[Moderator.] Henry Daggett Esq[r] was chosen Moderator.

Voted to adjourn and meet again immediately at the Court House in said New Haven.

---

1. Leonard E. Wales (1788 - 1823) was a Yale graduate who studied law and practised in New Haven. He served as City Attorney from 1819 - 1821. He died of Typhus Fever, unmarried, in 1823. See, Dexter, *Biographical Sketches of the Graduates of Yale College,* Vol. 6: 165 - 166.

2. White Haven Church is today known as the United Church on the Green. It was the site of a famous 1800 Phi Betta Kappa oration by Abraham Bishop, son the long-term town clerk and former mayor. The younger Bishop's oration was banned at Yale, but allowed by the church. It advocated the separation of church and state in Connecticut, which would become a reality in 1818. See, "A Brief History of the United Church on the Green in New Haven," http://storage.cloversites. com/unitedchurchonthegreenucc/documents/2014-11-14%20A%20Brief%20History%20of%20 The%20United%20Church%20on%20the%20Green%20in%20New%20Haven%20revised%20 10-19-2014.pdf.

[Accounts.] Having met at the Court House. The Selectmen exhibited a statement of the town accounts for the past year which was accepted and ordered to be lodged on file.

Selectmen. Voted. That Samuel Punderson, Andrew Kidston, Eleazer Foster, Anson Clinton and Eli Hotchkiss be appointed Selectmen.

Grandjurors. Voted That Leonard E. Wales, Ralph I. Ingersoll, Sereno E. Dwight, Zacheus Cande, Anthony P. Sanford be Grand jurors.

Listers. Voted That Truman Woodward, William A. Babcock, Walter Budington, Timothy Bishop, William McCrackin, Ebenezer Johnson Junr, Nehemiah Kimberly, Jonas F. Merwin, Hervey Sanford, Levi Tuttle, Eli Ives, Sereno E. Dwight, Joseph Punderson Hotchkiss, Thomas Hull and Clement Goodale be Listers.

[Lister.] Voted, that Timothy Bishop be excused from serving as a Lister and that John C. Bush be appointed in his room.

Surveyers of highways. Voted. That Anthony P. Sanford, William Hotchkiss, Elnathan Atwater, Luther Bradley, Laban Smith, Medad Osborn, Eliakim Kimberly, Isaac Dickerman, Nathan Platt, Ebenezer Townsend, Nathaniel Ferrand Clark & Andrew Kidston be Surveyors of highways. Voted that Andrew Kidston be excused from serving as Surveyor – and that Henry Daggett Junr be appointed in his stead.

[p. 38] Tithingmen. Voted. That Stephen Twining, Lent Bishop, William Leffingwell, Jesse Alling, Luther Bradley, Charles Bostwick, James Henry, Hezekiah Howe, Samuel Sacket, Anthony P. Stanford, William Peckham, Reuben Hall, Jacob Wolf, Bradford Smith and James F. Merwin be Tithingman.

Constables. Voted. That John Skinner, Josiah B. Morse, Benjamin R. Fowler and Eliakim Kimberly be appointed Constables.

Fenceviewers. Voted. That Hezekiah Hotchkiss, Stephen Rowe, Isaac Dickerman, William Brintnall, Anson Clinton, Gillead Kimberly, Nathan Platt and Henry Monson be Fence-viewers.

Poundkeepers. Voted. That John Scott, Thomas Peck, James B. Reynolds, Nathan Platt, Medad Culver, Chauncey Alling, Cheney Ames and Elias Alling be appointed pound keepers.

[Treasurer.] Voted. That Nathan Beers be Treasurer.

[Sealer of Weights and Measures.] Voted. That Isaac Munson be sealer of weights and measures.

Agents. Voted, that the Selectmen be appointed Agents for the Town for the year ensuing and that either of them with the consent of the majority be authorized to appear*[,]* sue and defend*[,]* or act as Agents aforesaid.

Church. Upon the Petition and the Representation of Trinity Church in New Haven shewing they have it in contemplation to erect a new Church on or near the corner of the western half of the Public square next south of the Court house, as soon as their circumstances will enable them conveniently to do it, and praying this town to pass a vote consenting thereto.

<u>Voted</u>, that this town do consent that s^d Society may there erect such building.[1]

[p. 39] Town Meeting. Voted, that the annual Town meetings be held in future on the second or third mondays in November according to the notification of the Selectmen.

Tax. <u>Voted</u>, that a Tax of five cents on the dollar be laid on the List 1812, and be made payable on the first day of february 1813.

Collector. Voted, that John Skinner be appointed Collector of the town tax – also Collector of the State tax.

Highways. Voted, that seven hundred and fifty dollars be allowed for improving and repairing highways throughout the town.

Committee. Voted, that Simon Baldwin, Thaddeus Beecher and James Merriman, be appointed a Committee to make an appropriation of that portion of said seven hundred and fifty dollars which may be allowed for the purpose of improving and repairing the highways between the rivers.

Certified by Elisha Munson Clerk

---

1. Trinity Episcopal Church was designed by Ithiel Town, a pioneer in the Gothic Revival Style in America. The church was the first Gothic Revival Style church in the country, and was constructed over a two-year period. The church was consecrated in February of 1816. .See, "Trinity's Architecture," Trinity on the Green website, http://trinitynewhaven.org/architecture/.

Encroachments.[1] Voted, that the powers of the Committee who were appointed to remove encroachments according to the Statute be continued.

Voted, to adjourn till the 4th Monday of Ins[r] Dec[r] and meet at the Court House at 2 oClock P.M.

[DECEMBER 28, 1812]

AT A TOWN MEETING HOLDEN (BY ADJOURNMENT) AT THE STATE HOUSE IN NEW HAVEN ON THE 4th MONDAY OF DECEMBER 1812.

[Moderator.] Henry Daggett Esq[r] being Modertor.

[Lister.] Voted, that Doct[r] Eli Ives be released from serving as Lister and that Charles Sherman be appointed in his room.

[Selectmen.] Whereas the Selectmen of the town have heretofore been accustomed to meet twelve half days in the year viz[t] on the first mondays of each month and charge nothing for their services.

Voted, that the Selectmen for the year ensueing be authorized *[p. 40]* to charge for their services on those days which they have heretofore been accustomed to give for the benefit of the public.

[Surveyor of highways.] Voted, that Lewis Alling be appointed a surveyor of highways.

[Meeting House.] Upon the Representation and petition of Simeon Baldwin and Eleazer Foster for and in behalf of the United Society of White haven and Fair-haven requesting the absent of this town to erect a new meeting house at such place on the corner where Fair haven meeting house now stands as shall be legally assigned.

Voted, that this town do consent that said Society their erect such meeting house. Whereas the First ecclesiastical society in New Haven have represented to this Meeting that they are about to erect a new Brick Meeting house at or near where the old one stood praying for a licence and consent of the town that they may extend the Walls of said New House westerly of the founda-

---

1. This committee was formed to deal with property disputes, easements, and other legal matters.

tion of said old one. Therefore <u>Voted</u>, that this town do consent that said first ecclesiastical society may extend the walls of their said new meeting house, as far westerly of the foundation of the old Meeting house as their convenience may require — provided however this licence & consent do not vary or affect the rights of individuals.[1]

[DECEMBER 28, 1812][2]

[Oysters and Clams.] A By Law regulating the fishery of Oysters and Clams.

AT A TOWN MEETING HOLDEN IN NEW HAVEN ON THE 28TH DAY OF DECEMBER 1812.

Voted that no person or persons be permitted between the 1st day of May and the 10th day of October 1812 to take, gather or collect any Oyster shells or Oysters in or upon any of the flats, beaches, rivers, creeks, harbors[,] or waters, within the limits of the town of New Haven; nor any long clams on Dragon Flatts except as hereafter provided, on pain of forfeiting for each and every such offence the sum of Seven Dollars.

That no person or persons shall catch Oysters within the limits of the town of New Haven at any season of the year except in *[the]* months of December *[p. 41]* and January without culling out the shells and small Oysters at or near the place where said Oysters were taken on pain of forfeiting for each & every such offence the sum of seven Dollars.

[Voted] That John Rowe, Charles Lewis, Seth Barnes, Stephen Rowe, Cheney Ames, Ezra Smith, Anson Clinton, Phinehas Andrus and Levi Curtiss be a Committee to superintend the catching of Oysters and Clams within the limits aforesaid; who shall have authority granted to them or either of them, within the time limited aforesaid to grant a permit or permits in writing, thereby licensing the person therein named, to take the quantity of Oysters or long clams therein

---

1. Designed by Ithiel Town in the post-Georgian or Federalist style, Center Church on the Green was built between 1812 - 1814. It was the fourth Congregationalist meeting house on that location. Because of its expansion, art of the church was built over a portion of the New Haven burial ground. Known as the Crypt, those 137 grave sites, including some of New Haven's founders, are protected by the church's foundation and can be visited by the public at certain times of the year. The remaining graves outside the church were relocated to the Grove Street Cemetery in 1821. See, "Center Church on the Green," Center Church website, http://centerchurchonthegreen.org/history/.
2. The town clerk recorded this entry out of chronological order.

mentioned, at any place in such permit specified

Provided that no such permit for Oysters shall be granted between the first day of May and the tenth day of October 1813 unless upon a certificate under the hands of a Physician, that the Oysters will be conducive to the health of the person for whose benefit the permit shall be requested, nor shall such permit be more than one Bushel, or be in force more than 24 hours from its date; and if any person shall take a larger quantity than is specified in any such permit, such person shall incur the penalty as provided for taking without a permit.

That no person shall drive any kind of Carriage in or upon any of the Oyster Banks, where Oysters are growing, within the before mentioned limits, at any season of the year, on pain of forfeiting seven Dollars for every such offence.

That the penalties and forfeitures incurred by any breach of the above regulations shall belong to the Treasury of the town of New Haven, and that Leonard E. Wales Esquire be appointed agent for the town to enquire after at his discretion, to prosecute for the town in their name and at their expences all breaches of the foregoing regulations and that it be made the duty of the said Committee to make complaint to said agent, of all breaches of said regulations that shall come to their knowledge.

Adjourned without day.

Certified by Elisha Munson – Clerk

[NOVEMBER 22, 1813]

P. 42] AT THE ANNUAL TOWN MEETING LEGALLY WARNED AND HOLDEN AT THE COURT HOUSE IN THE TOWN OF NEW HAVEN ON THE 22ᴰ DAY OF NOVEMBER 1813, AT TWO o'CLOCK P.M.

Moderator. Henry Daggett Esqʳ was chosen Moderator.

Accounts. The Selectmen exhibited a statement of the Town accounts which was accepted and ordered to be lodged on file.

Selectmen. Voted, that Samuel Punderson, Eleazer Foster, Mathew Read, Eliakim Kimberly and John Hunt Junʳ be appointed Selectmen.

Grand jurors. Voted, that Leonard E. Wales, Ralph I. Ingersoll, Sereno E. Dwight,

Anthony P. Sanford and Samuel Clark be appointed <u>Grand jurors</u>.

[Listers.][1] Voted, that Charles Sherman, ~~Truman Woodward, William A. Babcock, Walter Budington, William McCrackan~~, Ebenezer Johnson Jun[r], Nehemiah Kimberly, Jonas F. Merwin, ~~Hervey Sanford~~, Levi Tuttle, Sereno E. Dwight, Joseph Punderson Hotchkiss, Thomas Hull, Clement Goodale and John Bush be appointed <u>Listers</u>.

Surveyors. <u>Voted</u>, that Anthony P. Sanford, Ambrose Ward, Nathan Peck, Laban Smith, Isaac Tomlinson, Isaac Dickerman, Medad Osborn, Nehemiah Kimberly, Nath[l] F. Clark, Nathan Platt, Ebenezer Townsend & Edward Alling be appointed Surveyors of highways.

Tythingmen. <u>Voted</u>, that Luther Bradley, Charles Bostwick, James Henry, Hezekiah Howe, Charles Sherman, Mathew Read, Lemuel Bradley, William E. Thompson, William Peckham, Lent Bishop, Delauzan Deforest, Elihu Sanford Jun[r], Bradford Smith, Jonas F. Merwin, Jeremiah M. Atwater and Lewis Hotchkiss be appointed <u>Tythingmen</u>.

Constables. <u>Voted</u>, that John Skinner, Josiah B. Morse, Benjamin R. Fowler, Ebenezer Weed & Nathan Platt, Anth[y] P. Sanford & Walter Budington be <u>Constables</u>.

[p. 43] <u>*Fence Viewers.*</u> <u>Voted</u>, that Hezekiah Hotchkiss, Stephen Rowe, Isaac Dickerman, William Brintnall, Gillead Kimberly, Nathan Platt, Enos Smith and Henry Monson be appointed Fence-Viewers.

Pound keepers. <u>Voted</u>, that John Scott, Thomas Peck, James B. Reynolds, Nathan Platt, Chauncey Alling, Cheney Ames, Medad Culver, Elias Alling and Ezra Barnes be appointed <u>Pound keepers.</u>

Sealer. Voted, that Isaac Munson be appointed be appointed a sealer of weights & measures.

Treasurer. Voted, that Nathan Beers be appointed <u>Treasurer</u>

Agents. Voted, that the Selectmen be appointed Agents for the town the ensuing year and that either of them with the consent of the majority be authorized to appear, sue, and defend or act as Agents aforesaid.

---

1. The town clerk listed a number of names, then crossed them out.

Tax. Voted that a tax of five cents on the dollar be laid on the List for the year 1813 – and become payable on the first day of february, 1814.

Collector. Voted, that John Skinner be appointed Collector of the State Tax – Also Collector of said Town tax.

Highways. Voted that the Selectmen be authorized to lay out seven hundred and fifty dollars in repairing and improving highways throughout the town.

Voted to adjourn till the 3 Monday of december next at 2 oClock – P.M.

Certified by Elisha Munson Clerk

[DECEMBER 20, 1813]

AT A TOWN MEETING HOLDEN IN NEW HAVEN (BY ADJOURN-MENT) ON THE 3ᵈ MONDAY OF DECEMBER 1813.

[Moderator.] Henry Daggett Esqʳ being Moderator.

Listers released. The following persons were released from serving as Listers viz.
Hervy Sanford
Walter Budington
Truman Woodward
William McCrackan
William A. Babcock

[p. 44] Listers. The following persons were appointed Listers viz.
Anthony P. Sanford
James Hunt
James Atwater
John H. Jacobs
William H. Elliot
Charles Bostwick
Samuel Willmont
Charles Lewis
David Ray
Lewis Hotchkiss

Tythingmen. Voted, that David Ray, Edward Carr and Isaac Gilbert be appointed Tythingmen.

Sexton. Voted, that Joseph Alley[1] be appointed sexton in the room of John Claus dec^d.[2]

Lands near the Market. Application being made to the meeting for a lease of a piece of Public land on the West side of Union Street opposite the market.

Voted, that it is inexpedient to lease said land it being the opinion of this meeting that the same is necessary for the accommodation of the Market.

School House. Voted. — that the Inhabitants of Hotchkiss town[3] so called in Westfield school district have liberty to continue their school house where it now stands in the highway on the top of the hill near the Dwelling house of Isaac Thomas and have liberty to occupy so much of the vacant ground Easterly of the school house on the top of the bank as may be necessary for a wood yard and a place to erect a necessary for the use of the school – under direction of Captn Samuel Punderson. Provided the same do not incommode the highway and this permission is to be continued during the pleasure of the town.

[DECEMBER 20, 1813]

Byelaw. A By-Law regulating the Fishery of oysters and Clams.
AT A TOWN MEETING HOLDEN IN NEW HAVEN ON THE 20TH DAY OF DECEMBER 1813.[4]

Oyster-act. Voted, that no person or persons be permitted, between the 1st day of May and the 10th day of October *[p. 45]* 1814 to take, gather[,] or collect any Oysters in or upon any of the flats, beaches, rivers, creeks, harbors[,] or waters within the limits of the town of New Haven nor any long clams on Dragon

---

1. Joseph Alley (1762/8 - 1829) was the husband of Esther Bradley (1795 - 1843). There is a discrepancy as to his birthdate. Jacobus notes it was March 2, 1768 , while the Hale Collection has it as 1762/3. Alley was a communicant of Center Church.
2. In addition to serving as sexton of Center Church, John Claus (1736 - 1813) was a veteran of the American Revolution as a member of the 20th Regiment of Militia in Captain Bradley's artillery company. See, U.S., Revolutionary War Rolls, 1775-1783, Regiment: 20th Regiment of Militia, 1779-1781 (Folder 184) - Johnson's Regiment of Militia, 1778 (Folder 216).
3. The early name of Westville.
4. As the town clerk likely recorded this meeting after the fact he apparently failed to note that it was a continuation of the meeting noted on page 323.

Flats, except as hereafter provided on pain of forfeiting for each and every such offence the sum of seven dollars.

That no person or persons shall catch Oysters within the limits of the town of New Haven, at any season of the year, except in the months of December & January, without culling out the shells and small Oysters at or near the place where said Oysters were taken, on pain of forfeiting for each and every such offence the sum of seven dollars.

That no person shall at any season of the year, catch long clams with oysters, longs or clams foresd.

That John Rowe, Charles Lewis, Seth Barnes, Chaney Ames, Ezra Smith, Phineas Andrews and Levi Curtis be a committee to superintend the catching of oysters and clams within the limits aforesaid; who shall have authority granted to them or either of them, within the time limited aforesaid, to grant a permit or permits in writing, thereby licensing the person therein named to take the quantity of oysters or long-clams therein mentioned, at any place in such permit specified.

Provided that no such permit for oysters shall be granted between the first day of may and the 10th day of October, 1814, unless upon a certificate under the hand of a Physician, that the oysters will be condusive to the health of the person for whose benefit the permit shall be requested, nor shall such permit be for more than one bushel, or be in force more than 24 hours from its date. And if any person shall take a larger quantity than is specified in one such permit, such person shall incur the penalty as provided for taking without a permit.
That no person shall drive any kind of carriage in or upon any of the oyster banks, where oysters are growing within the before mentioned limits, at any season of the year, upon pain of forfeiting seven dollars for every such offence. That the penalties and forfeitures incurred by any breach of the above regulations, shall belong to the *[p. 46]* Treasury of the town of New Haven and that Leonard E. Wales Esq' be appointed agent for the town, to enquire after and at his discretion to prosecute for the town, in their name and at their expences, all breaches of the foregoing regulations; and that it be made the duties of the said Committee to make complaint to the said Agent, of all breaches or said regulations that shall come to their knowledge.

         Adjourned without day – Elisha Munson Clerk

[MAY 9, 1814]

AT A TOWN MEETING HOLDEN IN NEW HAVEN ON THE 9ᵀᴴ DAY
OF MAY 1814.

Moderator. Dyer White Esquire was chosen Moderator.

Khine-poch.¹ Voted, that the Selectmen of the town employ Doctʳ S. Fansher² to
inoculate with the kine-pock such of the Inhabitants as may attend for that purpose at the places to be designated by the Selectmen and that the same be done
at the expence of the town provided. Doctʳ Fancher will undertake at a sum not
exceeding twenty five cents for each person.

Adjourn'd without day. Certified by Elisha Munson Clerk

[NOVEMBER 28, 1814]

AT A THE ANNUAL TOWN MEETING LEGALLY WARNED AND
HOLDEN AT THE COURT HOUSE IN NEW HAVEN ON THE 28ᵗʰ DAY
OF NOVEMBER 1814, AT 2 o'CLOCK P.M.

[Moderator.] Henry Daggett Esqʳ was chosen Moderator.

[Accounts.] The Selectmen exhibited a statement of the Town accounts – it was
read, accepted and lodged on file.

Selectmen. Voted, that Samuel Punderson, Eleazer Foster, Mathew Read, John
Hunt Junʳ and Eliakim Kimberly be appointed Selectmen.

Grand jurors. Voted that Ralph I. Ingersoll, Serino Dwight, Anthony P. Sanford,
Samuel Clark & Roger Sherman Baldwin³ be appointed Grand jurors.

---

1. In 1796, Edward Jenner began inoculating humans with matter from a cowpox against smallpox.
Two years later a Jenner associate, Henry Cline, used dried vaccine material from Jenner to successfully inoculate against the disease, and from that point on, inoculations became more widespread.
2. Dr. Sylvanus Fansher (1770 - 1846) was a Connecticut physician and leading advocate of inoculation
against smallpox. He was born in Plymouth, CT, and died in Hartford in 1846. See, Sylvanus Fansher,
Record of Inoculation for the Kine Pox, 1810-1831, MSS., Harvard Medical School, Countway Library,
Boston,MA. See also William Cothren, *History of Ancient Woodbury, Connecticut* (1854), pp. 135 - 136.
3. Roger Sherman Baldwin (1793 - 1863), graduated from Yale College in 1811. He held a number
of political and judicial appointment in Connecticut and is best remembered for serving as Connecticut's governor as well as his defense of the *Amistad* Africans in 1841.

Listers. <u>Voted</u>, that Ralph I. Ingersoll, Clement Goodale *[p. 47]* Anthony P. Sanford, James Hunt, James Atwater, John H. Jacobs, William H. Elliott, Charles Bostwick, Samuel Wilmot, Charles Lewis, David Ray, Edward Alling, Amos Johnson, Zerah Hawley, Justus Harrison, Newton Stevens and Jonas Fowler Merwin be <u>Listers</u>.

Surveyors of Highways. Voted, that Anthony P. Sanford, Nathan Peck, Laban Smith, Isaac Tomlinson, Isaac Dickerman, Ambrose Ward, Nehemiah Kimberly, ~~Laban Smith~~, Jonas F. Merwin, Nathan Platt, Ebenezer Townsend and Edward Alling be <u>Surveyors</u> of highways.

Tythingmen. <u>Voted</u>, that Luther Bradley, Lent Bishop, Jonathan Maltby, Charles Bostwick, Sidney Hull, Elisha Punderson, Richard B. Law, Solomon Johnson, Silas Hotchkiss, Jesse Alling, Isaac Gilbert, Joseph Alley, William Peckham, John Beach, Stephen Huggins, Eliakim Kimberly and Jonas F. Merwin be <u>Tythingmen</u>.

Constables. <u>Voted</u>, that John Skinner, Josiah B. Morse, Benjamin R. Fowler, Ebenezer Weed and Nathan Platt be appointed – <u>Constables</u>.

Fence Viewers. <u>Voted</u>, that Hezekiah Hotchkiss, Stephen Rowe, Isaac Dickerman, William Brintnall, Gillead Kimberly, Nathan Platt, Enos Smith, Henry Munson and Joseph Munson be <u>Fence Viewers</u>.

Pound-keepers. <u>Voted</u>, that John Scott, Thomas Peck, James B. Reynolds, Nathan Platt, Chauncey Alling, Cheney Ames, Medad Culver, Elias Alling and Ezra Barnes be appointed <u>Pound keepers</u>.

Sealer. <u>Voted</u>, that Leverit Griswold be appointed a <u>Sealer of Weights and Measures</u>.

Treasurer. Voted, that Nathan Beers be appointed Treasurer.

[Agents.] Voted, that the Selectmen be appointed <u>Agents</u> for the Town the ensuing year and that either of them (with the consent of the majority) be authorized to appear, sue and defend*[,]* or act as Agents aforesaid.

[p. 48] Tax. Voted, that a Tax of five cents on the dollar be laid on the List for the year 1814, and that said Tax become payable on the 1ˢᵗ day of Febʸ 1815.

Collector. Voted, that John Skinner be Collector of the above Tax. <u>Voted</u>, that

John Skinner be appointed Collector of the State Taxes.

Highways & Bridges. Voted, that the sum of five hundred dollars be appropriated for the purpose of repairing highways and bridges.

Voted to adjourn till the 4ᵗʰ monday of Decmʳ next at 2 oClock P.M.
                                   Certified by — Elisha Munson Clerk

[DECEMBER 26, 1814]

AT A TOWN MEETING HOLDEN AT THE COURT HOUSE IN NEW HAVEN (BY ADJOURNMENT) ON THE FOURTH MONDAY OF DE-CEMBER 1814.

[Moderator.] Henry Daggett Esqʳ being Moderator.

New Highways. The Selectmen exhibited a report respecting several new high-ways near the Village of Dragon¹ which report was read, considered & accepted. Whereupon — Voted that said highways be established as public highways – provided they can be opened without any expence to the town. (see report on the next page.)

Tithingman. Voted, that Jacob Wolf be appointed a Tythingman.

Petition. A petition from several of the inhabitants of the Town of Milford, requesting a new highway to be laid out in the west part of New Haven to run across the West Meadows &c. was read & considered[.] After debate a vote was passed to do nothing on the subject.

Samˡ Punderson's Sallary. Voted, that the Samuel Punderson's Sallary for oversee-ing and purchasing supplies for the Alms-House be increased and that the sum to be added to his Sallary be left to the discretion of the Selectmen.

[p. 49] Report on highways &c a Survey. We the subscribing Selectmen for the town of New Haven report that we have surveyed and laid out the following highways near the village of Dragon (viz.) A highway by the river, extending Northerly from the highway opposite the house owned by Samuel Pierpont to the west end

---

1. Village of Dragon is Fair Haven Heights. It was originally located where the Ferry Street Bridge now crosses the Quinnipiac River.

of Dragon Bridge. We run the west line of the highway on the East side of the dwelling houses, which front the East River, touching those which present the most Easterly till we come to the land leading to Dragon Bridge, we then set off 30 feet and run the East line, parallel to the first described, and made the road 30 feet wide throughout.[1]

We then passed to the North side up the road near Dragon Bridge and laid out a new Highway under the bank: beginning between the Dwelling house & Store of John Rowe, we run Northerly, by the East end of said Rowe's house and gardens, about one chain and thirty two links from thence 71° 95 links to a post, from thence A[2] 14° W. 1. 86 links to a point 10 links East of the Northeast corner of Levi Grannis' dwelling house, from thence in a direct line 5,8° 0 to two small cedar trees, from thence 4° four chains & fifty links to a stone near the foot of the hill and then continued the highway up the hill five chains & sixty links to a New highway hereafter described. We then returned to the stone at the foot of the hill and continued the highway under the bank viz. we run A 57° E 4.25 to a cedar tree, from thence A 21° E 1.89 to a cedar bush, from thence A 18° E 2.64 to a willow tree at the South East corner of Cheney Ames' Dwelling house, from thence A 2.20 to a stake from thence A 12° E 4.16 to the land *[of]* Jonathan Maltby. We then set off two rods in width and run a line parallel to the above described line and two rods distant from it to form the Easterly line of the highway. We then proceeded to the dwelling house of Cheney Ames *[p. 50]* and laid out a new highway in front of said house three rods wide and seven from the East river 80 ft about half a mile through the lands of William Brintnall and Chaney Ames to an ancient four rod highway which runs through the <u>Neck</u>.[3]

We then Proceeded to that part of the road *[...]* to Dragon Bridge which is nearly opposite to Stephen Rowe's and laid out a New Highway 2 1/2 rods wide, the course being 3° 88 & and passing between the new building lately errected Chancellor Kingsbury and the dwelling house of Stephen Rowe about 85 rods to a new highway crossing the lands of Stephen Rowe & William Brintnall*[.]*[4]

Eleazer Foster |

---

1. In margin of records an unknown hand wrote "South Font St."
2. An abbreviation for Azimuth, referring to the number of degrees from north (or other reference direction) that a line runs, measured clockwise. A link, meanwhile, measured 7.92 inches, while a chain contained 100 links and measured 66 feet.
3. Written in the margin is "Pine St," which today runs from Front Street to Monroe Street.
4. Again in the margin is written "Clinton Ave," likely now the area near Clinton Park in Fair Haven.

John Hunt 2ᵈ   }   Selectmen
Matthew Read

[Oyster & Clams.] A Bye-Law regulating the Fishing of Oysters and Clams. <u>Voted</u>, that no person or persons be permitted, between the first day of May, and the 10ᵗʰ day of November, 1815, to take, gather*[,]* or collect any Oyster shells or Oysters in or upon any of the flats, beaches, rivers, creeks*[,]* or harbors, or waters within the following limits, in the town of New Haven, Viz. Northerly of a line drawn from the old ferry house in New Haven to the dwelling house of Jacob Mallery, in East Haven on pain of forfeiting for each and every such offence the sum of <u>seven</u> dollars.

That no person or persons from & after the first day of May, until the first day of October 1815, shall take or cause to be taken any Oysters in or upon any of the flats, beaches, rivers, creeks, harbor waters, or shores within the limits of the town of New Haven, nor any long clams on Dragon flats, excepting as hereafter provided, on pain of forfeiting <u>seven</u> dollars for each offence.

That no person or persons shall catch Oysters within the limits of the town of New Haven at any season of the year except in the months of December and January, without culling out *[p. 51]* shells and small Oysters, at or near the place where said Oysters were taken on pain of forfeiting for each and every such offence the sum of <u>seven</u> dollars.

That Thomas Painter, Ezra Smith, Stephen Rowe, Levi Tuttle, Isaac Tomlinson, Walter Budington, Charles Lewis, Phinehas Andrews, and be a committee to superintend the catching of Oysters & Clams within the limits aforesaid, who shall have authority granted to them, or either of them within the times limited aforesaid to grant a permit or permits in writing, thereby licencing the person therein named to take the quantity of Oysters or long clams therin mentioned, at any place in such permit specified; <u>Provided</u>, that no such permit for Oysters shall be granted between the first day of May and the first day of October, 1815 unless upon a certificate under the hand of a physician that the Oysters will be conducive to the health of the person for whose benefit the permit shall be requested, nor shall such permit be for more than one bushel, or be in force more than twenty four hours from its date; and if any person shall take a larger quantity than is specified in any such permit such person shall incur the penalty as provided for taking without a permit.

That no person shall drive any kind of carriage in or upon any of the Oyster Banks where Oysters are growing within the before mentioned limits, at any season of the year on pain of forfeiting <u>seven</u> dollars[.]

That the penalties and forfeitures incurred by any breach of the above regulations shall belong to the treasury of the town of New Haven and that Roger Sherman Baldwin Esq[r] be appointed agent for the town to enquire after, & at his discretion, to prosecute for the town in their name and at their expence, all breaches of the foregoing regulations; and that it be made the duty of said Committee to make complaint to the said agent of all breaches of s[d] regulations that shall come to their knowledge. Adjourned without day — certified by

Elisha Munson Clerk.

[p. 52]   *[JUNE ?, 1815]*

AT THE ANNUAL MEETING OF THE MAYOR, ALDERMEN, COM-
MON COUNCILMEN AND FREEMEN FOR THE CITY OF NEW
HAVEN LEGALLY WARNED AND HELD AT THE COURT HOUSE IN
SAID NEW HAVEN ON THE *[...]* DAY OF JUNE 1815.

[Moderator.] The Hon[ble] Elizur Goodwrich the Mayor being Moderator.

Error — See the Record Book for the City.[1]

[NOVEMBER 27, 1815]

AT THE ANNUAL TOWN MEETING HOLDEN AT THE COURT-
HOUSE IN NEW HAVEN ON THE 27TH DAY OF NOVEMBER 1815.

[Moderator.] Henry Daggett Esq[r] chosen Moderator.

[Town Accounts.] The Selectmen exhibited a statement of the Town accounts for the past year which was accepted and ordered to be lodged on file.

Selectmen. Voted that Samuel Punderson, Eleazer Foster, Matthew Read, John Hunt 2[d] & Eliakim Kimberly be appointed Selectmen.

Grandjurors. Voted, that Sopha Staples, Serino E. Dwight, Roger S. Baldwin, John D. Fowler, Dennis Kimberly, John Beach, and Samuel Clark be appointed Grandjurors.

---

1. No explanation for this remark by the town clerk is provided.

Listers. Voted, that Ralph J. Ingersoll, Clement Goodell, Anthony P. Sanford, James Hunt, James Atwater, John H. Jacocks, William H. Elliot, Charles Bostwick, Samuel Wilmont, Charles Lewis, David Ray, Amos Johnson, Asa Alling, Solomon Johnson, Newton Stevens, Levi Beecher, Zerah Hawley & Elisha Benham be appointed Listers.

Tithingmen. Voted that Ebenezer Weed, Hezekiah Howe, Josiah B. Morse, Joseph Alley, John Beach, Isaac Gilbert, Sidney Hull, Lent Bishop, Elihu Munson, Bradford Smith, Jacob Wolf & Jonas F. Merwin be appointed Tithing-Men.

Surveyors of Highways. Voted that Anthony P. Stanford, Nathan Peck, Laban Smith, Isaac Tomlinson, Isaac *[p. 53]* Dickerman, Ambrose Ward, Nehemiah Kimberly, Jonas F. Merwin, Nathan Platt, Ebenezer Townsend, Levi Beecher and William McCracken be appointed Surveyors of highways.

Constables. Voted that John Skinner, Josiah B. Morse, Benjamin R. Fowler, Ebenezer Weed and Nathan Platt be appointed Constables.

Fence–viewers. Voted that Hezekiah Hotchkiss, Stephen Rowe, Isaac Dickerman, William Brintnall, Eliakim Kimberly, Nathan Platt, Enos Smith, Henry Munson and Joseph Munson be appointed Fence Viewers.

Poundkeepers. Voted that John Scott, Thomas Peck, James B. Reynolds, Nathan Platt, Chauncey Alling, Cheney Ames, Medad Culver and Elias Alling be appointed Poundkeepers.

Sealer. Voted that Leveritt Griswold be sealer of weights and measures.
Treasurer. Voted, that Nathan Beers be Treasurer.

Agents. Voted that the Selectmen be appointed Agents for the town for the year ensuing and that either of them with the consent of the majority be authorized to appear, sue and defend*[,]* or act as Agents aforesaid.

Tax. Voted that a tax of five cents on the dollar be laid on the list for the year 1815 and become payable on the first day of Feburary 1816.

Collector. Voted that John Skinner be appointed collector of the town tax — also collector of the State tax.

[Highway Repairs.] Voted that 500 dollars be appropriated for the repairs of high-

ways in the town of New Haven to be laid out in the town at the discretion of the Selectmen.

[p. 54] [Old Burying Ground Fence.] Voted that Elisha Munson, Luther Bradley & Eleazer Foster be a Committee to enquire respecting the fence around the old Burying Ground and ascertain at whose expence it has been heretofore erected and in what manner it may be repaired.[1]

Voted to adjourn till the 4th monday of December at 2 °Clock PM. Certified by [...][2]

[DECEMBER 25, 1815]

AT A TOWN MEETING HELD BY ADJOURNMENT IN NEW HAVEN ON THE 25TH DAY OF DECEMBER 1815.

[Moderator.] Henry Daggett Esq[r] was chosen Moderator.

Listers. Voted — That James Hunt, James Atwater and Levi Beecher be excused from serving as Listers and that Leman Dunning be appointed a Lister.

Tythingmen. Voted — that Ebenezer Johnson Jun[r], Oliver Beach and Elijah Rowe be appointed Tythingmen.

Poundkeeper. Voted that John Rowe be appointed Poundkeeper.

By-law regulating the fishing of oysters & clams. Voted — that no person or persons be permitted between the first day of April and the 20th day of November 1816, to take[,] gather[,] or collect any oyster shells or oysters, in or upon any of the flats[,] beaches, rivers, creeks, harbors[,] or waters within the following limits in the town of New Haven Viz.— Northerly of a line drawn from the old Ferry House in New Haven to the old ferry wharf in East-Haven, on pain of forfeiting for each and every such offence the sum of seven dollars.

That no person or persons, from and after the first day of April, until the 20th day of October 1816, shall take or cause to be taken, any Oysters, in or upon

---

1 The ancient burial ground graves that remained outside of the rebuilt Center Church remained until 1820. In that year the town levied a tax to move what remained of the headstones to the Grove Street Cemetery. See, Thomas Plunkett, "The New Haven Burying Ground A Brief History and Discussion of the Grove Street Cemetery," website, http://www.smithie.com/nhcemetery.html.
2. The clerk failed to certify the record with his signature..

one of the flats, beaches, rivers, creeks, harbors, water[,] or shores, within the limits of the town of New Haven nor any long clams on Dragon flats, excepting as hereafter provided, on the pain of forfeiting seven dollars for each offence.

[p. 55] That no person or persons shall catch oysters within the limits of the town of New Haven, at any season of the year, without culling out the shells & small oysters from the longs, as they are taken up and throwing the same overboard when taken, on pain of forfeiting for each and every offence the sum of seven dollars.

That Thomas Painter, Ezra Smith, Stephen Rowe, Levi Tuttle, Isaac Tomlinson, Walter Buddington, Charles Lewis, Phinehas Andrews & Russell Hotchkiss be a committee to superintend the catching of oysters and clams within the limits aforesaid; who shall have authority granted to them, or either of them, within the time limited aforesaid, to grant a permit or permits in writnig, thereby licensing the person therein named, to take the quantity of oysters or long claims therein mentioned at any place in such permit specified: Provided that no such permit for Oysters shall be granted between the first day of April and the tenth day of October 1816 unless upon a certificate under the hand of a Physician that the oysters will be condusive to the health of the person for whose benefit the receipt shall be requested nor shall such permits be for more than one bushel, or be in force for more than twenty four hours from its date, and if any person shall take a larger quantity than is specified in any such permit, such person shall incur the penalty as provided for taking without a permit.

That not person shall drive any kind of carriage in or upon any of the Oyster Banks where Oysters are growing, within the before mentioned limits at any season of the year, on pain of forfeiting seven dollars.

That the penalties and forfeitures incurred by any breach of the above regulations shall belong to the Treasury of the town of New Haven; and that Roger Sherman Baldwin Esq[r] be appointed agent for the town, to enquire after and at his discretion to prosecute for the town, in their name and at their expence all breaches of the foregoing regulations; and that it be made the duty of said committee, to make complaint to said agent, of all breaches [p. 56] of said regulations, that shall come to their knowledge.

Adjourned without day — certified by Elisha Munson Clerk.

[NOVEMBER 25, 1816]

AT THE ANNUAL TOWN MEETING HOLDEN AT THE COURT-HOUSE IN NEW HAVEN ON THE 25TH DAY OF NOVEMBER 1816.

[Moderator.] The Honble Elizur Goodrich was chosen Moderator.
[Clerk.] Elisha Munson Clerk.

[Town Accounts.] The Selectmen exhibited a Statement of the Town Accounts for the year past — accepted & ordered to be lodged on file.

Selectmen. Voted — that Samuel Punderson, Eleazer Foster, Solomon Collis, Matthew Read & Eliakim Kimberly be appointed Selectmen.

Grandjurors. Voted — that Sophos Staples[1], David Ray, Samuel J. Hitchcock, John Barlow, Bryan Clark and John D. Fowler being appointed Grand jurors

Listers. Voted — that Ralph I. Ingersoll, Anthony B. Sanford, Asahel Tuttle, ~~Charles Bostick~~, Lucius Atwater, Normand [?] Dexter, Roger Sherman Baldwin, Roger S. Skinner[2], Aaron Thomas Junr, Elisha Benham, Asa Alling, John Rowe, ~~Clement Goodall~~, Elisha Punderson, Eli Ives, Charles Lewis, Elisha Davis & Leman Dunning be appointed Listers.

Tythingmen. Voted — That David Ritter, Hezekiah Howe, Oliver Deming, Samuel P. Davis, Joseph Alley, Charles Bostwick, Jacob Wolf, John Beech, Bradford Smith, Enos Smith, Clement Goodell & Joseph Munson be appointed Tythingmen.

Surveyors of Highways. Voted — That Anthony P. Sanford, Nathan Peck, Laban Smith, Asahel Tuttle, Leman Dunning, Ebenezer Townsend, Bradford Smith, Laban Smith 2^d, Elisha Benham, Levi Beecher, Leman Hall & Elisha Punderson be appointed Surveyors of Highways.

---

1. Sohos Staples (1789/91 - 1826) of Canterbury, CT, , graduated from Yale College in 1809, became an attorney practicing in New Haven, then moved to Sparta, GA, in 1817. He married Sarah Abercrombie in January of 1826, but he died in July of that same year. See, Dexter, *Biographical Sketches*, VI: 281.
2. Roger S. Skinner (1795 - 1838) graduated from Yale in 1813 and attended Litchfield Law School. He was admitted to the bar in 1816 and served as clerk of the New Haven City and County courts for a number of years before moving to New York in 1828. He died while visiting Peru, Illinois, in 1838.

[p. 57] Constables. Voted — that John Skinner, Josiah B. Morse, Benjamin R. Fowler, Erastus Osborn,[1] Nehemiah Kimberly & Ebenezer Fowler be appointed Constables.

Fence viewers. Voted — That Hezekiah Hotchkiss, Isaac Dickerman, William Britnall, Enos Smith, Stephen Prindle, Joseph Munson & Henry Munson be appointed Fence Viewers.

Pound Keepers. Voted, That John Scott, Thomas Peck, Chancey ~~Alling~~, Medad Culver, James B. Reynolds, Elias Alling, Nathan Platt & Cheney Ames be appointed Pound keepers.

Sealer. Voted — That Leveritt Griswold be appointed sealer of weights and measures.

Treasurer. Voted — That Nathan Beers be appointed Treasurer.

Agents. Voted — That the Selectmen be appointed Agents for the Town, for the year ensuing, and that either of them with the consent of the majority, be authorised to appear, sue and defend[,] or act as agents aforesaid.

Tax. Voted — That a tax of five cents on the dollars be laid on the list 1816 and that the same be made payable on the first day of Feburary 1817 — and that John Skinner be collector of said Tax. Voted — That John Skinner be collector of the State tax.

Highways. Voted — That five hundred dollars be appropriated for repairs of highways in the Town of New Haven to be laid out at the discretion of the Selectmen. Voted to adjourn till the last Tuesday in December to meet at the Court House at two oClock P.M.

Certified by Elisha Munson Clerk.

[DECEMBER 31, 1816]

AT A TOWN MEETING HELD AT THE COURT HOUSE IN NEW HAVEN BY ADJOURNMENT ON THE 31ST DAY OF DECR AD 1816.

---

1. Erastus Osborn (1785 - 1868) became famous for leading a raid on Yale Medical School in 1824 to retrieve the body of a young West Haven woman, Bethsheba Smith, which had allegedly been taken by Yale staff or students for dissection. See, http://www.thenewjournalatyale.com/2005/11/a-grave-offense/

[p. 58] [Moderator.] Cha[s] Denison Esq[r] was chosen Moderator.

Bank. Voted unanimously that it is the wish of this Town that an office of Discount & Deposit of the Bank of the United States be established in the City of New Haven.[1]

Committee. Voted Unanimously that Me[ssrs] James Hillhouse, Abraham Bishop, Eli Whitney,[2] John Nicoll and William Bristol Esq[rs] be a committee to take such measures to procure the location of said Branch in the City of New Haven as they may deem expedient and proper.

Oysters. Voted — that Eleazer Foster, John Rowe and Charles Lewis be a Committee to take into consideration the expediency of removing young Oysters from the vicinity of Dragon bridge up the River with a view of enlarging the oyster beds & if they judge it expedient to enlarge said beds, to superintend the removal of said Oysters.

Oysters & Clams. Voted that Eleazer Foster, Simeon Baldwin, John Rowe, Charles Lewis, Samuel J. Hitchcock, Leonard E. Wales and John Skinner be appointed a Committee to examine the By-laws relative to the catching *[of]* Oysters and Clams & take into consideration the expediency of making amendments & alterations in said Laws and make report at some future meeting.

Lister. Voted, that Clement Goodell be excused from serving as a Lister & that Zina Hotchkiss be appointed a Lister in his room.

Lister. Voted, that Charles Bostwick be excused from serving as Lister and that Beriah Bradley be appointed a Lister in his room.

Pound-keeper. Voted, that Chauncey Alling be excused from serving as Pound keeper and that Jesse Alling be appointed Pound keeper in his room.

By-law regulating the fishery of Oysters & Clams. The following By-law regulating the fishery of Oysters & Clams was passed viz.

[p. 59] Voted, that no person or persons be permitted between the first day of

---

1. The Second Bank of the United States opened in February 1816. New Haven failed to raise enough capital in its bid to open a branch of the bank, which, instead opened in Middletown, CT, in 1817. See, Federal Reserve of Philadelphia, *The Second Bank of the United States* (2010), p. 8.
2. Eli Whitney (1765 - 1825) needs little introduction as the inventor of the cotton gin. A Yale graduate (1792), Whitney's cotton gin and advocacy of interchangeable parts revolutionized American industry.

April and the 20th day of November 1817 to take, gather, or collect any Oyster shells or oysters, in or upon any of the flats, beaches, rivers, creeks, harbor, or waters within the following limits in the town of New Haven viz. Northerly of a line drawn from the Old Ferry house in New Haven to the old Ferry wharf in East-Haven, on pain of forfeiting for each and every such offence the sum of seven dollars.

That no person or persons, from and after the first day of April, until the 10th day of October 1817 shall take, or cause to be taken, any Oysters, in or upon any of the flats, beaches, rivers, creeks, harbours[,] waters[,] or shores within the limits of the town of New Haven or any long clams on Dragon flats, excepting as hereafter provided, on pain of forfeiting seven dollars for each offence.

That no person or persons shall catch oysters within the limits of the town of New Haven at any season of the year without culling out the shells and small oysters from the longs as they are taken up, and throwing the same overboard where taken on pain of forfeiting for each and every such offence the sum of seven dollars.

That Thomas Painter, Ezra Smith, Levi Tuttle, Isaac Tomlinson, Walter Budington, Charles Lewis, Russell Hotchkiss & John Rowe, be a committee to superintend the catching of oysters and clams within the limits aforesaid, who shall have authority granted to them or either of them within the term limited aforesaid to grant a permit or permits in writing, thereby licencing the person therein named, to take the quantity of oysters or long clams therein mentioned at any place in such permit specified. Provided that no Such permit for oysters shall be granted between the first day of April and the tenth day of October 1817, unless upon a certificate under the hand of a physician, that the oysters will be conducive to the health of the person for whose benefit the permit shall be requested; nor shall such permit be for more than one bushel ,or be in force for more than twenty four hours from its date, and if any person shall take a larger quantity *[p. 60]* than is specified in any such permits such person shall incur the penalty as provided for taking without a permit.

That no person shall drive any kind of carriage in or upon any of the oyster-banks, where oysters are growing within the before-mentioned limits at any season of the year, on pain of forfeiting seven dollars.

That the penalties & forfeitures incurred on any breach of the above regulations, shall belong to the Treasury of the town of New Haven, and that Roger

Sherman Baldwin Esq' be appointed agent for the town, to enquire after and at his discretion to prosecute for the Town in their name and at their expence, all breaches of the foregoing regulations; and that it be made the duty of said Committee to make complaint to said agent of all breaches of said regulations that shall come to their knowledge.

Adjourned without day.

Certified by Elisha Munson Clerk

[NOVEMBER 24, 1817]

AT THE ANNUAL TOWN MEETING HOLDEN AT THE COURT HOUSE IN NEW HAVEN ON THE 24ᵀᴴ DAY OF NOVEMBER 1817.

[Moderator.] Henry Daggett Esq' was chosen Moderator.

[Clerk.] Elisha Munson Clerk.

Selectmen' exhibition of acct'. The Selectmen exhibited a statement of the town accounts which was read, accepted, and ordered to be lodged on file in the town clerks office.

Selectmen. Voted, that Solomon Collis, Isaac Gilbert, Henry Ward, Lent Bishop, Anthony P. Sanford, Elisha Punderson, *[and]* Charles Bostwick be Selectmen.

Grand jurors. John Beech, Elisha Sanford, Eben' Johnson Jun', Charles K. Shipman, Oliver Clark and Stephen Bunnell be appointed Grandjurors.

Listers. Voted, that Normand Dexter, Lucius Atwater, R.S. Skinner, Samuel R. Crane, Jacob Wolfe, Aaron Thomas Jun', Nathan Platt, Andrew *[p. 61]* Kidston, Caleb Mix, Zina Hotchkiss, Charles W. Alling, John Rowe, Elihu Sanford, David Kimberly & Beriah Bradley be appointed Listers.

Tything men. Voted, that David Ritter, Samuel P. Lewis, Hezekiah Howe, Hezekiah Augur 2ᵈ, Jacob Wolfe, John Hempsted, John Beach, David B. Spencer, Leonard A. Daggett,[1] John B. Davis, Bradford Smith, Enos Smith, Sydney

---

1. Leonard Augustus Daggett (1790 - 1867) graduated from Yale in 1807, studied law, and was a prominent merchant and teacher in New Haven. Like his father before him, his three sons also attended Yale.

Hull, *[John?]* Meloy, Clement Goodwll, Ezra Stiles Hubbard, Wm Barth & Eldad Gilbert be appointed <u>Tything men</u>.

Surveyors of highways. <u>Voted</u>, that Jonas Merwin, Nathan Peck, Asahel Tuttle,
Laban Smith, Dan Tolles, Luther Bradley, Elisha Benham, Nathan Platt, Normand Dexter, Levi Beecher & Eleazer Hotchkiss Junr be appointed surveyors
of highways.

Constables. Voted that John Skinner, Horace Beach, Benjamin R. Fowler, Erastus
Osborn, Ebenezer Fowler and Nehemiah Kimberly be appointed <u>Constables</u>.

Fence Viewers. Voted that Hezekiah Hotchkiss, Isaac Dickerman, Isaac Tom-
plinson, Enos Smith, Henry Munson, Stephen Prindle and Joseph Munson be
<u>Fence Viewers</u>.

Pound keepers. <u>Voted</u> that Augustus Frisbie, Henry Munson, Clement Goodale,
James B. Reynolds, Elias Alling, Nathan Platt, Cheney Ames, Elisha Dickerman, John A. Thomas and Jesse Alling be <u>Pound-keepers.</u>

Sealer. Voted that Leverit Griswold be sealer of Weights & Measures.

Treasurer. Voted, that Nathan Beers be appointed Treasurer.

Agents. Voted, that the Selectmen be appointed <u>Agents</u> for the Town for the
year ensuing and that either of them with the consent of the majority be authorized to appear, sue and defend*[,]* or act as Agents aforesaid.

Tax. Voted, that a tax of six cents on the dollar be laid on the list for the year
1817, payable on the 1st day of February 1818, and that John Skinner be Collector of said tax.

Collector. Voted that John Skinner be collector of the State Tax.

[p. 62] Highways. Voted, that the Selectmen lay out in repairing highways in
the town of New Haven, at their discretion, any sum, not exceeding three
hundred dollars.

Voted to adjourn till the last monday of december next & meet at the State
house in s^d town at 2 oClock, P.M.

[DECEMBER 29, 1817]

AT A TOWN MEETING HOLDEN BY ADJOURNMENT AT THE STATE
HOUSE IN NEW HAVEN ON THE 29TH DAY OF DECR 1817.

Moderator. Doctr Levi Ives was chosen Moderator.

Selectman. Voted, to excuse Col[.] Elisha Punderson[1] from serving as a Selectman
for the year ensuing.

Lister. Voted, that William Mix be appointed a Lister.

Poundkeeper. Voted, that Thomas Maccumber Junr be appointed a Poundkeeper.

Selectman. Voted, that Eleazer Foster be appointed a Selectman.

Geese. Voted, that from the first day of January 1818, till the first day of November 1818, no Geese be suffered to go at large within the limits of New Haven
unless they be yoked with a yoke fifteen inches long, and if any Geese be found
so at large without such yoke they shall be considered damage feasant and liable
to be impounded.

Voted that the Poundage for every Goose so taken damage feasant be 6¼ cents
each.

Constitution. Resolved — That the Representatives of this town in the next General Assembly be, and they are hereby requested to use their influence and exertions that measures be immediately taken for forming a written Constitution
of Civil Government for the State of Connecticut. And that the Town Clerk
furnish said Representatives with a certified copy of the foregoing resolution.[2]

A By-Law Regulating the fishing of Oysters and Clams. At a Town Meeting held in
NewHaven on the 29th day of December 1817, Voted *[p. 63]*

[Oysters and Clam Act.] Voted, that no person or persons be permitted between

---

1. Col. Elisha Punderson (1790 - 1864) served as colonel of the 2nd Regiment, known as the New
Haven "Grays" from 1817 - 1821. See, Jerome B. Lucke, *History of the New Haven Grays, from Sep. 13,
1816, to Sept. 13, 1876* (New Haven: Tuttle, Morehouse & Taylor, 1876), pp. 21 -27
1. This entry is in a different hand than Elisha Munson. The records also do not include a copy of
the New Haven resolution concerning the state constitution.

the first day of April & the 20ᵗʰ day of November, 1818 to take, gather, or collect any oyster shells or oysters, in or upon any of the flats, beaches, rivers, creeks, harbours*[,]* or waters, within the following limits in the Town of New Haven, — viz. — northerly of a line drawn from the old ferry house in New Haven to the old ferry wharf in East Haven, nor southerly of a line drawn from the dwelling house of Amasa Goodyear, in the oyster point quarter, to the point of the beach, on pain of forfeiting for each & every such offence the sum of Seven dollars.

That no person or persons from and after the first of April untill the 10ᵗʰ day of October 1818 shall take or cause to be taken, any oysters in or upon any of the flats, beaches, creeks, harbors, waters*[,]* or shores, within the limits of the Town of New Haven, nor any long clams on Dragon flatts (except as hereafter provided) on pain of forfeiting seven dollars for each offence.

That no person or persons shall catch oysters within the limits of the Town of New Haven, in any season of the year, without culling out the shells & small oysters from each longsfull necessarily, as they are taken up, either from a board attached to the canoe or boat, or from the longs, and throwing the same overboard where taken on pain of forfeiting for each and every such offence the sum of seven dollars.

That Thomas Painter, Ezra Smith, Levi Tuttle, Isaac Tomlinson, Walter Budington, Charles Lewis, Russell Hotchkiss, John A. Rowe, Stephen Bunnell, Robert Talmadge, Joel Goodyear, Jared Richards and Chauncey Smith, be a committee to superintend the catching of oysters & clams within the limits aforesaid, who shall have authority granted to them or either of them within the term limited aforesaid, to grant a permit or permits in writing thereby licencing the person therein named, to take the quantity of oysters or long clams therein mentioned at any place in such permit Specified.

Provided, that no such permit for oysters shall be granted between the *[p. 64]* the first day of April & the tenth day of October 1818 unless upon a certificate under the hand of a physician that oysters will be conducive to the health of the person for whose benefit the permit shall be requested; nor shall such permit be for more than one bushel or be in force for more than twenty four hours from its date. And if any person shall take a larger quantity than is Certified in such permit, such person shall incur the penalty as provided for taking without permit.

That no person shall drive any kind of carriage in or upon any of the oyster banks where oysters are growing within the before mentioned limits, at any season of the year on pain of forfeiting Seven dollars.

That the penalties & forfeitures incurred by any breach of the above regulations shall when recovered, belong, one moiety[1] thereof, to the treasury of the Town, and the other moiety to the person who shall have first given information of such breach to said Committee or to the agent for the Town.

That Roger Sherman Baldwin Esq[r] be appointed agent for the Town to inquire after &c at his discretion to prosecute for the Town in their name & at their expence, all breaches of the foregoing regulations; and that it be made the duty of said Committee to make complaint to said agent of all breaches of s[d] regulations that shall come to their knowledge.

Adjourned without day – Certified by
E. Munson Clerk

[JULY 4, 1818]

Convention & Constitution. AT A TOWN MEETING LEGALLY WARNED AND CONVENED IN NEW HAVEN ON THE 4TH DAY OF JULY 1818, in conformity to a Resolves of the General Assembly for choosing Delegates to attend a Convention to be holden at Hartford on the 4th Wednesday of August next to take into consideration the subject of forming a Constitution of Civil government for this State the Freemen of s[d] town (elected W[m] Bristoll Esq[r] Moderator of the Meeting &c).

[p. 65] Delegates. [M]ade choice of Will[m] Bristoll and Nathan Smith[2] Esq[rs] to represent this town in said Convention.

Adjourned without day – certified by E. Munson Clerk.

[OCTOBER 5, 1818]

AT A TOWN MEETING LEGALLY WARNED AND HELD IN NEW HAVEN ON THE FIRST MONDAY OF OCTOBER 1818.

---

1. Moiety means each of two parts of something that can be divided.
2. Nathan Smith (1770 - 1835) was a graduate of the Litchfield Law School, prosecuting attorney for New Haven, and U.S. Senator from 1833 - 1835.

[Constitution.] Pursuant to a Resolve of Assembly passed at the May session of the General Assembly AD 1818 and the direction of the Convention of Delegates held pursuant to said Resolve on the 4th Wednesday of August last to take into consideration the Constitution of Civil government recommended by said Convention.

[Moderator.] The hon[ble] William Bristol was chosen Moderator of the Meeting. *Constitution.* The constitution of Civil Government was by the Town Clerk submitted to the consideration of the qualified voters of said Town for their probation and ratification, and the question being taken there were in favour of approving and ratifying said Constitution <u>four hundred and thirty votes</u> of the qualified voters present at said meeting — and against ratifying and approving said Constitution of Civil government <u>two hundred and eighteen votes</u> of such quallified voters.[1]

Adjourned without day   certified by Elisha Munson Clerk

[NOVEMBER 30, 1818]

AT THE ANNUAL TOWN MEETING HELD AT THE COURT HOUSE IN THE TOWN OF NEW HAVEN ON THE 30TH DAY OF NOV[R] 1818.

Moderator. Charles Denison[2] Esq[r] was chosen Moderator.

Clerk. Elisha Munson was chosen Clerk..

Statement of Accounts. The Selectmen exhibited statements of the expenditures and receipts of the Town during the past year, which were read – after a lengthy debate –

<u>Voted</u>, that the Hon[ble] Simeon Baldwin, Ralph J. Ingersoll Esq[r] and Capt[.] Samuel Punderson be a Committee to investigate the statement of the receipts

---

1. The new state constitution was ratified by the various towns through the month of October and called for the separation of church and state in Connecticut. It also allowed for universal white manhood suffrage. Full universal suffrage for all males came following the Civil War. Women would not receive the right to vote until 1920, 102 years after the ratification of this vote.

2. Charles Denison (1778 - 1825) graduated Yale College in 1798, became an instructor at William College, then returned to New Haven to practice law. He was a member of the Connecticut General Assembly from (1809 to 1820), serving as Clerk of the Lower House (1811-1814) and Speaker of the House (1815-1817). See, https://www.cga.ct.gov/hco/books/State_Officers_Members_CT_1776-1881.pdf.

and expenditures of the Town during the past year and *[p. 66]* report to some future meeting.

Selectmen. Voted that Isaac Gilbert, Anthony P. Sanford, E. Foster, Ralph I. Ingersoll, John Rowe, Thomas Ward and Laban Smith be appointed Selectmen.

Grand-jurors. Voted that John Beach, Charles A. Ingersoll,[1] Henry C. Flagg,[2] Samuel R. Crane, Oliver Clark & Scovil Hinman be appointed Grand-jurors.

Listers. Voted, that Beriah Bradley, Elihu Sanford, Caleb Mix, Andrew Kidston, Eli B. Austin, William Granger, Stephen Bunnel, Zina Hotchkiss, John Rowe, Fredrick Le Forge, Enos Smith & Nathan Platt be appointed Listers.

Tythingmen. Voted, that David Ritter, Samuel P. Davis, John Hempsted, Hezekiah Howe, John Beach, James F. Barnes, Bradford Smith, Enos Smith, Anthony H. Sherman, Lyman Smith, Joseph B. *[...]*[3], Solomon Woodruff, Fredrick L^{e}Forge, Jesse Alling, Elihu Hitchcock, David Hinman, William A. Thompson, James Brewster, William Fairchild Junr and Asa Bradley be appointed Tythingmen.

Surveyors of highways. Voted that Jonus Merwin, Nathan Peck, Leman Dunning, Asahel Tuttle, James Reynolds, Stephen Alling, Seth Barnes, John Hunt, Ebenezer Townsend, Elisha Punderson, Caleb A. Townsend, Clement Goodall, Laban Smith of West Haven, Levi Beecher and Nathan Platt be Surveyors of highways.

Constables. Voted, that Horrace Beach, Erastus Osborn, Ebenezer Fowler, David Butler, Jonathan Atwater and Thomas Atwater be appointed Constables.

Fence viewers. Voted that Hezekiah Hotchkiss, Isaac Dickerman, Isaac Tomlinson, William Powel, Edmund Smith, Henry Monson & Joseph Prindle be appointed Fence viewers.

---

1. Charles A. Ingersoll (1797/8 - 1850) received a M.A. in law from Yale in 1826. He was clerk of court for the United States District Court and the United States Circuit Court for the District of Connecticut from 1820 to 1853. He was a probate judge in New Haven from 1829 to 1853, and a state's attorney for Connecticut from 1849 to 1853. See, *Biographical Directory of Federal Judges*, a public domain publication of the Federal Judicial Center.

2. Henry C. Flagg (1790/92 - 1863) graduated from Yale College in 1811, served as editor of *The Connecticut Herald*, and mayor of New Haven from 1834-39. See, Dexter, *Biographical Sketches of the Graduates of Yale College,* VI: 384 - 386.

3. Left blank.

Pound-keepers. Voted that Elisha Dickerman, Augustus Frisbie, Henry Monson, Clement Goodell, Thomas Maucumber, *[p. 67]* Thomas Peck. Amasa Goodyear, James Reynolds, Elias Alling, Thomas Atwater and Nathan Platt be <u>Pound keepers</u>.

Sealer. <u>Voted</u>, that Leverit Griswold be sealer of weights and measures.

Treasurer. <u>Voted</u>, that Nathan Beers be appointed <u>Treasurer</u>.

West-bridge. <u>Voted</u>, that Eleazer Foster, Elisha Punderson and John Hunt Jun[r] be a Committee to examine the West bridge near Hotchkisstown and report make to the next meeting.[1]

[Accounts] Committee. <u>Voted</u> that Anthony P. Sanford, Henry W. Edwards and Samuel R. Crane, be a Committee to ascertain what sum it will be expedient to raise to pay the debts now oweing from the town and meet the expenditures for the ensueing year – also devise some expeditious mode of collecting the taxes.

Collector. <u>Voted</u> that Horace Beach be appointed Collector of the State Tax. Voted to adjourn till the last monday of decem[r] next and meet at the Court house at two oClock P.M.

Certified by Elisha Munson Clerk.

[DECEMBER 28, 1818]

AT A TOWN MEETING, HOLDEN BY ADJOURNMENT, AT THE STATE HOUSE IN NEW HAVEN ON THE 28TH DAY OF DECEMBER, 1818.

[Moderator.] Levi Ives Esq[r] was chosen Moderator.

Bridge. The Committee who were appointed at the last meeting to examine the West bridge near Hotchkiss town made their Report which was accepted.

Statement of Accounts. The Committee who were appointed a Committee to investigate the Statement of the Receipts & Expenditures of the Town during

---

1. The clerk inverted the words "report " and "make." Hotchkisstown was the early name for Westville. The bridge in question is now likely the Whalley Avenue bridge crossing the West River near Fitch Street on the edge of Edgewood Park in New Haven. See, Osterweis, p. 487. Also see, https://www.google.com/maps/place/Blake+St,+New+Haven,+CT/.

the past year made Report, which was read — and after debate, accepted and lodged on file.

Tax. The Committee who were appointed to ascertain what sum it would be expedient to raise by tax to pay the debts now oweing from the Town and meet the expenditures for the ensuing year made a verbal Report... after a lengthy debate.

Taxes. Voted that a Tax of eight cents on the dollar be laid on the list for the year 1818, and that John Skinner be Collector of said Tax — and that the Tax become payable on the first day of *[p. 68]* febuary 1819.

Constable. Voted that John Skinner be appointed Constable for the ensuing year.

Selectmen excused. Voted. That Capt Laban Smith, Eleazer Foster Esqr and John Rowe be excused from serving as Selectmen.

Selectmen appointed. Voted that Samuel Huggins be appointed a Selectman for the year ensuing.

Listers. Voted, that Roger S. Skinner be appointed a Lister for the ensuing year. Voted, that Hezekiah Auger and John Fitch be appointed Listers.

Poundkeeper. Voted that John Rowe be appointed a Pound keeper.

Constable. Voted, that Zina Hotchkiss be appointed a Constable.

Bye-Law Regulating the Fishery of Oysters and Clams. At a Town Meeting held in New Haven on the 28th day of December 1818:

Voted, That no person or persons be permitted, between the first day of April & the twentieth day of November 1819, to take, gather, or collect any oystershells or oysters, in or upon any of the flats, beaches, rivers, creeks, harbours, or waters within the following limits in the town of New Haven, viz. northerly of a line drawn from the old ferry-house in New Haven to the old ferry wharf in East Haven — nor southerly of a line drawn from the dwelling house of Amasa Goodyear, in the Oysterpoint quarter to the point of the beach on pain of forfeiting for each & every such offence the sum of sixteen Dollars.

That no person or persons, from an after the 1st day of April until the 10th day of October, 1819, shall take or cause to be taken any oysters in or upon, on of the flats, beaches, creeks, harbours, waters[,] or shores, within the limits of the town of New Haven, nor any long clams on Dragon flats, (except as hereafter provided) on pain of forfeiting sixteen Dollars for reach offence.

That no person or persons, shall catch oysters within the limits of the town of New Haven, at any season without culling out the shells & small oysters from each tongsfull successively, as they are taken up,either from a board attached to the canoe or boat or from the tongs and throwing the same over-board where taken, on pain of forfeiting for each and every such offence the sum of sixteen Dollars.

That no person or persons shall catch oysters within the limits of the town of New Haven, at any time, in the night season, between *[p. 69]* the setting & rising of the sun, on pain of foreiting for each offence, the sum of sixteen Dollars.

That Thomas Painter, Ezra Smith, Levi Tuttle, Isaac Tomlinson, Walter Buddington, Charles Lewis, Russel Hotchkiss, John Rowe, Stephen Bunnell, Robert Talmadge, Amasa Goodyear, Jere Richards & Chauncy Smith, be a committee to superintend the catching of oysters and clams within the lim-its aforesaid; who shall *[have]* authority granted to them or either of them, within the term limited aforesaid, to grant a permit or permits, in writing, thereby liciencing the person named, to take the quantity of oysters or long clams therein mentioned, at any place in such permit specified — Provided, That no such permit for oysters shall be granted between the first day of April & the 10th of October, 1819, unless upon a certificate, under the hand of a physician, that oysters will be conducive to the health of the person for whose benefit the permit shall be requested; nor shall such permit be for more than one bushel, or be in force for more than twenty-four hours from its date. And if any person shall take a larger quantity than is specified in such permit, such person shall incur the penalty as provided for taking without a permit.

That no person shall drive any kind of carriage in or upon any of the oyster banks where oysters are growing, within the before mentioned limits at any season of the year, on pain of forfeiting sixteen Dollars.

That the penalties & forfeitures incurred by any breach of the above regulations, shall when recovered, belong, one moiety thereof to the treasury
of the town & the other moiety to the person who shall have first given
information of such breach to said committee, or to the Agent for the town.

That Roger Sherman Baldwin, Esq. be appointed Agent for the town, to
inquire after & at his discretion to prosecute for the town, in their name and
at their expence, all breaches of the foregoing regulations; & that it be made
the duty of said Committee to ask complaint to said Agent of all breaches
of said regulations that shall come to their knowledge.

Adjourned without day — Certified by — Elisha Munson
Clerk.

[MAY 5, 1819]

AT A TOWN MEETING WARNED AND HELD AT THE COURT HOUSE
IN NEW HAVEN ON THE 5TH DAY OF MAY 1819.

[Moderator.] Isaac Mills[1] Esquire was chosen Moderator.

[West Haven and North Milford.] A Petition from the Inhabitants of the Parishes
of West Haven and North Milford was read & considered.[2]

Whereupon — Voted, that this Town will not oppose the Petition of Ichabod
A. Woodruff, Nathan Platt and others for the incorporation of a New Town,
But that it is proper an Agent should be appointed to attend to the aforesaid
Petition and procure proper provisions for the maintenance of the Bridges and
the support of the poor, for the establishment of the dividing lines and in rela-
tion to the fishery of Oysters and Clams. Voted, that R. I. Ingersoll and Charles
Bostwick Esq[rs] and Capt. Thomas Ward be Agents for the above purpose.

Adjourned without day.   Elisha Munson Clerk.

---

1. Isaac Mills (1767 - 1843) was a 1786 graduate of Yale College, who studied law and became one
of New Haven's leading citizens as an attorney, judge, and founder of Center Church. See, Dexter,
Biographical Sketches of the Graduates of Yale College, Vol. 4: 498 - 499.
2. This petition led to the eventual incorporation of the town of Orange in 1822, which included
North Milford and West Haven. West Haven did not gain its own independence until 1921, and was
the last town in the state to do so. See, Malia, *Visible Saints, passim.*

[OCTOBER 4, 1819]

AT A LEGAL TOWN MEETING, HELD AT THE COURT HOUSE IN NEW HAVEN ON THE 4ᵀᴴ DAY OF OCTOBER 1819.

[Moderator.] Levi Ives Esquire was chosen Moderator.

Assessors. After the reading of the Laws, the following persons were chosen to be Assessors viz. Elisha Munson, Henry Ward, Anthony P. Sanford, William Mix, and Elisha Punderson.

[p. 70] [Board of Relief.] And the following persons were chosen to be the Board of Relief viz. Isaac Gilbert, John Miles, John Rowe, Nathan Peck & Andrew Kidston.

Adjourned without day.

Certified by — Elisha Munson Clerk

[NOVEMBER 22, 1819]

AT THE ANNUAL TOWN MEETING LEGALLY WARNED AND HELD AT THE STATE HOUSE IN THE TOWN OF NEWHAVEN ON THE 22ᵈ DAY OF NOVᴿ 1819.

[Moderator.] The Honᵇˡᵉ David Daggett was chosen Moderator.

[Clerk.] Elisha Munson Clerk.

Accounts. The Selectmen exhibited a statement of the receipts and expenditures of the Town during the last year which was read and considered.

[Accounts Committee.] Voted that James Goodrich, Abraham Bishop[1], and Simeon Baldwin be appointed a Committee to investigate said statement of Receipts and expenditures and Report to some future meeting.

---

1. Abraham Bishop (1763 - 1844) graduated from Yale in 1778, was admitted to the bar in 1785, and is known as a leading, but controversial, figure in the American Enlightenment movement. A champion of women's rights and emancipation, Bishop served as collector of the port of New Haven and is credited as the founder of Wooster Square. See, https://yalealumnimagazine.com/articles/4379-abraham-bishop.

Selectmen. <u>Voted.</u> That Elisha Punderson, Isaac Gilbert, Ralph I. Ingersoll, Nathan Peck and Henry Denison be appointed Selectmen.

Grandjurors. Voted. That Dennis Kimberly, John Beach and Roger S. Baldwin be appointed Grand-jurors.

Tythingmen. <u>Voted.</u> That Grindley Harisson, Isaac Dickerman Jun[r], Solomon C. Woodruff, Sidney Hull, John Skinner, William Peckham, Thomas Macumber, Anthony H. Sherman, John Hempsted, John M. Barlow, Elias Gilbert, William Barth, Erastus Hoadley, Roswell Reynolds, Jeremiah Barnett, Falame Meloy,[1] Nemeiah Kimberly, James Reynolds, Wm. Kimberly, Isaac Wise and Isaac English be appointed Tythingmen.

Surveyors of highways. Voted, that Caleb A. Townsend, Laban Smith, Samuel Huggins, Nathan Platt and Elisha Punderson be appointed Surveyors of highways.

Constables. Voted that John Skinner, John Scott, Ebenezer *[p. 71]* Fowler, Horace Beach, Thomas Atwater, Nehemiah Kimberly and David Butler be Constables. *[Treasurer.]* Voted that Nathan Beers be appointed Treasurer.

Fence-viewers. Voted, that Stephen Ball, Henry Monson, Jesse Buck, Hezekiah Hotckiss, Aaron Thomas, Joseph Prindle, Silas Hotchkiss & Medad Atwater Jun[r] be appointed Fence Viewers.

Pound-keepers. Voted. That Elisha Dickerman, Henry Monson, John Rowe, Clement Goodell, Augustus Frisbie, Nathan Platt, Alva Gaylord and James Reynolds be appointed Pound keepers.

Sealers. Voted that, Leverit Griswold and William Mansfield Jun[r] be appointed sealers of Weights & Measures.

Collector. Voted –That John Skinner be appointed Collector of the State tax – Also Collector of the Town tax.

Com[tee] d' Slavery. Voted. That the Hon[ble] David Daggett, the Hon[ble] Simeon Baldwin and Seth P. Staples Esq[r] be appointed to take into consideration the expediency of presenting a memorial to Congress relative to the introduction

---

1. Falame Meloy (1792 - 1872) was a veteran of the War of 1812, spouse of Amarilla Richards (1789 - 1861), and a resident of Orange.

of Slavery into any new State, and Report to the next meeting.[1]

Poor. Voted, that the above named Committee and the Selectmen of the Town be appointed to take into consideration the subject of supplying those of the poor who remain out of the Almshouse.

A Survey. A survey of a continuation of Fleet Street extended southerly on to Union Wharf was read and submited to the consideration of the Meeting. Whereupon — Voted — That said survey be accepted and approved, provided no expence be incuoed *[sic.]* by the Town in opening and making the continuation of said Street.

Voted that this meeting be adjourned till the last monday of December next & meet at the Court house at 2 oClock P.M.

Certified by Elisha Munson Clerk

[DECEMBER 27, 1819]

[p. 72] AT A TOWN MEETING HOLDEN AT THE COURTHOUSE IN NEW HAVEN (BY ADJOURNMENT) ON THE 27TH DAY OF DECEMBER 1819.

[Moderator.] The Honble David Daggett being Moderator. New Haven

Selectmen. Voted, that two persons be added to the present number of Selectmen.

[Selectmen.] Voted that Thomas Ward be appointed a Selectman. Voted that John Rowe be appointed a Selectman.

Constables. Voted that Elisha Munson be appointed Constable. Voted that Jonathan Atwater be appointed Constable.

Surveyors of highways. Voted, that John Hubbard be appointed Surveyor of highways. Voted that William A. Thompson be a Surveyor of highways.

Poundkeeper. Voted that Thomas Macumber be appointed Pound keeper.

---

1. Among the three men on the committee, David Daggett was then serving as Connecticut's senator. Simeon Baldwin served on the Connecticut Supreme Court of Errors and was a supporter of colonization for African Americans. Seth P. Staples was a distinguished attorney and founder of what became Yale University Law School.

Grand-jurors. Voted, that Charles A. Ingersoll and Stephen Bunnel are appointed Grand-jurors.

Accounts. The Committee appointed at the last meeting to examine the Statement of the Selectmen relating to the Receipts and expenditures of the Town during the past year made their Report which was read and considered. Voted, that said Report be accepted & approved.

Report d' Survey. A survey of the widening of Water Street at the head of Union Wharf particularly of the land lately owned by Thaddeus Beecher was read and considered. Whereupon Voted that the Report on [the] survey be accepted and approved provided no expence be incurred by the Town in opening or widening said Street and no expence relative to the land described in said survey.

Slavery. The existence of Slavery in the United States, being in the opinion of this meeting, an evil of great magnitude, they consider it the high and solemn duty of the government of this free and enlightened nation, to prevent, by all institutional means, the expansion of it.

It is thereupon — Resolved that in the opinion of this meeting the United States Congress have the undoubted right to prohibit the admission of Slavery into any State or Territory hereafter to be formed and admitted into the United States.

Resolved that of the opinion of this meeting the Omission of Slavery into any such State or Territory, would be opposed to the Genius and spirit of our Government, and injury to the highest interests of the Nation.

Resolved, that the Senators and Representatives from this *[p. 73]* State in Congress, be respectfully and earnestly requested to use their most strenuous exertions to prevent the further extention of slavery in the United States.

It is further resolved that the Town Clerk cause a copy of these Resolutions to be transmitted to one of our Senators one a like copy to one of our Representatives to be submitted to the respective Houses of Congress.[1]

---

1. These resolutions were in response to the Congressional debate over the admission of the Missouri territory as a slave-holding state. Northern states, and New England in particular, opposed the expansion of slavery, as each slave would be counted as three-fifths of a person, thus providing the South with an advantage when it came to the number of Congressional representatives chosen, which were based on population. The issue was settled, at least for the time being, by the passage of The Missouri Compromise, which became law in 1821. See, http://www.historynet.com/missouri-

Bankruptcy. To the Honble the Senate and House of Representatives of the United States of America in Congress assembled. The Petition of the Chamber of Commerce of New Haven in the State of Connecticut humbly shewth that in their opinion, it has become highly expedient that a uniform law on the subject of Bankruptices should be enacted by Congress.[1]

The wise and good men who framed the Constitution of the United States, made express provision in that instrument, for such laws, believing no doubt that the time would come, when the exercise of that power would be not only fit but highly necessary. In the opinion of your Petioners that time has already come, laws the benefit of insolvent debtors exist in allmost every State in the Union. The Provisions of these laws are vary variant from each other in the several States, in many instances complex and capable of being understood only by those who are obliged to expound them.

In the extensive commerce existing between distant parts of the United States and between the individuals of this nation and individuals of other nations the experience of every day shews the wisdom of the provisions in the Constitution above mentioned & executed supposing the power of Congress not exercised.

The embarrisments experienced throughout the commercial world produced by causes well understood by the member of you honorable body, are every where seen and every where felt and perhaps in no Country to a greater degree than in the United States. Individual Bankruptcies, and individual sufferings in consequence of this state of things are common to all our towns, cities and villages.

The Petitioners forbear to dwell eminently on other subject they feel an entire confidence that by an extended and elaborate discussion of it they could afford to your honorable body no new light, nor by any manifestation of zeal, secure a more favorable attention to this request than the wisdom and *[p. 74]* patriotism of Congress will be ever ready to yield to the reasonable request of any portion of the people of this Country. They will only declare

---

compromise.
1. Congress repealed the Bankruptcy Act of 1800 in 1803, citing its high costs and corruption. Individual states were then left to fill the void, causing years of lawsuits among debtors and creditors from different states. That changed in 1819 when the U.S. Supreme Court ruled that state courts could not dismiss debts from other states. See, Federal Judicial Center, *The Evolution of U.S. Bankruptcy Law,* http://www.rib.uscourts.gov/newhome/docs/the_evolution_of_bankruptcy_law.pdf.

their entire conviction of the propriety and neccesity of an immediate exercise by Congress of the powers vested in them to pass uniform laws on the subject of bankruptcies.[1]

Dated at Newhaven this 27ᵗʰ December 1819.
From the Chamber of Commerce
Isaac Tomlinson President

[DECEMBER 27, 1819]

AT A TOWN MEETING HOLDEN AT THE COURTHOUSE IN NEW HAVEN (BY ADJOURNMENT) AT NEW HAVEN ON THE 27TH OF DECEMBER 1819.

[Moderator.] The Honble David Daggett *being Moderator.*

Selectmen. Voted that two persons be added to the present number of Selectmen.

[Selectmen.] Voted that Thomas Ward be appointed a Selectman. Voted that John Rowe be appointed a Selectman.

Constables. Voted that Elishu Munson be appointed Constable. Voted that Jonathan Atwater be appointed Constable.

[Bankruptcies.] The Petition of the Chamber of Commerce having been read and considered. Voted that this Town approve thereof and that the Senators and the representatives of this State in Congress be requested to promote the object there of by using their influence to procure laws on the subject of — bankruptcies, to be passed.

It is further resolved that the town clerks cause a copy of the foregoing petition and resolution to be transmitted to one of the Senators and a like copy to one of the Representatives of this state in Congress to be submitted to the respective Houses of Congress.

Tax. Voted that a tax of six cents on a dollar be laid on the list of 1818 and made payable on the first day of February 1820.

---

2. Spurring on the Chamber of Commerce's petition was the first national financial crisis known as the Panic of 1819. See, Murray N. Rothbard, *The Panic of 1819 (1962), pp. 1 - 24.*

[Oysters and Clams.] A Bylaw regulating the fishery of Oysters and Clams. Voted That no person or persons be permitted between the first day of April and the 20 day of November 1820 to take, gather, or collect any oyster shells or oysters in or upon any of the flats, beaches, rivers, creeks, harbours or waters, within the following limits in the town of New haven going northerly on a line drawn from the old ferry house in New Haven to the Old Ferry wharf in East Haven nor southerly of a line drawn from the Dwelling house of Amasa Goodyear in the Oyster Point Quarter, to the point of the beach nor any round clams in the West River on pain of forfeiting for each and every such offense the sum of seven dollars – That no person or persons from and after the first day of April until the 10th day of October 1820. Shall take or cause to be taken any oysters, in or upon any of the flats, beaches, creeks, harbours, waters, or shores within the limits of the town of New Haven, nor any long clams *[p. 75]* claims on Dragon flats (except as is hereafter provided) on pain of forfeiting seven dollars for each offense.

By law of Oysters and Clams. That no person or persons shall catch oysters within the limits of the town of New Haven at any season of the year without culling out the shells and small Oysters from each tongs full successively, as they are taken up either from a board attached to the canoe or boat or from the tongs and throwing then same overboard where taken, on pain of forfeiting for each and every such offense the sum of seven dollars.

That no person or persons shall catch oysters within the limits of the town of New Haven at any time in the night season between the setting and rising of the sun on pain of forfeiting for each and every offense the sum of seven dollars.

That Thomas Painter, Ezra Smith, Levi Tuttle, Isaac Tomlinson, Walter Budington, Charles Lewis, Russell Hotchkiss, John Rowe, Stephen Bunnell, Robert Talmadge, Joel Goodyear, Gere Richards, and Chauncey Smith be a committee to superintend the catching of Oysters and Clams within the limits aforesaid; who shall have authority appointed to them, or either of them within the term limited aforesaid to grant a permit or permits in writing, thereby licensing the person or persons in writing, thereby licensing the person or persons therein named to take the quantity of Oysters or long clams therein mentioned at any place in such permit specified, Provided that no such permit for oysters shall be granted between the first day of April and the 10th day of October 1820, unless upon a certificate maid in the hand of a Phicisian that Oysters will be conducive to the health of the person for whose benefit the permit shall be requested; nor hall such permit be for more than one bushel, on be in force for more than twenty four hours from to date. And of any person shall take a larger quantity than so specified in such permit such person shall incur the penalty as is provided for taking without a permit.

That no person shall drive any kind of carriage on or upon any of the Oyster banks where oysters are growing *[p. 76]* growing, within the before mentioned Limits at any season of the year, on pain of forfeiting seven dollars.

That the penalties and forfeitures incurred by any breach of the above regulations shall belong to any person who shall sue for and prosecute the same to effect. – Adjourned without day.

Certified by Elisha Munson Clerk

Introduction To Freemen's Meetings of New Haven 1769 - 1826

The first known version of a Freeman's Oath administered in the North Amer-icn colonies appeared on the face of a half sheet of paper printed in Cambridge, Massachusetts, in 1639.

The historical significance of that small document can not be overestimated. It "afforded printed evidence that nowhere in it is any reference made to the King's Majesty, or of allegiance to any power on earth save that of their own Government as constituted."[1]

New Haven settlers agreed to a similar Freeman's Oath in 1639that was equally radical in its omission to the King:

> Yow shall neither plott, practise, nor consent, to any euill, or hurt, against this Jurisdiction, or any part of it, nor against The Civill Gouerment here estab-lished: And if you shall know any person or persons wch intend, plott, or con-spire anything, wch tends to the hurt, or prjudice, of the same, you shall timely discouer the same to Lawfull Authority here established, and you shall assist, and be helpfull, in all the affaires of the Jurisdiction, and by all meanes shall promoue the publique wellfare of the same, according to yor place, abillity, and opportunity; you shall giue due honor to the Lawfull Magistrats, and shall be obedient, and subject, to all the wholesome Lawes, and Orders, allready made, or wch shall be hereafter made, by Lawfull Authority afforesaide, and that both in yor person, and estate, and when you shall be duely called, to giue yor vote, or suffrage, in any Election, or touching any other matter, wch concerneth this Common wellth, yow shall giue it, as in yor conscience, you shall judg may con-duse to the best good of the same.[2]

Some 126 years prior to the Declaration of Independence, American colonists were already pledging their fidelity to a New World order. In New Haven that meant Freemen in full standing in the Congregational Church as well as Plant-ers, 21 years and older with a certain amount of taxable property that earned them the right to vote in town meetings. In some form those same criteria remained in place until Connecticut drafted its first state constitution in 1818 that officially separated the affairs of the Congregational Church from the State of Connecticut.

---

1. Charles Evans, " Oaths of Allegiance in Colonial New England," Reprinted from the *Proceedings of the American Antiquarian Society for October, 1921* (Wooster, MA, The Davis Press, 1922), *http://www.gutenberg. org/files/53843/53843-h/53843-h.htm#h45a.*
2. *Ibid.*

Freemen's Meetings of New Haven
1769 - 1826[1]

[September 19, 1769]

At a freemans meeting in New Haven Sepr 19th 1769, the following persons were admitted freemen & Sworn in the freemens meeting.

Gad wells, Seth Downs, William Pluymart, Benjamin Alling, John Troop, John Sanford, Caleb Clark, James Hull, David Osborn, Henry Barns, Saml Holt, John Brocket J^r, Eben^r Brocket, Saml Ives, James Heaton, Saml Potter, Stephen Moltrop, Enos Granis, Hezekiah Pierpoint, Jesse Ludinton, Isaac Brocket, Jacob Hitchcock, Daniel Rexford Ju^r, Joseph Holt, Samuel Davenport, Israel Potter, Jonathan Barns, Ichabod Russel, Isaac Granis, Elip^t Pardee, Aaron Page, Isaac Moltrop, Daniel Clark, Caleb Cooper, Seth Barns, Daniel Holt, Asher Maltrop, Jesse Wolcot, James Bishop, Abel Brocket, Stephen Ives, Jacob Tharp, Abel Tharp, Stephen Pardee, Francis Browne, Titus Tharp, Joseph Turner, William Mansor, Moses Wills, Elihu Sperry and Revd Jonathan Edwards.

[April 9, 1770]

At a freemans meeting in New Haven april 9th 1770.

The following persons were admitted freemen & took ye freemens oath in the meeting. James Todd J^r, Isaac Tharp J^r, Sam^{ll} Martin, Saml Wales, Nehimiah Toles, Peter Eastman, Lemuel Bradly, Obed Blackslee, Phileman Smith, Silas Kimberly, Rutherford Trowbridge, Peter Perkins, Elihu Hotchkis, Zina Bradly, Levi Tuttle, Elihu Rogers, Titus Peck, Lazarus Toles, Hez^h Tuttle, David Beecher, Aner Ives, Saml Downs, Edward Perkins, Tim^o Lounsbury, Hez^h Sperry & William Glen.

[September 18, 1770]

At a meeting of the Freemen in the Town of New Haven Sepr 18th 1770 the following persons were admitted freemen and took the freemens oath in the meeting. Saml Chew, Robert Grant, Moses Austin and Israel Bishop.

[April 3, 1771]

At a meeting of the freemens in the Town of New Haven April 3^d 1771 the following persons were admitted freemen and took the oath by Law Provided

---

1. Before being unbound, the volume of New Haven Town Records covering the years 1769 - 1807 included the Freemen's Meetings, from 1769 - 1826 in the back of the volume.

in the meeting. Joseph Lyman, Nathan Strong, Caleb Mix, Daniel Willmot, John Row, Abram Norton, Job Todd, Saml Clark, Joseph Hotchkis, Titus Mansfield, William Crane, Elias Shipman, Nathl Beech, James Ives J^r, John Beecher J^r, and Jesse Stevens.

[September 17, 1771]

At a meeting of the Freemen of the Town of New Haven Sepr 17 1771 the following persons were admitted freemen & took the freemens Oath in the meeting. Sam^{ll} White, Hez^h How, John Wolcot, William Sanford, John Denison, Phin^s Bradly J^r, and Sam^{ll} Hotchkiss.

[April 13, 1772]

At a meeting of the freemen of the Town of New Haven april 13th 1772 the following persons were admitted freemen and took the oath by Law Provided in the meeting. John Lewis, John Trumble, Theop^s Munson J^r, Hez^h Tuttle, Ezra Tuttle, William Scot, James Plant, Stephen Mix, David Mix, Saml Mix, Saml Wilmot, Stephen Bristoll, Sam^{ll} Sherman, John Miles, Enoch Jacob, Joel Thorp, Pierpoint Edwards, Paul Noyes, Jos Humaston, Giles Pierpoint, Saml Newton, and Sam^{ll} Griswald.

[September 15, 1772]

At a meeting of the freemen of the Town of New Haven Sepr 15th 1772 the following persons were admitted freemen and took the freemens oath. Benjamin Pierpoint, Enos Brocket, Caleb Hitchcock J^r, Titus Frost, Thomas Wooster & Mr Nathl Sherman.

[April 13, 1773]

At a meeting of the freemen of the Town of New Haven april 13th 1773 the following persons were admitted freemen and took the freemens oath. The Revd Allen Mather, Phileman Marry, Amos Sheppard, Titus Barns, James Turner, Robt Fairchild, James Prescott, Russel Clark, John Sherman, Henry Dagget, Thomas Ives, Joel Brad1y, Dan^{ll} Tallmadge J^r, Solomon Tuttle, Eben^r Barns, John Davenport, John Hill and Caleb Doolittle.

[September 21, 1774]

At a meeting of the freemen of the Town of New Haven Sepr 21st 1774 the following persons were admitted freemen and took the freemens oath. Mark Levinsworth, Jesse Blackslee, Jabez Tuttle, Levi Cooper, John Robinson, Saml Smith, Eben^r Blackslee, Maj^r Lines, Stephen Ives and David Phipps.

[April 11, 1774]

At a meeting of the freemen in the Town of New Haven April 11th 1774 The following persons were admitted freemen and took the freemens oath in the meeting. Job Potter, Solomon Williams, Tim° Dwight, Achilles Mansfield, Obed Johnson, Willm Sherman J^r, Barnabas Mulford, Thomas Atwater, Nath^11 Fitch, Ezekiel Tuttle, Joseph Dickerman, John Hubbard, Joseph Collins, Stephen Cooper J^r, Benjamin Hull, Titus Bradly, Charles Bradly, Hez^h Warner, Daniel Bontueou, Robert Woodhouse, Gold Sherman, Elisha Mix, Abr^m Heminway, John McClive, Saml Clark J^r, Caleb Geer, Asa Sperry, Zacheus Candee, Asael Kimberly, Epheram Turner, Seth Peck, Azariah Perkins Jr., Eben^r Heaton J^r, Joel Hotchkiss J^r, Tim° Heaton, Titus Goodyear, Abr^m Thompson J^r, Josiah Mansfield, Willm Sperry, David Mulford, Eben^r Bradly, Thad^s Clark, Edward Jacob Smith, Ichabod Bishop and John Thompson.

[April 10, 1775]

At a meeting of the Freemen of the Town of New Haven April the 10th 1775, the following persons were admitted Freemen, and took the freemens Oath. Abner Bristol, Willmot Bradley, Justus Johnson Fitch, David Clark, David Munson, David Smith, Benjamin Peck, James Humaston, Roger Peck, Timothy Ball Junr, Joseph Prindle, John Russel, Enoch Newton, Joseph Beecher Junr, Jason Bradley, Joseph Gilbert, Ebenezer Todd, Jonathan Tuttle, John Horton Junr, Gaskell Woodward, John Wooden Junr, Elijah Osborne, Jonathan Roberts, Saml Smith, Elijah Prindle, Nehemiah Johnson, Edmund Clark, Gamaliel Benham, Reuben Thomas, John Fuller, Samuel Allen, Edward Rossfelt , Elisha Alling, Abel Atwater, Isaiah Blakesley, Jotham Allen, Samuel Townsend, Timothy Brown, Enos Dickerman, Obed Bradley, Timothy Tharp, Rosseter Griffen, Oliver Smith, Stephen Herrick, Joseph Hull, Nathaniel Kimberly, Jared Hemmingway, Richard Hood, Buckminster Brintnal, Eleazer Oswould, Roger Alden, Hezekiah Sabin Junr, John Chandler, , Nathaniel Tuttle, John Smith, Israel Wheeler, Simeon Sperry, Samuel Nevins, Timothy Andrews J^r, William Walter, John Logus, Timothy Dickerman, Enoch Moulthrop, John Bradley, Jason Wooden, Nathaniel Wooden, Philemon Toles, Eliakim Mallery, George Dudley, Benjamin Wooden Junr, Daniel Russel, Leverit Hubbard Junr, John How, Thomas Burrell, Ebenezer Huggins, Levi Chidsey, Noadiah Carrington, Hezekiah Smith, Isaac Mallery, Bela Strong, Hezekiah Bradley, Levi Pardy, William Grannis, Saml Thompson, Saml Molthrop, Ebenezer Chidsey, Lemuel Sperry, Jacob Pardy, William Everton, Asa Bradley, Benjamin Bur[blank], Jesse Beecher, Solomon Sackett, John Sely, Isaac Smith, Timothy Thompson, Abner Row, Joseph Hemmingway, Moses Hemmingway, Samuel Hemmingway, James Peck Junr, Hope— Cretendon, Joseph Peck, Stephen Brockett, John Woodward Junr, Dan Todd, Lent Sperry, Joseph Granniss, Daniel Hull,

Eli Sacket, Jared Sherman, Timothy Bradley, Noah Atwater, Jared Bradley, Joel Gilbert, Elnathon Toles, John Prindle, Alven Bradley, Sam[l] Sperry.

[September 19, 1775]

At a meeting of the Freemen of the Town of New Haven September the 19th 1775. the following persons were admitted Freemen and took the Oath required by law, viz. Mess[rs] Peter Bonticou[1], Sollomon Phipps, John Culver, Chauncey Dickerman, Abraham Turner, Christopher Hughes, John Platt, John Parker, Jeremiah Platt, Thomas Punderson Jun[r], Samuel Broome, Joel Gilbert, Jesse Denison, Benjamin English Jun[r].

[September 15, 1778]

At a meeting of the Freemen of the Town of New Haven September 15th 1778. the following persons were admitted Freemen and took the Oath required by law, viz. John Whiting, Charles Chauncey, Jonathan Ingersoll, Jeremiah Atwater, John Gills, Seth Peck, Jotham Tuttle, Jacob Tharp, Titus Todd, James Sherman, Mathew Gilbert, Isaac Sherman, Job Todd, Nathan Beers, John Warner, William Plymert, Giles Dayton, Titus Bradley, Timothy Lounsbury, Phinehas Bradley Jun[r].

[April 12, 1779]

At Freemens meeting, in the Town of New Haven, the 12th day of April 1779, the following persons were admitted Freemen and took the Oath required by law. David Gilbert, Jesse Ford, Gamaliel Bradley, Jonas Prentice, Joseph Mix, Jonah Hotchkiss, Abner Austin, Abram Chidsey, Elisha Alling, Thomas Green, Major Lines,[2] Levi Ives, Gamaliel Benham, Joseph Beecher.

[April 20, 1780]

At a meeting of the Freemen in the Town of New Haven April the 20th 1780. the following persons were admitted Freemen and took the Oath required by Law. Medad Atwater, Hezekiah Dickerman, Dudley Baldwin, William Lockwood, Joel Barlow,[3] David Austin J[r], Medad Osborn, Glover Ball, Medad Beecher, David Tharp, Ezra Stiles, Jun[r], John Scott, Evelyn Pierpoint, Benjamin Beech, Ezra Ives, Richard Woodward, Eli Leavensworth, David Beecher, Enos Todd, Elisha

---

1. Captain Peter Bonticou (1738 - 1779) was master of the ship *Hawke* when he was captured and imprisoned aboard the prison ship *Jersey*. He escaped, but contracted smallpox and died in Huntington, L.I. in 1779. See, Frederic Gregory Mather, *The Refugees of 1776 from Long Island to Connecticut*, p. 241.

2. This appears to be a mistake on the part of the clerk. A Major Lines was previously recorded taking the Freeman's Oath in 1774. No other Major Lines fitting the time frame has been located.

3. Joel Barlow (1754 - 1812) was a 1778 Yale graduate, newspaperman, poet, and diplomat.

Chapman, Philip Daggett, John Ball, William Mansfield, Henry Peck, Gabriel Hotchkiss, John Robinson, Levi Ray, Hezekiah Sperry, Joseph Bradley, Calvin Heaton, Joel Barnes, Nathaniel Story, Ichabod Russel, Lazarus Toles. Peter Perkins, Asa Goodyear, Ephraim Humaston, Abraham Augur, William Munson.

[April 7, 1783]

At a meeting of the Freemen in the Town of New Haven April 7th 1783. the following persons were admitted freemen and took the oath required by law. Stephen Alling, John Sloan, Amaziah Jocelin, Enos Johnson, William Miles, Benjamin Downs, Timothy White, David Sanford, Daniel Tuttle, Hezekiah Augur, Hezekiah Beecher, Sacket Gilbert, Nathaniel Downs, John Johnson, David Hotchkiss, Ebenezer Johnson, Amos Gilbert, Eleazer Hotchkiss, John Perkins, John Russel, Joel Hough, Aaron Bradley, William Noyes, Josiah Talmage, Caleb Ives, Gurden Turner, Nathan Oaks, James Dickerman, John Andrews, Philemon Augur, Zuatous Blackslee.

[September 16, 1783]

At Freemens meeting September 16th 1783 the following persons were admitted Freemen and took the oath required by law. Samuel Newton, Daniel Russell, Timothy Bull, Jonathan Atwater.

[April 12, 1784]

At a meeting of the Freemen in the Town of New Haven April 12th 1784. the following persons were admitted Freemen and took the Oath required by Law. Joshua Perry, Stephen Ball, Leveret Hubbard, Thomas Howel, John Miles Junʳ, Thomas Burrill, Henry Daggett Junʳ, Henry Mansfield, Elihu Lyman, William Joseph Whiting, Solomon Pinto, James Rice, Theophilus Goodyear, Eleada Sanford, Joseph Gorham, Alling Cooper, Joseph Bracket, John Sanford, Titus Tharp, Enoch Ray, David Grannis, Eber Ives, Richard Bracket, [blank] Barns, Jotham Wlliams, Jared Mansfield, Leverit Hubbard Junʳ, Amos Blakesley, Asa Hotchkiss, Isaac Dickerman, Nathaniel Dayton, Philemon Blaksley, Richard Cutler, Levi Hubbard, Christian Hanson, Henry Cunningham, John Miles 3ᵈ, Hannover Barney, John Trowbridge, Elias Stilwill, Rositer Griffin, Samuel Green, Stephen Hotchkiss, Samuel Clark, Parsons Clark, Simeon Baldwin, Bela Hubbard, William Powel, Jedediah Moss[1], Samuel Nesbit, Richard Ell, Thomas Rice, Asa Austin, James Pierpoint, Thomas Sanford, Michael Baldwin, Ezra

---

1. Jedediah Morse (1761 - 1826) graduated from Yale in 1786 with an M.A. in theology. He is best known for geography textbooks and became known as the father of American geography. He was the father of Samuel Morse, the painter and telegraphy pioneer. See, https://en.wikipedia.org/wiki/Jedidiah_Morse.

<u>Stiles</u>, Samuel Darling, Charles Prindle, Phineas Andrus.

[September 21, 1784]

At a meeting of the Freemen of the Town of New Haven, September 21st 1784, the following persons were admitted Freemen and took the oath required by Law. Obadiah Hotchkiss Jun[r], Ezra Ford, Christopher Todd, Samuel Pierpoint, Oliver Blakeslee, Samuel Sacket, , Joel Barnes, Joshua Barnes Jun[r], Caleb Blakeslee, Caleb Smith, Isaiah Bracket, Daniel Hull, Hezekiah Hotchkiss, Walter Munson.

[April 11, 1785]

At a meeting of the Freemen in the Town of New Haven April 11th 1785. the following persons were admitted Freemen and took the oath required by Law. Abraham Bishop, Thaddeus Peritt, Job Perrit, Henry F. Channing[1], Parsons Clark, Jesse Gilbert, Isaac Stiles, Lewis B. Sturges, James Bassett Jun[r], Timothy Bassett, Dan Ives, Thomas Bird, Ebenezer Pamerlee, George A. Bristol, Jun[n] Dayton Jun[r], Stiles Curtiss, Samuel Barnes, Daniel Brown, Amos Peck, Allen Ives, Moses Peck, Jesse Tuttle, Thomas Pierpoint, John Frost Junr., Edmund Bradley, Joseph Hotchkiss, Hiel Peck, Alven Bradley, Pember Jocelin, Bethuel Todd.

[September 20, 1785]

At Freemens meeting September 20th 1785, the following persons were admitted freemen and took the oath. John Heyliger, Timothy Phelps, Eli Alling, John Atwater, William Griffin, Jesse Bassett, Daniel G. Phipps, Joseph Drake.

[April 10, 1786]

At Freemens meeting April 10th 1786. the following persons were admitted Freemen and took the freemens Oath. John Atwater, Abel Morse, Joel Goodyear, Samuel Whittlesey, David Daggett, Nathaniel Rosseter, Jonathan Leavit, Barna*[bus]* Bidwell, Isaac Bassett.

[September 19, 1786]

At a meeting of the Freemen September 19th 1786. Dyer White was admitted freeman and took the Oaths required by Law.

[April 9, 1787]

1787. At a meeting of the Freemen of the Town of New Haven April 9th 1787.

---

1. Henry F. Channing (1760 - 1840) graduated from Yale in 1782 and soon became an influential minister at Newport, RI, where is was an early proponent of Unitarianism. See, http://uudb.org/articles/henrychanning.html.

The following persons were admitted freemen and took the Oath required by Law. Samuel Austin Jun[r,1] Joseph Denison, Ebenezer Alling, Nathaniel Smith, Harth Ramsdale, Eldad Mix, Eli Hotchkiss, Samuel Howel.

[April 9, 1787]

At a meeting of the Freemen of the Town of New Haven April 9th 1787. the following persons were admitted freemen. Peter Woodward, George Brown.

[April 7, 1788]

1788. At a meeting of the Freemen of the Town of New Haven the following persons were admitted freemen, April 7th 1788. and took the Oath required by law. Benjamin Sanford, Sturges Burr, Hezekiah Wetmore, Jeremiah Atwater 3[d], Jeremiah Smith, Jesse Turner, Joseph Merwin, Justus Smith, Benajah Thomas.

[September 16, 1788]

At a meeting of the Freemen of the Town of New Haven the following persons were admitted freemen and took the Oath required by law September 16th 1788. Daniel Read, John Bishop, Eneas Munson Jun[r], Peleg Sanford, Eli Beecher, Israel Munson Jun[r], Stephen Ball Jun[r].

[April 13, 1789]

1789. At a meeting of the Freemen of the Town of New Haven April 13th 1789. the following persons were admitted freemen and took the Oath required by law. Ralph Isaacs, Jeremiah Mason, Isaac Ives, Isaac Augur, Frederick Hunt. Also at Freemens meeting September 15th 1789. Roger Sherman was admitted freeman.

[April 12, 1790]

1790. At a meeting of the Freemen of the Town of New Haven April 12th 1790 the following persons were admitted freemen and took the Oath required by Law. Jonas Prentice Jun[r], John Smith, Eli Bullard, Jonas Sisson, Prince Briant Hall, Nathaniel Eliot, Luther Fitch, Henry J. Cooledge, William Bills, Ambrose Ward Jun[r], Stephen Trowbridge 3[d].

[September 21, 1790]

At Freemens meeting September 21st 1790. the following persons were admitted freemen and took the Oath required by Law. Heaton Huggins, Abraham Tuttle,

---

1. Samuel Austin (1760-1830), graduated Yale in 1783. He served as minister of the Fair Haven Church from 1786 - 1790, then as president of the University of Vermont from 1815 - 1821. From 1821 assumed the pulpit at the First Congregational Church of Newport, RI serving until 1825. See, https://snaccooperative.org/ark:/99166/w6b00nmv.

NEW HAVEN TOWN RECORDS

Samuel Covert, Roswell Woodward, Benjamin Prescott, Ezra Daggett, John Warner Jr., Timothy Atwater, Peter DeWit, Joseph Mix, Amaziah Lucas, John Tapping, Marcus Merriman, Ezra Lines, Robert Townsend, Benjamin Graniss.

[September 20, 1791]
1791. At a meeting of the Freemen of the Town of New Haven on the 20th day of September 1791 the following persons were admitted freemen and took the oath required by Law. Christopher K. Allikoke, Benjamin Wooster, Elisha Munson, Nathaniel Kimberly, Gillead Kimberly, William Brown, Joseph Strong, Roswell Judson, John Peck.

[April 9, 1792]
1792. At Freemens meeting April 9th 1792. the following persons, were admitted freemen and took the Oath required by Law. Thomas Painter, Josiah Stebbins, John Russ and Hezekiah Mix.

[April 8, 1793]
1793. At a meeting of the Freemen of the Town of New Haven April 8th 1793. the following persons were admitted freemen and took the Oath required by Law.. Jonathan Walter Edwards,[1] Elijah Waterman, William G. Hubbard and John Leak.

[September 16, 1793]
At a Freemens meeting September 16th 1793. the following persons were admitted Freemen and took the Oath required by Law. William Austin, Kneeland Townsend, Justus Butler, Jesse Camp, Ichabod Lord Skinner,[2] Samuel Lathrop, William Trowbridge, Francis Bolling.

[April 7, 1794]
At Freemens meeting on the 7th of April 1794. the following persons were admitted freemen and took the oath required by Law. William Hart[3], John Nicoll, Eli Whitney, Levi Ives Junr, John Sergeant, Nathan Smith, Solomon Mudge, Napthali Daggett, Joseph Lynde, Stephen Trowbridge Junr.

1. Son of the Rev. Jonathan Edwards and Mary Porter Edwards, Jonathan Walter Edwards (1772 - 1831) was a 1789 Yale graduate, lawyer, judge, and state representative in the Hartford area. See, https://www.findagrave.com/memorial/95614704/jonathan-walter-edwards.
2. Ichabod L. Skinner (1767 - 1852) graduated Yale in 1793 and was respectively a minister, lawyer, engineer, and teacher. He died in Broioklyn, NY in 1852. See, https://www.findagrave.com/memorial/50062239/ichabod-lord-skinner.
3. Rev. William Hart (1772 - 1836) graduated from Yale in 1792.

[September 14, 1794]

At Freemens meeting in New Haven September 14th 1794. the following persons were admitted freemen and took the oath required by Law Luther Bradley, William Baldwin, Abraham Dummer.

[..... , 1795]

At Freemens meeting in N. Haven A.D. 1795 the following persons were admitted Freemen, viz. John Sherman and Benjamin Beecher.

[April 11, 1796]

At Freemens meeting in N. Haven April 11th 1796 the following persons were admitted freemen and took the oath. Lyman Hotchkiss, Erastus Ripley, Jeremiah Atwater 4th, Isaac Jones Junr.

The following Lists contain the names of those persons who have been admitted Freemen of the Town of New Haven since the commencement of the year 1797. and who have taken the Oath required by Law at the time of their admission.

April 10th 1797
Anson Clinton
Daniel Salter
Nathan Platt
David Bristol Junr
David Dickson
Isaac Townsend Junr
Isaac M. Wales
Hezekiah Howe

September 18th 1797
Diodate Mix
Daniel Barnes
Joseph Munson
James Munson
William Scott
William S. Hotchkiss

April 10th 1798
William Mix

Henry Lynde
Asahel Tuttle Junr
Asahel Tuttle
Daniel Colliss
John Miller
Austin Denison

April 18th 1798
Bradford Hubbard
Gold Smith
Stephen Atwater
John Meloy
David Benham
Nathan Platt
David Bristol Junr
Ward Atwater
Alexander Bradley
Stephen S. Twining
James Alling
Thomas Smith

William Pinto

Nathan Howel

Amos Alling

Chauncey Alling

Joel Pardy

Edward Alling

Jabez Dwight

Samuel Bishop Jun[r]

Lyman Beecher

Seth P. Staples

John Niles

Amos Benedict

Nathaniel Lyon

[p. 345] Elijah Alling

Dan Huntington

Zacheriah Lewis

Solomon Daviss

William Rhodes

Solomon Pinto

Joseph Merwin Jun[r]

Oliver Sherman

David Larabee

Samuel Hughes

Robert Brown Jun[r]

Merrit Clark

Asahel Thomas

Silas Alling Jun[r]

Abner Kirby

John Richards Jun[r]

David Trowbridge

Philemon Peckham

William Wallace

Stephen Prindle

David Bristol

Samuel Horton

Elihu Monson

Joel Downs

Miles Hotchkiss

Isaac Monson

David Beecher Jun[r]

Stephen Thompson

Leverit Stevens Jun[r]

Punderson Hotchkiss

Samuel Clark Jun[r]

Oliver Clark

September 17th 1798

Asa Lyman

John P. Austin

Solomon Collis

Amos Townsend

Elnathan Atwater

Abraham Bradley 3rd

John Huggins

John Whittlesey

Thomas Ward

Ezra Smith

Isaac Townsend

Hervey Mulford

John S. Edwards

Josiah Merrick

Clark Sage

April 8th 1799

John Hunt

Charles Bostick

Ellis Viel

Elijah Gilbert

Joseph Alley

Jonathan Atwater

Henry Meloy

David W. Youngs

Jared Thompson

Aaron Forbes

Wlliam Brintnall

Claudius Herrick

John H. Lynde

John Swathel

John Cook

Ebenezer G. Marsh

Jeremiah Day
Gold S. Silliman
[p. 346]
Henry Davis
James Murdock
Timothy Bishop
Samuel Barnet
James Henry
Edmund French Junr
Henry Ward
Jonas Merwin
Benjamin Bragg

September 16th 1799
Daniel Green
Joseph Thompson
Charles Denison
Samuel Pardee
Moses Humpherville

April 7th 1800
Samuel Huggins Junr
Reuben Rice
Ebenezer Townsend Junr
Joel Atwater
Noah Barber
George Peckham
William Daggett
Elisha Dickerman
Samuel Gorham
William Fitch
James Gilbert
Amos White
Charles Whittlesey
Elijah Hotchkiss
Stephen Lines
Thomas Howel

September 15th 1800
Stephen Row

Nathaniel Grannis
Amos Hill
Nathaniel Harrisson
Samuel B. Hine
Daniel Smith
Abel Denison
Israel Kimberly
Jesse Alling
William Thompson
Henry Monson
Daniel Hodge
Justus Bradley
Darius Higgins
Caleb Miller
John Hunt 3^d
Anthony P. Sanford
William Bristol
William Turner
Isaac Chase
Jesse B. Mix
Levi Goodsell
Asa Potter
Joshua Newel
William Mansfield Junr
Eliakim Benham
[p. 347] William Hull
Joel Walter
William Noyes Junr
Justus Hotchkiss
Enos Johnson Junr
James Cockran
Linus Kimberly
Jonah Bradley
Peter Johnson Junr
David Downs
Amasa Goodyear
Isaac Smith
Richard Downs
Cornelius Thomas
John Munson Page

Simeon Newton

Jabez Dwight

Thomas Pardy

Amos Downs

Levi Beecher

Jonathan Alling

William Mathews

Enos Smith

Thomas Downs

John Platt

Uri Tuttle

John Staples

Shadrach Brooks

Titus Sanford

David Hull

Thomas Hull

Jesse Hunt

Samuel Hull

Walter Brown

Farrand Clark

Laban Smith Jun[r]

Samuel Pool

Jehiel Holms

Joseph Wetmore

John Morriss

Ichabod Smith

Eliphlet Luddington

Isaac Pinto

Benjamin Bakenwell

Eli Cone

Abner Tuttle

Enoch Ives

Ezra Barns

Cornelius Ball

Gideon Kimberly

Peter Clark

John Benedict

April 13th 1801

Ezra Hotchkiss

Daniel Hubbard

David Dorman

Thomas Townsend

September 21st 1801

Nathaniel S. Lewis

Zebul Bradley

Elisha Bradley

David Gillet

Benjamin Burritt

Chauncey Daggett

Henry W. Edwards

Elijah Crane

[p. 348] April 12th 1802. admitted

Stephen Hotchkiss

George Hotchkiss

Henry Denison

Charles Austin

Bancroft Fowler

Shuball Bartlett

David Eli

George Fitch

Leveritt Hubbard

Elihu Ives

Mathew Read

John Fitch

John Buckley

James Thompson Jun[r]

Richard Gorham

Amasa Dorman

Moses Beecher

Silas Baldwin

Levi Sperry

John Scott Jun[r]

Samuel Merriman

Timothy Gilbert

September 20th 1802

De Lauzun De Forrest

Timothy Dwight Junr

Daniel Bishop

David D. Field

Joseph Ward

Elisha Hammond

Benjamin W. Dwight

April 11th 1803. admitted

Abraham Jarvis[1]

Eldad Gilbert

Daniel Collins

Ebenezer H. Collins

James Goodrich

Andrew Kidston

Isaac Thomas

Benjamin Forbes

Thomas Green J^r

William Fairchild

Alexander Langmuir

John Trowbridge

John Davenport

Giles Cooper

Alvah Kennedy

Charles Short

Gilbert Totten

Gad Peck

Daniel Truman

Philemon Harrisson

Agur Tomlinson

John Ball

Abraham Johnson

Kierstead Mansfield J^r

Silas Kimberly

Eliakim Kimberly

Elias Alling

Ransom Lines

Ezra Tuttle

James Bonticou

Thaddeus Alling

Amos Johnson

Abner Alling

Calvin Turner

Benjamin Merriman

[p. 349] Israel Terrill

William Smith

Aaron Thomas

Chauncey Smith

Richard Thomas

Lewiss Hepburn

Abraham Bassett

William McCracken Jr.

William Babcock

Chancey Bunce

Caleb Hotchkiss

Asa Thomas

Stephen Brown

Thaddeus J. Clark

Elihu Daggett

Abraham Heaton

David Ritter

Clark Sibley

Simeon Marble

Jabez Brown

William Sherman

Samuel Plant

Russell Graniss

Asa Bradley

Joseph J. Brown

September 19th 1803. Admitted

Nathaniel Storer

Nathan Oaks

Elisha Hull

Samuel Willmot Junr

William Townsend

---

[1]Abraham Jarvis (1738 - 1813) was the second Episcopal Bishop of Connecticut.

April 9ᵗʰ 1804. admited
Ebenezer Johnson Junʳ
Nathaniel Fitch
Russell Hotchkiss
Horace Austin
Ezekiel Chidsey
William Stanley
Parsons Gorham
Eli Osborne
Raphael Dickenson
Daniel C. Banks
Jeremiah Bishop
John H. Jacobs
Pelatiah W. Peritt
George Munson
Lemuel Baldwin

Septemʳ 17ᵗʰ 1804. admited as Freemen
Job Atterbury
George Dummer
William L. Bakewell
William Howel
William Dougall
Richard Cutler Junr
Wyllys Hotchkiss
Russell Osborne
Jeremiah Osborne
David Griffin
Jacob Goodsell
Anthony H. Sherman
William Peckham
William Fitch Junʳ
James Ward
Aaron Thomas
Daniel Thomas

Dan Tolles
[p.350]
William Ventris
Elihu Smith
Horace Kimberly

April 8ᵗʰ 1805 admitted as Freemen
Jeremiah Evarts
Clark Bissell[1]
James Howard
Oliver Steel[2]
William W. Burwell
Elihu Spencer
Edard Graniss
Elijah Davis

Septʳ 16ᵗʰ 1805 admitted as Freemen
Ashbel Stillman Junʳ
William Gorham
William Sherman Junʳ
Sherlock Austin
Bethel Tuttle
Willet Bradley
Josiah Deming

April 7ᵗʰ 1806 admitted as Freemen
Eleazer Foster
Jared Bradley
Comfort Williams
David A. Sherman
Charles Sherman
Seth Barnes
Levi Tuttle
Fredᵏ Wᵐ Bishop
Jerry Walter

---

[1] Clark Bissell (1772 - 1857) was a Yale graduate, class of 1806, Admitted to the bar in 1809, he served in the state legislature, as a state Supreme Court Justice, and as Governor from 1847 - 1848.

[2] Oliver Steele (1781 - 1826) was a boolseller and publisher of several newspapers, including New Haven's *Connecticut Herald* from 1804 - 1816.

Andrew Tuttle

[September 15, 1806]

At a Meeting of the Freemen of the Town of New Haven Septr 15th 1806, the following persons were admited Freemen of this State and took the Oath required by law, viz. -

Stephen Huggins
Ebenezer Huggins Jun
Asaph Dunbar
Eli Ives[1]
Andrew Farrell
Daniel Brown
Samuel Fields
Thomas Dougall
William H. Eliot
John Knowles
Marquiss D. L .F. Foster[2]
Sidney Hull
Abraham Thompson Junr
Samuel Barney

[April 13, 1807]

At a Meeting of the Freemen of the Town of New Haven April 13th 1807 the following persons were admited Freemen of this State *[p. 351]* and took the Oath required by law, viz.

Mills Day
William Pardee
Charles Atwater
James Atwater
Minot Augur
John Beecher
Henry Benedict

Abel Burritt Junr
Joseph Trowbridge
John Shipman
Hervey Sanford
Charles Trowbridge
William Kilby
Henry Sherman
Nathl Downs
Willm W. Lamson
Lemuel Deming
Oliver Deming
Eli Townsend
Robert Townsend
Leman Hall
Caleb Sperry
Isaac Tomlinson

[September 21, 1807]

At a meeting of the Freemen of the Town of New Haven on the 21st day of September 1807. The following persons were admitted Freemen of the State of Connecticut and took the Oath provided by Law.

Nehemiah Bradley
Jonathan C. Porter
John Rowe
Emanuel Hopkinson
Jacob Chapman
William Cutler
Zacheus Candee
Isaac Darling
Birdseye Peck
David Molthrop
Norman Dexter

---

[1] Eli Ives (1779 - 1861) was a 1799 Yale graduate who then studied medicine under his father, Levi, as well as Drs. Benjamin Rush and Casper Wistar in Philadelphia. Eli practiced medicine in New Haven for over 50 years. He was instrumental in the founding of Yale Medical School, The New Haven Medical Society, and served as President of the American Medical Society in 1860.

[2] The town clerk was referring to DeLazun DeForest.

Daniel Rose
Leverit Gill
Patrick Mitchel
George Hepburn
John S. Holland
           Attest Elisha Munson Town
Clerk

[April 11, 1808]
At a Meeting of the Civil Authority
and Selectmen of the Town of New
Haven on the 11th day of April 1808,
the following persons Inhabitants
of said Town were found qualified
by Law to be made freemen of this
State. viz.
Aaron Ogden
Benjamin Prime
Nehemiah Bradley
Justus Harrisson
Caleb A. Townsend
[p. 352] John Mantle
Jesse Pardy
Lenos Bassett[1]
Joseph N. Clark
Miles Punderson
William Love
Lester Kimberly
Joseph Sears
Nehemiah Kimberly
Amos Smith
Samuel Langdon
Edmund Langdon
Merriam Tuttle
Lucius Atwater
Amos Trowbridge

Adonijah Thomas
Elias Thomas
Jacob Ward
Henry Austin
David Kimberly
Samuel B. Northrup
Thomas Camby
Nehemiah Carrington
Stephen Richards
Jacob Wolfe
James Hunt
Jonathan Brigden
Henry Trowbridge
Eli Bradley
John Dwight
Certified by Elizur Goodrich asst
Attest Elisha Munson Clerk

[September 19th 1808]
At a meeting of the Freemen of the
Town of New Haven legally warned
and held at New Haven on the 19th day
of September 1808. The Civil Authority
and Selectmen examined the qualifica-
tions of the following persons and ad-
mitted them to become freemen of the
State of Connecticut. viz.
William W. Woolsey
Thomas Punderson Junr
William Northrop
Henry Hartley
Willm Henry Ruggles Pynchon
John Derrick
Certified by Elizur Goodrich
Chairman
Attest - Elisha Munson Town Clerk

---

[1] While the clerk clearly wrote "Lenos Bassett," the editor believes this was Enos Bassett (1784 - 1821). There was an Linas Bassett in North Haven at ther time, but he was 11 years of age in 1808.

[2] The Rev. Thomas Punderson (1783 - 1848) was a Yale graduate (Class of 1804), who went on to an illustrious career as a Congregational minister in Pittsfield, MA and Huntington, CT.

[April 10ᵗʰ 1809]

At a meeting of the Civil Authority and Selectmen of New Haven April 10ᵗʰ 1809, the following persons were found to be qualified to be free.

William Brown of the City of New Haven
Eli Mix Junʳ
Simeon Hoadley
James Parker
Samˡ A. Foot
Elisha Benham
Henry Huggins

[p. 353] [April 10ᵗʰ 1809]

Thomas Peck
Josiah Pardy
William E. Thompson
George Moss
Samuel Gorham
Bradford Smith
Michael G. Hotchkiss
Phinehas B. Thayre
Henry Wells
John Brumham
Henry Eld
Philemon Smith
Alson B. Crane
Certifyed by Elizur Goodrich
A true copy - E. Munson Town Clerk

[September 18, 1809]

The following persons were admitted Freemen of the State of Connecticut on the 18th of September 1809 by the Authority and the Selectmen of the Town of New Haven in open Freemans Meeting.
Leonard E. Wales
New Haven - Septʳ 18ᵗʰ 1809

Test. David Daggett
Presiding Authority

[April 9, 1810]

At a meeting of the Civil Authority and Selectmen of New Haven April 9ᵗʰ 1810, the following persons were admitted Freemen of the State of Connecticut. viz.
Asa Buddington
James Gorham
Jesse West
Elisha Loomis
Thaddeus Clark Junʳ
James English
    Certified - by David Daggett Presiding Authority Recorded by Elisha Munson, Town Clerk

[September 17ᵗʰ 1810]

At a Meeting of the Civil Authority and Selectmen of the Town of New Haven on the 17ᵗʰ Septʳ 1810, the following person was duly admitted and made a freeman of this State being duly qualified and sworn.
Joseph Barker
Attest - David Daggett presiding Authority

[April 8 1811]

The following Persons appeared and were found qualified to be made free of this State and were sworn accordingly under the direction of the Civil Authority and Selectmen of the Town of New Haven.
William Walter Junʳ
Joel Matoon
Eli Gilbert

Henry Butler
Stephen Dickerman
    certified by
Elizur Goodrich Assistant & Presiding Officer

[p. 354] [September 16, 1811]
At a meeting of the Civil authority and Selectmen of the Town of New Haven Septr 16, 1811, the folowing persons were admitted freemen of this State, Viz.
Elisha Punderson
Elihu Sanford
Jonas F. Merwin
Joseph Stevens
    Test David Daggett
    Presiding Officer
Recorded by Elisha Munson Town Clerk

[April 13, 1812]
At a Freemans Meeting holden at New Haven on the 13th of April 1812, the following persons were adrnited Freemen of this State viz
Allen Fitch
Hezekiah Gorham
Norman Hayden
Attes^t David Daggett Assis^t and presiding Authority.
Recorded by Elisha Munson Clerk

[September 21, 1812]
At a Freemans Meeting holden at New Haven this 21st day of September 1812. the following persons were admitted Freemen of this State.
Isaac English
Jared Goodsell

Augustus Wm Maltley
Attest David Daggett Presiding Officer Recorded by Elisha Munson Town Clerk

[April 12, 1813]
At a Meeting of the Civil Authority and Selectmen of the town of New Haven April 12th 1812 the following persons were admitted freemen of this State in open Freemens meeting.
Ralph I. Ingersoll
Chas Hequembough Junr
Leonard A. Daggett
George Miles
Benjamin Sherman
Thaddeus Thomas
Samuel Chatterton
Ezekiuel Hotchkiss
Reuben Hall
James Bradley Junr
Caleb Mix
Sereno E Dwight
    David Daggett
    presiding Authority
N Haven April 13th 1813.
Recorded by Elisha Munson Clerk

[September 20, 1813]
This may certify that at a freemens meeting duly warned and holden at New Haven on the 20th of september 1813.
    William Dwight
was admitted a freemen and sworn accordingly Septr 20th 1813.
    David Daggett
    Presiding officer
Recorded by Elisha Munson Clerk

[p. 355]   [April 11, 1814]
At a Meeting of the Civil Authority and Selectmen of New Haven the following persons, were found qualified according to law and were admitted as Freemen of this State On this 11ᵗʰ day of April 1814.
Ebenezer Weed
Solomon Phipps
Jabez Barnett
Saphos Staples
          Certified by
                    Elizur Goodrich Assisᵗ
          Recorded by Elisha Munson
          Clerk

[September 19, 1814]
At a meeting of the Civil Authority and Selectmen of the Town of New Haven September 19ᵗʰ 1814 the following persons were found qualified for admission as Freeman of this State and were sworn accordingly, viz.
William Austin Junʳ
          Certified by Elizur
          Goodrich Chairman
          Recorded by Elisha Munson
          Clerk

[April 10, 1815]
At a Meeting of the Civil Authority and Selectmen of the town of New Haven in open freemens Meeting April 10ᵗʰ 1815 the following persons were found qualified to be admitted Freemen of this State and sworn accordingly viz.
Revᵈ Samuel Merwin
Roger Sherman Baldwin
Timothy Chittenden

Elam Hull
Fredrick LeForge
Leveritt Griswold
Thomas Atwater Junʳ
Samuel R. Crane
Certified by
          Elizur Goodrich
          Presiding officer,
          Record by *[...]*

[September 18, 1815]
The following persons were admitted to be Freemen of this State by the Civil Authority and Selectmen of New Haven. - September 18ᵗʰ 1815
John D. Fowler
Nathaniel Bacon
George F. Whiting
Russel Boothe
Joseph Taylor
Glover Mansfield
          certified by
                    Elizur Goodrich
                    Presiding Officer,
          Recorded by
                    Elisha Munson Clerk

[p. 356] [April 8, 1816]
At a meeting of the Civil Authority and Selectmen of the Town of New Haven on the 8ᵗʰ day of april 1816, the following persons were admitted freemen of this State.
Jared Doolittle
Warham Bunnel
Dennis Kimberly
Samuel J. Hitchcock
John Gilbert
Jairhes *[Jarius]* Sanford
Benjamin Thompson

William Kenedy
Solomon Taylor
Alexander Coburn
Isaac Beers
Luther D. Cooks
Algernon S. Jones
David Novice
Erastus Hoadly
William Potter
Samuel Gilbert
William Pishall
Joseph Chipmars
Silas Benham
Arnold Candee
Joel Osborn
Chancellor Kingsbury
Thomas McCumbers
Jared Shattuck
Elah Gorham
Uri Ames
Levi Moulthrop
Joseph A. Bishop
Aner Thomas
Timothy Allen
Oliver Beach
Jotham Tuttle
David C. Fitch
William Thompson 2nd
Ithiel Towne
James Colson
Isaac Dickerman Junʳ
Eber Lines

certified by
Elizur Goodrich
Presiding officer
Recorded by Elisha Munson Clerk

[September 16, 1816]
At a meeting of the Civil Authority &
Selectmen of the town of New Ha-

ven September 16th 1816 the following
persons were admitted to be free of this
State viz.
Titus Street
Samuel F. Davis
Oliver Maltbie
Abiel H. Maltbie
Ezra Stiles Hubbard
John Daggett
Edwin Porter
Timothy P. Beers
Grindley Harrisson
Nathan S. Mead
William Granger
Roger S. Skinner
James S. Huggins
Egbert D. Peck
Ephraim Peck
[p. 357] George F. Read
Elias Hotchkiss
Marcus Merriman Junʳ
Robert Atwater
William Lewis Clark
Leman Chatfield
George Raymond
Samuel J. Clark
Reuben M. Beecher
James Dwight
Elias B. Bishop
David Austin
Ebenezer Haws
John Beach
Levi Alling
Elam C. Brown
Eleazer Gorham
Eli B. Austin
George Trowbridge
Timothy Fowler
John Davis
Clement Goodale

Eleazer Hotchkiss Junr
Isaac Mallery
Gaius Fenn
Elihu Atwater
Henry C. Flagg
George Smith
William Townsend
Alexander Harrison
Ammi Harrison Junr
Certified by
    Elizur Goodrich
Recorded by E. Munson Clerk

[April 7, 1817]
At a meeting of the Civil authority
& selectmen held in New Haven
april 7th 1817.
James L. Kingsley
Henry Oaks
George Ives
Theodosius Hunt
Charles K. Shipman
Nathaniel B. Smith
Denison Olmsted
Alexander M. Fisher
Samuel B. Ingersoll
John Thomas
Oliver Bryans
Wooster Hotchkiss
Austin Redfield
Thomas G. Woodward
Nathaniel Jocelyn[1]
Isaac Lacey
Legrand Cannon
Martin Graniss
Levi Stillman
Henry Parmelee
John Goldsmith

Demas Hotchkiss
Randolph Stone
William Wise
John Titsworth
[p. 358] Frederick Morgan
Ely Sperry
Alexis Painter
James Reynolds 2^d
Archibald Blakeslee
Horace H. Edwards
Samuel Punderson Junr
William Thompson
Cleaveland J. Salter
Henry Hotchkiss
Thomas Wright
Samuel Green
Samuel F. Bolles
Mason A. Durand
Stephen Bishop
Richard B. Law
James Peck
Philip Clime
Augustus B. Street
Timothy Ward
Benjamin R. Hall
Elias Smith
Jonathan Brigden
Giles Mansfield
Nathan Mansfield
William Creighton
Charles Munson
Isaac Bassett
Chauncey Clark
William Fairchild Junr
Roswell Trowbridge
Isaac Trowbridge
William Trowbridge
Newman Trowbridge

[1] Nathaniel Jocelyn (1796 - 1881), was an engraver, painter, and abolitionist best known for his portrait of the leader of the *La Amistad* rebellion, Joseph Cinqué also called Sengbe Pieh.

Richard Trowbridge

Eliphaz Gillett

Joseph Beecher

Allen Brown

John Bester Davis

Marcus J. Hotchkiss

Nathan Whiting

Timothy D. Williams

David B. Spencer

David Alling

.Horace Butler

William Lego

Samuel Short

William Stebbins

Ira Atwater

Freeman Pope

Nahum Haywood

Alva Keep

Enos Sperry

Newton Stevens

Daniel Main

George Kirtland

Joseph Todd

John Jones

George Bradley

Edward Budington

Miles Gorham

Bela Baldwin

[p. 359] Alvin Blakely

John Baldwin

Medad Culver

Gillead Alling

Peter Chatterton

William Kimberly

Matthias Hitchcock

William H. Jones

John A. Thomas

Sheldon Smith

John H. Anthony

Leander Cook

Samuel Johnson

Solomon Johnson

Lyman Benedict

Barnabas Benedict

Smith Tuttle

Virgil M. Dow

Jaremiah Barnet

Daniel F. Auger

Thaddeus Austin

John D. Brown

Lewis Bradley

Amos Thomas

Jared Richards

Amiel Camp

Horace Johnson

John Babcock 2ᵈ

Whiting Cooper

Certified by

Elizur Goodrich, Assistant

Recorded by Elisha Munson Clerk

[September 15, 1817]

At a Meeting of the civil authority and Selectmen in New Haven thls 15ᵗʰ day of September, 1817 the following persons were examined and found quallfled to be admitted as Free of this State viz.

Joseph Hotchkin

Jonathan Nicholson

Elliott Ward

Samuel Austin

John Hubbard

Francis Kimberly

Benjamin Fuller

George I. Tomlinson

Charles S. Tomlinson

John Mc Niel

Amos Goodsell

Elam Allen

James F. Barnes

Luther D. Fitch
Bryant Whittlesey
John P. Beers
Isaac Auger Jr.
Alfred S. Monson
Sherman Converse
Samuel Manson
Joshua Bennett
William K. Townsend
Sherman Blair
John H. Cook
Edwin E. Lewis
Isaac T. Wise
[p. 360] Sylvester Jones
David Kempton
Alfred Heglegar
John Hayes
James E. Parker
Simeon Francis
Henry Scott
Johnson Ford
William Cannon
Eben N. Thompson
John S. Bradley
Stephen A. Maltbie
John Babcock 2ᵈ
William Way
Thomas Cook
Augustus Frisbie
Edward Hotchkiss
Thomas Cook
Charles J. Allen
Lefotus Day
Samuel C. Johnson
Elias S. Townsend
Samuel Wadsworth
Josiah Stone

James Brewster
Samuel Scott
Ebenr. D. Barney
John M. Garfield
Levi Atwater
Sherman Bradley
Charles Collins
Grove Smith
Amos A. Gilbert
Selah Short
Phinehas Ferrill
David D. Swift
Recorded by E. Munson Clerk
certified David Daggett P officer
continued in New volume[1]

[1817]
A list of persons who have lodged
certificates with the town clerk of
New Haven that they had been
admitted freemen of the State of
Connecticut
Newton Wheeler
Joseph Stone
Merick Linsley
Joel Atkins
Irijah Ferril
Samuel Sperry
Stephen Tyler
Malachi Tyler
William Danielson
Isaac Smith
Hervey Hemingway
Abraham S. Fowler
David Bacon
Austin Gurley
Simeon Maniel

---

[1]Although the town clerk noted that freemen's meetings were continued in a new volume, they actually ran for an additional half-page in the original volume with a scattering of entries through 1826.

Amasa Porter
Amiel Camp
James H. Linsley
Anson Hubbard
David Thomas
Harvey Hoadley
Selah Short
Daniel S. Gladding
Chancey Ripley

[1818]
David Butler
William W. Boardman
Charles Cotter

[1820]
Roswell Goodwin
Philo Taylor
Nathan Benjamin
William Ward

[1821]
Oliver Hotchkin

[1824]
George Y. Cutler

[1826]
Levi Baldwin

Index

(* following name denotes military service)

362

Austin, Asa (1747 - 1820); freeman, 363; questioned for remaining in town during British invasion, 83; tithingman, 129, 164, 172, 188, 201, 213, 227

Austin, Charles; freeman, 370

Austin, David; freeman, 378

Austin, David, Jr.* (1732 - 1801); agent for British invasion sufferers, 120; Articles of Association, 38; boundary committee, 128, 156; bridge committee, 177, 179, 180; committee for poor, 173; committee for relief of Boston, 37; committee of correspondence, 35; committee of inspection, 49; committee on commercial interests, 6–7; committee on New Haven - Woodbridge boundaries, 128, 156; committee on poor, 129, 145, 173, 188, 194; committee on salary for rate collector, 73; committee on smallpox, 189; committee to admit former Loyalists, 121–123; committee to divide town, 107, 110; committee to settle accounts, 128–129, 134; committee on confederation of the United States, 65; defense committee, 102–103; Dragon Bridge committee, 151, 159–163, 169, 177–180; freeman, 362; grand juror, 22, 133; hospital committee, 189–190; lister, 73, 107, 114, 118; lottery manager, 93, 100; overseer of poor, 145; released as lottery manager, 100; replaced as lister, 79; salary committee for rate collector, 73; surveyor, 151; town agent, 120, 129; town moderator, 132, 137, 157; town treasurer, 115, 118, 124, 129, 134, 139, 143, 150, 158, 172, 188; workhouse committee, 158

Austin, Eli B. (1792/3 - 1842); freeman, 378; lister, 344

Austin, Elijah (1750 - 1794); committee on poor, 134; grand juror, 151; lister, 139

Austin, Henry (1782 - 1852); freeman, 374

Austin, Horace (1777 - 1824); freeman, 372

Austin, John* (1736 - 1794); committee to clothe army, 78; constable, 51, 53, 62, 73; inspector of provisions, 90; lister, 86, 98; rate collector, 51, 52, 108; refuses rate collector post, 51, 109; refuses to serve as constable, 75; released as constable, 55; released as lister, 102; released as selectman, 120; selectman, 111, 118; tithingman, 193–194

Austin, John (1793 - 1833), 261

Austin, John P. (1774 - 1834); Yale (1794), 368; biography, 261n; constable, 263; constable, excused as, 264; fisheries overseer, 261, 265; freeman, 368

Austin, Jonathan* (1743 - 1823); sells land for work house, 165

Austin, Joshua* (1736 - ?); committee for bills of credit and Continental money, 93; committee of inspection, 49; committee on confederation of the United States, 65; committee on procuring uniforms, 69; committee on town defense, 70; committee to divide town, 107; grand juror, 113, 117; illicit trade, 94; inspector of provisions, 90; released as grand juror, 117

Austin, Martha (Denison) (1751 - 1833), 138

Austin, Moses (1733 - 1812); freeman, 359

Austin, Samuel (1734 - 1790); committee on provisions, 95

Austin, Samuel, Jr. Rev. (1760 - 1830); biography, 365n; freeman, 365; Yale (1783)

Austin, Samuel (1790 - 1830); freeman, 380

Austin, Sherlock (1776 - 1814); freeman, 372

Austin, Thaddeus (1782 - 1860); freeman, 380

Austin, William (1762 - 1833); fisheries overseer, 274, 281; freeman, 366; grand juror, 262; lister, 222, 227; tithingman, 209, 239

Austin, William, Jr. (1792/3 - 1870); freeman, 377

Azimuth; defined, 328

B

Babcock, Adam (1740 - 1817), 48, 49; Black Rock Fort, 47; committee about city, 17; committee for relief of Boston, 37; committee of inspection, 49; committee on Loyalists, 48; committee on Susquehanna, 30, 31; committee to procure gunpowder, 49–50; committee to promote commerce, 6, 7; lister, 23; town agent for defenses, 48

Babcock, John (1786 - 1839), 377; freeman, 380, 381

Babcock, William A.(1780 - 1814), 320, 322; freeman, 371; lister, 311, 316; released as lister, 322

Bacon, Nathaniel (1788 - 1823); freeman, 377

Bacon's Bill No. 2, 295

Bakewell, Benjamin (1767 - 1844); freeman, 370

tents, 58; orders towns to clothe troops, 78; orders towns to provide provisions to troops, 100; oysters, 233; permits Quinnipiac River Bridge, 148; poor, 179–180; procurement of tents, 56; provides funds for New Haven defense, 109; provides New Haven with firearms, 103; raises troops, 95; recommends county association for Committee of Inspection, 44; regulates prices, 58; revokes travel licences due to illicit trade, 94; Scarlet fever epidemic, 199; schools, 218; tax for army provisions, 102; U.S. Constitution, 138; votes to supply arms to New Haven and Yale, 47; work house, 168

Connecticut Journal, 29; Thomas Green, Jr., 29

Connecticut Medical Society, 244

Connecticut militia, 92; selectmen pay, 94

Connecticut money, 94

Connelly, Patrick (1727 - 1797)?; questioned on remaining in town during British invasion, 82

Constables, 8, 16, 17, 21, 22, 26, 39, 43, 50, 53, 55, 62, 73, 78, 85, 97, 106, 112, 118, 124, 128, 133, 138, 150, 159, 172, 187, 191, 193, 197, 201, 208, 212, 217, 239, 243, 249, 257, 263, 268, 271, 276, 288, 296, 300, 312, 316, 321, 326, 331, 334, 339, 344, 350, 351, 354

Constitution of 1818 (CT), 340–341, 342, 343; calls for separation of church and state, 343; New Haven votes to ratify, 342; universal white male suffrage, x, 343;

Constitution (U.S.); New Haven calls for ratification, 137–138

Continental Army; bonus for enlisting, 95; enlistments, 60 – 61; enlistments bonuses, 60; New Haven and, 103; New Haven protests draft, 101; New Haven supplies uniforms for, 61, 61 – 62; number of New Haven men in service, 96

Continental Association; New Haven supports boycott, 39

Continental Congress; bills of credit and Continental money, 93

Continental currency; British counterfeit, 175

Continental money, 94; forgeries of, 175; New Haven accepts, 93

Converse, Sherman (1789 - 1873); freeman, 381

Cook, David (1728 - 1807); refuses interview on remaining in town during British invasion, 83

Cook, George (1750 - 1794); questioned for remaining in town during British invasion, 83

Cook, Increase (1771 - 1814); grand juror, 289, 295; lister, 295, 300

Cook, John, 368; freeman, 368

Cook, John H. (1788 - 1850); freeman, 381

Cook, Leander (1792 - 1832); freeman, 380

Cook, Luther D., 378

Cook, Luther D. (1794 - 1866); freeman, 378

Cook, Thomas; freeman, 381

Cook, Thomas (1795 - 1860); freeman, 381

Cooledge, Henry J. (1766 - 1803); freeman, 365

Cooper, Alling (1741 - 1805); freeman, 363

Cooper, Caleb (1736 - 1810); freeman, 359

Cooper, Giles (1765 - 1815); freeman, 371

Cooper, Levi; freeman, 360; grand juror, 50; tithingman, 85, 99

Cooper, Samuel, Jr. (1722 - 1802); surveyor, 98, 124, 126

Cooper, Stephen, Jr. (1738 - 1816); freeman, 361

Cooper, Thomas* (1737 - 1808), 90; biography, 91

Cooper, Thomas Deacon (1702/3 - 1784); released as selectman, 126; surveyor, 55, 86

Cooper, Thomas , Jr. Ensign* (1737 - 1808); biography, 91n; committee of correspondence, 115; committee on procuring uniforms, 69 – 70; grand juror, 54, 91; inspector of provisions, 90; key keeper, 98, 119, 125, 129; lister, 2, 10, 54, 89, 92, 125, 129; released as grand juror, 92; selectman, 118, 124; surveyor, 63

Cooper, Whiting (1793 - 1853); freeman, 380

Coram, NY, 104

Cotton Gin, 336

Council of Safety, 72

Counterfeiting, 175

Coverly, John; tithingman, 302

Covert, Samuel (1760 - 1803); freeman, 366

Crane, Alson B. (1783 - 1810); freeman, 375

Crane, Samuel R. (1751 - 1829); accounts committee, 345; freeman, 377; grand juror, 344; lister, 338

Crane, William; freeman, 360

Creighton, William (1793 - 1824); freeman, 379

Crime; growth of in New Haven, 22

Crittendon, Hope; freeman, 361

Crocker, Daniel (1757 - 1831); tithingman, 139

Downs, Nathaniel (1702 - 1786); grand juror, 109; surveyor, 129

Downs, Nathaniel (1767/8 - 1836); freeman, 373

Downs, Nathaniel (1768 - 1836); freeman, 363

Downs, Nathaniel Jr. (1731 - 1801); surveyor, 17

Downs, Richard (1773 - ?); freeman, 369

Downs, Samuel (1720 - 1801); freeman, 359; grandjuror, 18; surveyor, 98, 119

Downs, Seth (1731 - 1795); freeman, 359; lister, 74; surveyor, 51, 86, 107

Downs, Thomas (1755 - 1812); freeman, 370

Dragon Bridge, 148, 156, 159 – 163, 169, 177 – 181, 187, 236 – 237, 249, 263, 267, 271, 273 – 276, 279, 313, 327, 328; financial burden, 264; lottery for, 173 – 175; originally Long Bridge, 169; tolls, 264, 270; town agents appointed for, 180; washed away, 272

Dragon (Fair Haven Heights), 145, 327

Dragon Flats, 265, 274, 289, 299, 303, 314, 329, 332, 337, 341, 346

Dragon Point, 148, 152, 156, 160; bridge, 151, 156; ferry, 18

Drake, Joseph (1737 - 1836); Dragon Bridge committee, 177; lister, 172, 188, 193, 257; schools, 223; selectman, 189, 193

Drake, Joseph (1764 - 1791); freeman, 364

Drake, William; leaves with British invaders, 83; refuses interview on remaining in town during British invasion, 83

Dudley, George; constable, 62, 63, 112

Dudley, George (1733 - ?); freeman, 361

Dummer, Abraham (1766 - 1815); freeman, 367; lister, 244

Dummer, George (1782 - 1853); freeman, 372

Dummer, Nathan* (1730 - 1813); biography, 125; key keeper, 125, 129, 133, 143, 151, 164, 173, 188, 194, 202, 208, 213–214, 217, 222; Rev. War veteran, 125; tithingman, 19

Dummer, Stephen (1755 - 1835); tithingman, 217

Dunbar, Asaph (1780 - 1814); freeman, 373

Duncomb, John, 229

Duncomb, Zachariah (1783 - 1839), 230; biography, 230

Dunning, Leman (1773 - 1833); lister, 332, 334; surveyor, 334, 344

Durand, Mason A. (1796 - 1832); freeman, 379

Dwight, Benjamin W. Dr. (1780 - 1850); freeman, 371; lister, 287; tithingman, 276; Yale (1799), 371

Dwight, Jabez (1774/75 - 1809); freeman, 368, 370

Dwight, James (1784 - 1863); freeman, 378

Dwight, John (1785 - 1832); freeman, 374

Dwight, Sereno E. (1786 - 1850); freeman, 376; grand juror, 316, 320, 325, 330; lister, 316, 321

Dwight, Timothy Jr.,; lister, 268

Dwight, Timothy Jr. (1752 - 1817); biography, 262n freeman, 361; grand juror, 262; lister, 268, 271; Yale (1744), 262

Dwight, Timothy Jr. (1778 - 1844); , 361; audit committee, 276; freeman, 371; town auditor, 279

Dwight, William (1791 - 1834); freeman, 376

East Haven, CT, 9, 18, 26, 135, 140, 160, 162, 170, 194, 223, 232, 233, 298, 303, 332, 336, 346; beacon erected, 45; boundary with New Haven, 227 – 228, 249, 253; creation as separate town, 127; Dragon Bridge, 236 – 237, 271; Old Ferry Wharf, 346; salt works, 64; taxes, 140 –1 41; town status, 110

East Haven River (Farm River); ferry, 76; lottery for bridge, 109; toll approved, 109, 110

Eastman, Peter (1746 - 1829); constable, 106, 112; freeman, 359; grand juror, 97; lister, 50, 62; tithingman, 27

East River, 115

East River Bridge, 24, 90, 121, 124, 136, 148, 152, 156, 159, 160, 169, 170, 173, 179, 194, 207, 211, 212, 213, 214, 218, 221, 222, 223, 253, 264. See Quinnipiac River bridge, 90, 115; lottery, 173, 173–175; lottery for, 100

Edwards, Henry W. (1779 - 1847); accounts committee, 345; biography, 243n; encroachments committee, 313; freeman, 370; grand juror, 243; lister, 244

Edwards, Horace H. (1782 - 1862); freeman, 379

Edwards, John S. (1778 - 1813); freeman, 368

Edwards, Jonathan Rev. (1745 - 1801); freeman, 359

Edwards, Jonathan Walter (1772 - 1831); biography, 366n; freeman, 366

Edwards, Pierpoint; Committee on confederation of the United States, 65

Perkins, Jonathan (1747 - post 1790); tithing-man, 74

Perkins, Peter (1741 - 1799); biography, 56n; committee for bills of credit and Continental money, 93; committee on procuring uniforms, 69; committee on town defense, 70; freeman, 359, 363; grand juror, 8; illicit trade, 94; inspector of provisions, 90; rate collector, 26; selectman, 97, 106, 112; surveyor, 56, 86

Perkins, Reuben (1745 - 1800); grand juror, 118; tithingman, 86, 99, 107

Perkins, Samuel (1756 - 1811); lister, 107

Perrit, Job (1751 - 1794); freeman, 364; tithing-man, 52, 99, 133

Perrit, Martin (1740 - 1816); tithingman, 124, 227

Perrit, Thaddeus (1753/4 - 1806); excused as selectman, 252; freeman, 364; lister, 209, 213; oyster overseer, 241; questioned on remaining in town during British invasion, 82; selectman, 252; shellfish overseer, 247; tithingman, 114

Perry, Joshua (1748 - ca. 1812)); freeman, 363

Peru, Illinois, 334

Pesthouse; for smallpox victims, 61

Phelps, Timothy; freeman, 364

Philadelphia, PA, 37, 138

Philemon, Marry; freeman, 360

Phipps, Daniel G. (1751 - 1838); freeman, 364

Phipps, David (1741 - 1825); freeman, 360

Phipps, Solomon (1745 - 1813); freeman, 362

Phipps, Solomon (1782 - 1834); freeman, 377

Pierpoint, Benjamin, 51, 360

Pierpoint, Benjamin (1738 - 1812); freeman, 360; grandjuror, 8; surveyor, 51, 124

Pierpoint, Evelyn (1755 - 1809); freeman, 362

Pierpoint, Giles (1741 - 1832), 22; Articles of Association, 38; committee on poor, 129; freeman, 360; surveyor, 129; tithingman, 55

Pierpoint, Hezekiah (1745 - ?); freeman, 359; surveyor, 17, 63

Pierpoint, James (1699 - 1776); biography, 12n; committee, 16; moderator, 12

Pierpoint, James (1761 - 1840); freeman, 363; mill owner, 125

Pierpoint, James, Rev. (1659 - 1714), 15

Pierpoint, John (1740 - 1805); grand juror, 85, 90;

rate collector, 28; refuses to serve as grandjuror, 57

Pierpoint, Joseph (1735 - 1824); committee of inspection, 39; grand juror, 54; mill owner, 125

Pierpoint, Thomas (1760 - 1795); freeman, 364; tithingman, 114

Pierpont, Evelin (1755 - 1809); fisheries overseer, 261, 265, 274, 281; lister, 224, 234, 239, 240, 244; oyster overseer, 238, 241, 247, 259, 290

Pierpont , James (1699 - 1776), 12

Pierpont, Samuel (1756 - 1821), 327; freeman, 364

Pine Rock fFeld, 149

Pine Street, 328

Pinto, Isaac 1777 - 1858); freeman, 370

Pinto, Jacob (1724 - 1806), 14; committee to increase commerce, 7

Pinto, Solomon (1758 - 1824); freeman, 363

Pinto, William (1760 - 1847); freeman, 368

Pishall [?], William; freeman, 378

Plainfield Path, 149

Plant, James (1742 - 1814); freeman, 360

Plant, Samuel (1772 - 1862); freeman, 371

Platt, Jeremiah (1744 - 1794); committee on Loyalists, 48; freeman, 362; Long Island native, 48

Platt, John (1752 - 1782), 362; freeman, 362, 370; surveyor, 51

Platt, John (1779 - 1835); freeman, 370

Platt, Nathan (1774 - 1840), 348; constable, 246, 268, 271, 321, 326, 331; fence viewer, 300, 312, 316, 321, 326, 331; freeman, 367; key keeper, 269, 271; key keeper, 277; lister, 338, 344; pound keeper, 288, 296, 301, 312, 316, 321, 326, 331, 335, 339, 344, 350; rate collector, 246; rate collector, released, 246; surveyor, 257, 263, 276, 312, 316, 321, 326, 331, 338, 344, 350

Pluymert (Pluymerth), William (1725 - 1810; freeman, 359, 362

Pool, Samuel (1765 - ?); freeman, 370

Poor, 134, 154, 164–165, 165–167, 173, 179–180, 189–191, 194, 201–203, 202–203, 208, 209, 214, 215, 217, 223–224, 229, 229–231, 233, 234, 239, 245, 301, 350; board of relief. *See also* board of relief; care of, 117, 148; com-

Trumble, John (Trumbull); freeman, 360

Trumbull, Benjamin Rev.* (1735 - 1820), 25; biography, 70; committee on town defense, 69–71; Freemen's Meeting Address, 25; Susquehanna claim, 34; town agent, 72; Yale (1759), 70

Trumbull, John (1756 - 1843); committee on confederation of the United States, 65

Trumbull, Jonathan (1710 - 1785); receives New Haven petition against military draft, 103

Tryon, William Maj. Gen.; leads British invasion, 80

Tucker, Noah (1747 - 1804); questioned on remaining in town during British invasion, 82

Turner, Abraham (1734 - 1796); freeman, 362

Turner, Calvin (1778 - 1825); freeman, 371

Turner, Ephraim (1730 - 1784); freeman, 361; grand juror, 62; surveyor, 2, 86, 361; tithingman, 19

Turner, Gurden (Gorden) (1746 - 1836); freeman, 363

Turner, Jabez (1756 - 1846); tithingman, 124

Turner, James (1727 - 1788); freeman, 360

Turner, Jesse (1746/7 - 1834); freeman, 365

Turner, Joseph (1745 - 1773); freeman, 359; key keeper, 3, 9, 18, 19, 23, 359

Turner, William (1777 - 1868); freeman, 369

Tuttle, Abigail; indigent, 131

Tuttle, Abner (1760 - 1813); freeman, 370

Tuttle, Abraham (1721 - 1799), 15; oyster overseer, 6, 11

Tuttle, Abraham (1750 - 1824); freeman, 365

Tuttle, Andrew (1785 - 1868); freeman, 373

Tuttle, Asahel (1767 - 1837), 367; bridge committee, 312; committee on poor, 272; encroachments committee, 313; freeman, 367; lister, 264, 287, 334; surveyor, 249, 338, 344; surveyor, 334; tithingman, 300

Tuttle, Ashael, Jr. (1775 - 1828); freeman, 367

Tuttle, Bethel (1779 - 1813); freeman, 372

Tuttle, Charles (c. 1749 - 1777); Rev. War solider, 40; tithingman, 40

Tuttle, Chloe (1738 - 1773), 191

Tuttle, Daniel; freeman, 363

Tuttle, Daniel (1702 - 1772); key keeper, 125; tithingman, 9

Tuttle, Ezekiel (1745 - 1783); freeman, 361

Tuttle, Ezra; freeman, 360

Tuttle, Ezra (1776 - 1859); freeman, 371

Tuttle, Hezehiah; committee to clothe army, 78; constable, 43; pound keeper, 42; rate collector, 100

Tuttle, Hezekiah 3d; surveyor, 119; tithingman, 118

Tuttle, Hezekiah (1743 - 1813); freeman, 359, 360; grand juror, 128

Tuttle, Isaac; surveyor, 129

Tuttle, Ithamer Capt. (1736 - 1817); grand juror, 8, 40; lister, 40

Tuttle, Jabez (1753 - 1799); freeman, 360

Tuttle, Jesse (1759 - 1848); freeman, 364

Tuttle, Joel (1718 - 1789); key keeper, 3, 9, 18, 23, 28, 40, 50, 54, 63, 75, 87, 98, 108, 114, 119; surveyor, 113

Tuttle, Jonathan (1728 - 1793); constable, 124; surveyor, 27, 40; tithingman, 124

Tuttle, Jonathan (1755 - 1822); freeman, 361

Tuttle, Joseph (1735 - 1813); inspector of provisions, 90; surveyor, 23, 27

Tuttle, Jotham (1752 - 1817); freeman, 362; tithingman, 86, 99

Tuttle, Jotham (1787 - 1832); freeman, 378

Tuttle, Levi (1751 - 1784); freeman, 359

Tuttle, Levi (1777 - 1842); fisheries overseer, 299, 303, 329, 333, 337–338, 341, 347, 355; freeman, 372; lister, 316, 321

Tuttle, Marion (1785 - 1850); freeman, 374

Tuttle, Nathaniel (1714 - 1780); surveyor, 23

Tuttle, Nathaniel (1742 - 1802); freeman, 361; grand juror, 54; lister, 114

Tuttle, Samuel (1727 - 1784); rate collector, 26; refuses interview for remaining in town during British invasion, 83; taken prisoner by British invaders, 83

Tuttle, Smith (1794 - 1863); freeman, 380

Tuttle, Solomon Deacon (1746 - 1828); freeman, 360; surveyor, 27, 55; tithingman, 19

Tuttle, Stephen (1716 - 1795); surveyor, 55

Tuttle, Titus (1731 - 1820); grandjuror, 54; Rev. War veteran, 40; surveyor, 40

Tuttle, Uri (1760 - 1826); freeman, 370

Tuttle, Uriah (1737 - 1822), 113; grand juror, 113; surveyor, 98

Twining, Stephen S. (1767 - 1832), 279; alms house, 301; almshouse, 296; bridge committee, 312; committee on poor, 223; commit